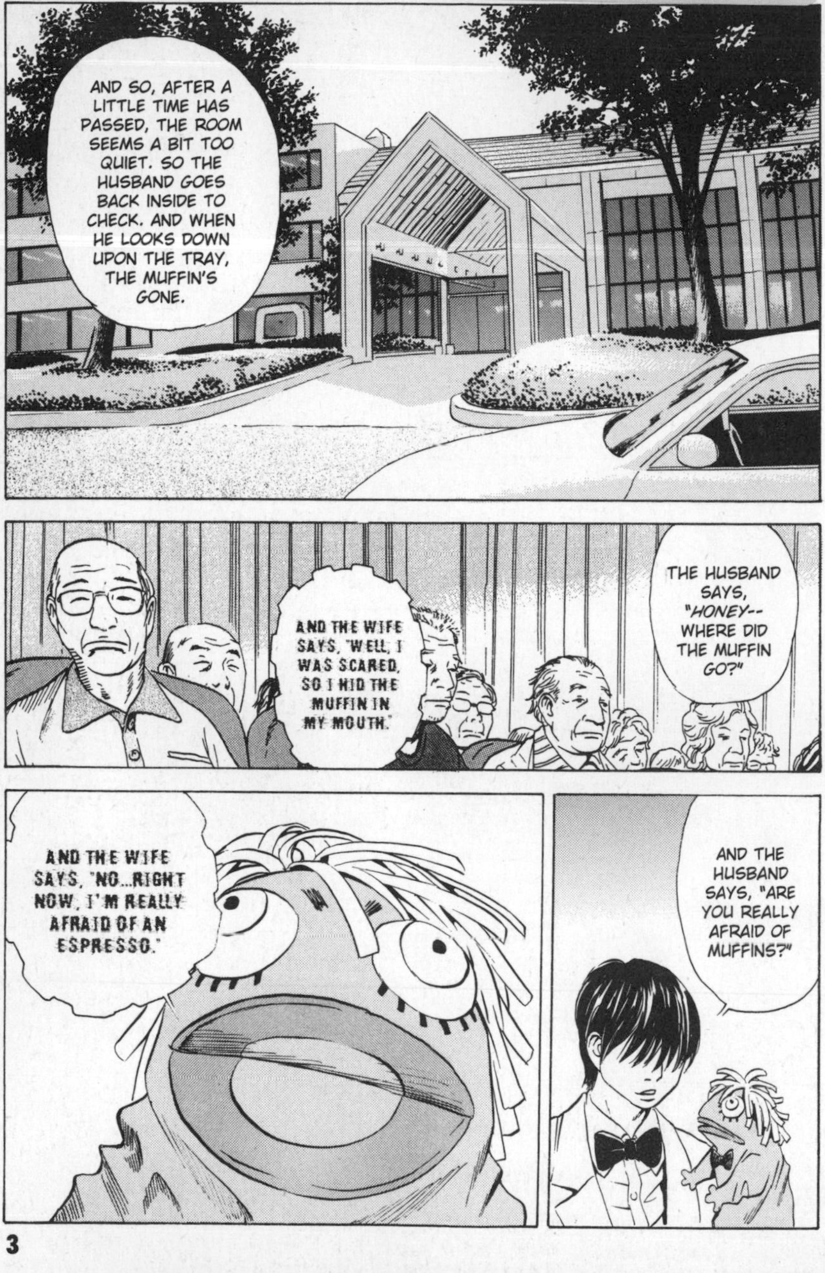
AND SO, AFTER A LITTLE TIME HAS PASSED, THE ROOM SEEMS A BIT TOO QUIET. SO THE HUSBAND GOES BACK INSIDE TO CHECK. AND WHEN HE LOOKS DOWN UPON THE TRAY, THE MUFFIN'S GONE.
THE HUSBAND SAYS, "*HONEY*-- WHERE DID THE MUFFIN GO?"
AND THE WIFE SAYS, "WELL, I WAS SCARED, SO I HID THE MUFFIN IN MY MOUTH."
AND THE HUSBAND SAYS, "ARE YOU REALLY AFRAID OF MUFFINS?"
AND THE WIFE SAYS, "NO...RIGHT NOW, I'M REALLY AFRAID OF AN ESPRESSO."

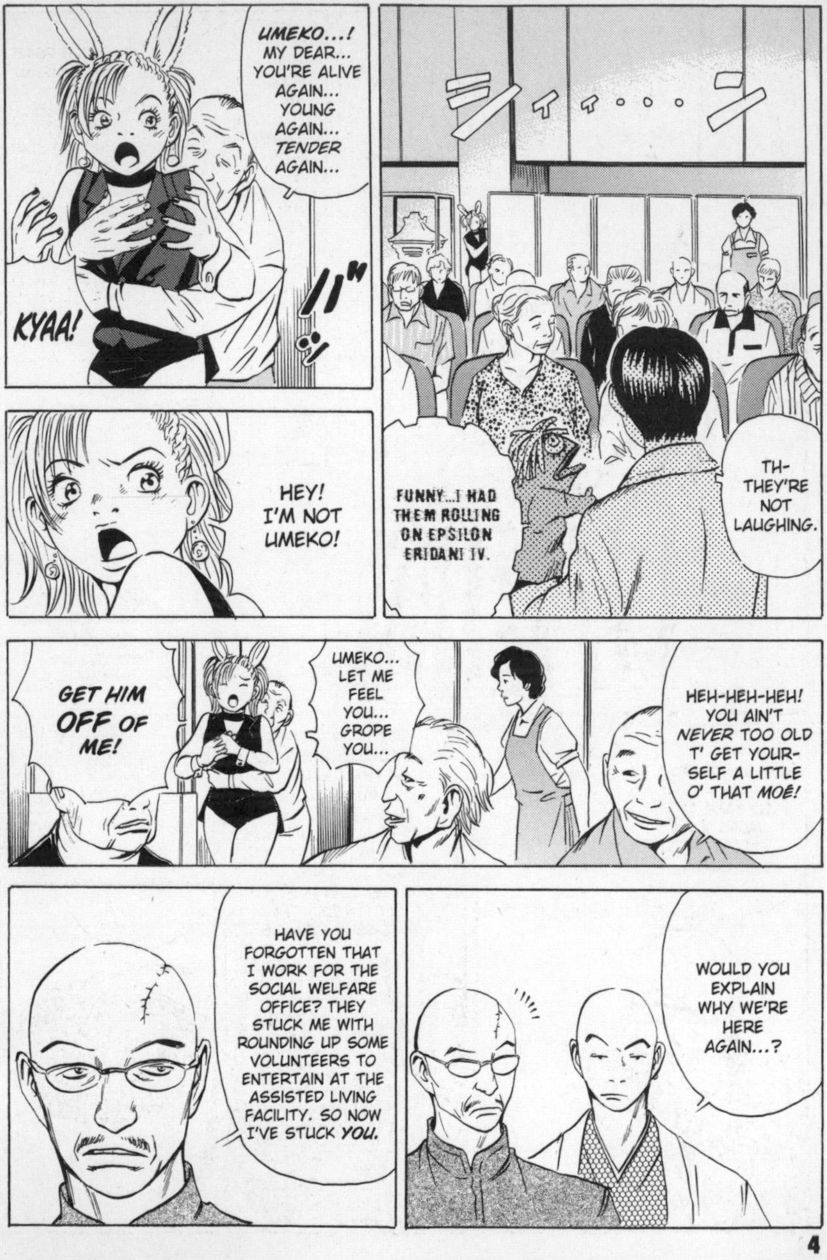
シィィ・・・ン
TH- THEY'RE NOT LAUGHING.
FUNNY...I HAD THEM ROLLING ON EPSILON ERIDANI IV.
UMEKO...! MY DEAR... YOU'RE ALIVE AGAIN... YOUNG AGAIN... TENDER AGAIN...
KYAA!
HEY! I'M NOT UMEKO!
HEH-HEH-HEH! YOU AIN'T NEVER TOO OLD T' GET YOURSELF A LITTLE O' THAT MOÉ!
UMEKO... LET ME FEEL YOU... GROPE YOU...
GET HIM OFF OF ME!
WOULD YOU EXPLAIN WHY WE'RE HERE AGAIN...?
HAVE YOU FORGOTTEN THAT I WORK FOR THE SOCIAL WELFARE OFFICE? THEY STUCK ME WITH ROUNDING UP SOME VOLUNTEERS TO ENTERTAIN AT THE ASSISTED LIVING FACILITY. SO NOW I'VE STUCK YOU.

contents

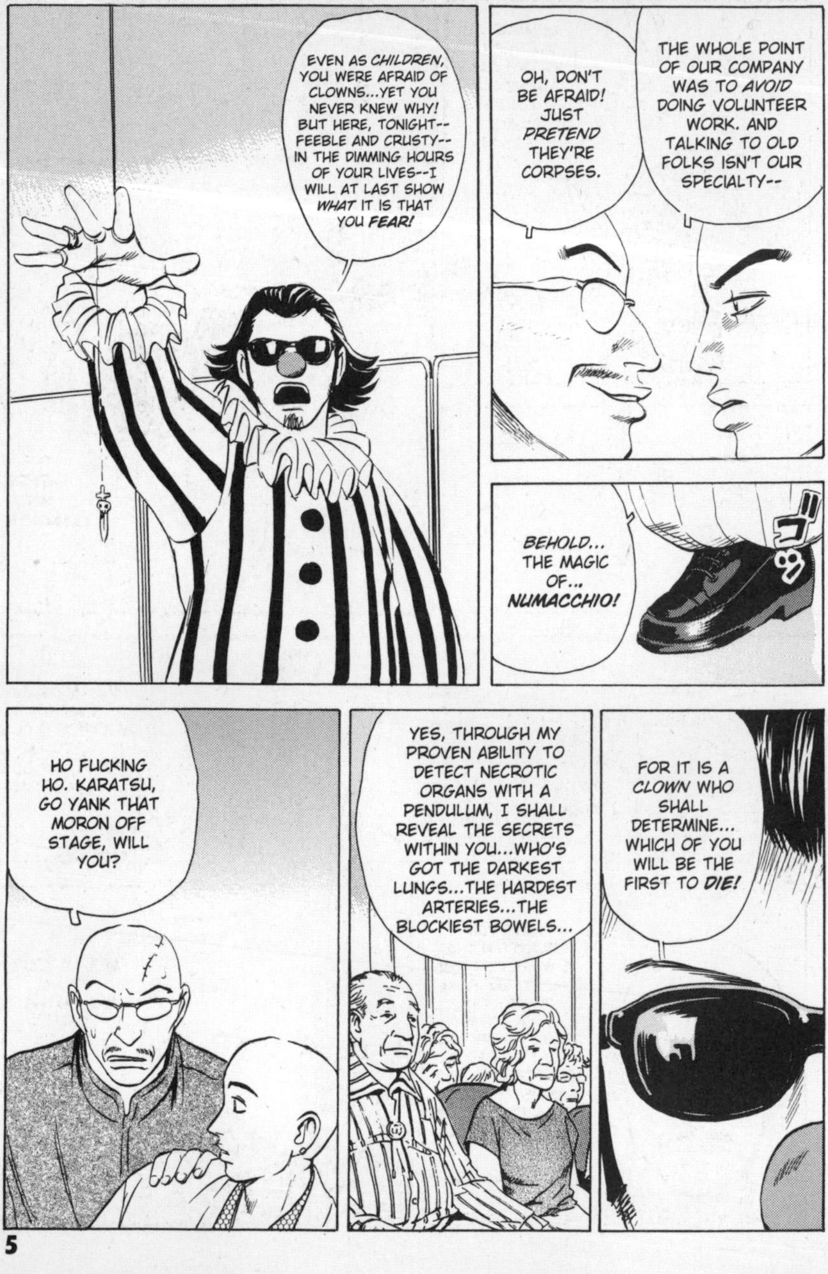
THE WHOLE POINT OF OUR COMPANY WAS TO *AVOID* DOING VOLUNTEER WORK. AND TALKING TO OLD FOLKS ISN'T OUR SPECIALTY--
OH, DON'T BE AFRAID! JUST *PRETEND* THEY'RE CORPSES.
BEHOLD... THE MAGIC OF... ***NUMACCHIO!***
EVEN AS *CHILDREN*, YOU WERE AFRAID OF CLOWNS...YET YOU NEVER KNEW WHY! BUT HERE, TONIGHT-- FEEBLE AND CRUSTY-- IN THE DIMMING HOURS OF YOUR LIVES--I WILL AT LAST SHOW *WHAT* IT IS THAT YOU ***FEAR!***
FOR IT IS A *CLOWN* WHO SHALL DETERMINE... WHICH OF YOU WILL BE THE FIRST TO ***DIE!***
YES, THROUGH MY PROVEN ABILITY TO DETECT NECROTIC ORGANS WITH A PENDULUM, I SHALL REVEAL THE SECRETS WITHIN YOU...WHO'S GOT THE DARKEST LUNGS...THE HARDEST ARTERIES...THE BLOCKIEST BOWELS...
HO FUCKING HO. KARATSU, GO YANK THAT MORON OFF STAGE, WILL YOU?

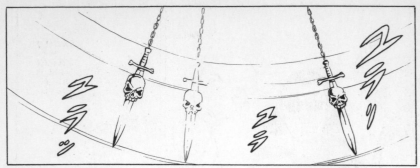

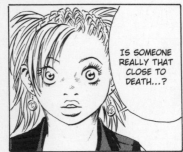

HEY... LOOK AT IT SWING!
WHAT ?!
IS SOMEONE REALLY THAT CLOSE TO DEATH...?
CLOSE... REALLY CLOSE!
!
HERE! WHOA! THIS GUY'S IN BAD SHAPE! AS MY MAN KENSHIRO WOULD SAY...YOU'RE ALREADY DEAD!

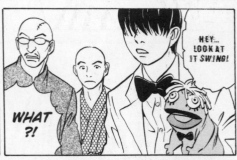

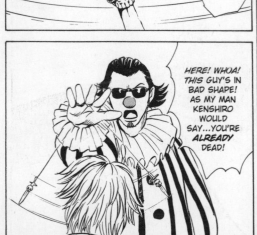

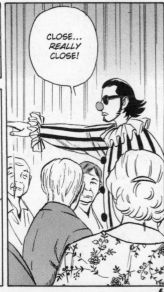

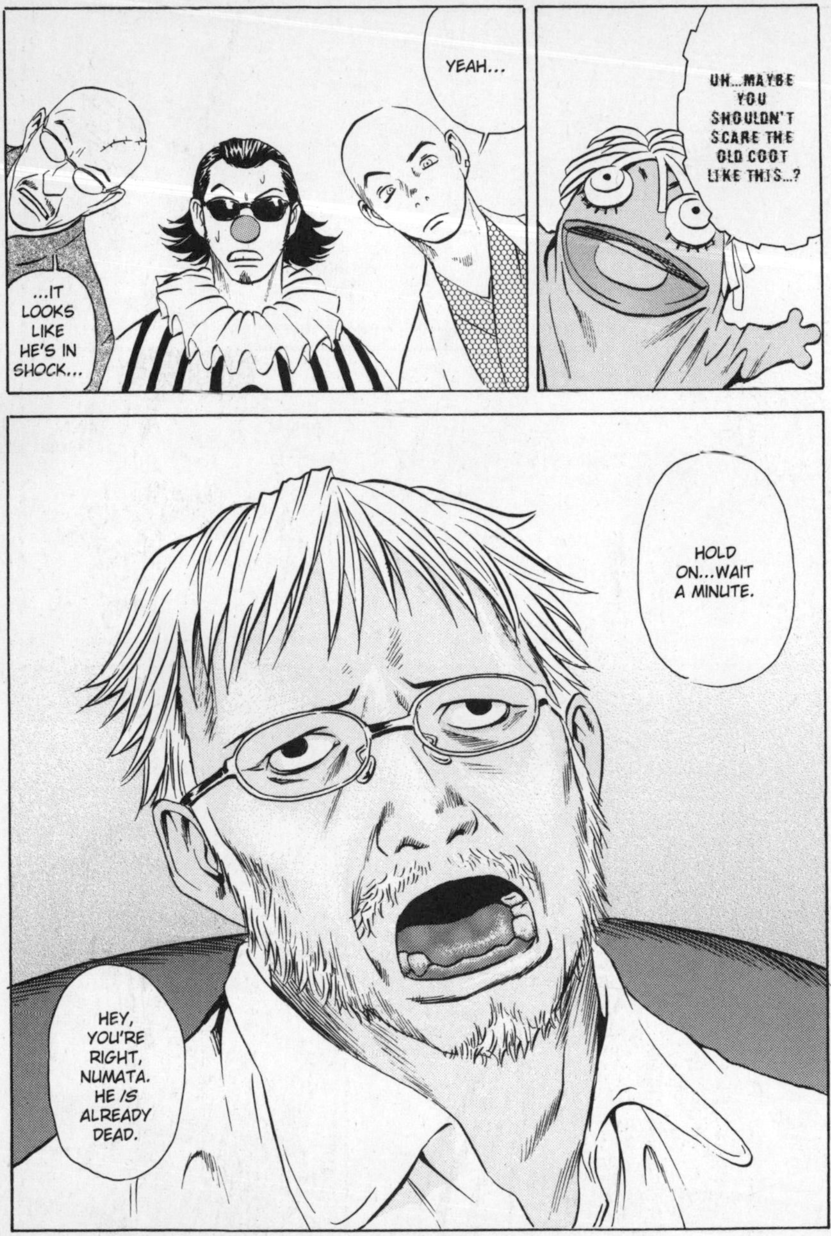
UH...MAYBE YOU SHOULDN'T SCARE THE OLD COOT LIKE THIS...?
YEAH...
...IT LOOKS LIKE HE'S IN SHOCK...
HOLD ON...WAIT A MINUTE.
HEY, YOU'RE RIGHT, NUMATA. HE *IS* ALREADY DEAD.

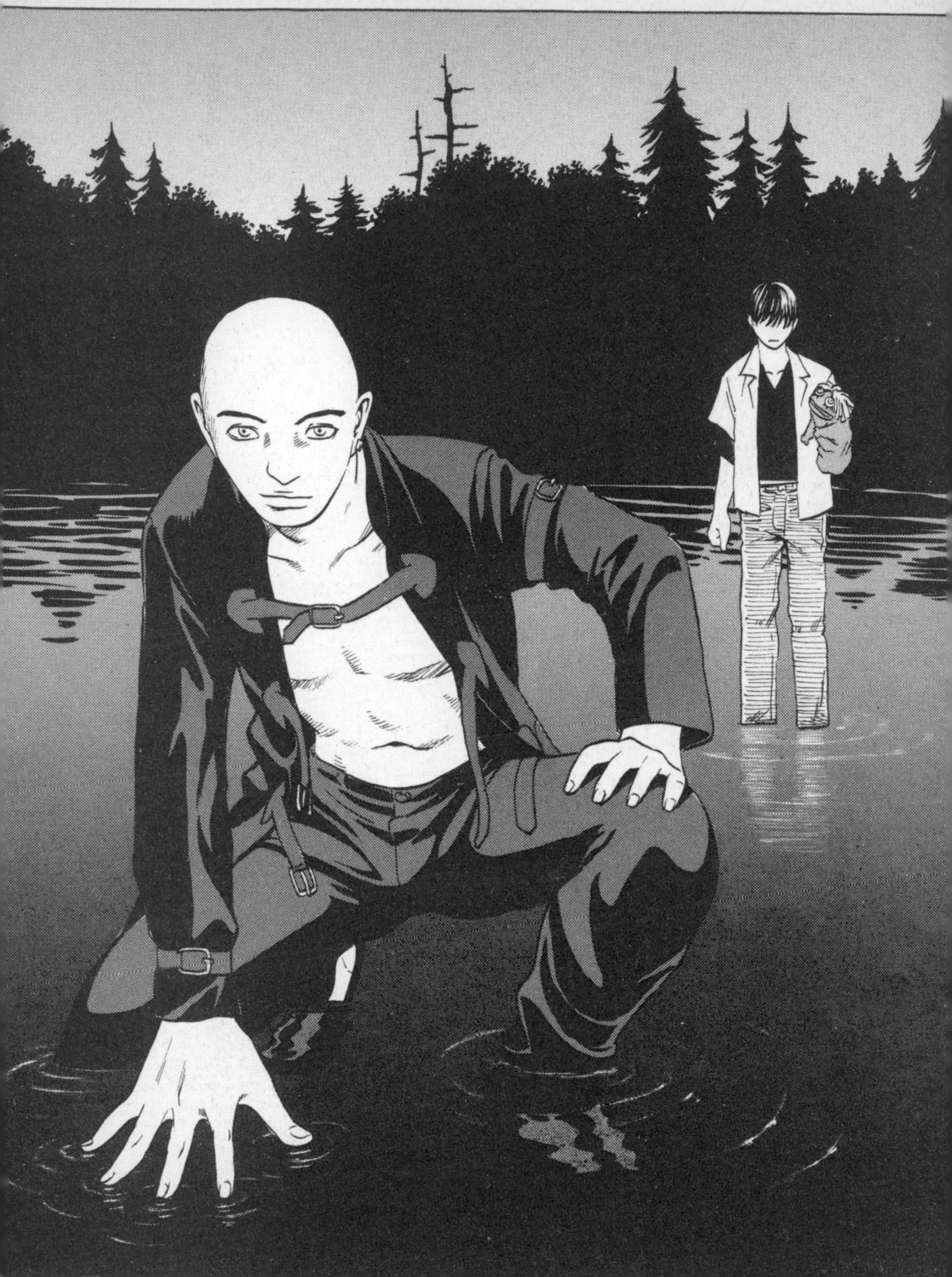

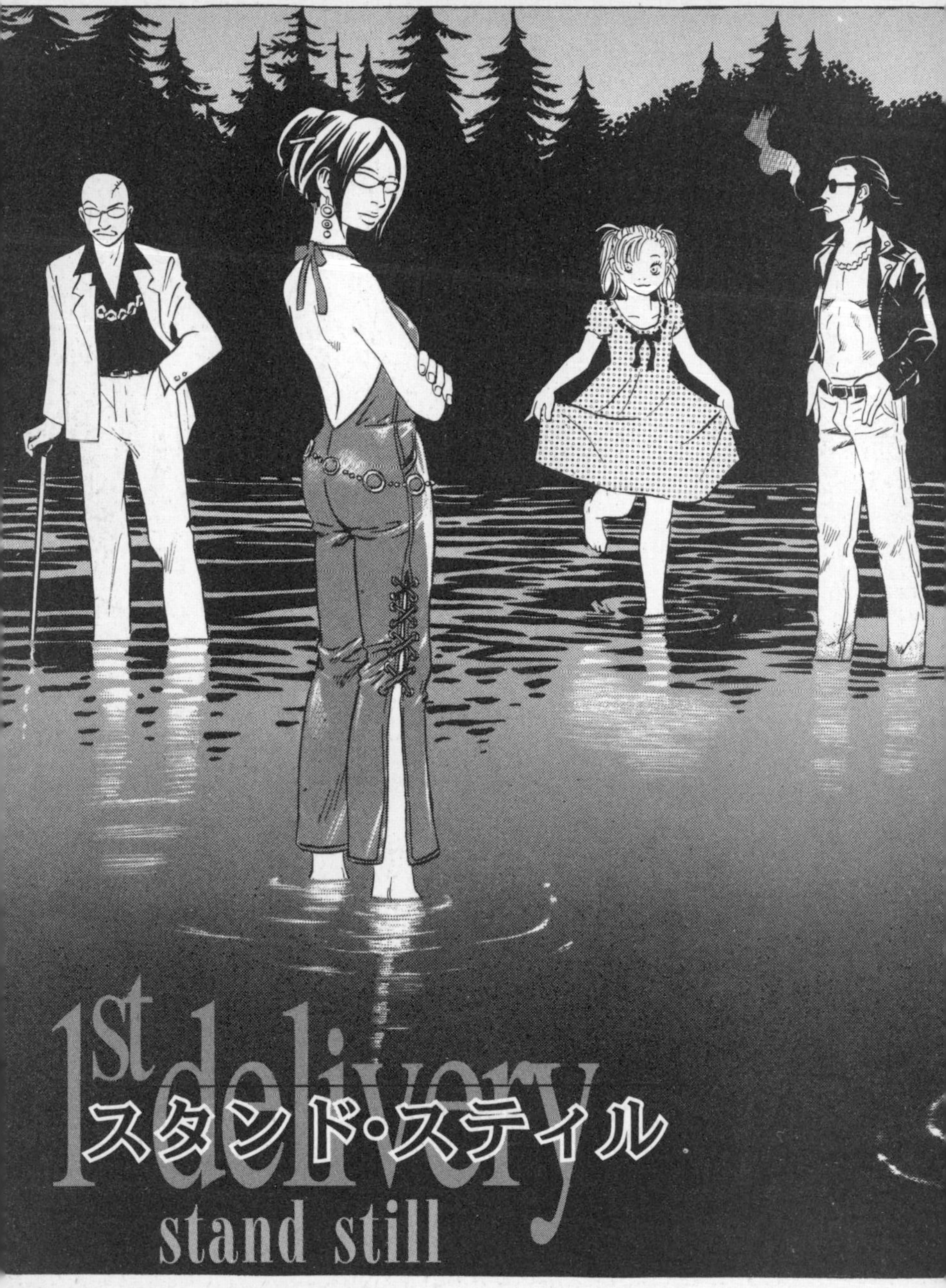
1st delivery
スタンド・スティル
stand still

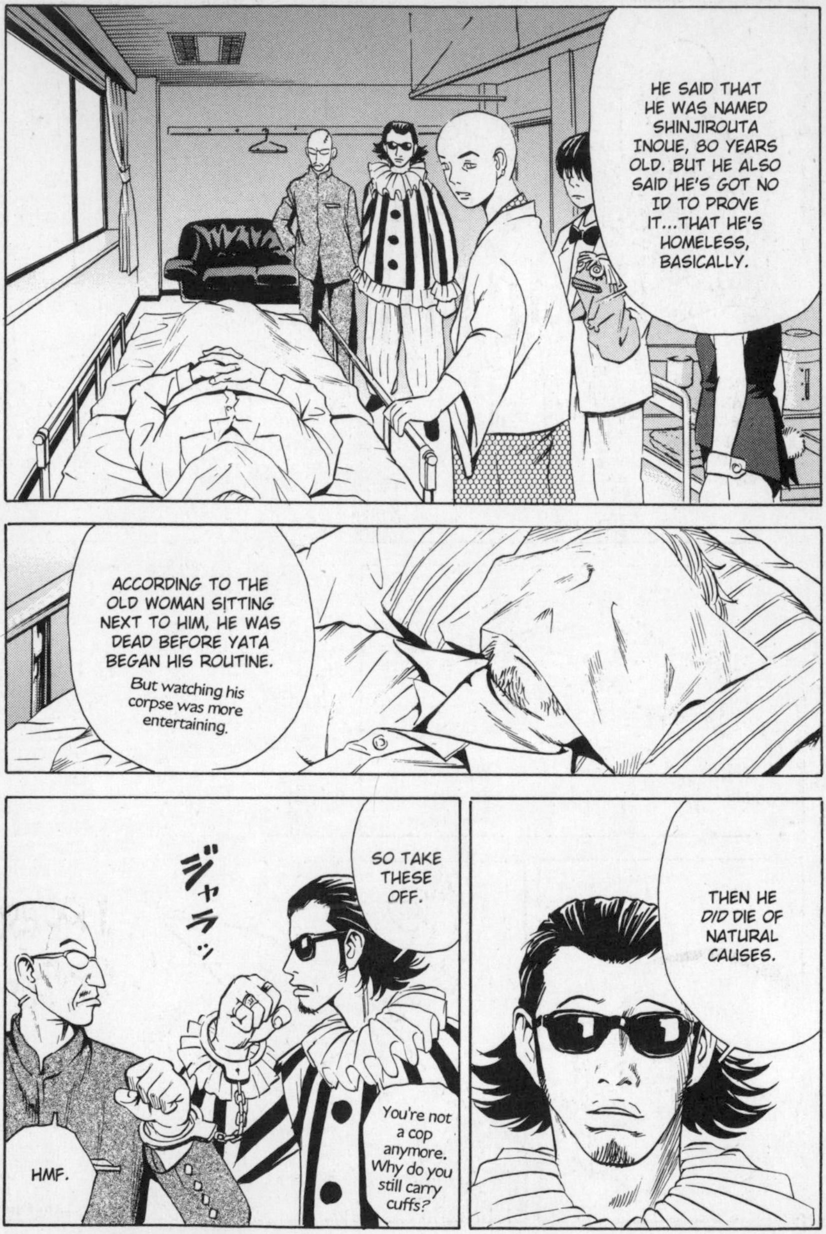
HE SAID THAT HE WAS NAMED SHINJIROUTA INOUE, 80 YEARS OLD. BUT HE ALSO SAID HE'S GOT NO ID TO PROVE IT...THAT HE'S HOMELESS, BASICALLY.
ACCORDING TO THE OLD WOMAN SITTING NEXT TO HIM, HE WAS DEAD BEFORE YATA BEGAN HIS ROUTINE.
But watching his corpse was more entertaining.
THEN HE *DID* DIE OF NATURAL CAUSES.
SO TAKE THESE OFF.
ジャラッ
You're not a cop anymore. Why do you still carry cuffs?
HMF.

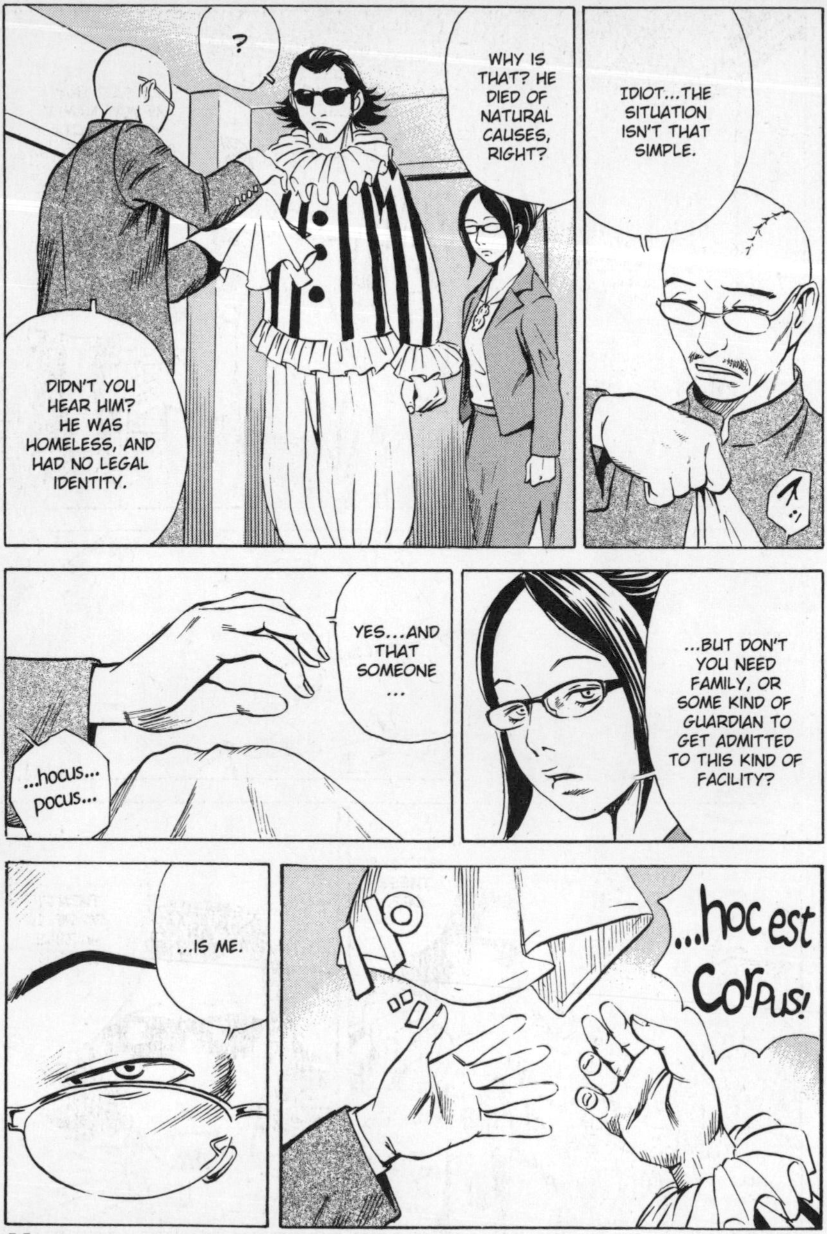
IDIOT...THE SITUATION ISN'T THAT SIMPLE.
WHY IS THAT? HE DIED OF NATURAL CAUSES, RIGHT?
?
DIDN'T YOU HEAR HIM? HE WAS HOMELESS, AND HAD NO LEGAL IDENTITY.
...BUT DON'T YOU NEED FAMILY, OR SOME KIND OF GUARDIAN TO GET ADMITTED TO THIS KIND OF FACILITY?
YES...AND THAT SOMEONE ...
...hocus... pocus...
...hoc est Corpus!
...IS ME.

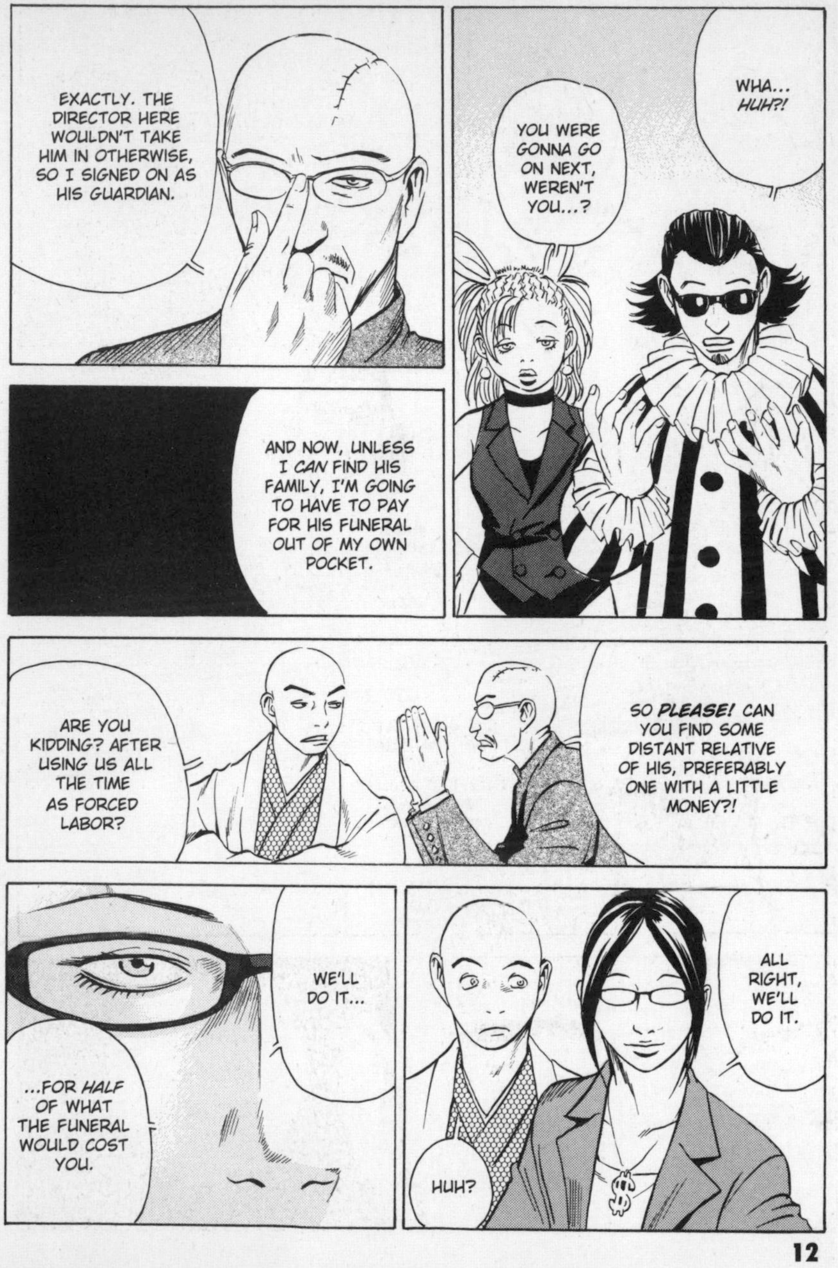
WHA... *HUH?!*
YOU WERE GONNA GO ON NEXT, WEREN'T YOU...?
EXACTLY. THE DIRECTOR HERE WOULDN'T TAKE HIM IN OTHERWISE, SO I SIGNED ON AS HIS GUARDIAN.
AND NOW, UNLESS I *CAN* FIND HIS FAMILY, I'M GOING TO HAVE TO PAY FOR HIS FUNERAL OUT OF MY OWN POCKET.
SO ***PLEASE!*** CAN YOU FIND SOME DISTANT RELATIVE OF HIS, PREFERABLY ONE WITH A LITTLE MONEY?!
ARE YOU KIDDING? AFTER USING US ALL THE TIME AS FORCED LABOR?
ALL RIGHT, WE'LL DO IT.
HUH?
WE'LL DO IT...
...FOR *HALF* OF WHAT THE FUNERAL WOULD COST YOU.

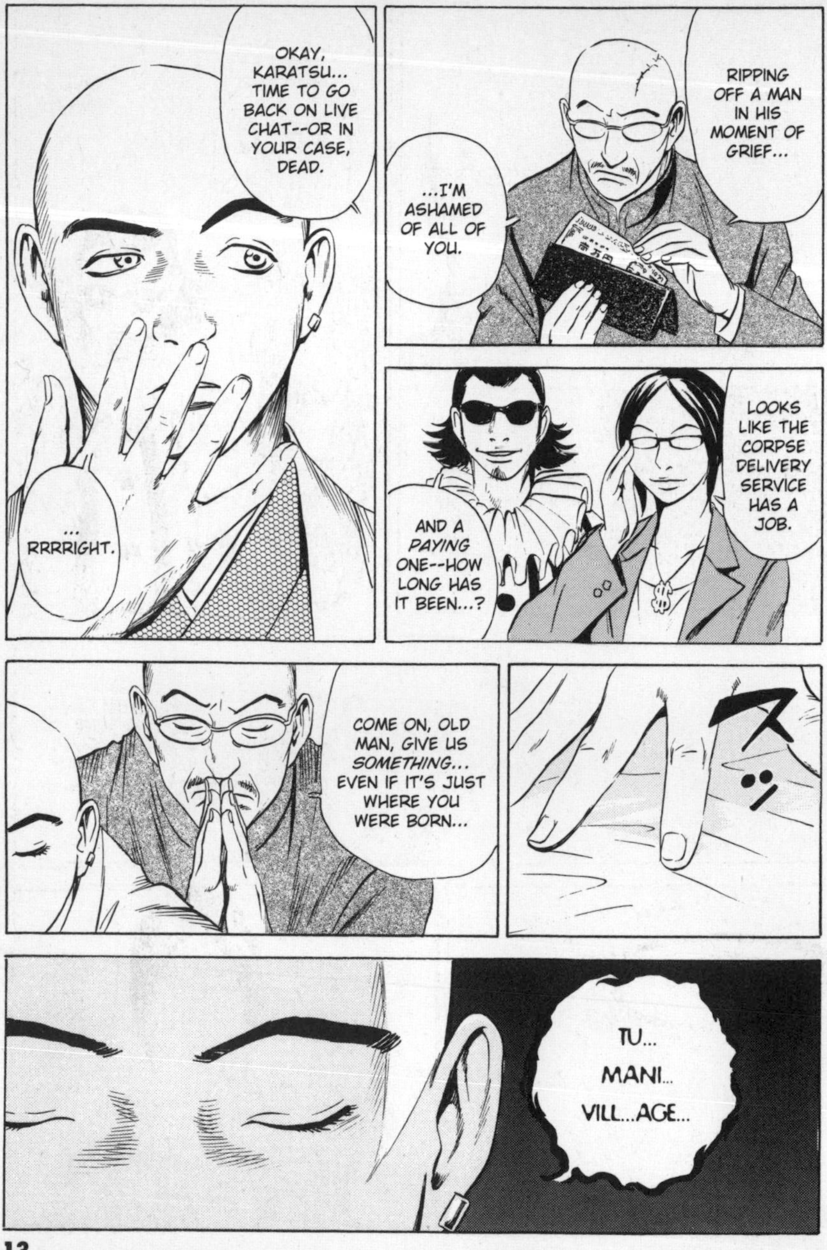
RIPPING OFF A MAN IN HIS MOMENT OF GRIEF...
...I'M ASHAMED OF ALL OF YOU.
LOOKS LIKE THE CORPSE DELIVERY SERVICE HAS A JOB.
AND A *PAYING* ONE--HOW LONG HAS IT BEEN...?
OKAY, KARATSU... TIME TO GO BACK ON LIVE CHAT--OR IN YOUR CASE, DEAD.
... RRRRIGHT.
スッ
COME ON, OLD MAN, GIVE US *SOMETHING*... EVEN IF IT'S JUST WHERE YOU WERE BORN...
TU... MANI... VILL...AGE...

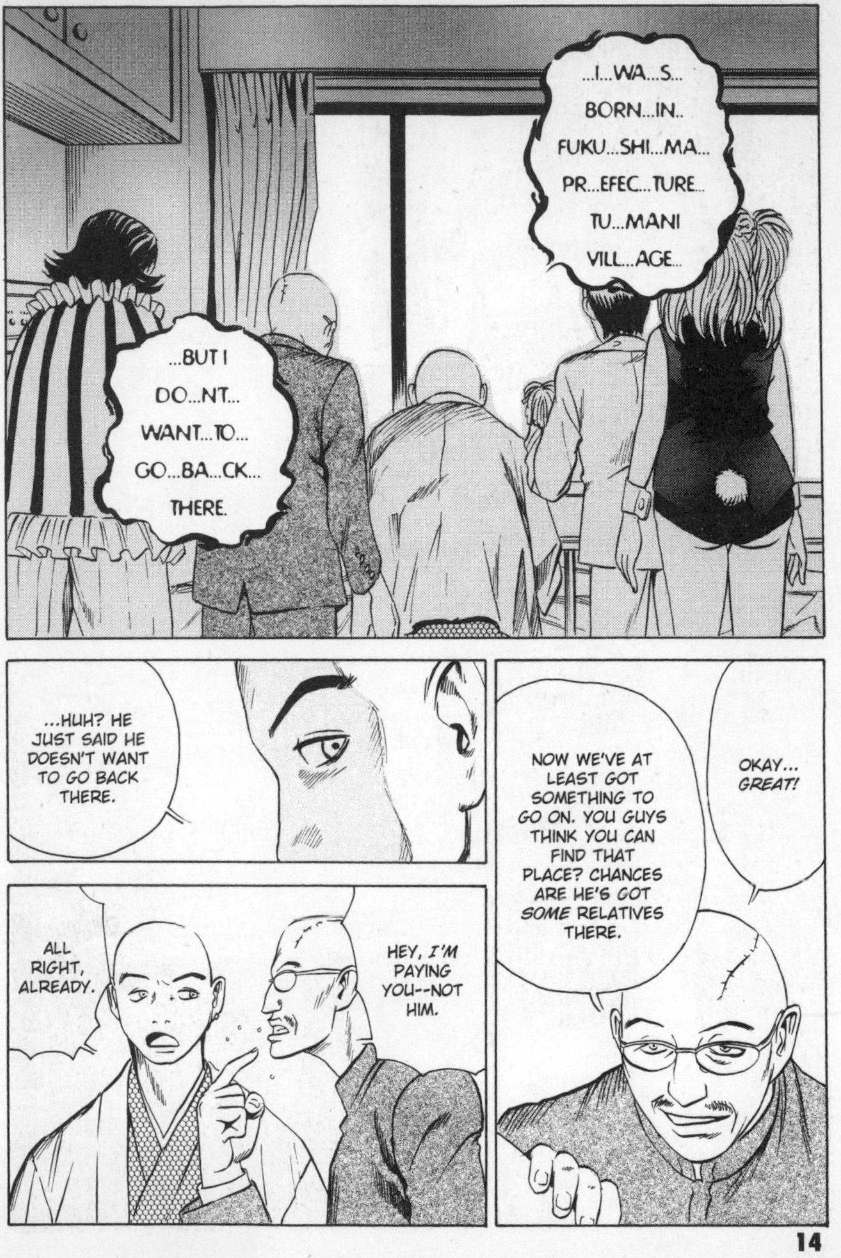
...I...WA...S... BORN...IN.. FUKU...SHI...MA... PR...EFEC...TURE... TU...MANI VILL...AGE...
...BUT I DO...N'T... WANT...TO... GO...BA...CK... THERE.
OKAY... GREAT!
NOW WE'VE AT LEAST GOT SOMETHING TO GO ON. YOU GUYS THINK YOU CAN FIND THAT PLACE? CHANCES ARE HE'S GOT SOME RELATIVES THERE.
...HUH? HE JUST SAID HE DOESN'T WANT TO GO BACK THERE.
HEY, I'M PAYING YOU--NOT HIM.
ALL RIGHT, ALREADY.

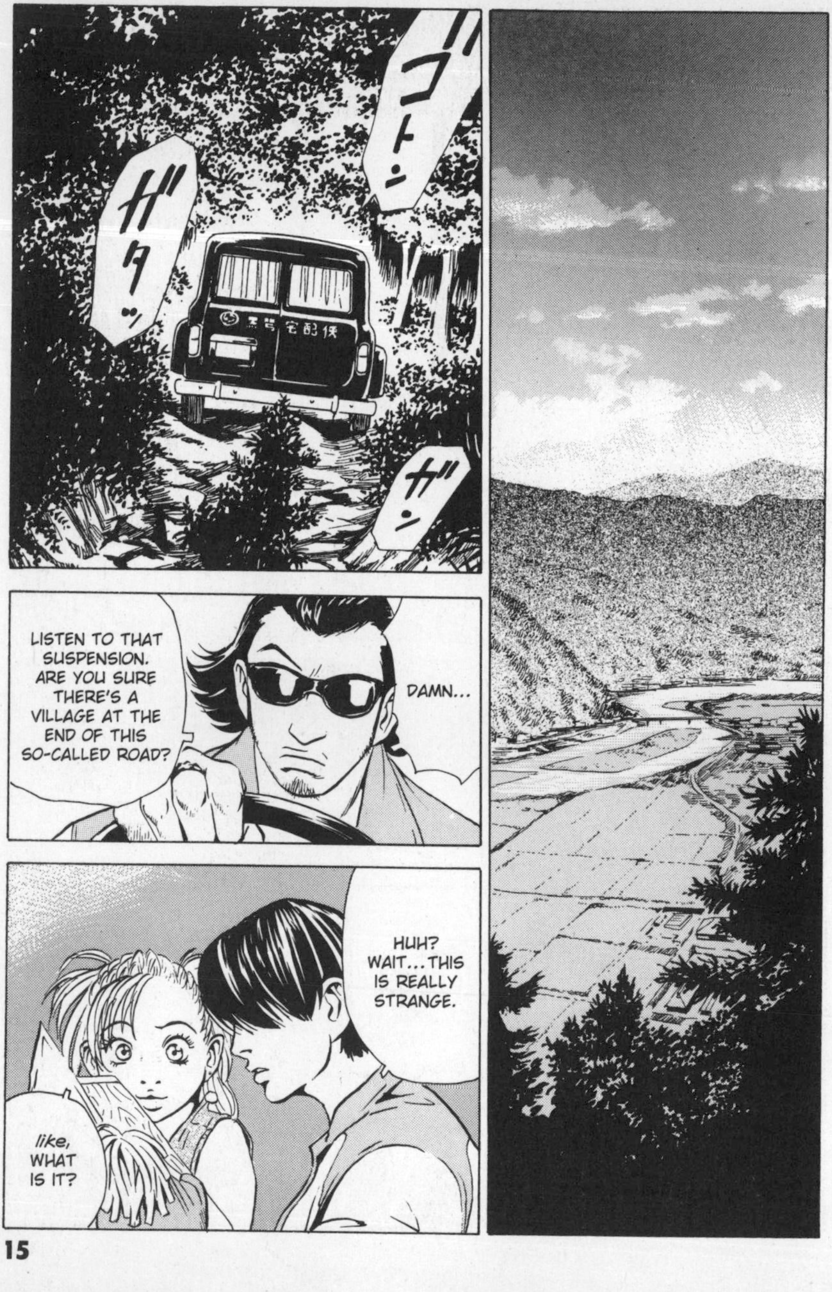

ゴトン
ガタッ
ガン
LISTEN TO THAT SUSPENSION. ARE YOU SURE THERE'S A VILLAGE AT THE END OF THIS SO-CALLED ROAD?
DAMN...
HUH? WAIT...THIS IS REALLY STRANGE.
like, WHAT IS IT?

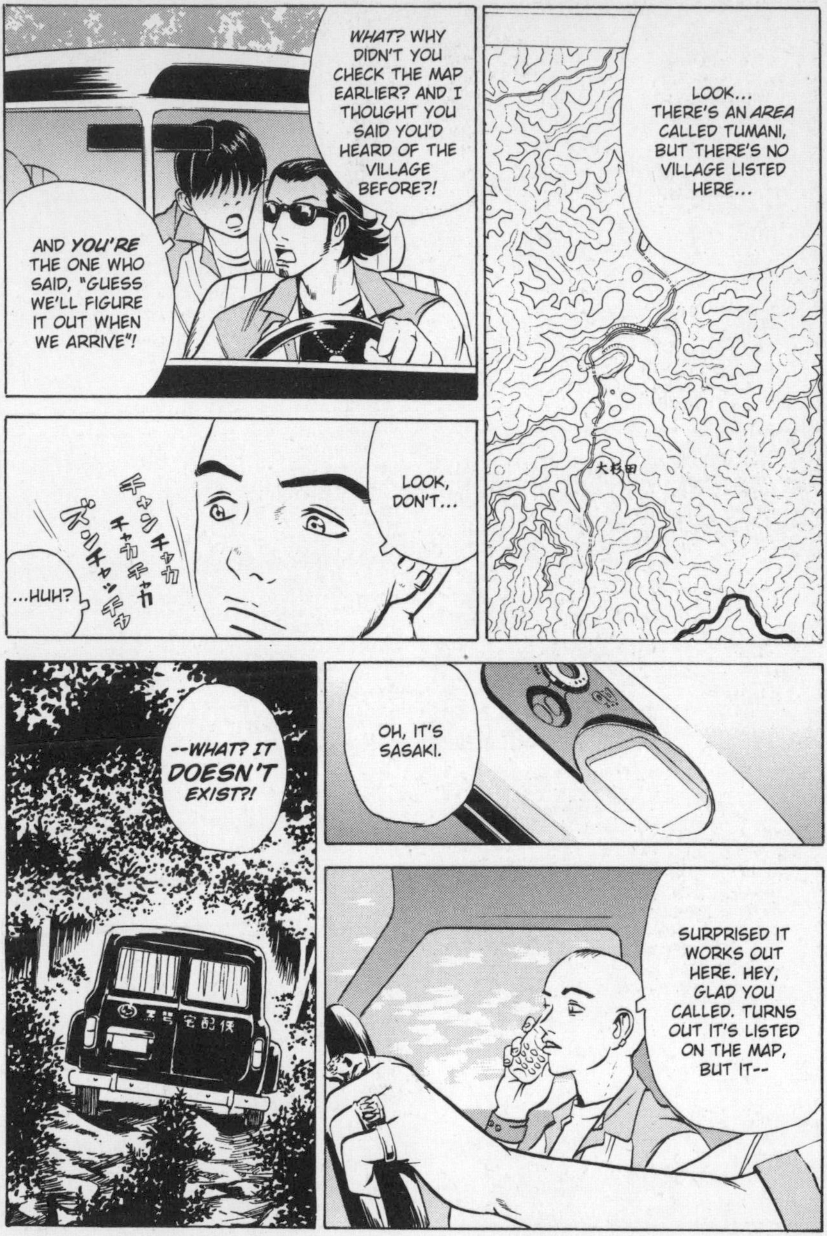
LOOK... THERE'S AN *AREA* CALLED TUMANI, BUT THERE'S NO VILLAGE LISTED HERE...
大杉田
WHAT? WHY DIDN'T YOU CHECK THE MAP EARLIER? AND I THOUGHT YOU SAID YOU'D HEARD OF THE VILLAGE BEFORE?!
AND ***YOU'RE*** THE ONE WHO SAID, "GUESS WE'LL FIGURE IT OUT WHEN WE ARRIVE"!
LOOK, DON'T...
チャンチャカ
チャカチャカ
ズンチャッチャ
...HUH?
OH, IT'S SASAKI.
SURPRISED IT WORKS OUT HERE. HEY, GLAD YOU CALLED. TURNS OUT IT'S LISTED ON THE MAP, BUT IT--
--WHAT? IT ***DOESN'T*** EXIST?!

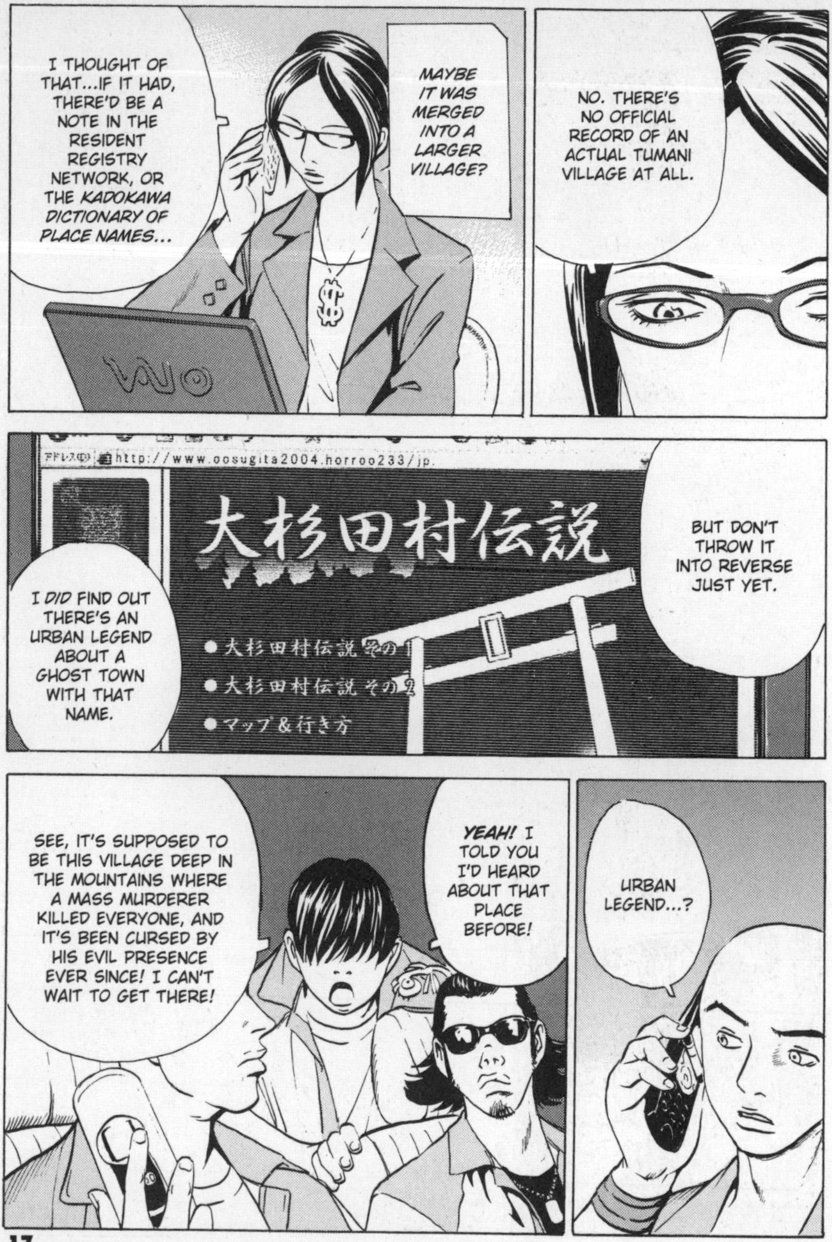
NO. THERE'S NO OFFICIAL RECORD OF AN ACTUAL TUMANI VILLAGE AT ALL.
MAYBE IT WAS MERGED INTO A LARGER VILLAGE?
I THOUGHT OF THAT...IF IT HAD, THERE'D BE A NOTE IN THE RESIDENT REGISTRY NETWORK, OR THE *KADOKAWA DICTIONARY OF PLACE NAMES*...
BUT DON'T THROW IT INTO REVERSE JUST YET.
http://www.oosugita2004.horroo233/jp.
大杉田村伝説
I *DID* FIND OUT THERE'S AN URBAN LEGEND ABOUT A GHOST TOWN WITH THAT NAME.
● 大杉田村伝説 その1
● 大杉田村伝説 その2
● マップ＆行き方
URBAN LEGEND...?
YEAH! I TOLD YOU I'D HEARD ABOUT THAT PLACE BEFORE!
SEE, IT'S SUPPOSED TO BE THIS VILLAGE DEEP IN THE MOUNTAINS WHERE A MASS MURDERER KILLED EVERYONE, AND IT'S BEEN CURSED BY HIS EVIL PRESENCE EVER SINCE! I CAN'T WAIT TO GET THERE!

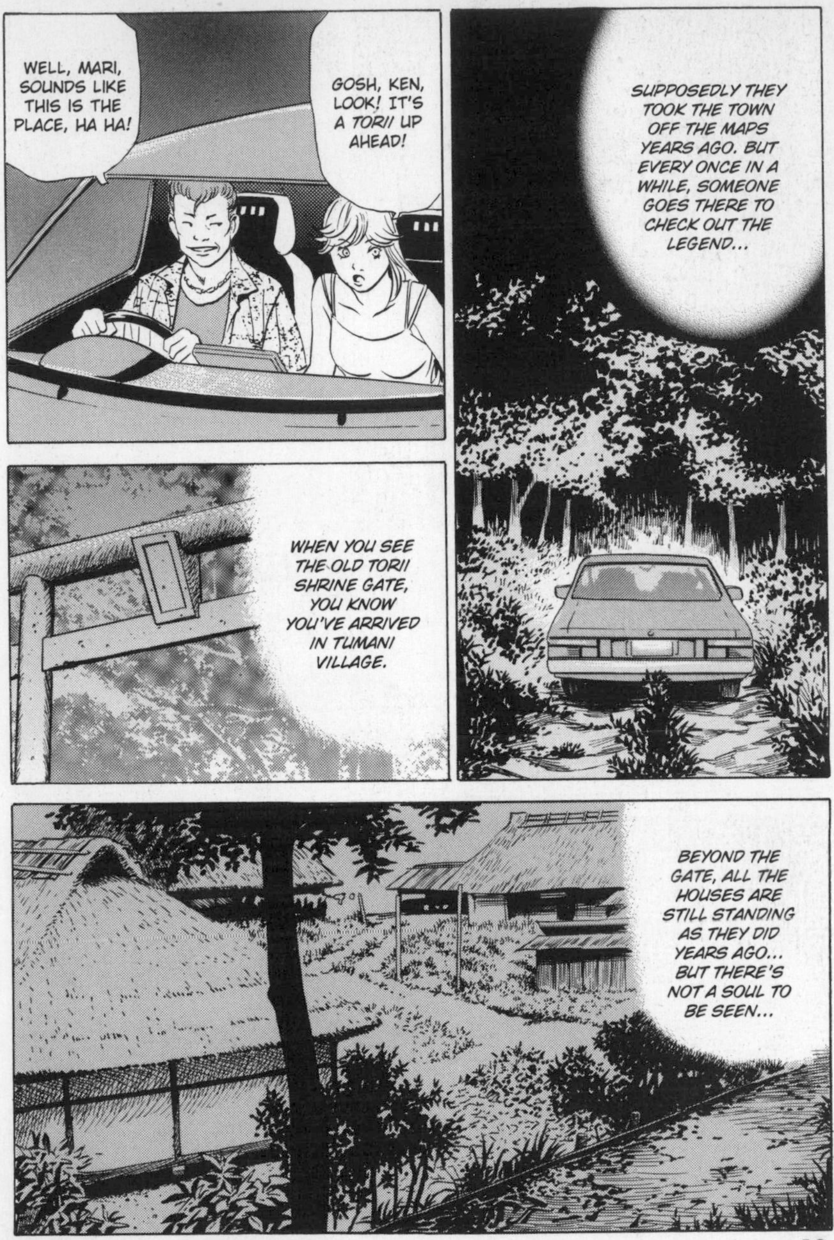
SUPPOSEDLY THEY TOOK THE TOWN OFF THE MAPS YEARS AGO. BUT EVERY ONCE IN A WHILE, SOMEONE GOES THERE TO CHECK OUT THE LEGEND...
GOSH, KEN, LOOK! IT'S A *TORII* UP AHEAD!
WELL, MARI, SOUNDS LIKE THIS IS THE PLACE, HA HA!
WHEN YOU SEE THE OLD TORII SHRINE GATE, YOU KNOW YOU'VE ARRIVED IN TUMANI VILLAGE.
BEYOND THE GATE, ALL THE HOUSES ARE STILL STANDING AS THEY DID YEARS AGO... BUT THERE'S NOT A SOUL TO BE SEEN...

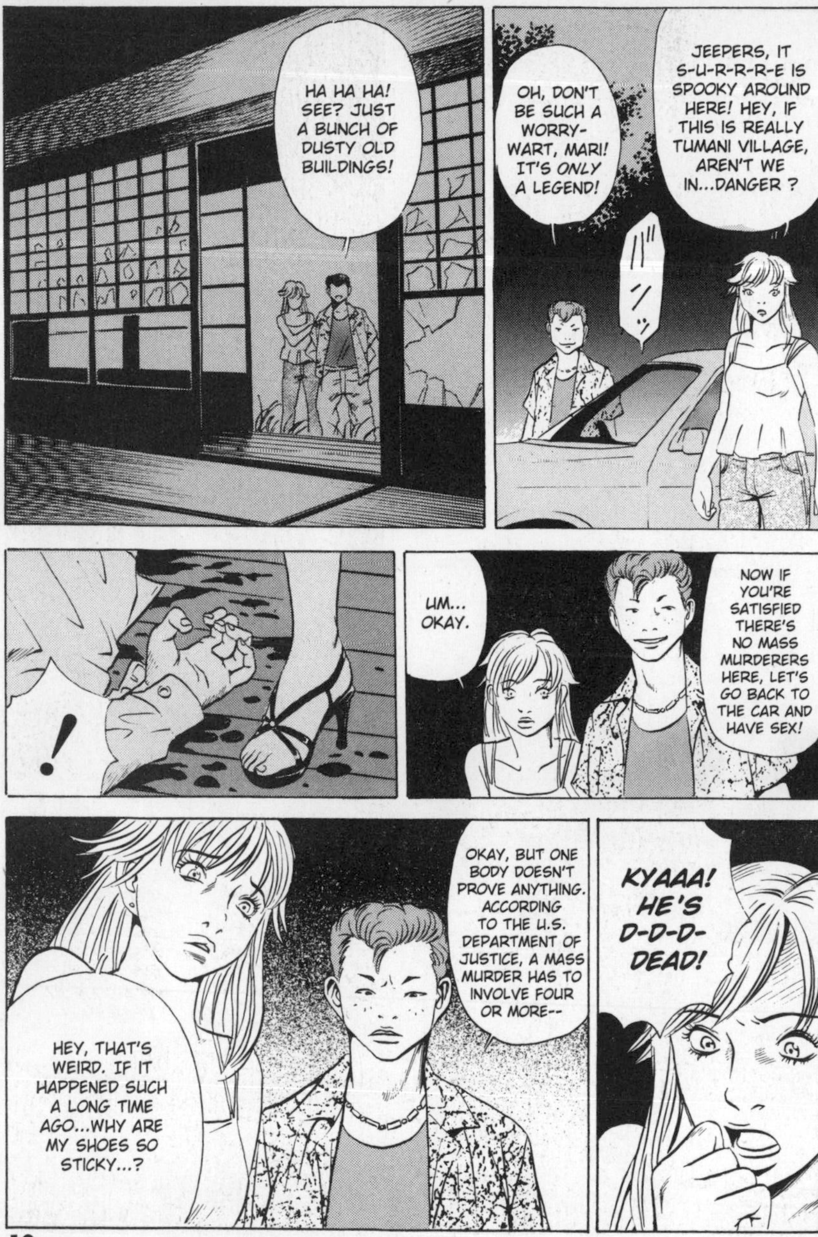
JEEPERS, IT S-U-R-R-R-E IS SPOOKY AROUND HERE! HEY, IF THIS IS REALLY TUMANI VILLAGE, AREN'T WE IN...DANGER ?
OH, DON'T BE SUCH A WORRY-WART, MARI! IT'S *ONLY* A LEGEND!
HA HA HA! SEE? JUST A BUNCH OF DUSTY OLD BUILDINGS!
NOW IF YOU'RE SATISFIED THERE'S NO MASS MURDERERS HERE, LET'S GO BACK TO THE CAR AND HAVE SEX!
UM... OKAY.
!
KYAAA! HE'S D-D-D-DEAD!
OKAY, BUT ONE BODY DOESN'T PROVE ANYTHING. ACCORDING TO THE U.S. DEPARTMENT OF JUSTICE, A MASS MURDER HAS TO INVOLVE FOUR OR MORE--
HEY, THAT'S WEIRD. IF IT HAPPENED SUCH A LONG TIME AGO...WHY ARE MY SHOES SO STICKY...?

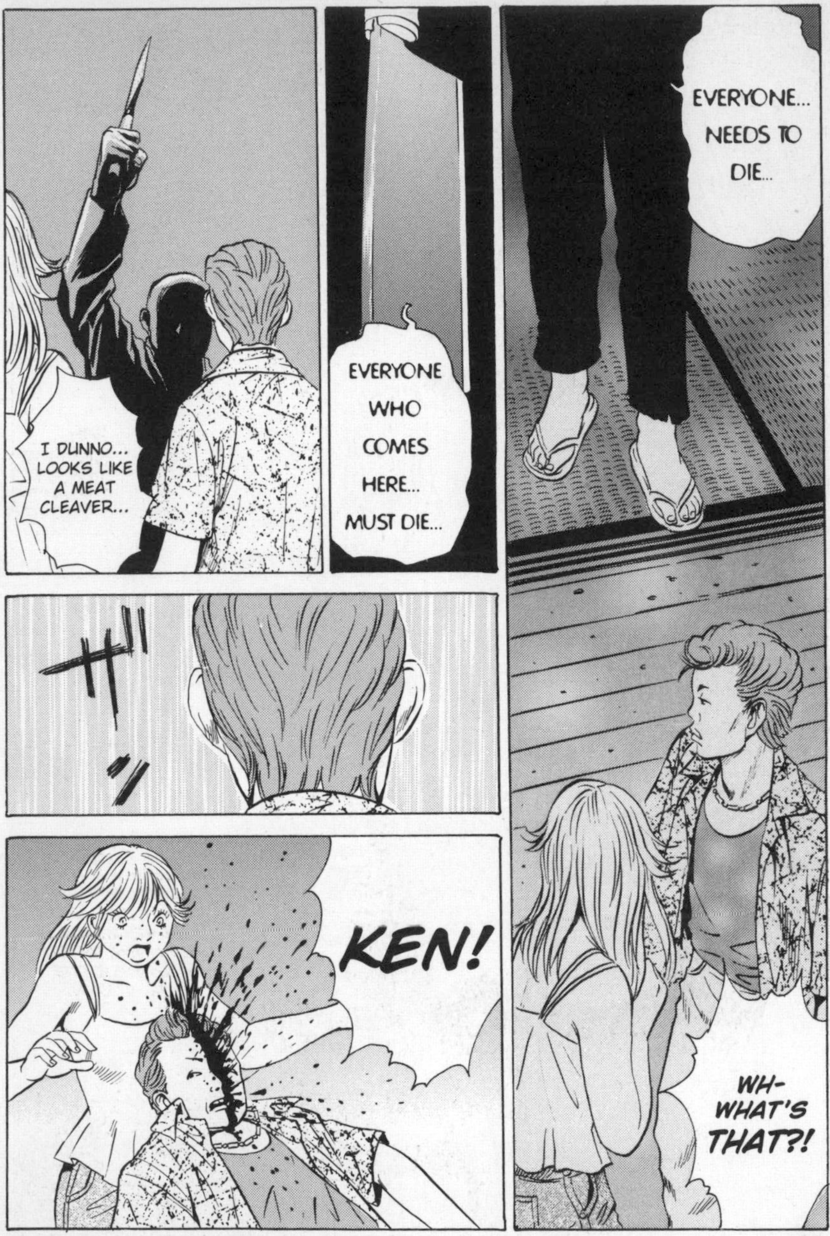
EVERYONE... NEEDS TO DIE...
EVERYONE WHO COMES HERE... MUST DIE...
I DUNNO... LOOKS LIKE A MEAT CLEAVER...
WH- WHAT'S THAT?!
KEN!

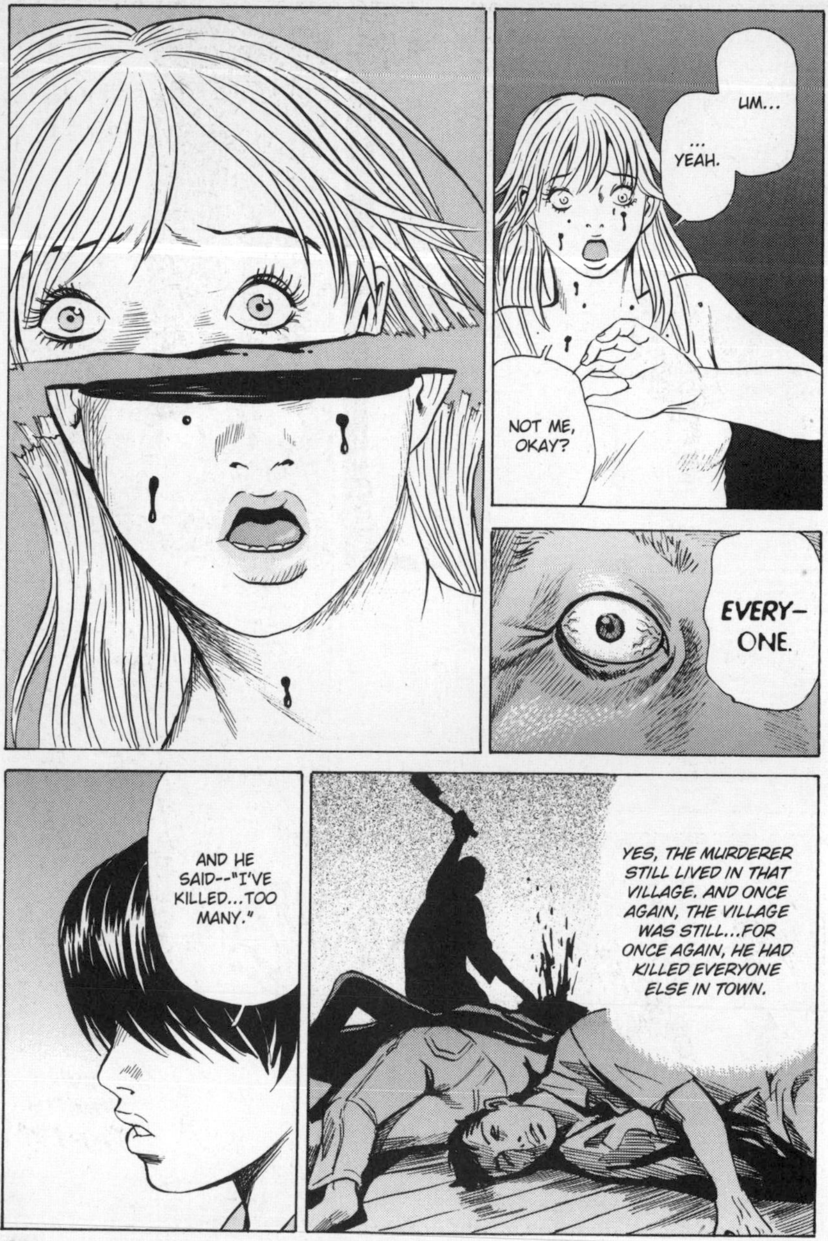
UM...
... YEAH.
NOT ME, OKAY?
EVERY-ONE.
YES, THE MURDERER STILL LIVED IN THAT VILLAGE. AND ONCE AGAIN, THE VILLAGE WAS STILL...FOR ONCE AGAIN, HE HAD KILLED EVERYONE ELSE IN TOWN.
AND HE SAID--"I'VE KILLED...TOO MANY."

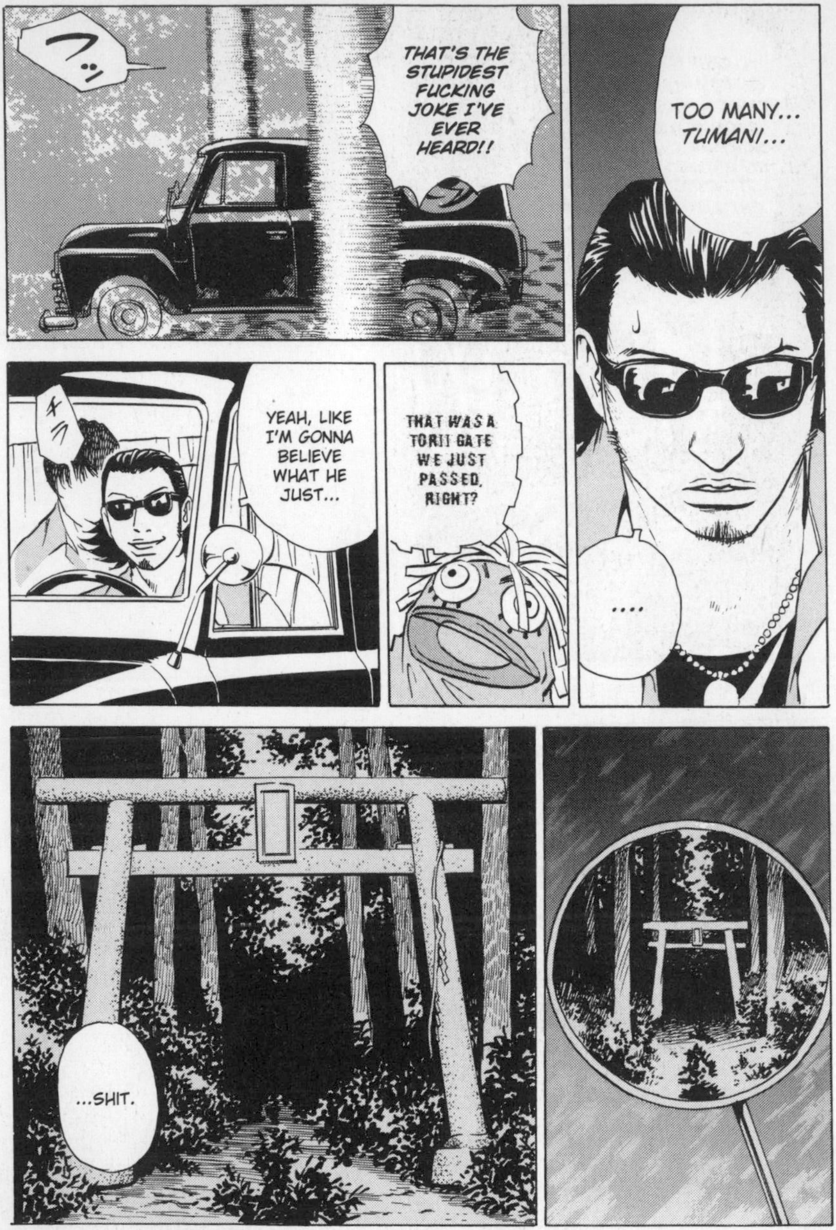
TOO MANY... TUMANI...
....
ヘッ
THAT'S THE STUPIDEST FUCKING JOKE I'VE EVER HEARD!!
THAT WAS A TORII GATE WE JUST PASSED, RIGHT?
YEAH, LIKE I'M GONNA BELIEVE WHAT HE JUST...
チラ
...SHIT.

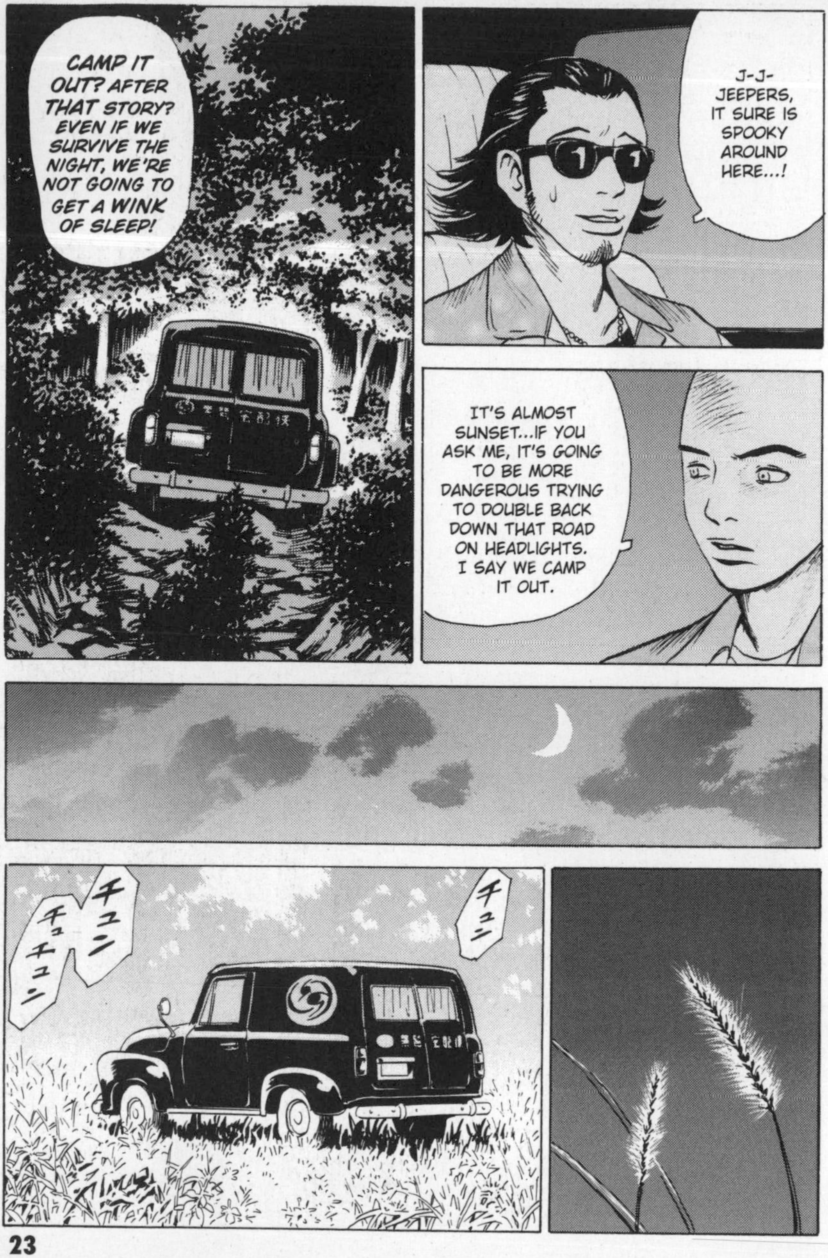
J-J-JEEPERS, IT SURE IS SPOOKY AROUND HERE...!
IT'S ALMOST SUNSET...IF YOU ASK ME, IT'S GOING TO BE MORE DANGEROUS TRYING TO DOUBLE BACK DOWN THAT ROAD ON HEADLIGHTS. I SAY WE CAMP IT OUT.
CAMP IT OUT? AFTER THAT STORY? EVEN IF WE SURVIVE THE NIGHT, WE'RE NOT GOING TO GET A WINK OF SLEEP!
チュン
チュン
チュチュン

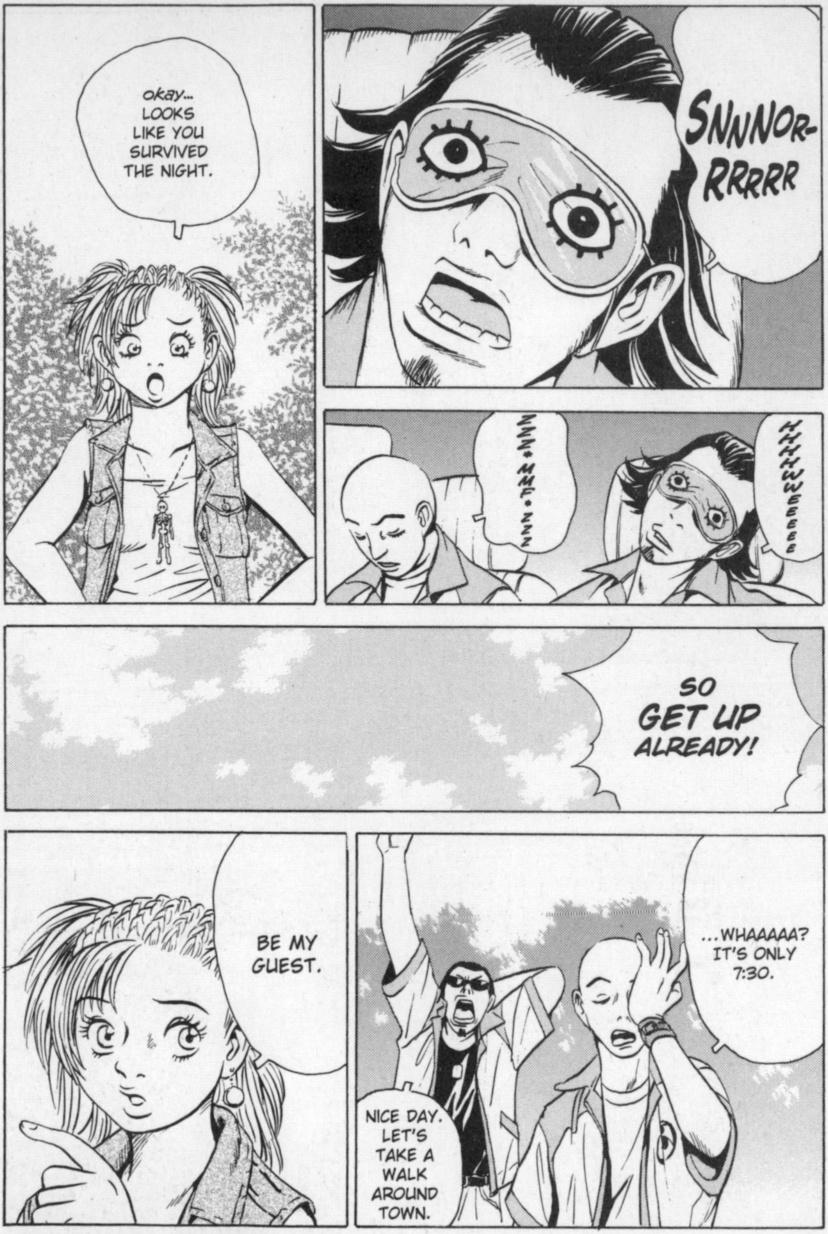
SNNNOR-RRRRR
HHHHWWEEEEEE
ZZZ*MMF*ZZZ
okay... LOOKS LIKE YOU SURVIVED THE NIGHT.
SO GET UP ALREADY!
...WHAAAAA? IT'S ONLY 7:30.
NICE DAY. LET'S TAKE A WALK AROUND TOWN.
BE MY GUEST.

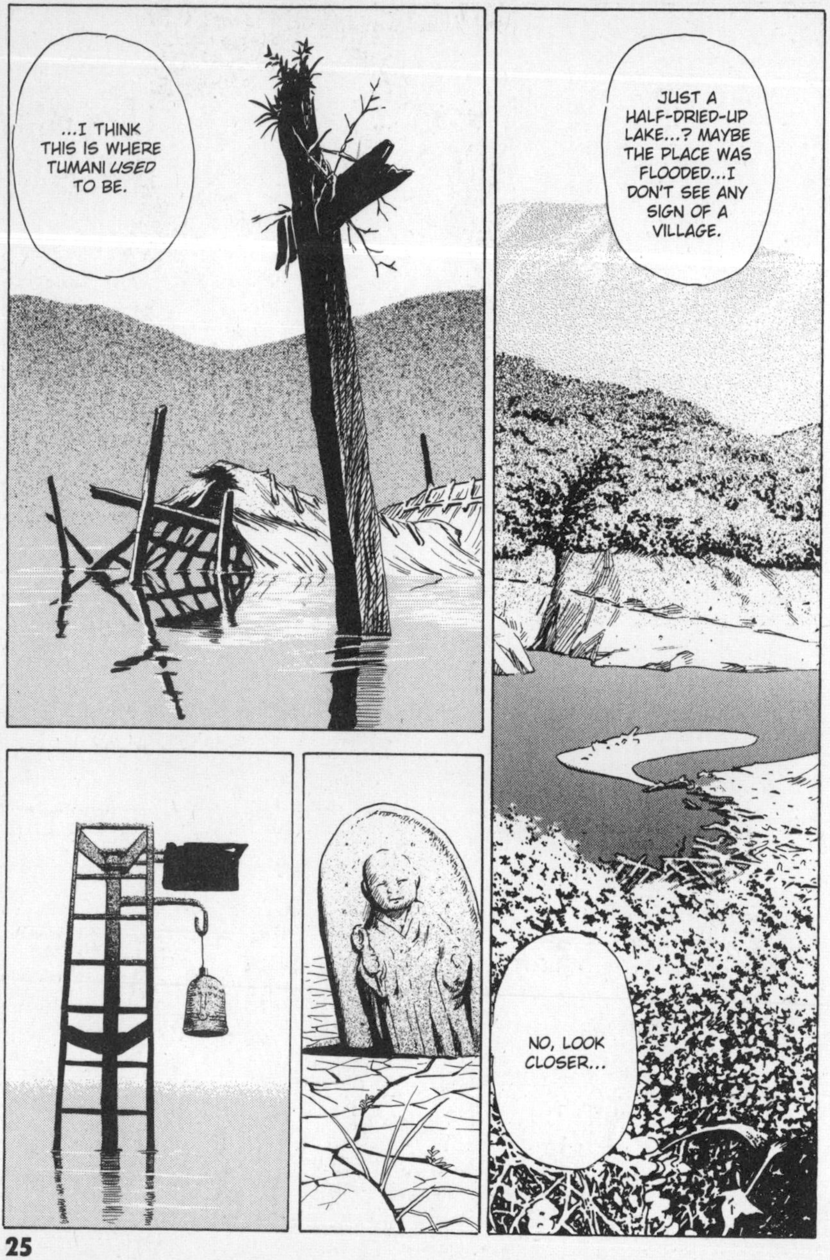
JUST A HALF-DRIED-UP LAKE...? MAYBE THE PLACE WAS FLOODED...I DON'T SEE ANY SIGN OF A VILLAGE.
NO, LOOK CLOSER...
...I THINK THIS IS WHERE TUMANI *USED* TO BE.

OLD COOKING POT...WELL, MAYBE THIS WAS IT, BUT IT SURE DOESN'T LOOK LIKE ANYONE'S AROUND TO GIVE THE OLD MAN A FUNERAL.
YEAH...AND COME TO THINK OF IT, HOW DO WE KNOW THIS REALLY WAS TUMANI?
ガポッ
WELL... IF THE STORY'S TRUE...
...MAYBE THERE'S SOME BODIES STILL AROUND...?
MY DOWSING STARTED THIS WHOLE THING...HEY, KARATSU, HOLD HIM A MINUTE...
...OKAY.
...LET'S SEE IF I CAN FINISH IT.
チャラン
HOLY... LOOK!
THERE'S GOT TO BE TWENTY... AT LEAST THIRTY CORPSES HERE!
ヒュン
ヒュン
ヒュン

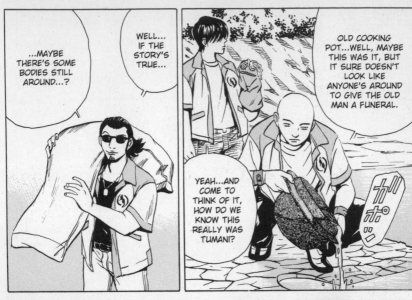

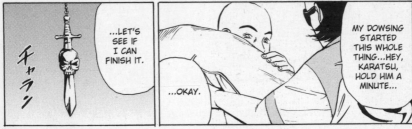

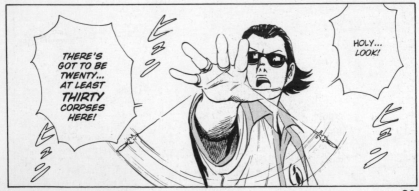

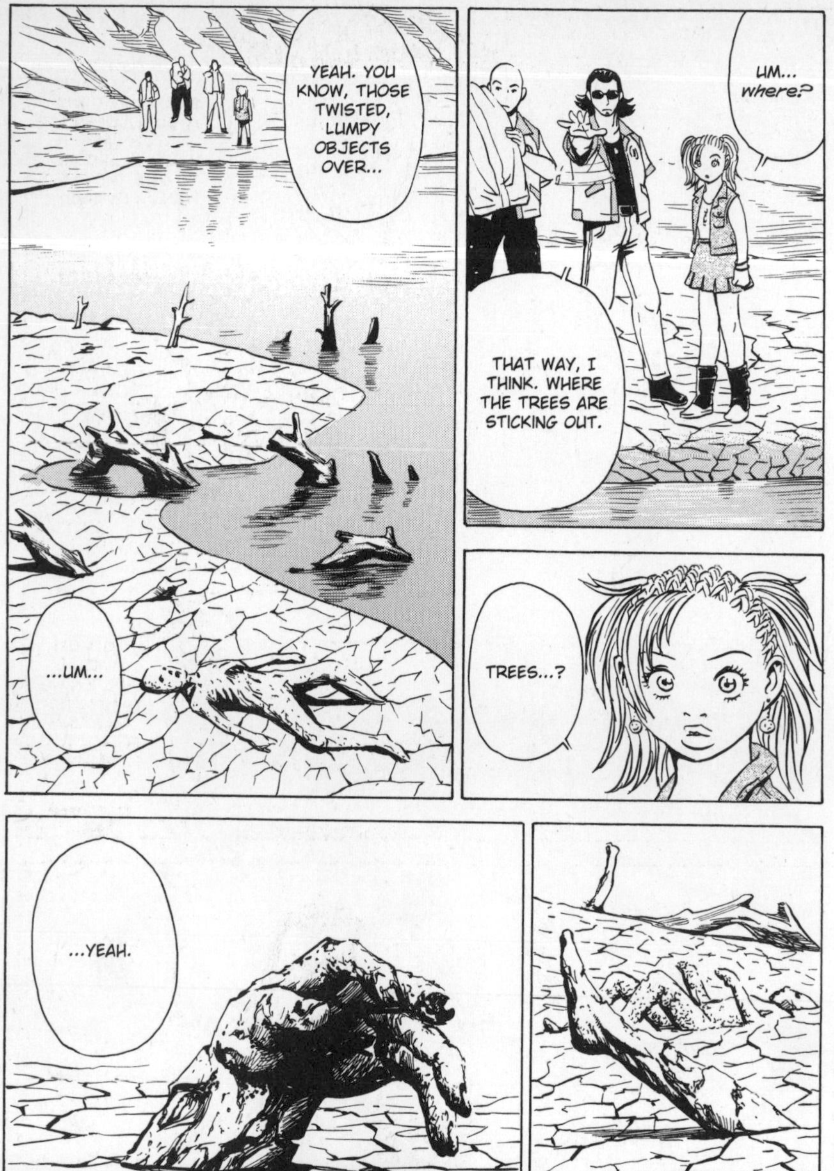
UM... *where?*
THAT WAY, I THINK. WHERE THE TREES ARE STICKING OUT.
TREES...?
YEAH. YOU KNOW, THOSE TWISTED, LUMPY OBJECTS OVER...
...UM...
...YEAH.

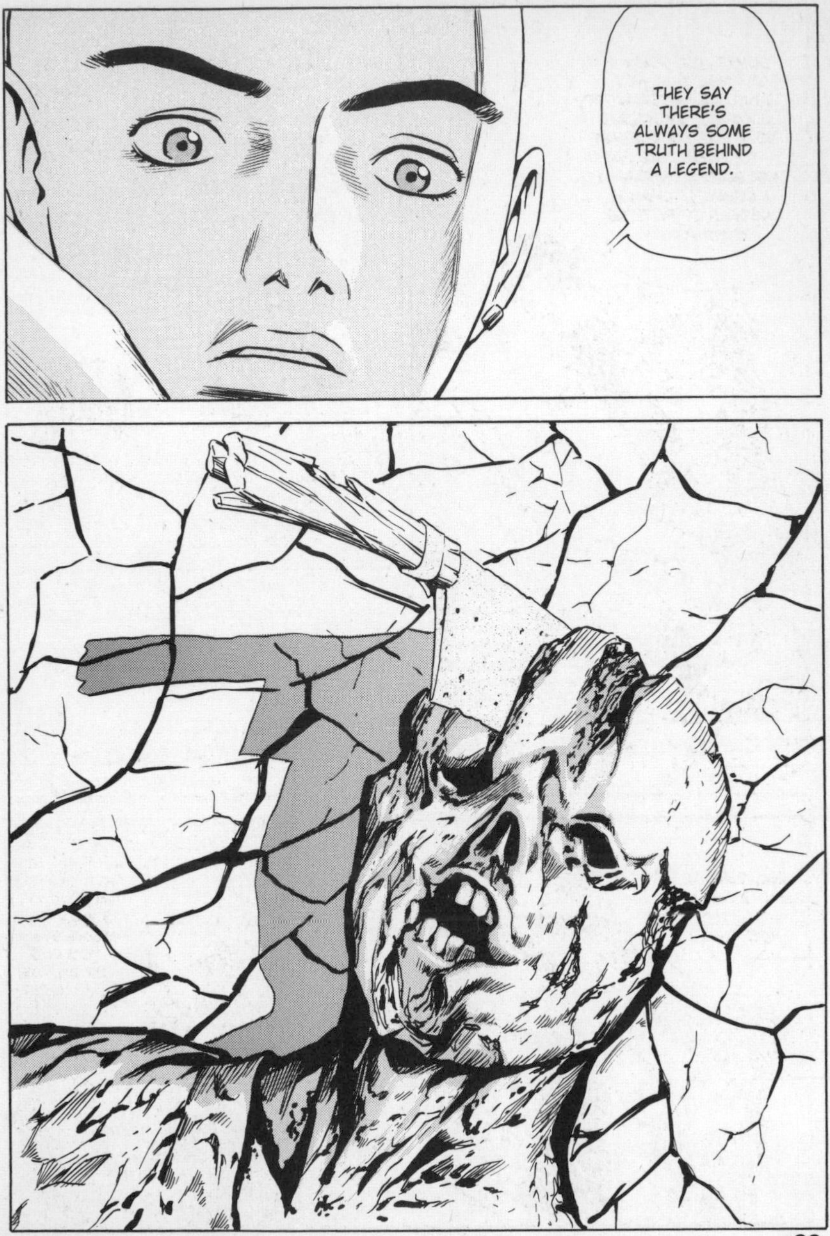
THEY SAY THERE'S ALWAYS SOME TRUTH BEHIND A LEGEND.

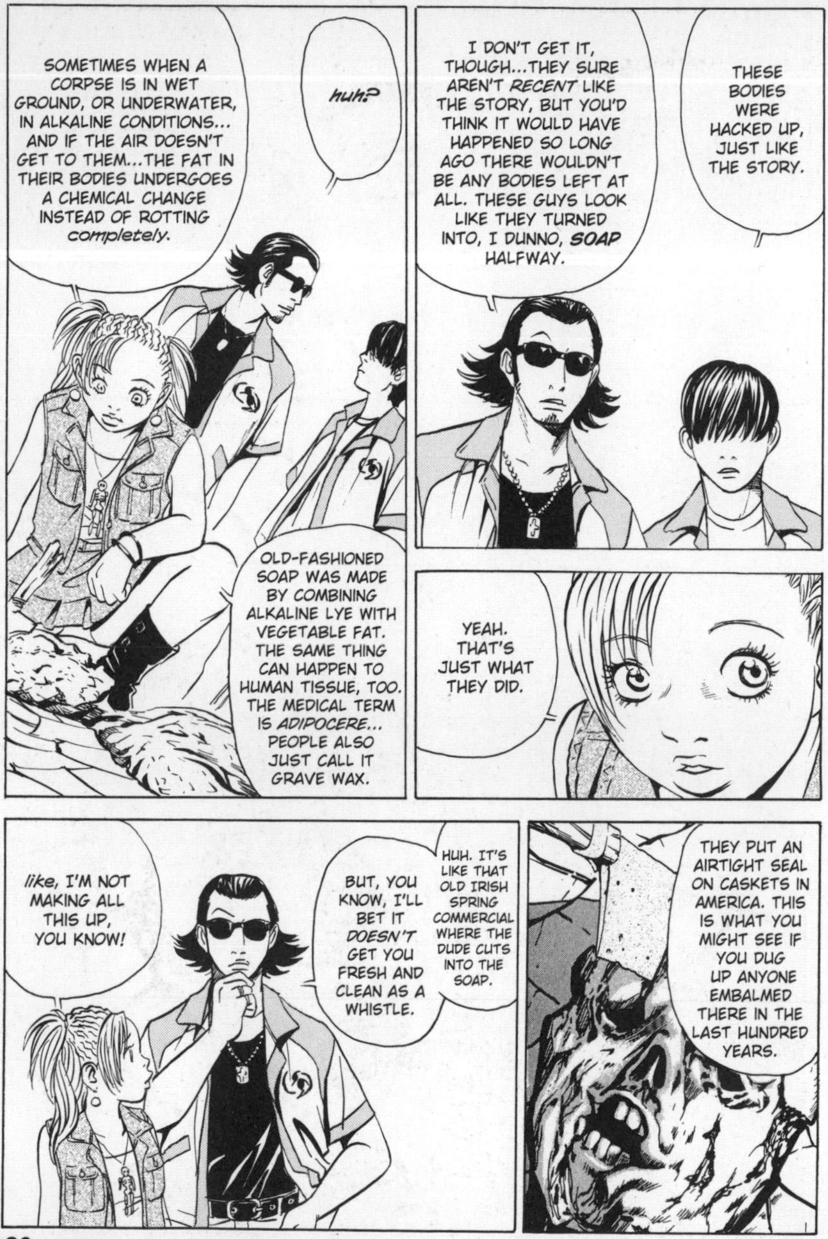
THESE BODIES WERE HACKED UP, JUST LIKE THE STORY.
I DON'T GET IT, THOUGH...THEY SURE AREN'T *RECENT* LIKE THE STORY, BUT YOU'D THINK IT WOULD HAVE HAPPENED SO LONG AGO THERE WOULDN'T BE ANY BODIES LEFT AT ALL. THESE GUYS LOOK LIKE THEY TURNED INTO, I DUNNO, ***SOAP*** HALFWAY.
YEAH. THAT'S JUST WHAT THEY DID.
huh?
SOMETIMES WHEN A CORPSE IS IN WET GROUND, OR UNDERWATER, IN ALKALINE CONDITIONS... AND IF THE AIR DOESN'T GET TO THEM...THE FAT IN THEIR BODIES UNDERGOES A CHEMICAL CHANGE INSTEAD OF ROTTING *completely*.
OLD-FASHIONED SOAP WAS MADE BY COMBINING ALKALINE LYE WITH VEGETABLE FAT. THE SAME THING CAN HAPPEN TO HUMAN TISSUE, TOO. THE MEDICAL TERM IS *ADIPOCERE*... PEOPLE ALSO JUST CALL IT GRAVE WAX.
THEY PUT AN AIRTIGHT SEAL ON CASKETS IN AMERICA. THIS IS WHAT YOU MIGHT SEE IF YOU DUG UP ANYONE EMBALMED THERE IN THE LAST HUNDRED YEARS.
HUH. IT'S LIKE THAT OLD IRISH SPRING COMMERCIAL WHERE THE DUDE CUTS INTO THE SOAP.
BUT, YOU KNOW, I'LL BET IT *DOESN'T* GET YOU FRESH AND CLEAN AS A WHISTLE.
like, I'M NOT MAKING ALL THIS UP, YOU KNOW!

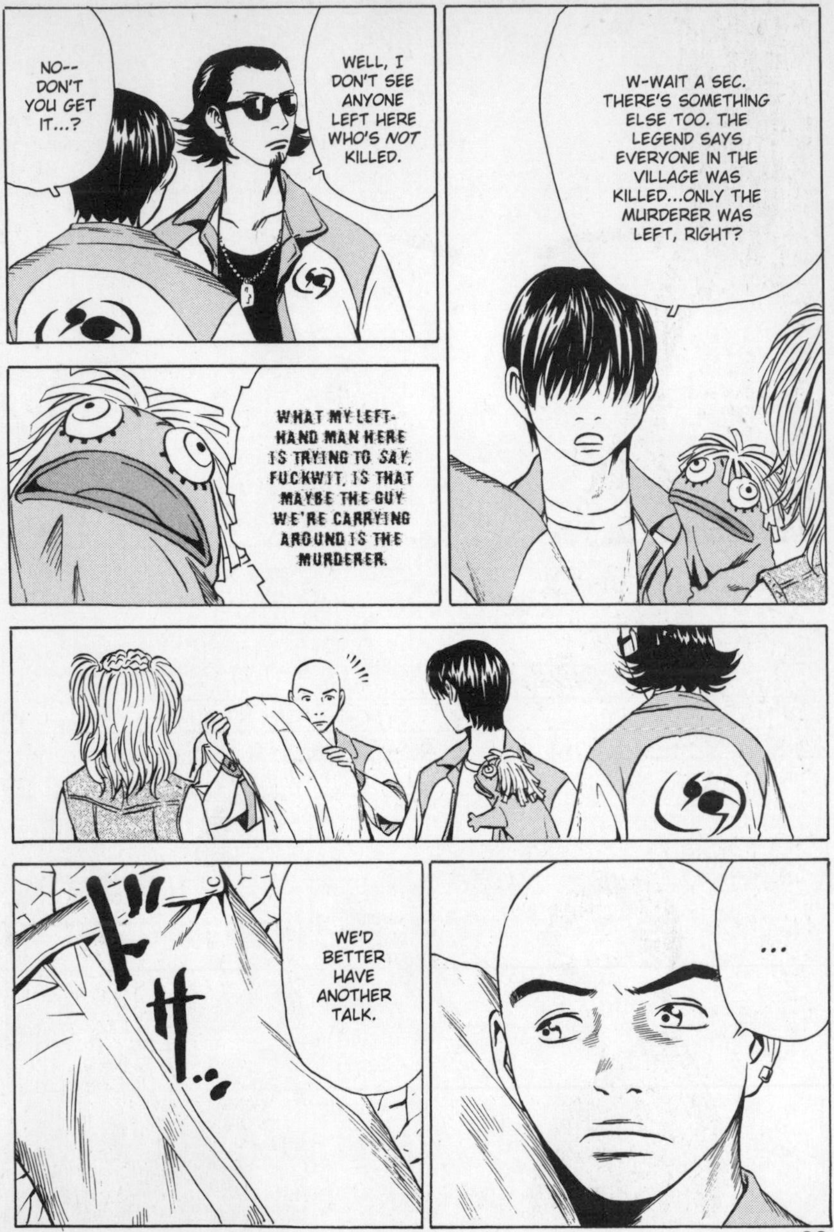

W-WAIT A SEC. THERE'S SOMETHING ELSE TOO. THE LEGEND SAYS EVERYONE IN THE VILLAGE WAS KILLED...ONLY THE MURDERER WAS LEFT, RIGHT?
WELL, I DON'T SEE ANYONE LEFT HERE WHO'S *NOT* KILLED.
NO-- DON'T YOU GET IT...?
WHAT MY LEFT-HAND MAN HERE IS TRYING TO SAY, FUCKWIT, IS THAT MAYBE THE GUY WE'RE CARRYING AROUND IS THE MURDERER.
...
WE'D BETTER HAVE ANOTHER TALK.

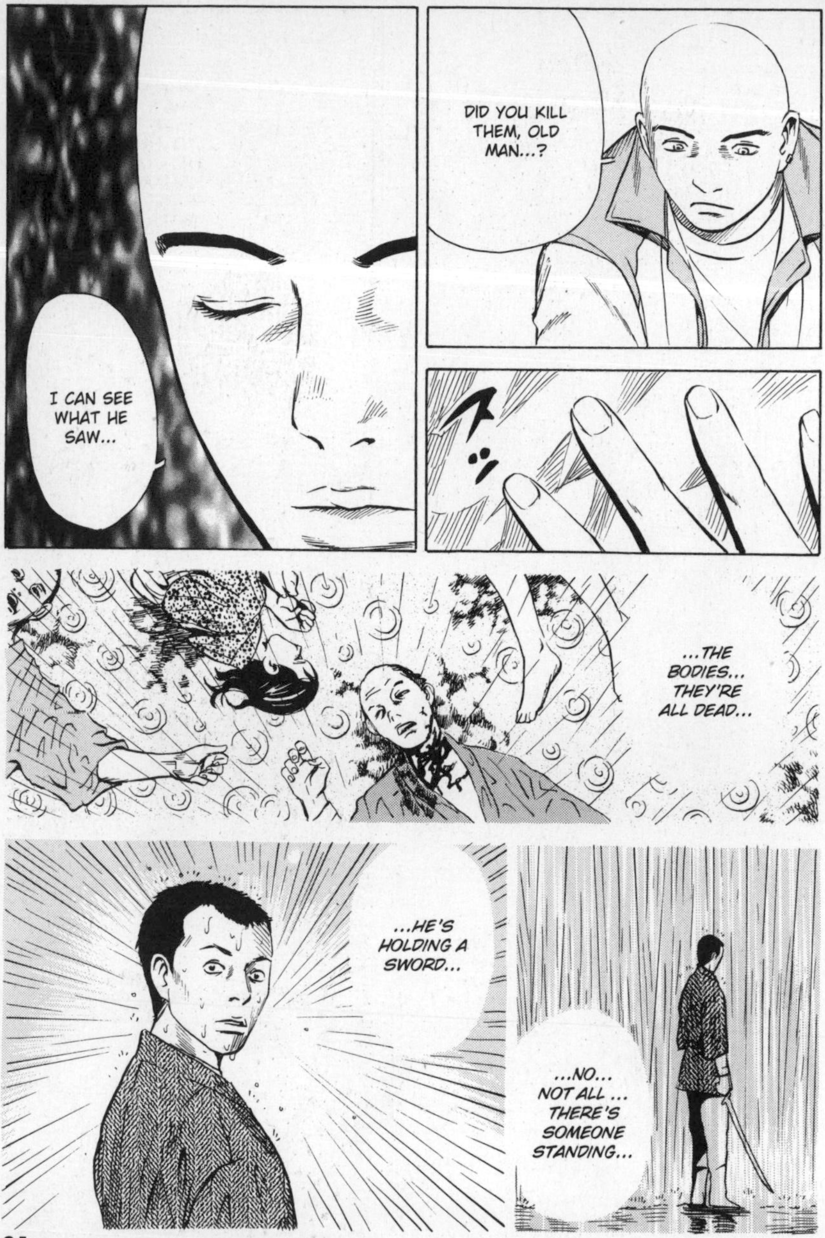
DID YOU KILL THEM, OLD MAN...?
I CAN SEE WHAT HE SAW...
...THE BODIES... THEY'RE ALL DEAD...
...NO... NOT ALL ... THERE'S SOMEONE STANDING...
...HE'S HOLDING A SWORD...

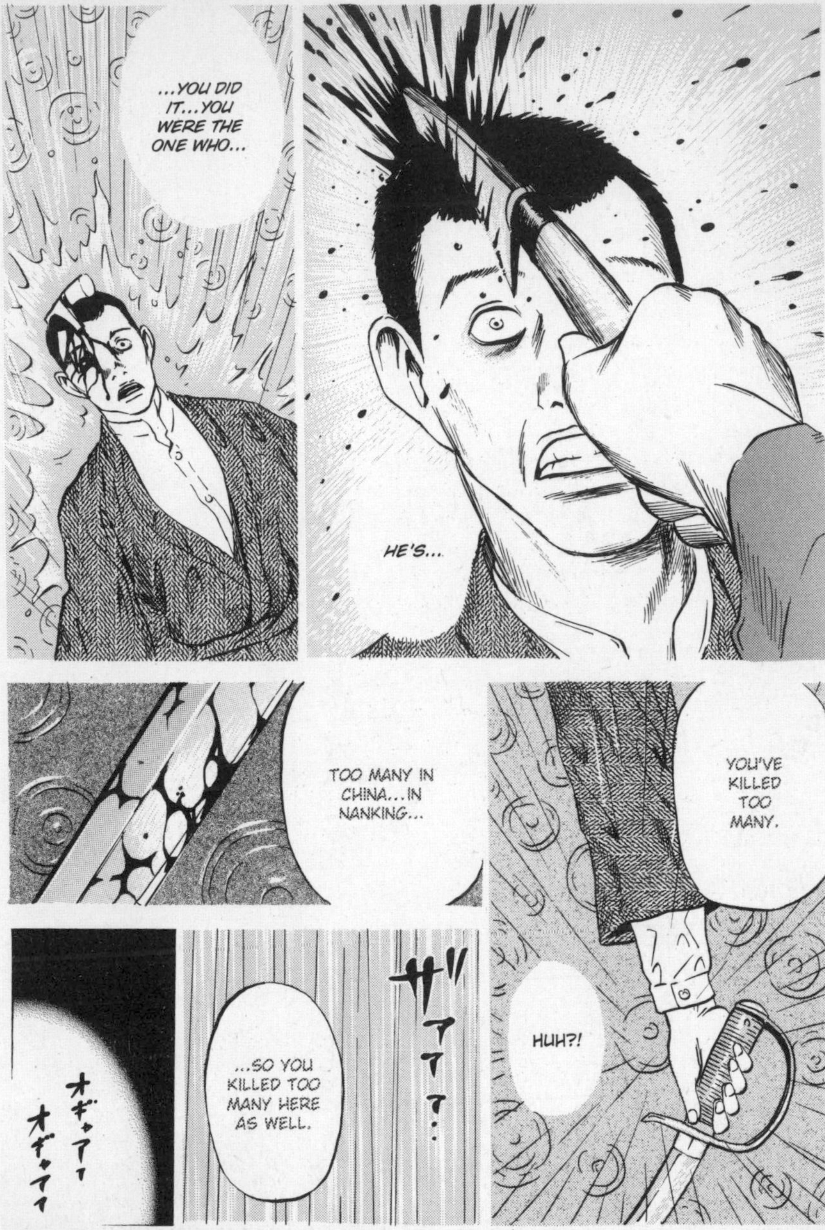
HE'S...
...YOU DID IT...YOU WERE THE ONE WHO...
YOU'VE KILLED TOO MANY.
HUH?!
TOO MANY IN CHINA...IN NANKING...
ザァァァ...
...SO YOU KILLED TOO MANY HERE AS WELL.
オギャァァ
オギャァァ

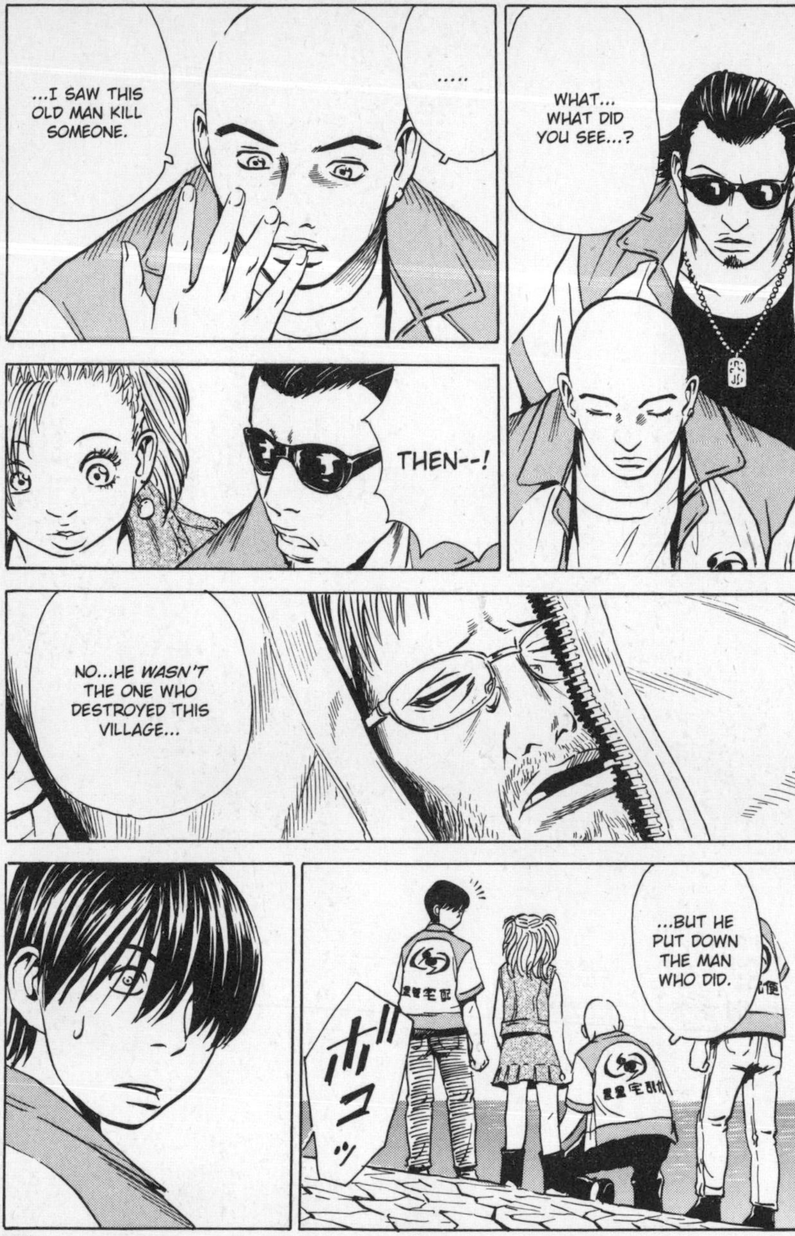
WHAT... WHAT DID YOU SEE...?
.....
...I SAW THIS OLD MAN KILL SOMEONE.
THEN--!
NO...HE *WASN'T* THE ONE WHO DESTROYED THIS VILLAGE...
...BUT HE PUT DOWN THE MAN WHO DID.
ボコッ

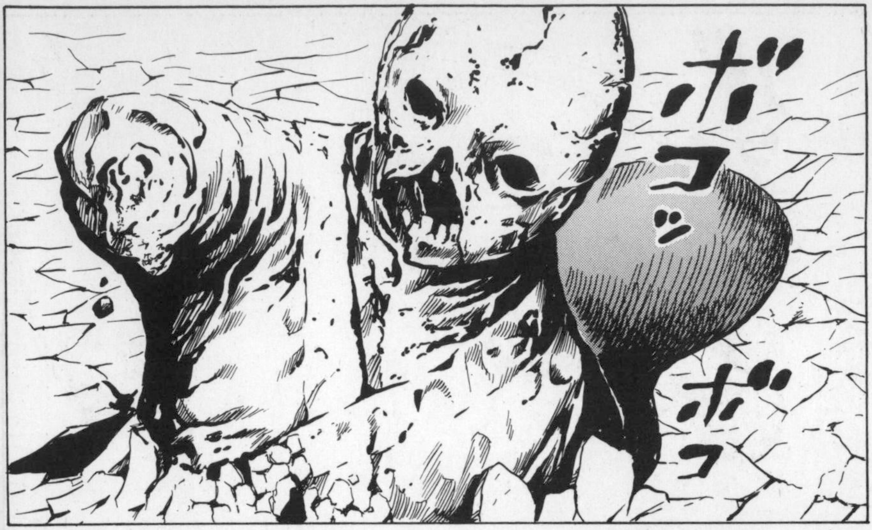
ボコッ
ボコ

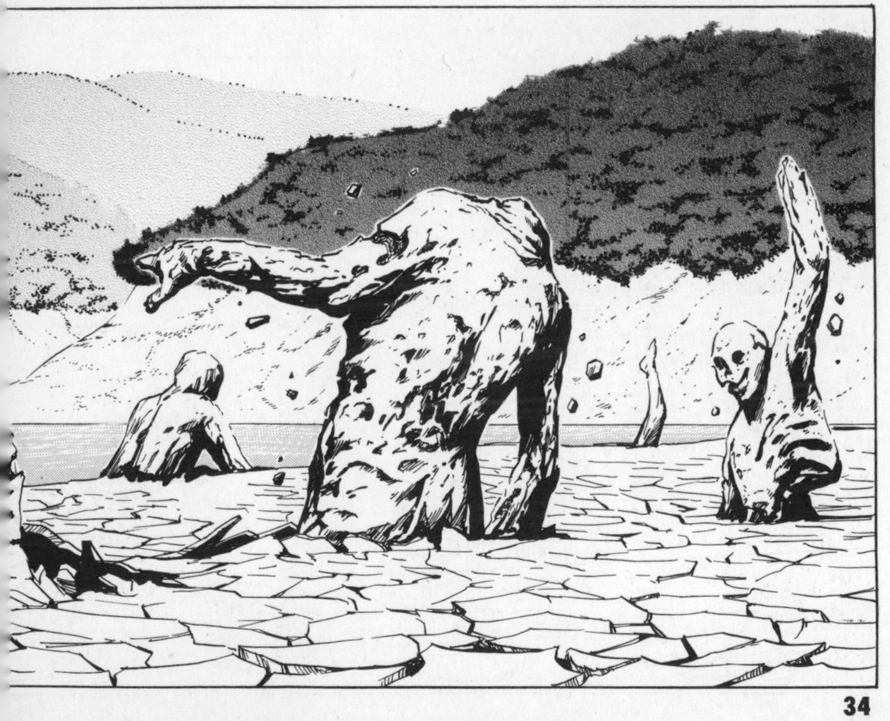

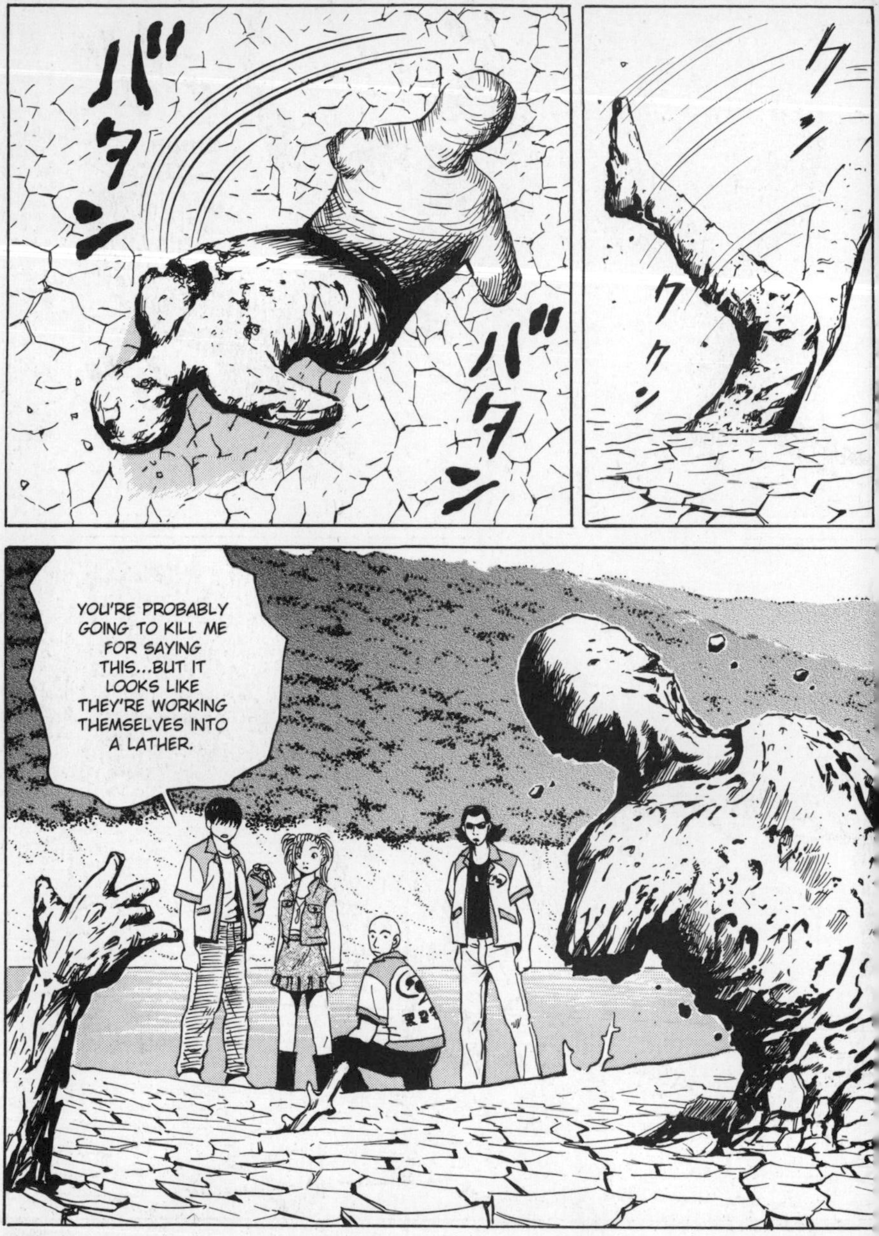
クン
ククン
バタン
バタン
YOU'RE PROBABLY GOING TO KILL ME FOR SAYING THIS...BUT IT LOOKS LIKE THEY'RE WORKING THEMSELVES INTO A LATHER.

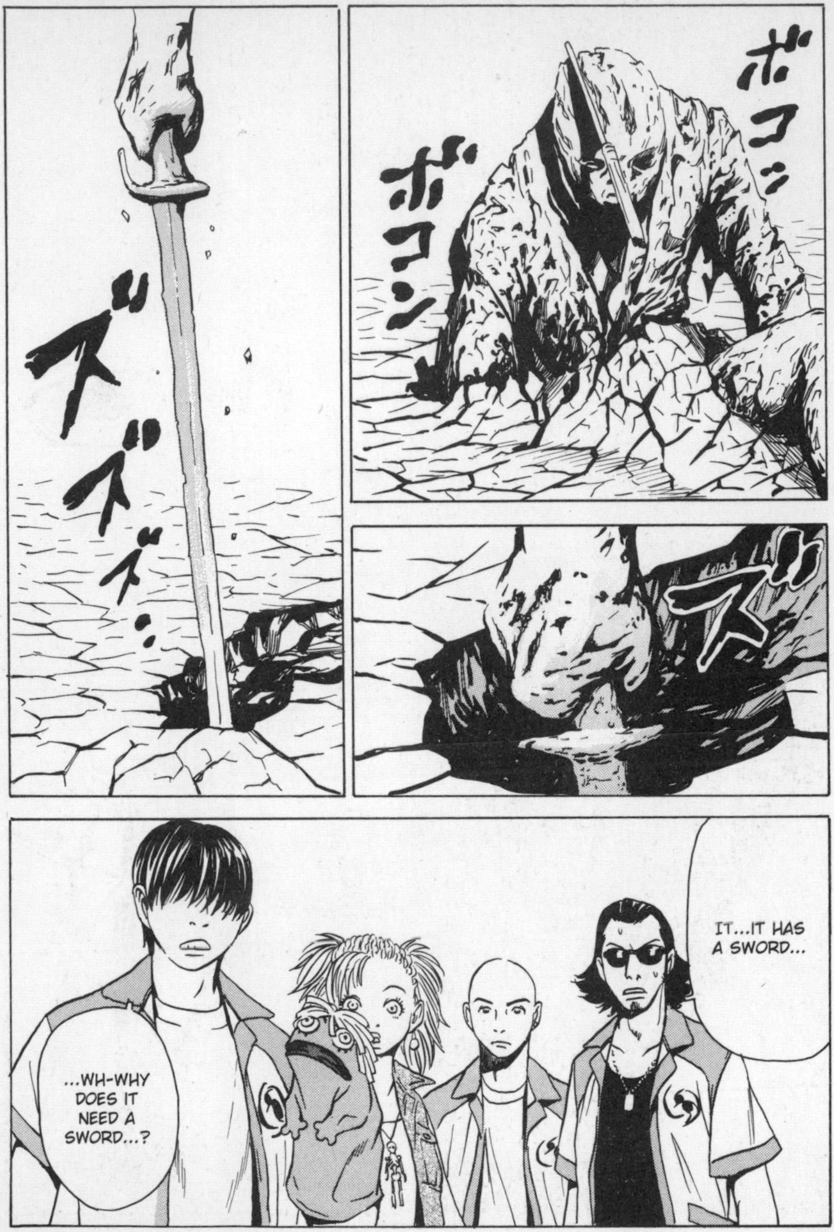
ボコッ
ボコン
ズッ
ズズズ…
IT...IT HAS A SWORD...
...WH-WHY DOES IT NEED A SWORD...?

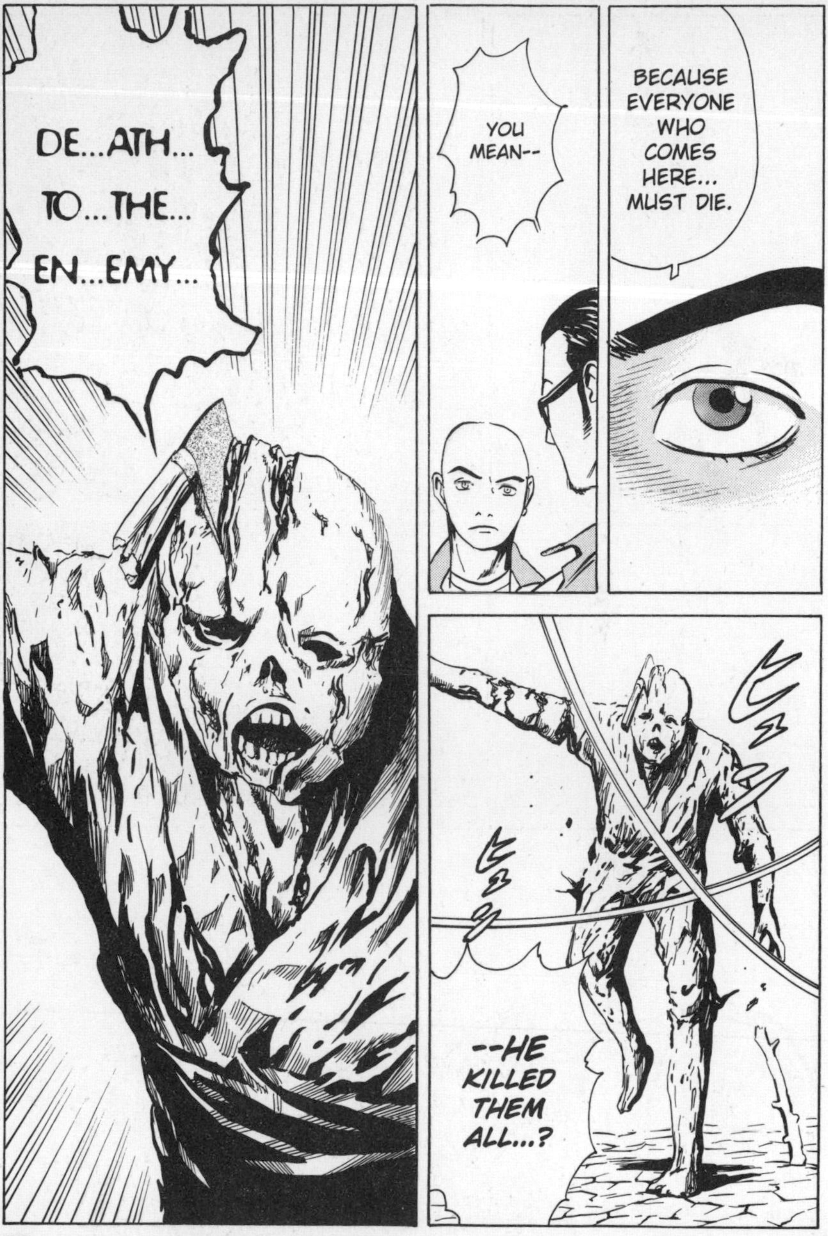
BECAUSE EVERYONE WHO COMES HERE... MUST DIE.
YOU MEAN--
--HE KILLED THEM ALL...?
DE...ATH... TO...THE... EN...EMY...

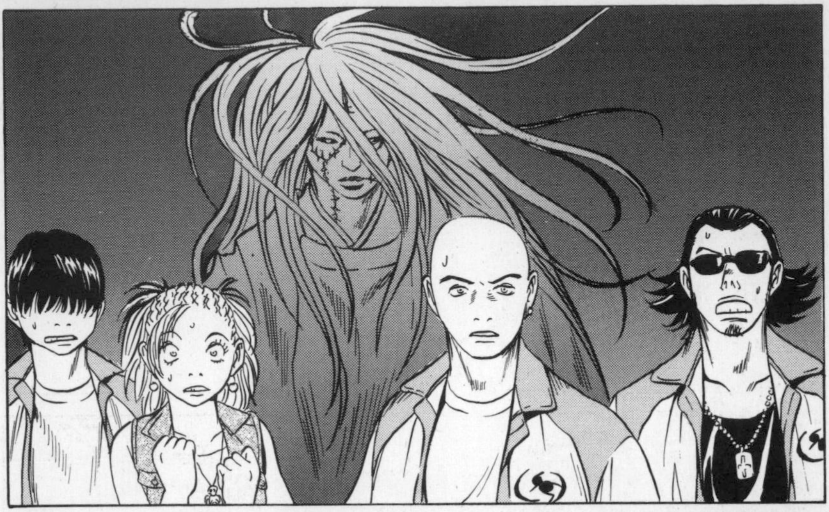

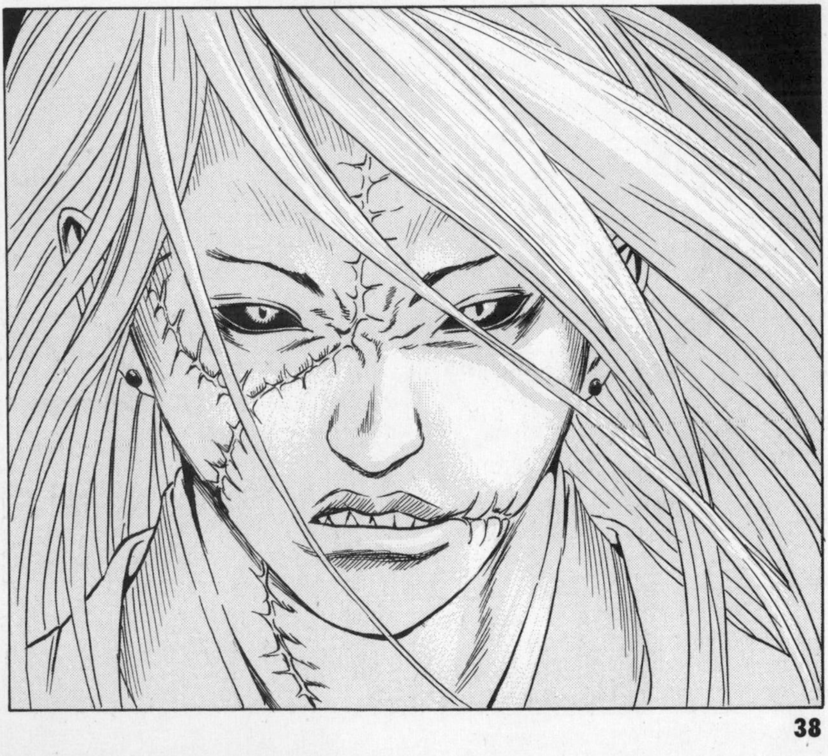

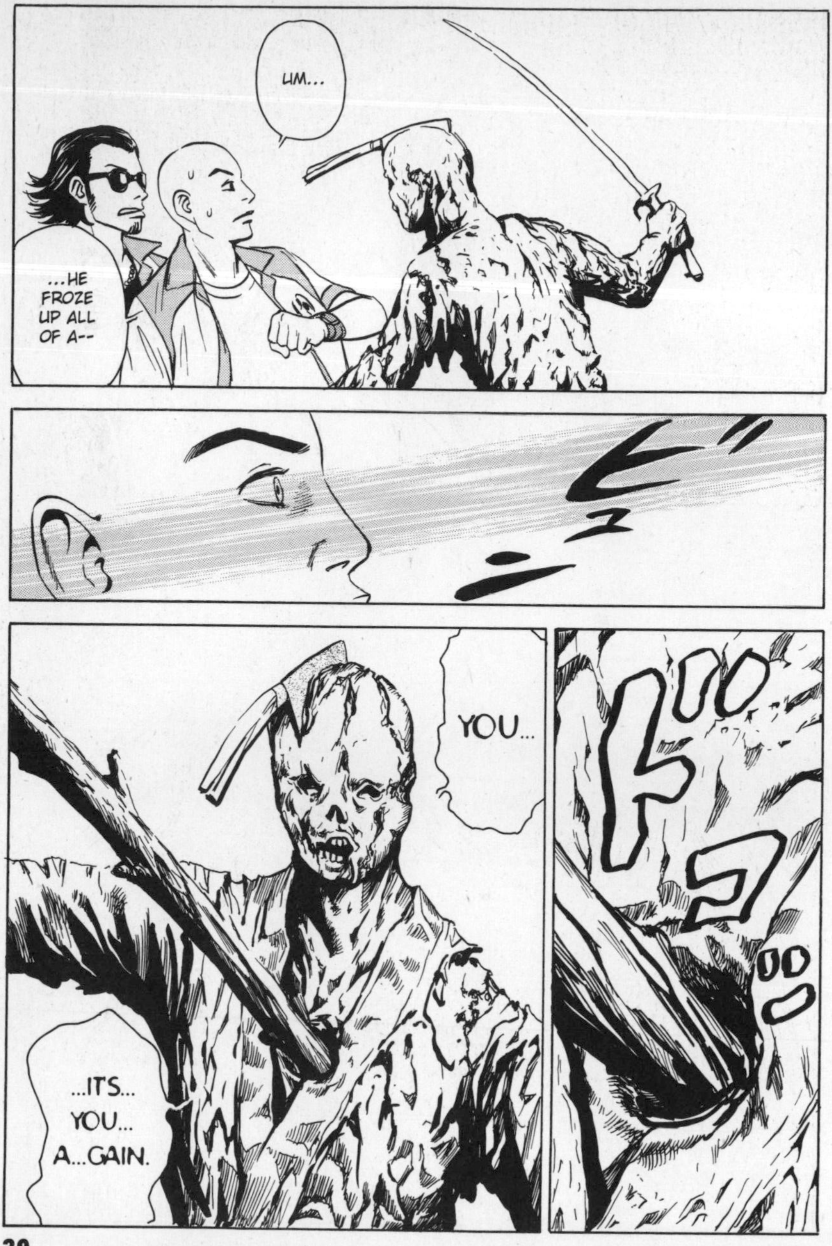
UM...
...HE FROZE UP ALL OF A--
YOU...
...IT'S... YOU... A...GAIN.

TH-
THANKS...

...OLD
MAN.

H-HE SAID
HE DIDN'T
WANT TO
COME BACK
HERE...

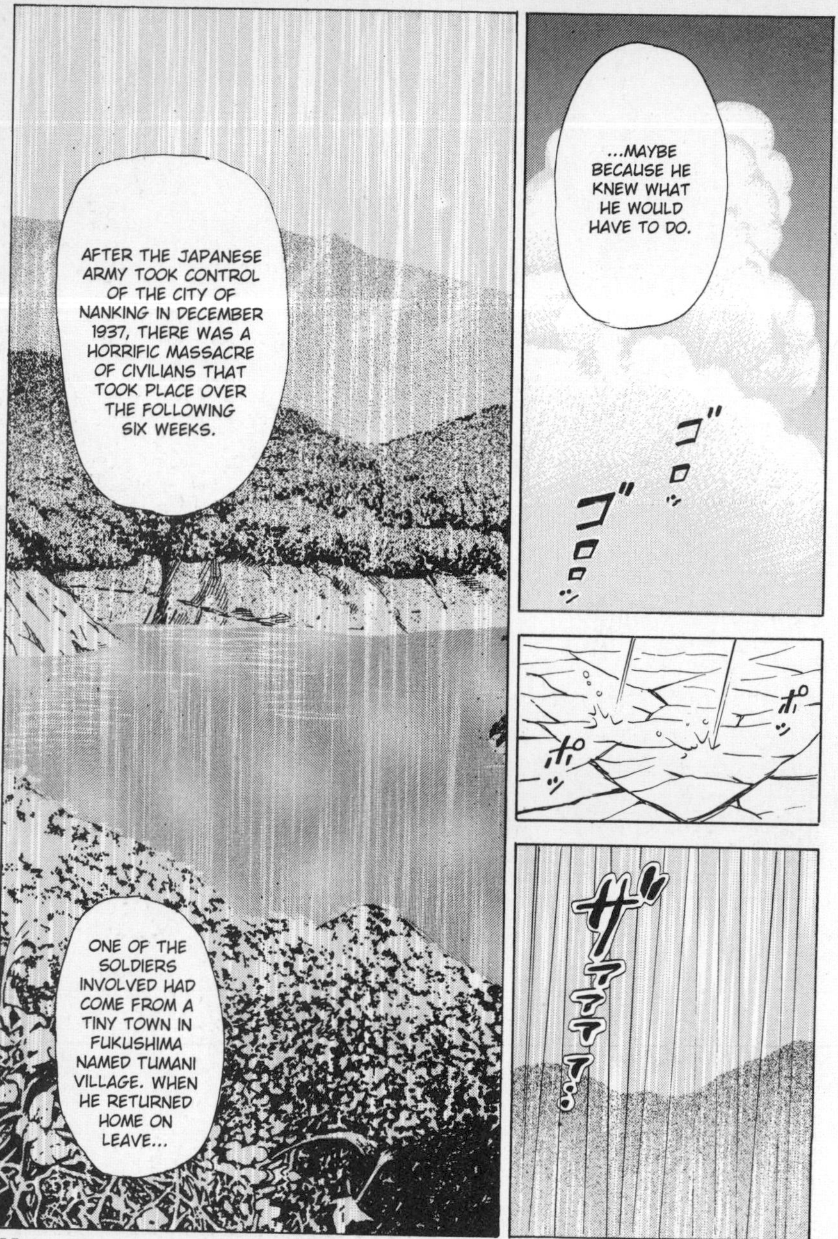
...MAYBE BECAUSE HE KNEW WHAT HE WOULD HAVE TO DO.
ゴロッ
ゴロロッ
ポッ
ポッ
ザァァァァ
AFTER THE JAPANESE ARMY TOOK CONTROL OF THE CITY OF NANKING IN DECEMBER 1937, THERE WAS A HORRIFIC MASSACRE OF CIVILIANS THAT TOOK PLACE OVER THE FOLLOWING SIX WEEKS.
ONE OF THE SOLDIERS INVOLVED HAD COME FROM A TINY TOWN IN FUKUSHIMA NAMED TUMANI VILLAGE. WHEN HE RETURNED HOME ON LEAVE...

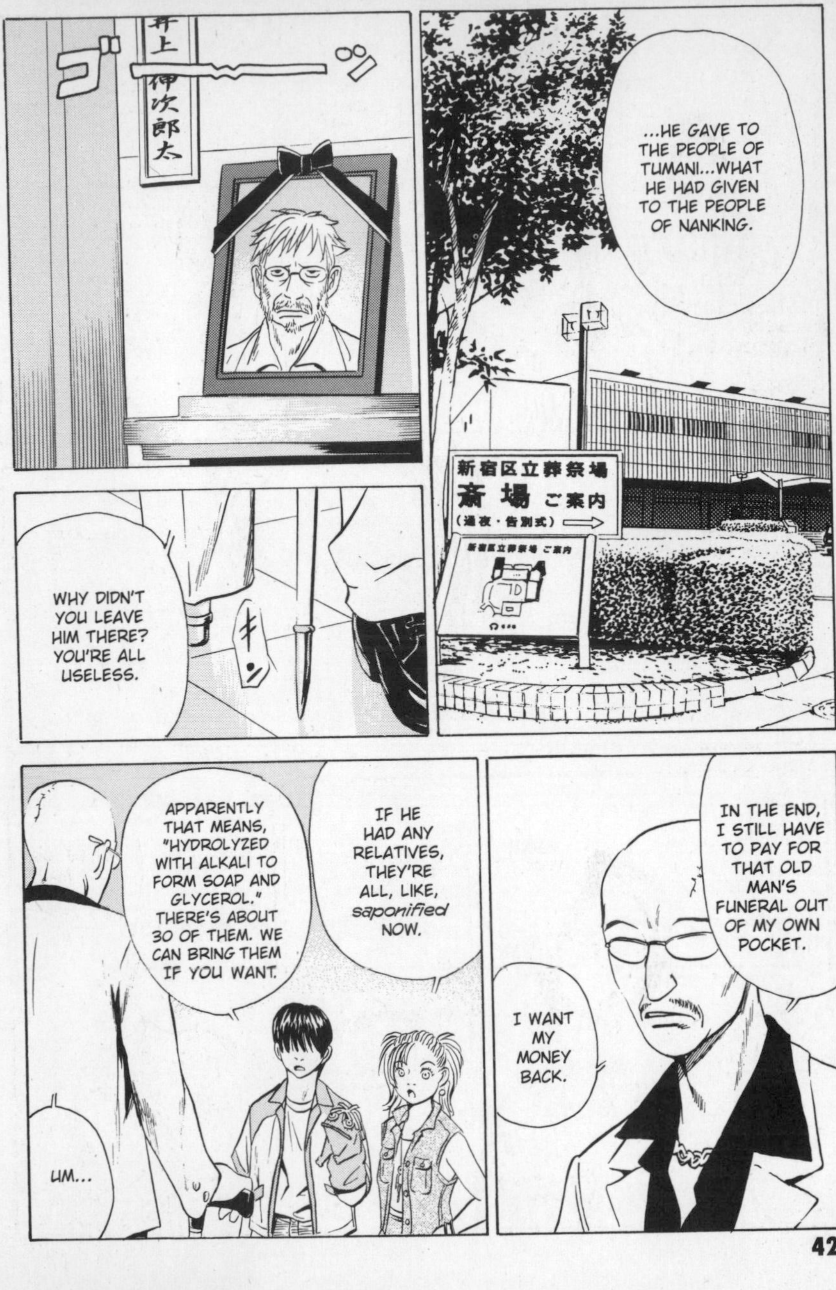
...HE GAVE TO THE PEOPLE OF TUMANI...WHAT HE HAD GIVEN TO THE PEOPLE OF NANKING.
新宿区立葬祭場
斎場 ご案内
(通夜・告別式)
新宿区立葬祭場 ご案内
WHY DIDN'T YOU LEAVE HIM THERE? YOU'RE ALL USELESS.
IN THE END, I STILL HAVE TO PAY FOR THAT OLD MAN'S FUNERAL OUT OF MY OWN POCKET.
I WANT MY MONEY BACK.
IF HE HAD ANY RELATIVES, THEY'RE ALL, LIKE, *saponified* NOW.
APPARENTLY THAT MEANS, "HYDROLYZED WITH ALKALI TO FORM SOAP AND GLYCEROL." THERE'S ABOUT 30 OF THEM. WE CAN BRING THEM IF YOU WANT.
UM...

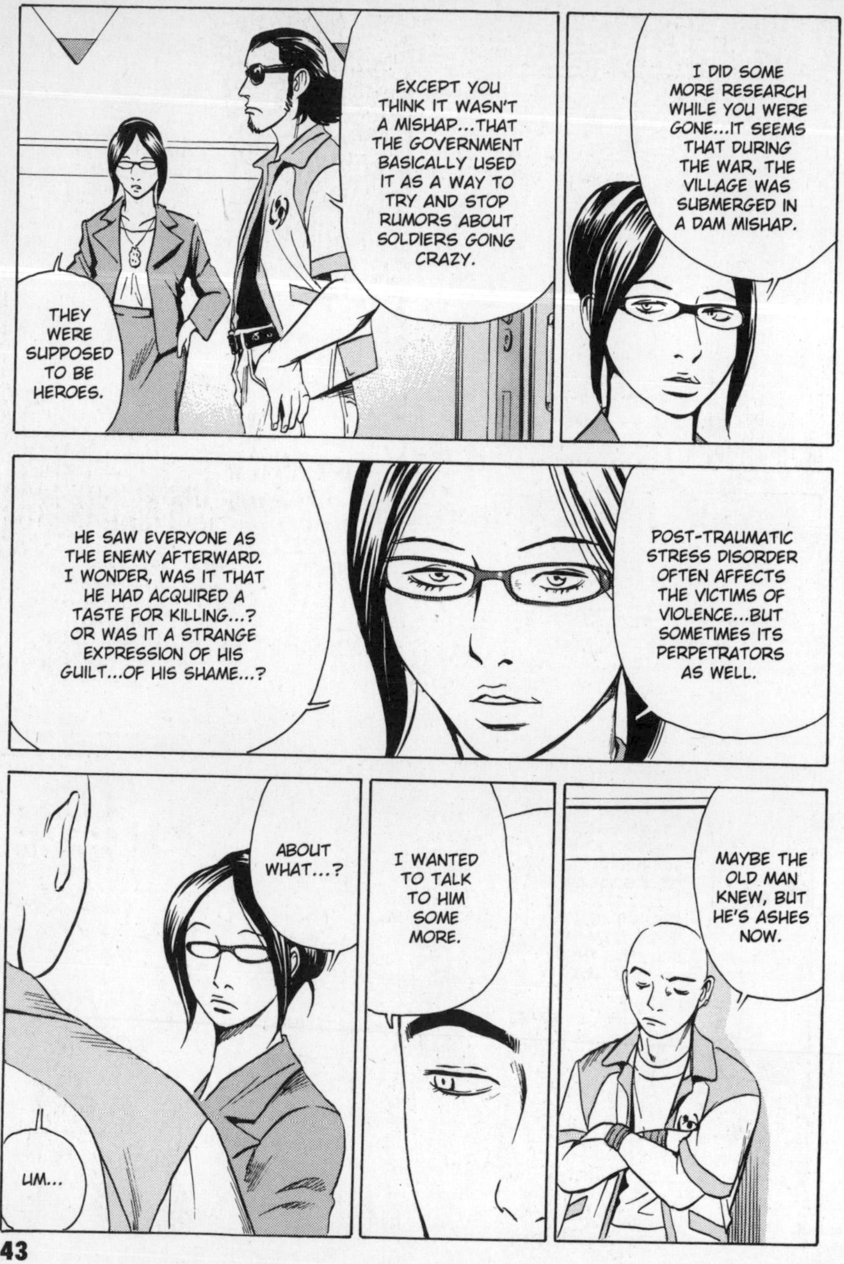
I DID SOME MORE RESEARCH WHILE YOU WERE GONE...IT SEEMS THAT DURING THE WAR, THE VILLAGE WAS SUBMERGED IN A DAM MISHAP.
EXCEPT YOU THINK IT WASN'T A MISHAP...THAT THE GOVERNMENT BASICALLY USED IT AS A WAY TO TRY AND STOP RUMORS ABOUT SOLDIERS GOING CRAZY.
THEY WERE SUPPOSED TO BE HEROES.
POST-TRAUMATIC STRESS DISORDER OFTEN AFFECTS THE VICTIMS OF VIOLENCE...BUT SOMETIMES ITS PERPETRATORS AS WELL.
HE SAW EVERYONE AS THE ENEMY AFTERWARD. I WONDER, WAS IT THAT HE HAD ACQUIRED A TASTE FOR KILLING...? OR WAS IT A STRANGE EXPRESSION OF HIS GUILT...OF HIS SHAME...?
MAYBE THE OLD MAN KNEW, BUT HE'S ASHES NOW.
I WANTED TO TALK TO HIM SOME MORE.
ABOUT WHAT...?
UM...

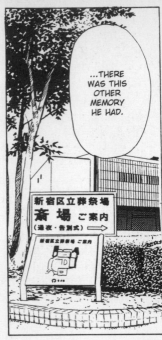

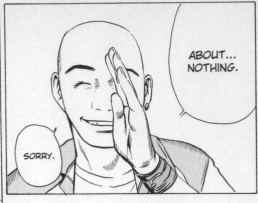

ABOUT... NOTHING.
SORRY.
WHY DON'T I BELIEVE YOU?
NOTHING... IT'S JUST...
...THERE WAS THIS OTHER MEMORY HE HAD.
新宿区立葬祭場
斎場 ご案内
(通夜・告別式)
新宿区立葬祭場 ご案内
ザァァ
DEAD... THEY'RE ALL DEAD...
オギャア
オギャア
!

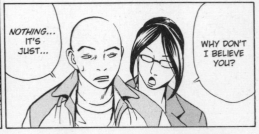

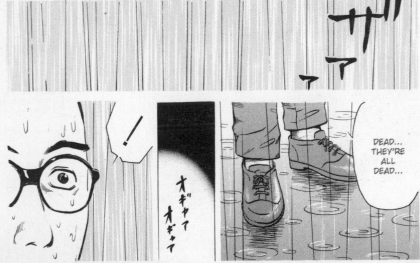

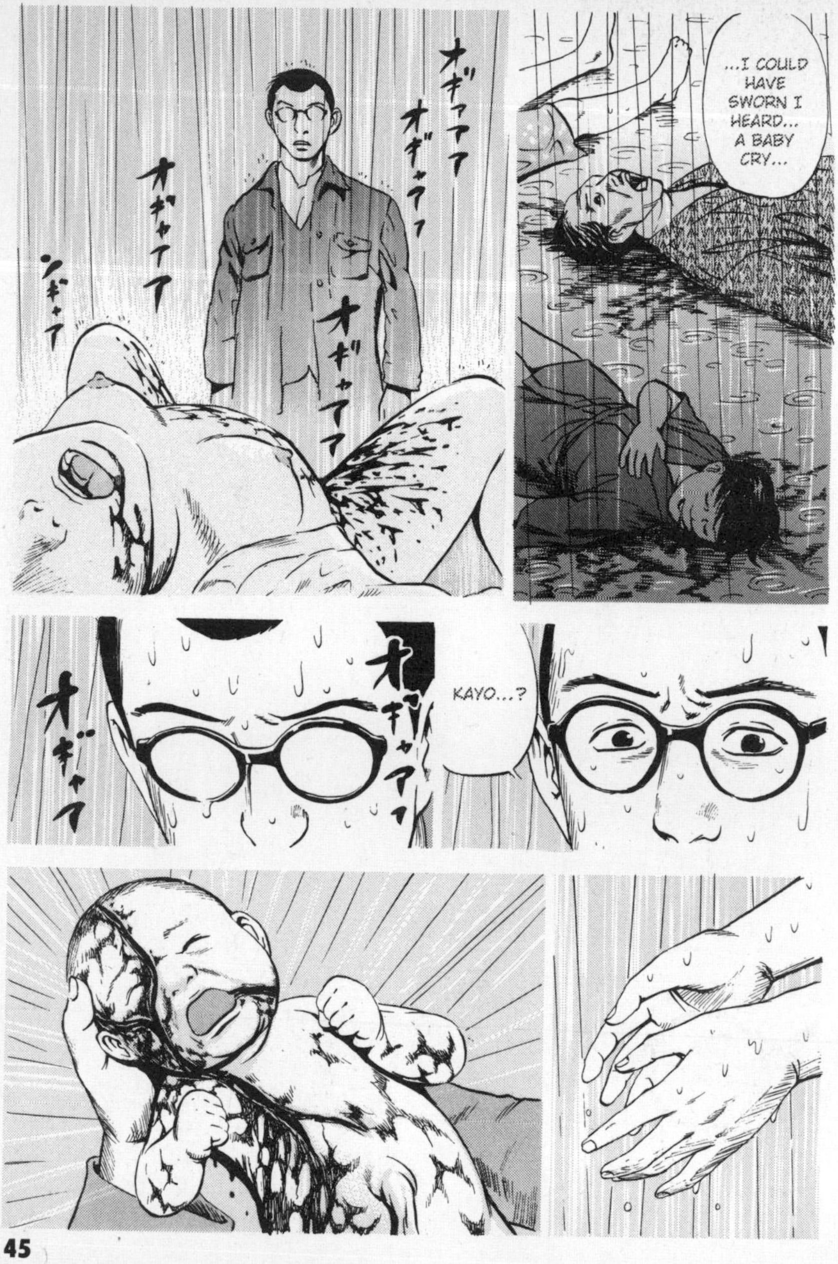
...I COULD HAVE SWORN I HEARD... A BABY CRY...
オギャアア
オギャアア
オギャアア
オギャアア
ンギャア
KAYO...?
オギャアア
オギャア

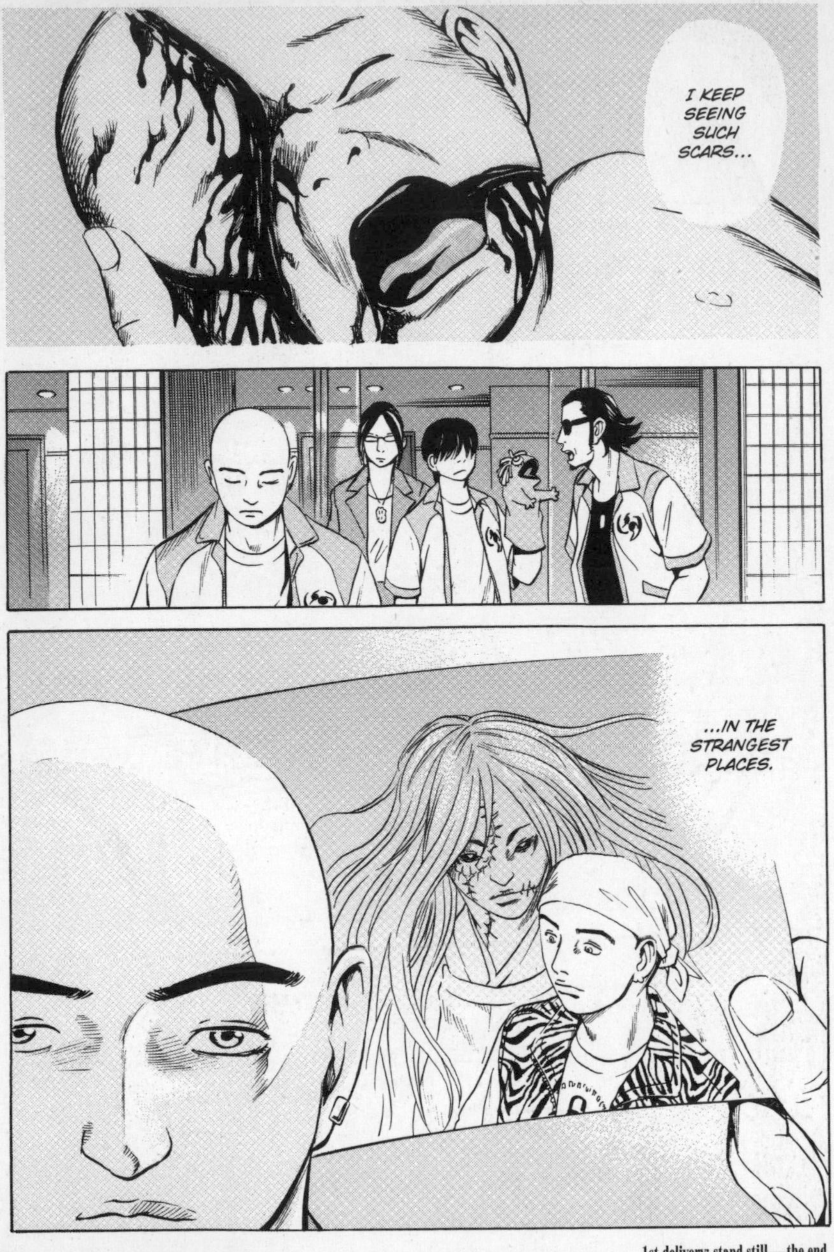
I KEEP SEEING SUCH SCARS...
...IN THE STRANGEST PLACES.

1st delivery: stand still—the end

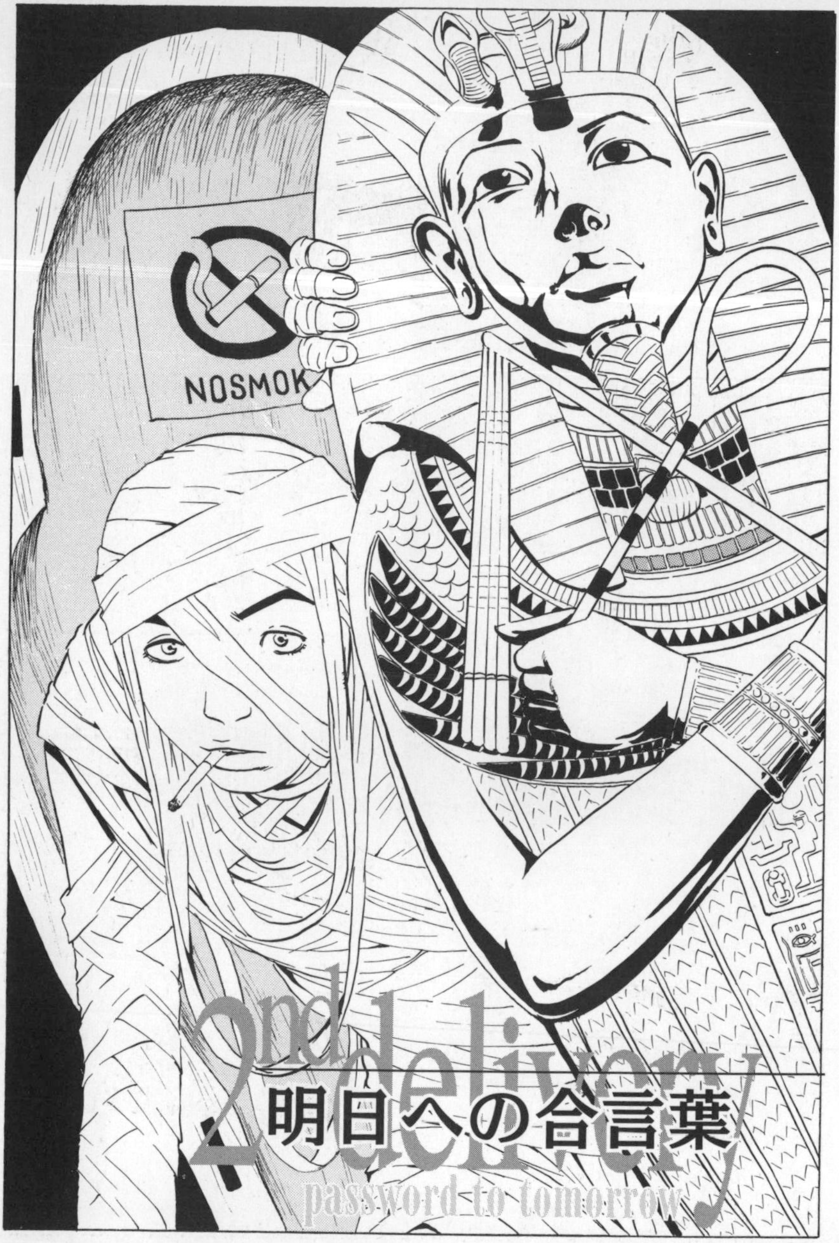
NOSMOK
2nd delivery
明日への合言葉
password to tomorrow

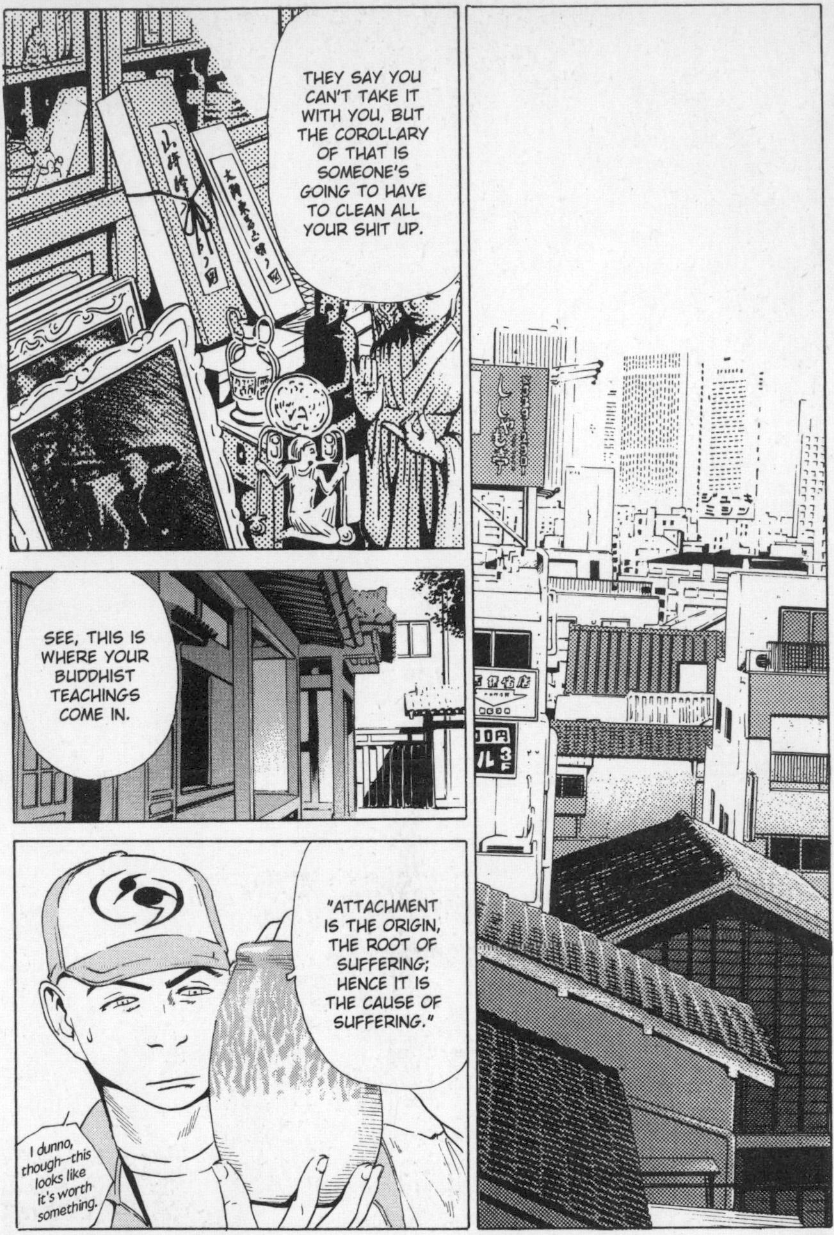
ジューキ
ミシン
THEY SAY YOU CAN'T TAKE IT WITH YOU, BUT THE COROLLARY OF THAT IS SOMEONE'S GOING TO HAVE TO CLEAN ALL YOUR SHIT UP.
SEE, THIS IS WHERE YOUR BUDDHIST TEACHINGS COME IN.
"ATTACHMENT IS THE ORIGIN, THE ROOT OF SUFFERING; HENCE IT IS THE CAUSE OF SUFFERING."
I dunno, though—this looks like it's worth something.

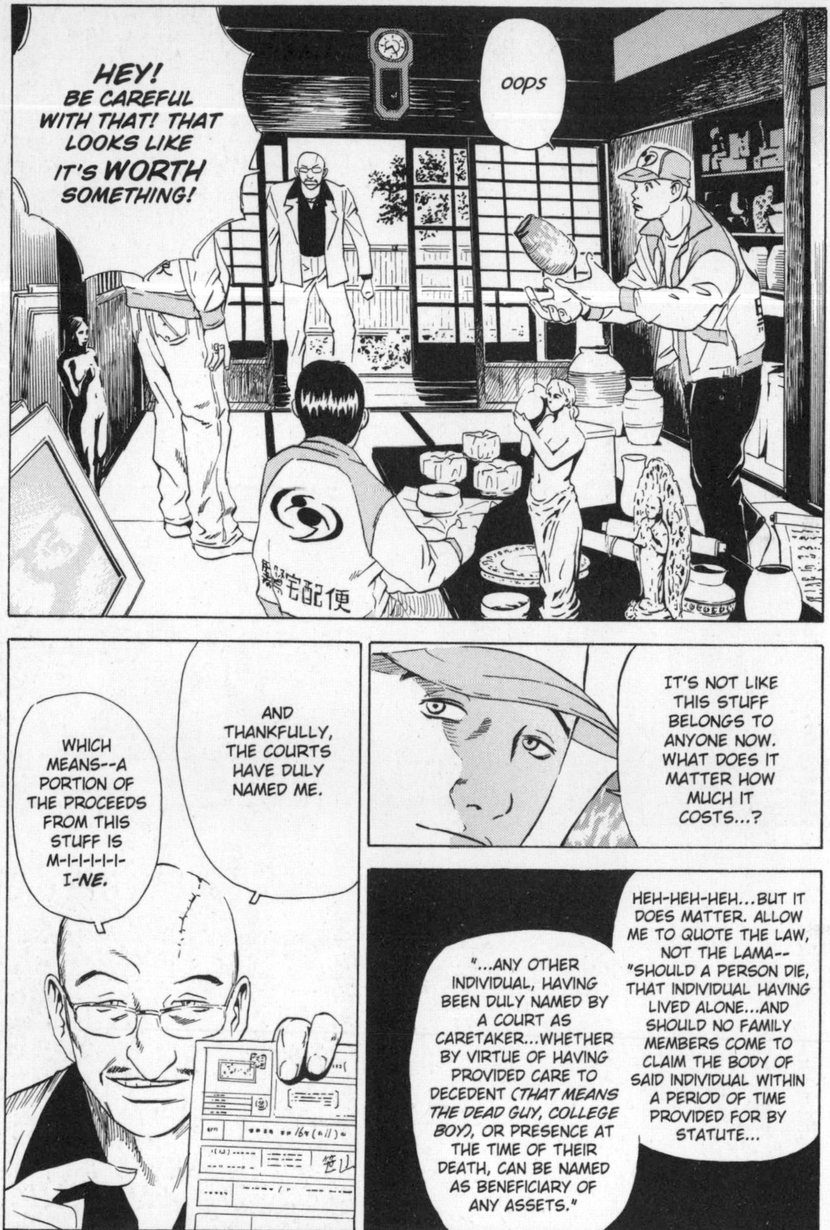
oops
HEY! BE CAREFUL WITH THAT! THAT LOOKS LIKE IT'S WORTH SOMETHING!
IT'S NOT LIKE THIS STUFF BELONGS TO ANYONE NOW. WHAT DOES IT MATTER HOW MUCH IT COSTS...?
HEH-HEH-HEH...BUT IT DOES MATTER. ALLOW ME TO QUOTE THE LAW, NOT THE LAMA-- "SHOULD A PERSON DIE, THAT INDIVIDUAL HAVING LIVED ALONE...AND SHOULD NO FAMILY MEMBERS COME TO CLAIM THE BODY OF SAID INDIVIDUAL WITHIN A PERIOD OF TIME PROVIDED FOR BY STATUTE...
"...ANY OTHER INDIVIDUAL, HAVING BEEN DULY NAMED BY A COURT AS CARETAKER...WHETHER BY VIRTUE OF HAVING PROVIDED CARE TO DECEDENT (THAT MEANS THE DEAD GUY, COLLEGE BOY), OR PRESENCE AT THE TIME OF THEIR DEATH, CAN BE NAMED AS BENEFICIARY OF ANY ASSETS."
AND THANKFULLY, THE COURTS HAVE DULY NAMED ME.
WHICH MEANS--A PORTION OF THE PROCEEDS FROM THIS STUFF IS M-I-I-I-I-I-I-NE.

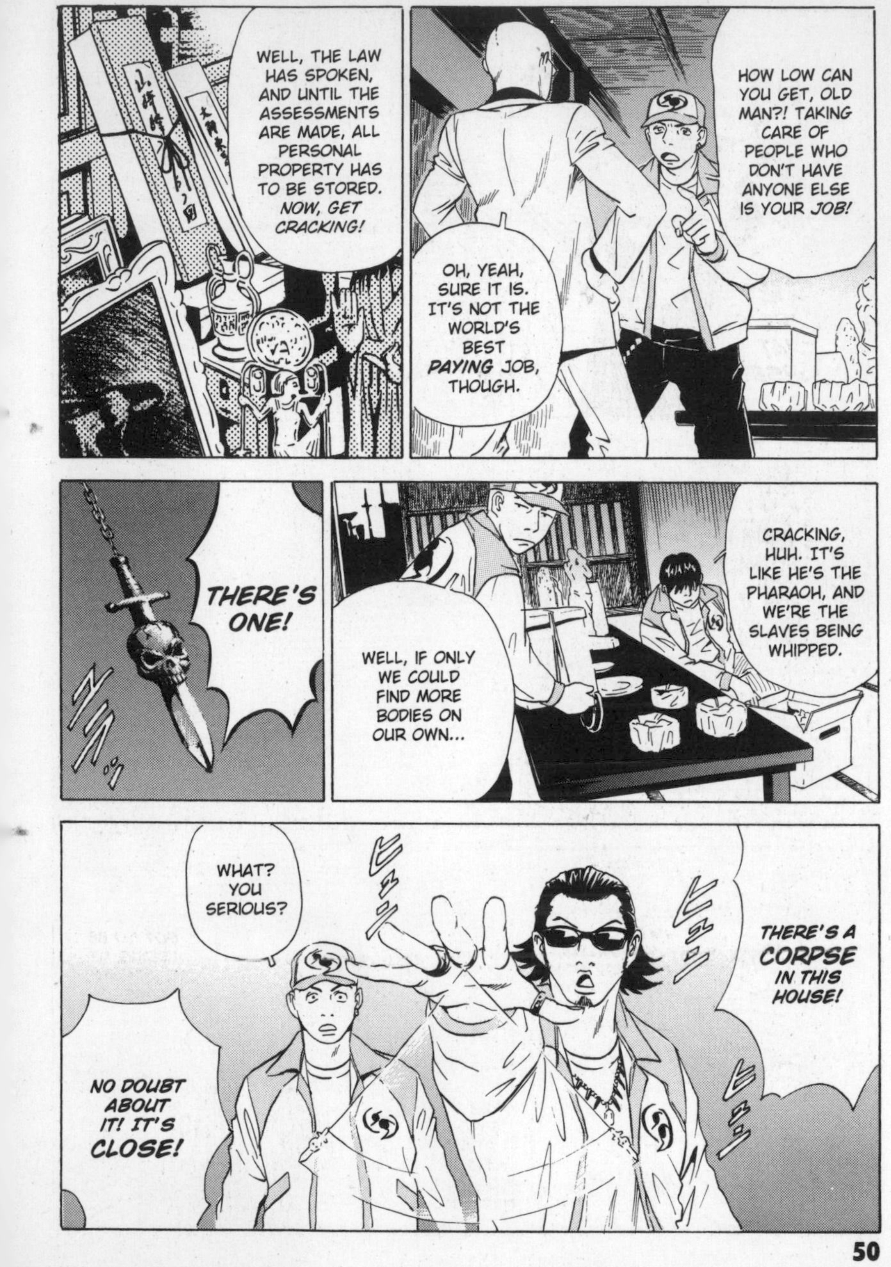
HOW LOW CAN YOU GET, OLD MAN?! TAKING CARE OF PEOPLE WHO DON'T HAVE ANYONE ELSE IS YOUR JOB!
OH, YEAH, SURE IT IS. IT'S NOT THE WORLD'S BEST PAYING JOB, THOUGH.
WELL, THE LAW HAS SPOKEN, AND UNTIL THE ASSESSMENTS ARE MADE, ALL PERSONAL PROPERTY HAS TO BE STORED. NOW, GET CRACKING!
CRACKING, HUH. IT'S LIKE HE'S THE PHARAOH, AND WE'RE THE SLAVES BEING WHIPPED.
WELL, IF ONLY WE COULD FIND MORE BODIES ON OUR OWN...
THERE'S ONE!
THERE'S A CORPSE IN THIS HOUSE!
WHAT? YOU SERIOUS?
NO DOUBT ABOUT IT! IT'S CLOSE!

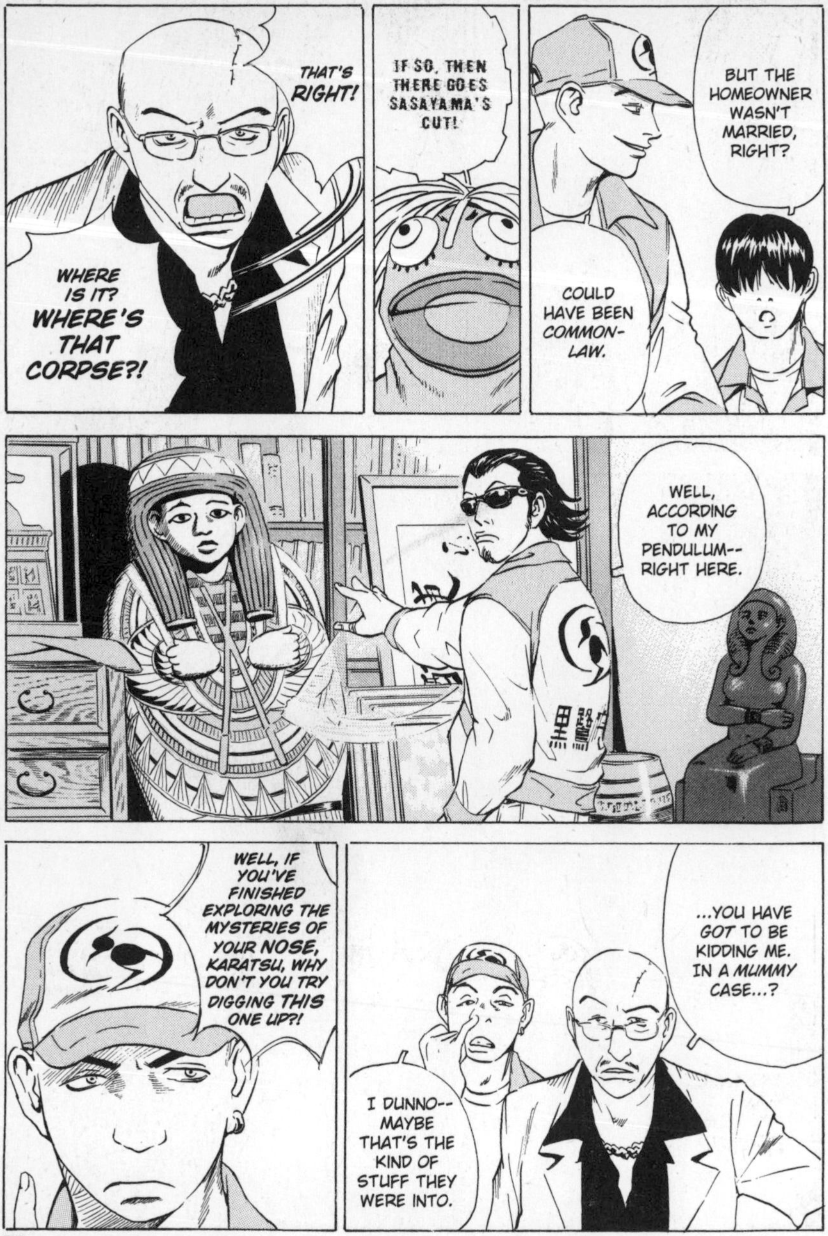
BUT THE HOMEOWNER WASN'T MARRIED, RIGHT?
COULD HAVE BEEN COMMON-LAW.
IF SO, THEN THERE GOES SASAYAMA'S CUT!
THAT'S RIGHT!
WHERE IS IT? WHERE'S THAT CORPSE?!
WELL, ACCORDING TO MY PENDULUM-- RIGHT HERE.
...YOU HAVE GOT TO BE KIDDING ME. IN A MUMMY CASE...?
I DUNNO-- MAYBE THAT'S THE KIND OF STUFF THEY WERE INTO.
WELL, IF YOU'VE FINISHED EXPLORING THE MYSTERIES OF YOUR NOSE, KARATSU, WHY DON'T YOU TRY DIGGING THIS ONE UP?!

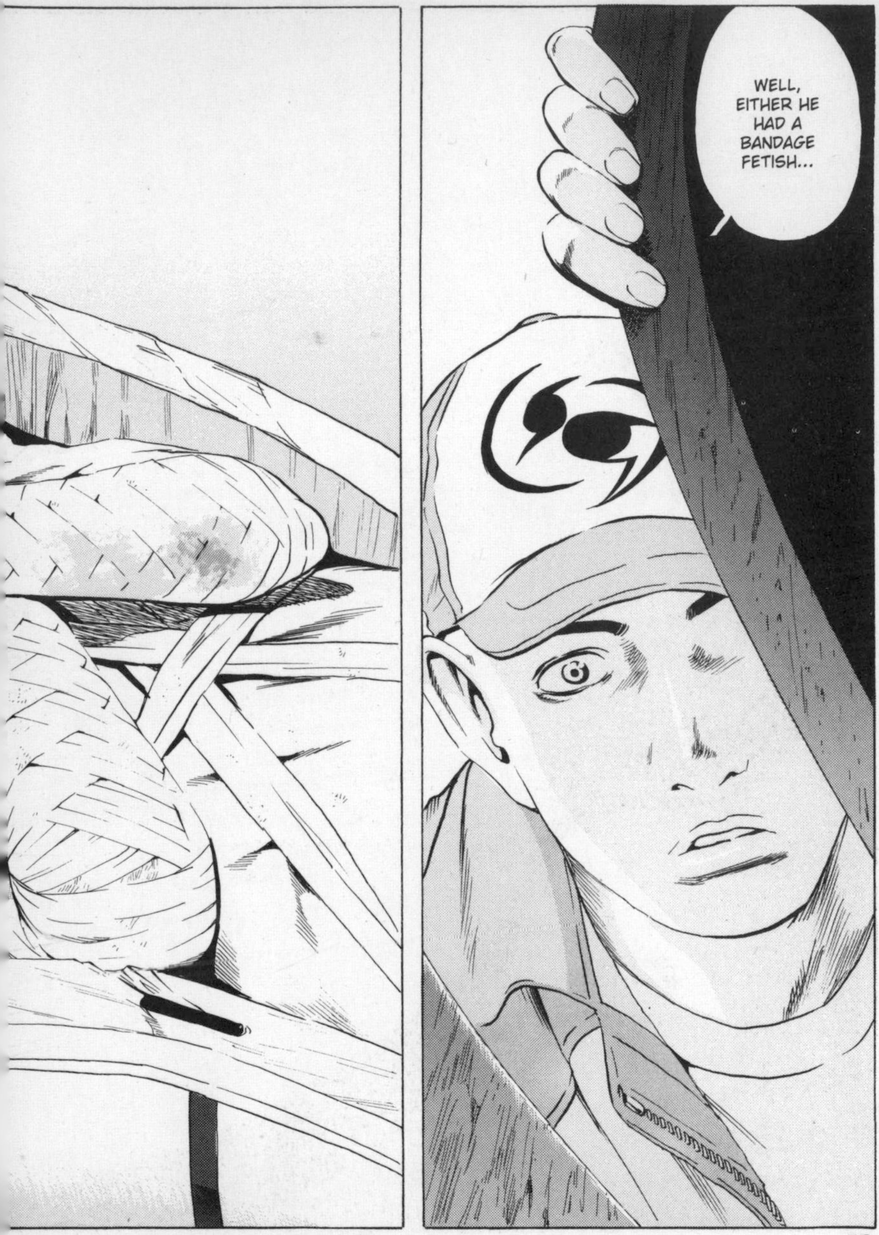
WELL, EITHER HE HAD A BANDAGE FETISH...

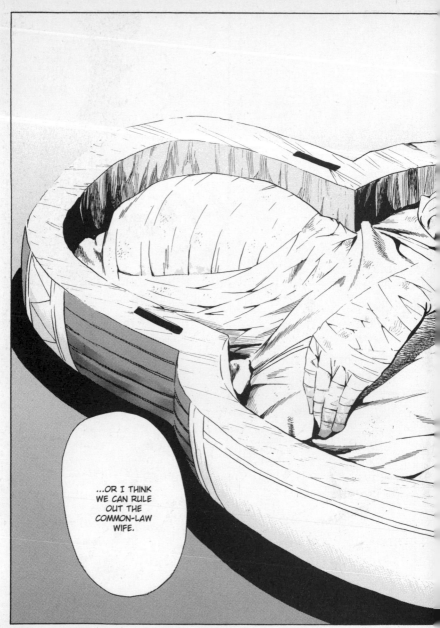

...OR I THINK WE CAN RULE OUT THE COMMON-LAW WIFE.

Can *you* finish 3
extra-large ramen...

TO WIN THE 10,000 YEN CHALLENGE?!?

(Sponsored by Your Student Cafeteria)

SO...
hnch...
IT WAS A
REAL...
shlorp...
MUMMY...
HUH...?

CHALLENGER
Makoto Numata

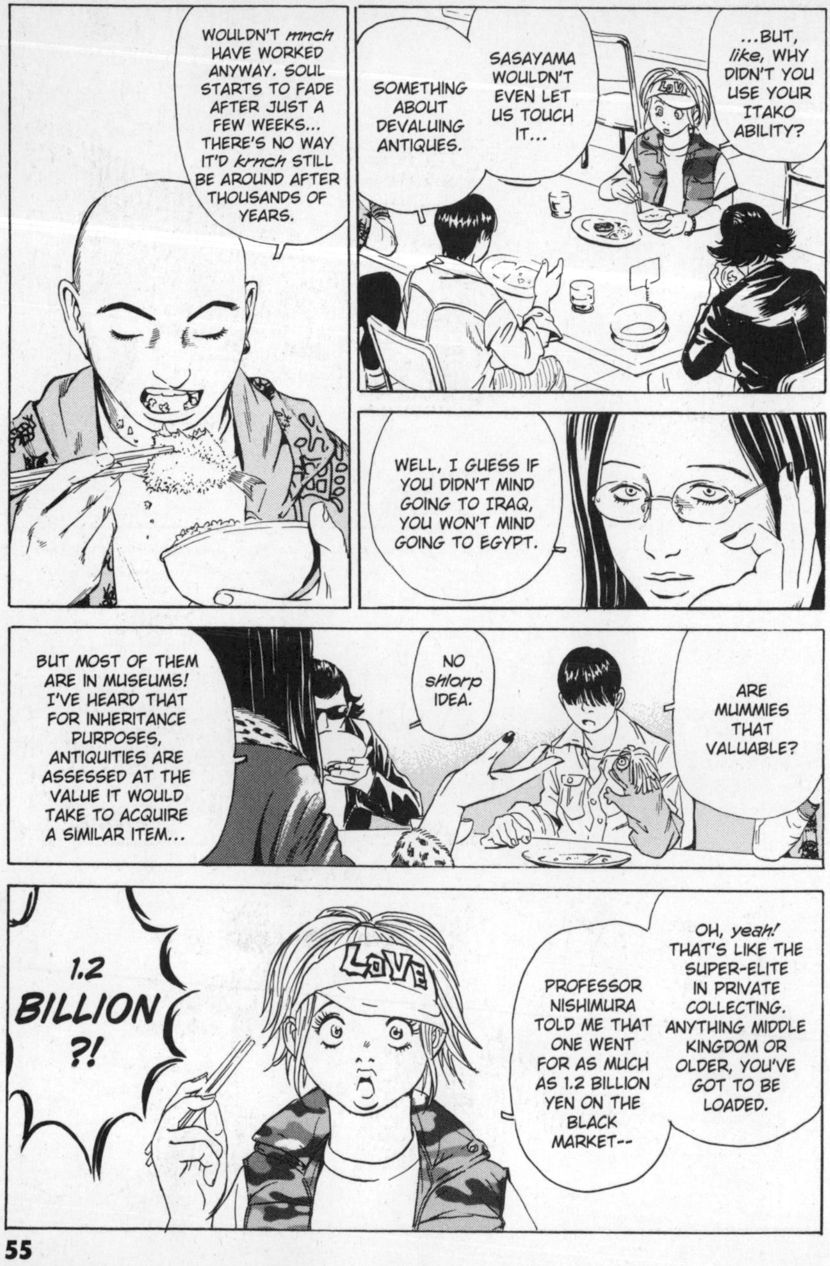
...BUT, *like*, WHY DIDN'T YOU USE YOUR ITAKO ABILITY?
SASAYAMA WOULDN'T EVEN LET US TOUCH IT...
SOMETHING ABOUT DEVALUING ANTIQUES.
WELL, I GUESS IF YOU DIDN'T MIND GOING TO IRAQ, YOU WON'T MIND GOING TO EGYPT.
WOULDN'T *mnch* HAVE WORKED ANYWAY. SOUL STARTS TO FADE AFTER JUST A FEW WEEKS... THERE'S NO WAY IT'D *krnch* STILL BE AROUND AFTER THOUSANDS OF YEARS.
ARE MUMMIES THAT VALUABLE?
NO *shlorp* IDEA.
BUT MOST OF THEM ARE IN MUSEUMS! I'VE HEARD THAT FOR INHERITANCE PURPOSES, ANTIQUITIES ARE ASSESSED AT THE VALUE IT WOULD TAKE TO ACQUIRE A SIMILAR ITEM...
OH, *yeah!* THAT'S LIKE THE SUPER-ELITE IN PRIVATE COLLECTING. ANYTHING MIDDLE KINGDOM OR OLDER, YOU'VE GOT TO BE LOADED.
PROFESSOR NISHIMURA TOLD ME THAT ONE WENT FOR AS MUCH AS 1.2 BILLION YEN ON THE BLACK MARKET--
1.2 BILLION ?!

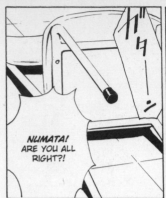

HHHKK! GRRGHH!
UH... NUMATA...?
NUMATA! ARE YOU ALL RIGHT?!
HE COULD BE CHOKING, BUT FROM THE LACK OF MOVEMENT, IT APPEARS MORE LIKE SHOCK.
HE'LL NEVER WIN THAT CONTEST NOW.
YATA! GET SOME WATER...!
LEAVE IT TO ME.

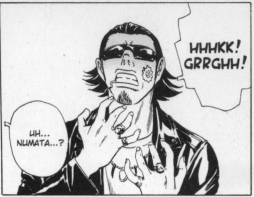

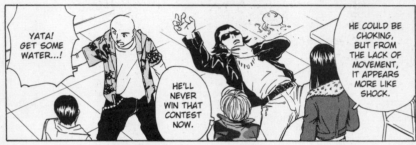

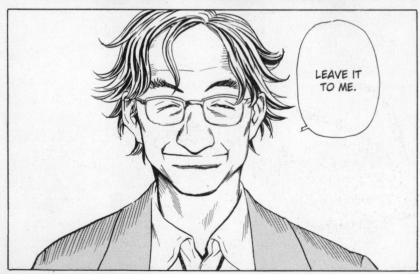

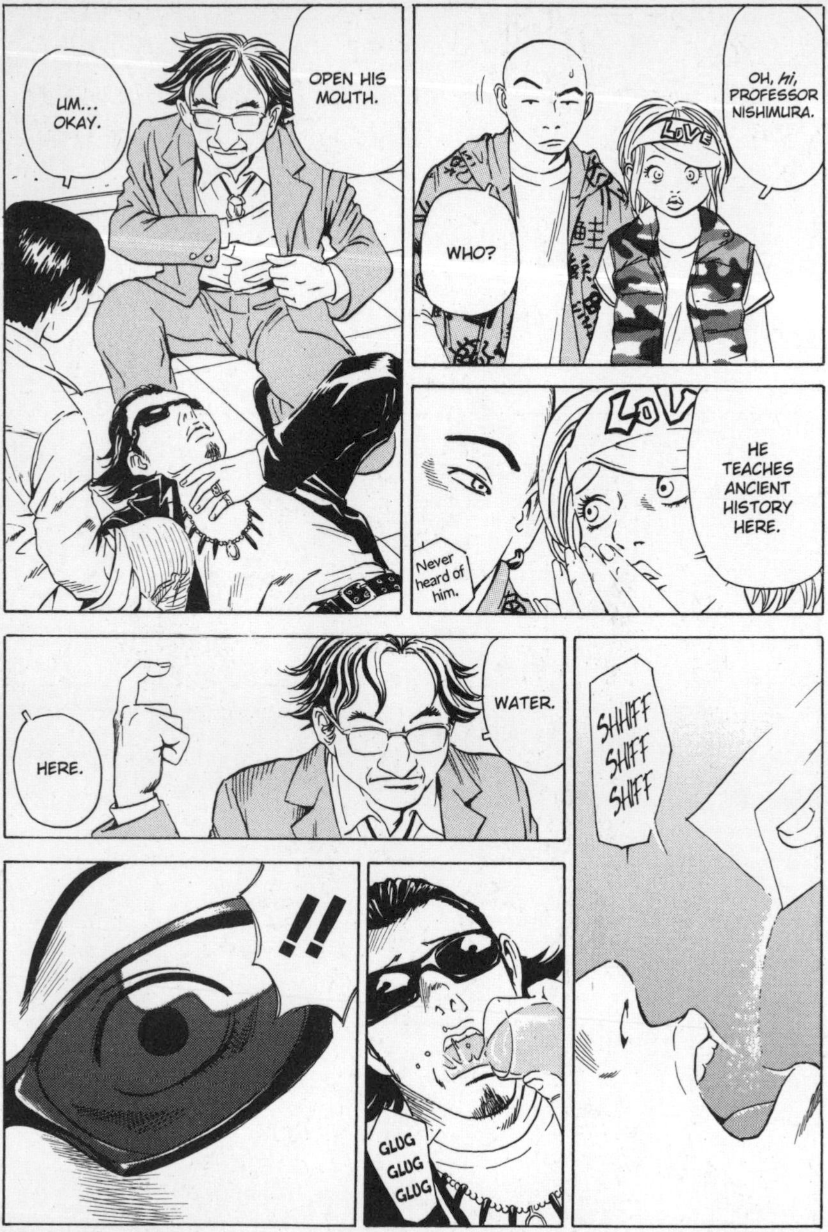
OH, *hi*, PROFESSOR NISHIMURA.
WHO?
HE TEACHES ANCIENT HISTORY HERE.
Never heard of him.
OPEN HIS MOUTH.
UM... OKAY.
SHHIFF SHIFF SHIFF
WATER.
HERE.
GLUG GLUG GLUG
!!

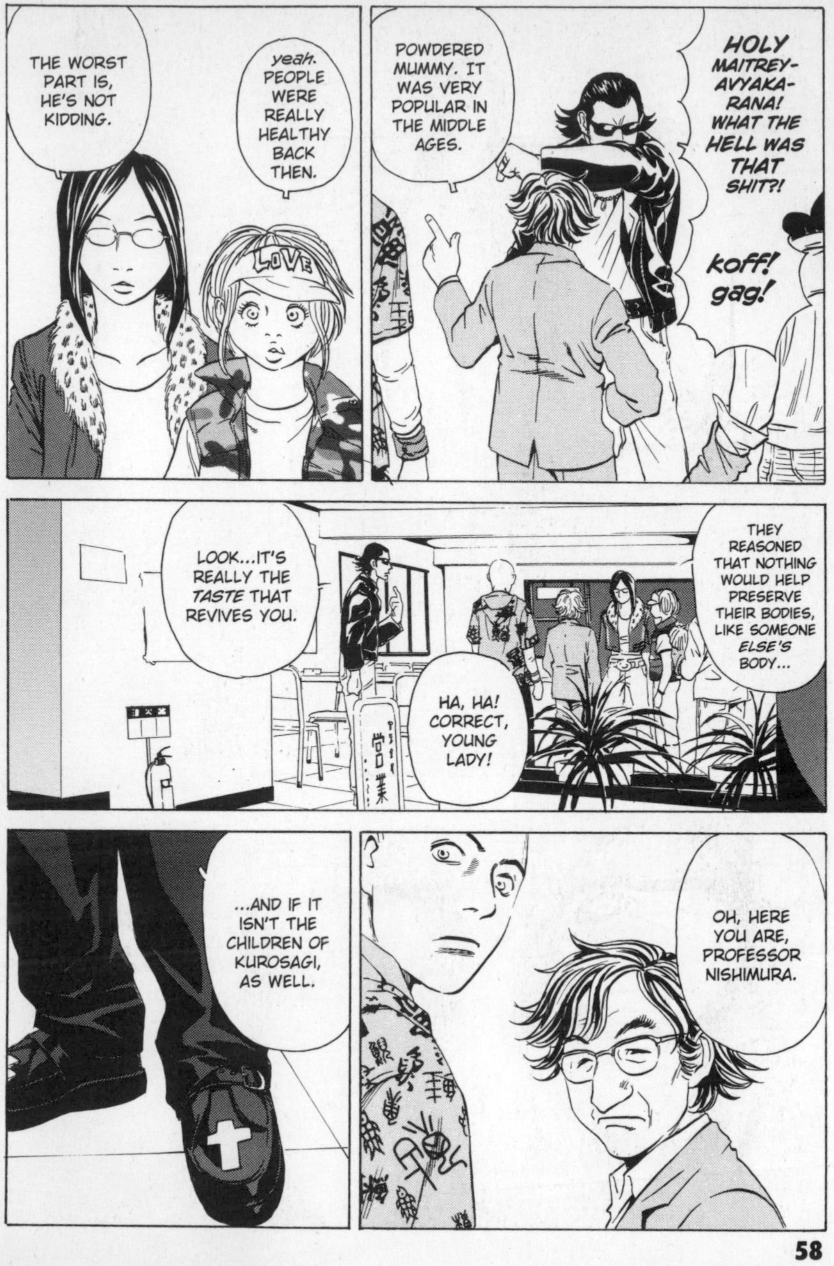
HOLY MAITREY-AVYAKARANA! WHAT THE HELL WAS THAT SHIT?!
koff! gag!
POWDERED MUMMY. IT WAS VERY POPULAR IN THE MIDDLE AGES.
yeah. PEOPLE WERE REALLY HEALTHY BACK THEN.
THE WORST PART IS, HE'S NOT KIDDING.
THEY REASONED THAT NOTHING WOULD HELP PRESERVE THEIR BODIES, LIKE SOMEONE ELSE'S BODY...
LOOK...IT'S REALLY THE TASTE THAT REVIVES YOU.
HA, HA! CORRECT, YOUNG LADY!
OH, HERE YOU ARE, PROFESSOR NISHIMURA.
...AND IF IT ISN'T THE CHILDREN OF KUROSAGI, AS WELL.

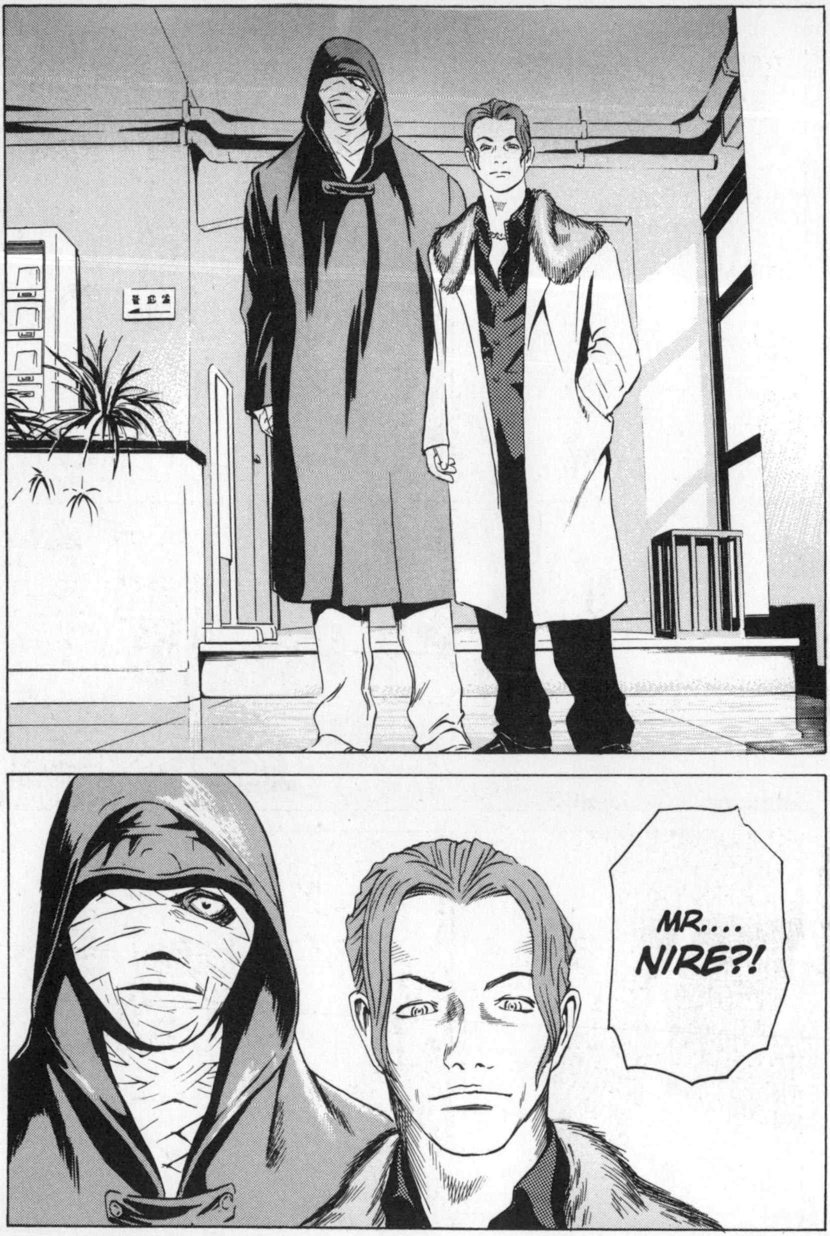
MR....
NIRE?!

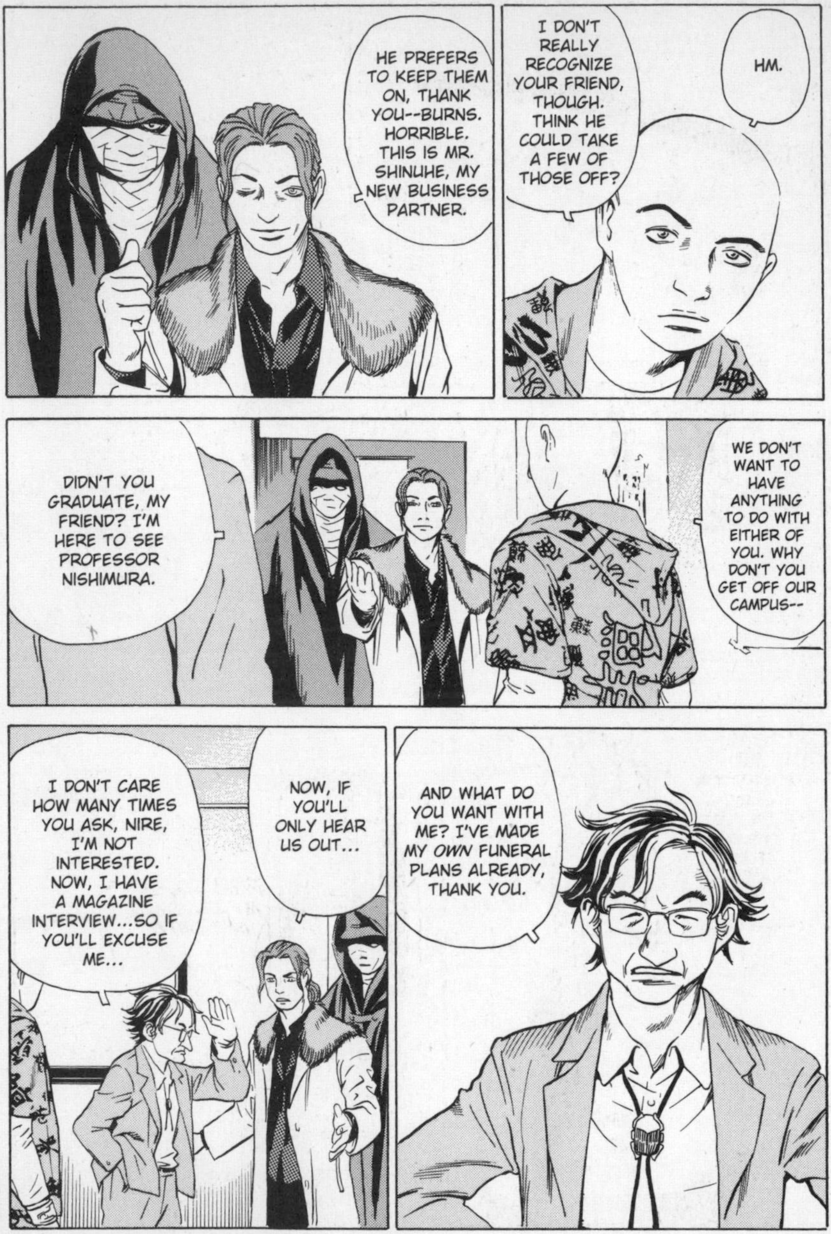
HM.
I DON'T REALLY RECOGNIZE YOUR FRIEND, THOUGH. THINK HE COULD TAKE A FEW OF THOSE OFF?
HE PREFERS TO KEEP THEM ON, THANK YOU--BURNS. HORRIBLE. THIS IS MR. SHINUHE, MY NEW BUSINESS PARTNER.
WE DON'T WANT TO HAVE ANYTHING TO DO WITH EITHER OF YOU. WHY DON'T YOU GET OFF OUR CAMPUS--
DIDN'T YOU GRADUATE, MY FRIEND? I'M HERE TO SEE PROFESSOR NISHIMURA.
AND WHAT DO YOU WANT WITH ME? I'VE MADE MY *OWN* FUNERAL PLANS ALREADY, THANK YOU.
NOW, IF YOU'LL ONLY HEAR US OUT...
I DON'T CARE HOW MANY TIMES YOU ASK, NIRE, I'M NOT INTERESTED. NOW, I HAVE A MAGAZINE INTERVIEW...SO IF YOU'LL EXCUSE ME...

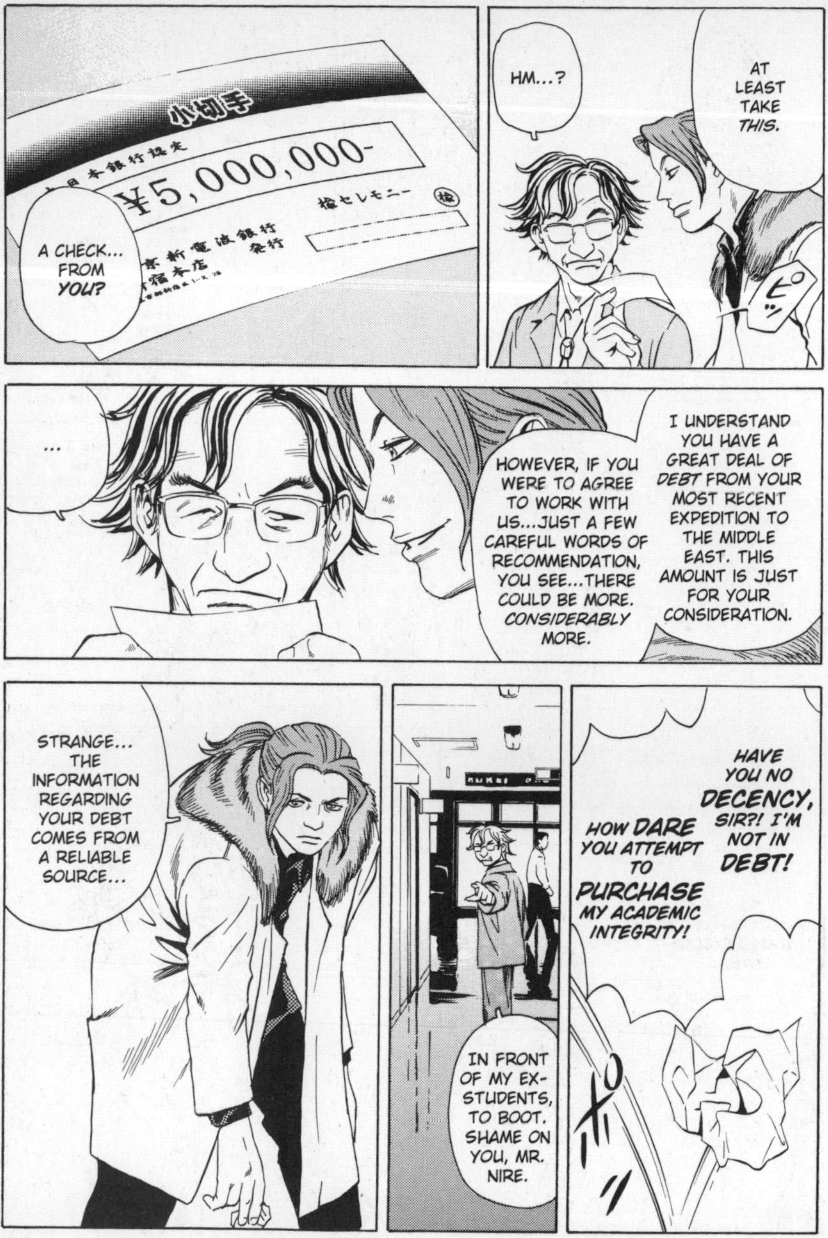
AT LEAST TAKE THIS.
HM...?
小切手
¥5,000,000-
A CHECK... FROM YOU?
I UNDERSTAND YOU HAVE A GREAT DEAL OF DEBT FROM YOUR MOST RECENT EXPEDITION TO THE MIDDLE EAST. THIS AMOUNT IS JUST FOR YOUR CONSIDERATION.
HOWEVER, IF YOU WERE TO AGREE TO WORK WITH US...JUST A FEW CAREFUL WORDS OF RECOMMENDATION, YOU SEE...THERE COULD BE MORE. CONSIDERABLY MORE.
...
HAVE YOU NO DECENCY, SIR?! I'M NOT IN DEBT!
HOW DARE YOU ATTEMPT TO PURCHASE MY ACADEMIC INTEGRITY!
IN FRONT OF MY EX-STUDENTS, TO BOOT. SHAME ON YOU, MR. NIRE.
STRANGE... THE INFORMATION REGARDING YOUR DEBT COMES FROM A RELIABLE SOURCE...

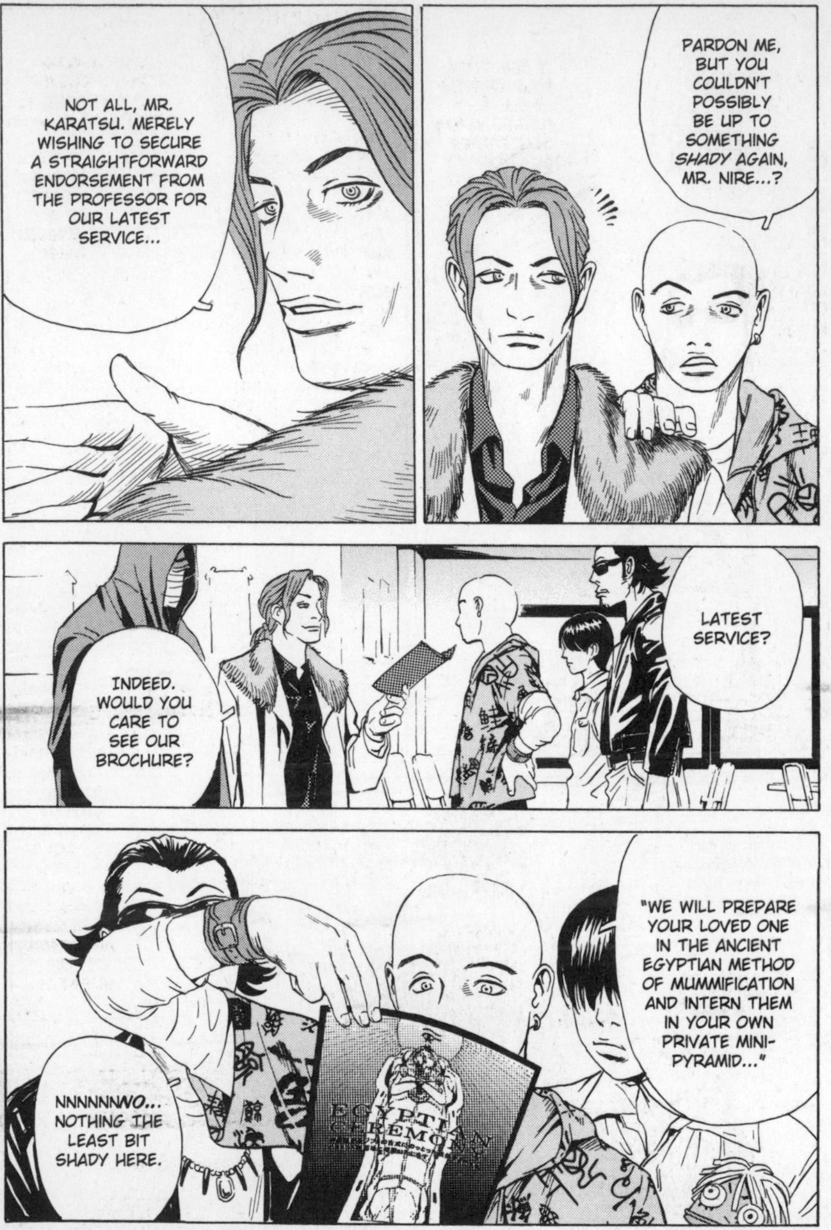
PARDON ME, BUT YOU COULDN'T POSSIBLY BE UP TO SOMETHING *SHADY* AGAIN, MR. NIRE...?
NOT ALL, MR. KARATSU. MERELY WISHING TO SECURE A STRAIGHTFORWARD ENDORSEMENT FROM THE PROFESSOR FOR OUR LATEST SERVICE...
LATEST SERVICE?
INDEED. WOULD YOU CARE TO SEE OUR BROCHURE?
"WE WILL PREPARE YOUR LOVED ONE IN THE ANCIENT EGYPTIAN METHOD OF MUMMIFICATION AND INTERN THEM IN YOUR OWN PRIVATE MINI-PYRAMID..."
NNNNNNN*NO*... NOTHING THE LEAST BIT SHADY HERE.

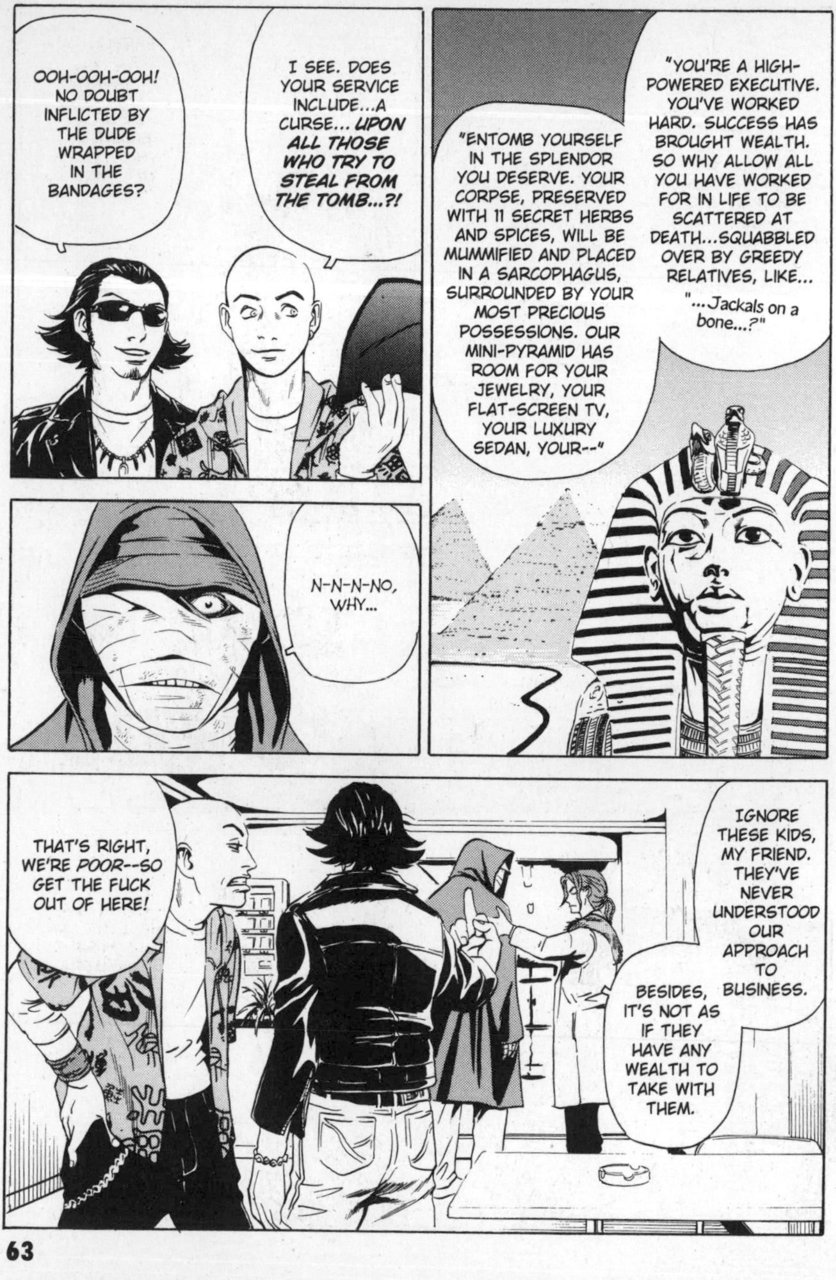
"YOU'RE A HIGH-POWERED EXECUTIVE. YOU'VE WORKED HARD. SUCCESS HAS BROUGHT WEALTH. SO WHY ALLOW ALL YOU HAVE WORKED FOR IN LIFE TO BE SCATTERED AT DEATH...SQUABBLED OVER BY GREEDY RELATIVES, LIKE...
"...Jackals on a bone...?"
"ENTOMB YOURSELF IN THE SPLENDOR YOU DESERVE. YOUR CORPSE, PRESERVED WITH 11 SECRET HERBS AND SPICES, WILL BE MUMMIFIED AND PLACED IN A SARCOPHAGUS, SURROUNDED BY YOUR MOST PRECIOUS POSSESSIONS. OUR MINI-PYRAMID HAS ROOM FOR YOUR JEWELRY, YOUR FLAT-SCREEN TV, YOUR LUXURY SEDAN, YOUR--"
I SEE. DOES YOUR SERVICE INCLUDE...A CURSE... *UPON ALL THOSE WHO TRY TO STEAL FROM THE TOMB...?!*
OOH-OOH-OOH! NO DOUBT INFLICTED BY THE DUDE WRAPPED IN THE BANDAGES?
N-N-N-NO, WHY...
IGNORE THESE KIDS, MY FRIEND. THEY'VE NEVER UNDERSTOOD OUR APPROACH TO BUSINESS.
BESIDES, IT'S NOT AS IF THEY HAVE ANY WEALTH TO TAKE WITH THEM.
THAT'S RIGHT, WE'RE *POOR*--SO GET THE FUCK OUT OF HERE!

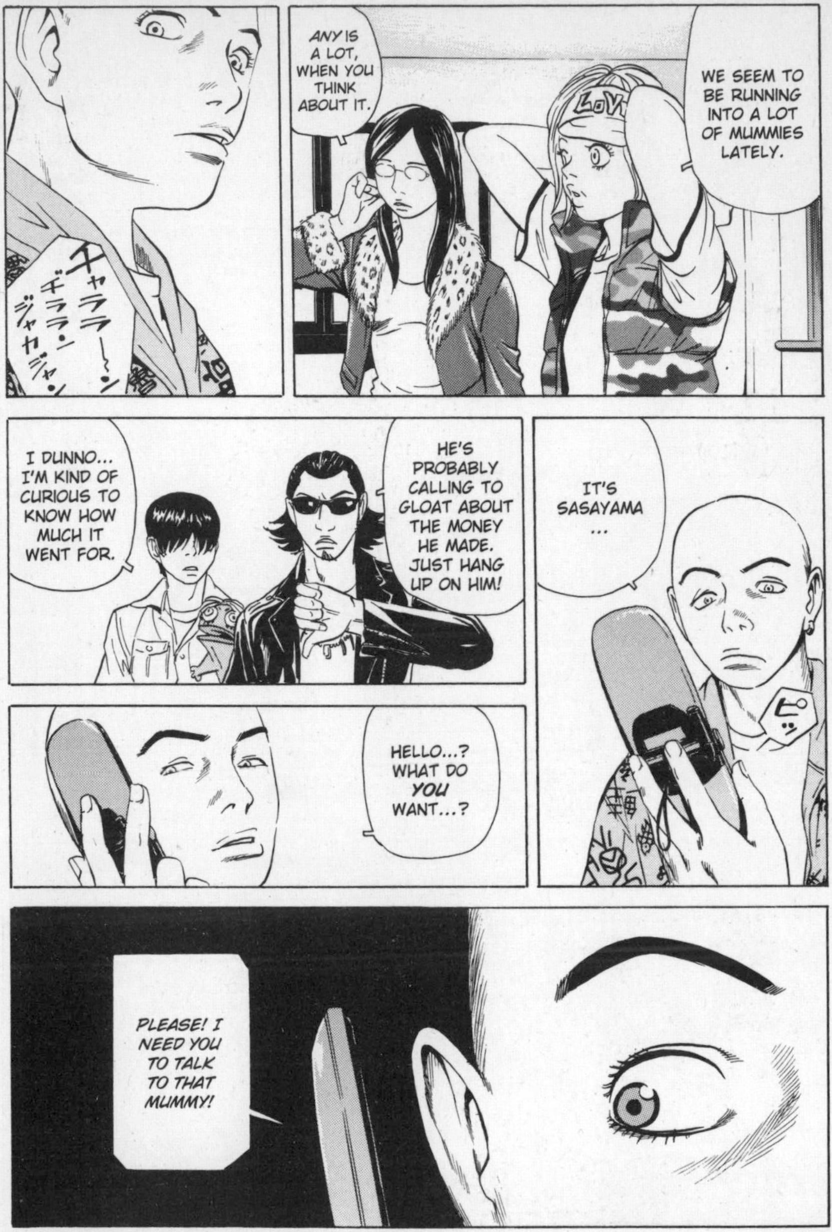
WE SEEM TO BE RUNNING INTO A LOT OF MUMMIES LATELY.
ANY IS A LOT, WHEN YOU THINK ABOUT IT.
ジャカジャン ギララ・ン キャララ～ン
IT'S SASAYAMA ...
HE'S PROBABLY CALLING TO GLOAT ABOUT THE MONEY HE MADE. JUST HANG UP ON HIM!
I DUNNO... I'M KIND OF CURIOUS TO KNOW HOW MUCH IT WENT FOR.
HELLO...? WHAT DO *YOU* WANT...?
PLEASE! I NEED YOU TO TALK TO THAT MUMMY!

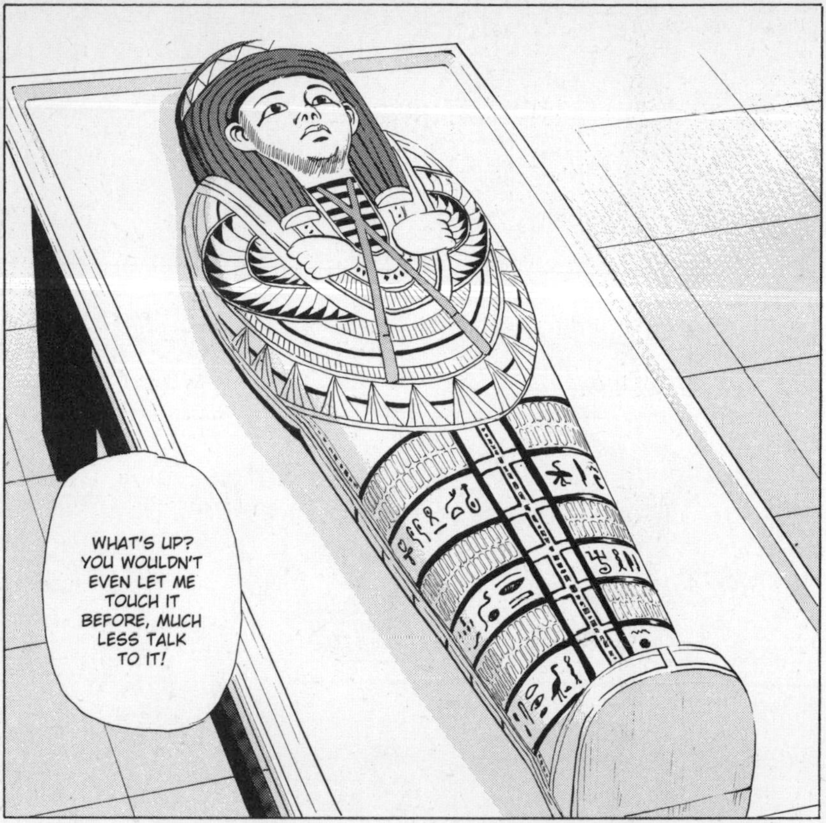
WHAT'S UP? YOU WOULDN'T EVEN LET ME TOUCH IT BEFORE, MUCH LESS TALK TO IT!

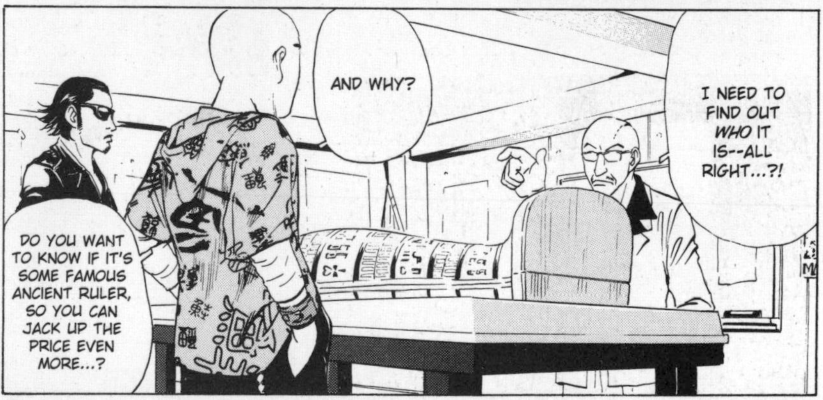
I NEED TO FIND OUT *WHO* IT IS--ALL RIGHT...?!
AND WHY?
DO YOU WANT TO KNOW IF IT'S SOME FAMOUS ANCIENT RULER, SO YOU CAN JACK UP THE PRICE EVEN MORE...?

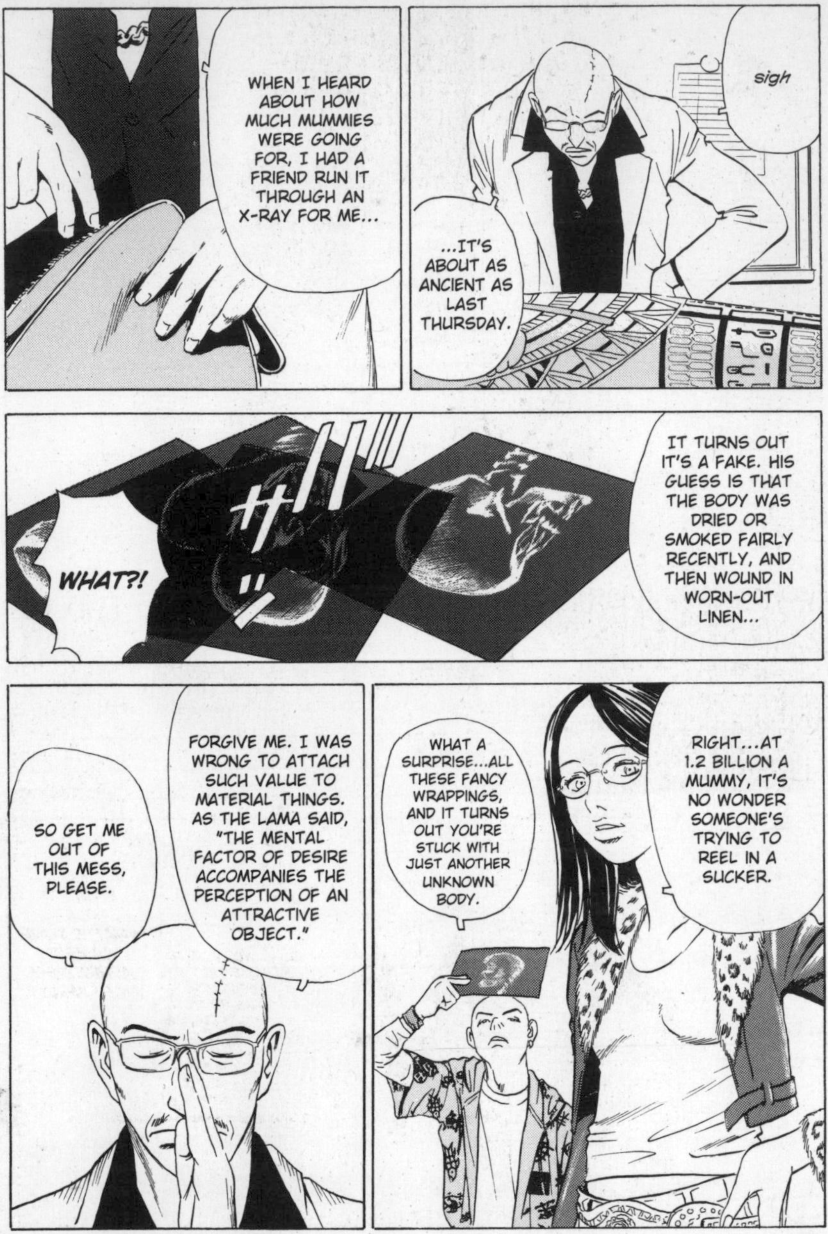
sigh
...IT'S ABOUT AS ANCIENT AS LAST THURSDAY.
WHEN I HEARD ABOUT HOW MUCH MUMMIES WERE GOING FOR, I HAD A FRIEND RUN IT THROUGH AN X-RAY FOR ME...
IT TURNS OUT IT'S A FAKE. HIS GUESS IS THAT THE BODY WAS DRIED OR SMOKED FAIRLY RECENTLY, AND THEN WOUND IN WORN-OUT LINEN...
WHAT?!
RIGHT...AT 1.2 BILLION A MUMMY, IT'S NO WONDER SOMEONE'S TRYING TO REEL IN A SUCKER.
WHAT A SURPRISE...ALL THESE FANCY WRAPPINGS, AND IT TURNS OUT YOU'RE STUCK WITH JUST ANOTHER UNKNOWN BODY.
FORGIVE ME. I WAS WRONG TO ATTACH SUCH VALUE TO MATERIAL THINGS. AS THE LAMA SAID, "THE MENTAL FACTOR OF DESIRE ACCOMPANIES THE PERCEPTION OF AN ATTRACTIVE OBJECT."
SO GET ME OUT OF THIS MESS, PLEASE.

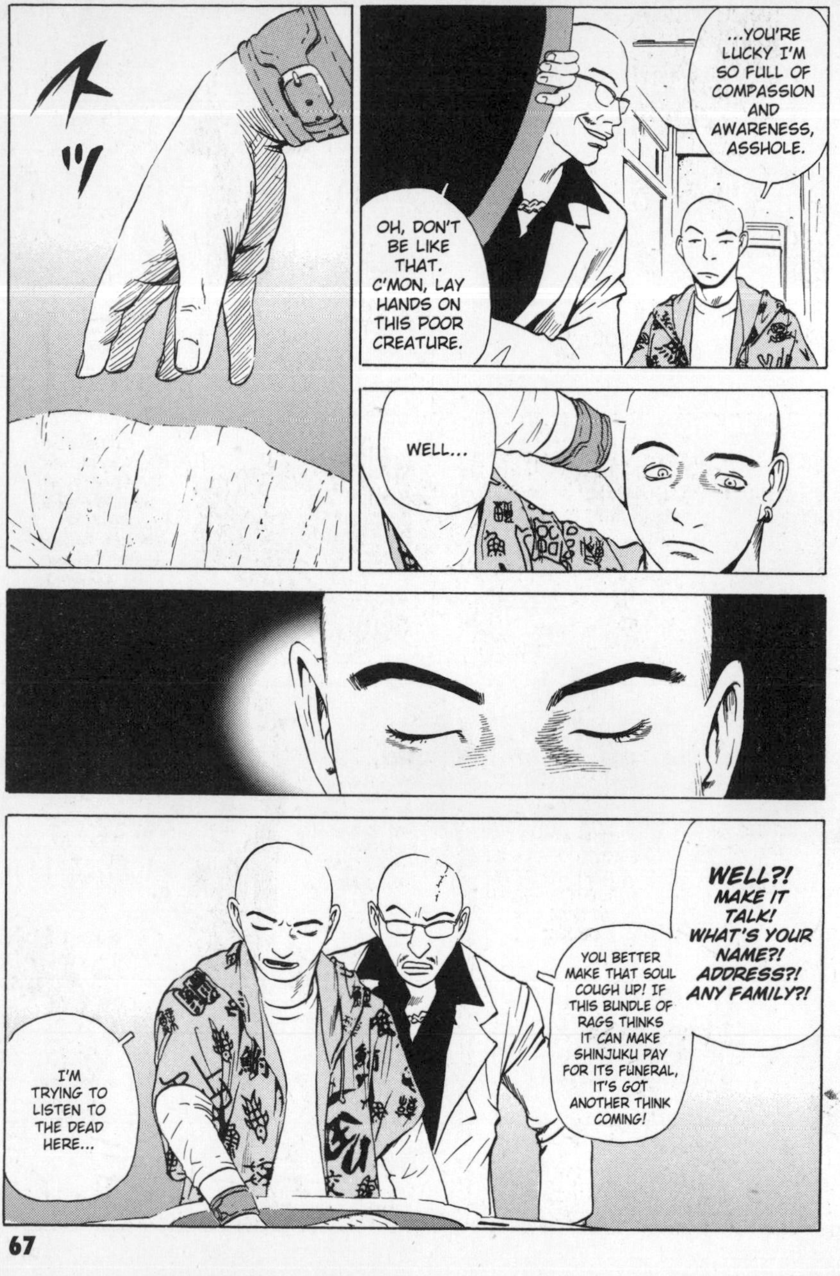
...YOU'RE LUCKY I'M SO FULL OF COMPASSION AND AWARENESS, ASSHOLE.
OH, DON'T BE LIKE THAT. C'MON, LAY HANDS ON THIS POOR CREATURE.
WELL...
スッ
WELL?! MAKE IT TALK! WHAT'S YOUR NAME?! ADDRESS?! ANY FAMILY?!
YOU BETTER MAKE THAT SOUL COUGH UP! IF THIS BUNDLE OF RAGS THINKS IT CAN MAKE SHINJUKU PAY FOR ITS FUNERAL, IT'S GOT ANOTHER THINK COMING!
I'M TRYING TO LISTEN TO THE DEAD HERE...

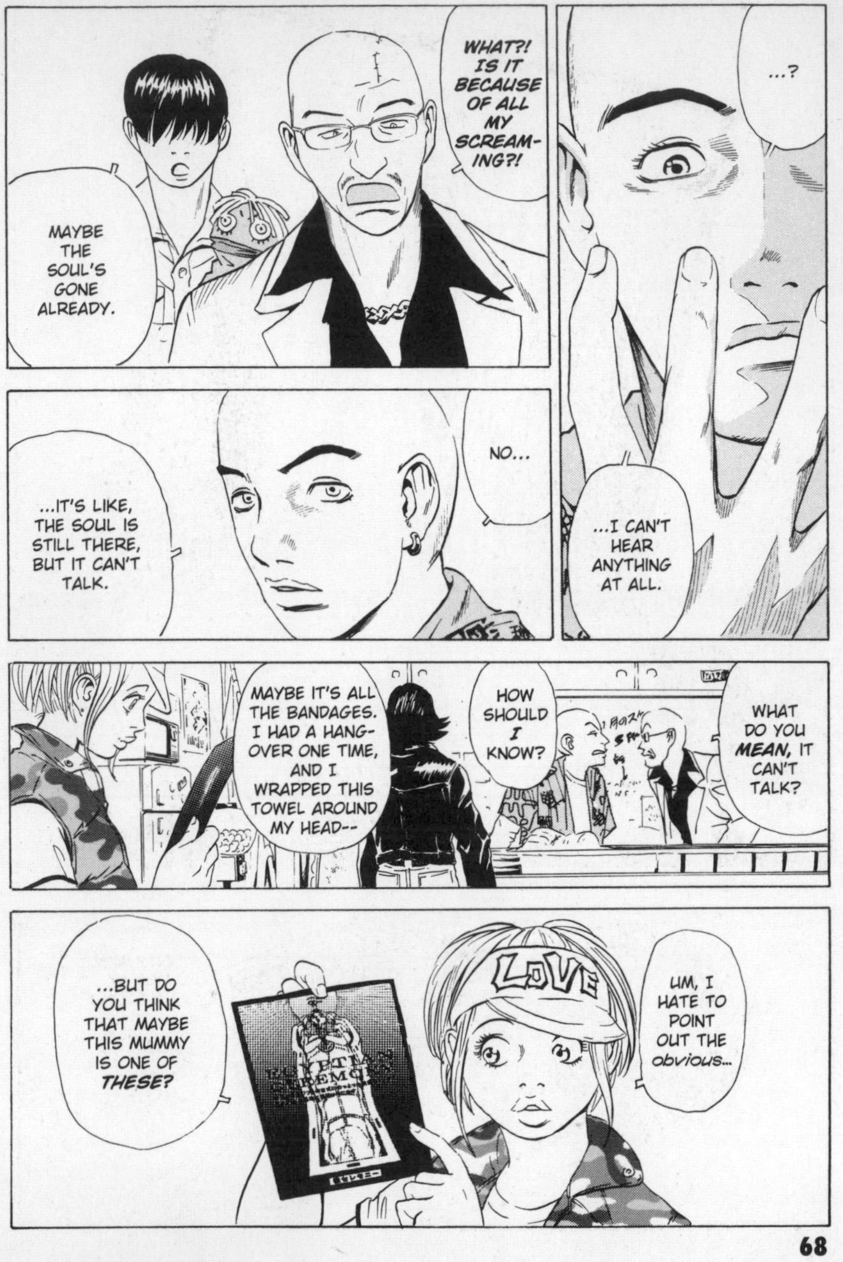
...?
...I CAN'T HEAR ANYTHING AT ALL.
WHAT?! IS IT BECAUSE OF ALL MY SCREAMING?!
MAYBE THE SOUL'S GONE ALREADY.
NO...
...IT'S LIKE, THE SOUL IS STILL THERE, BUT IT CAN'T TALK.
WHAT DO YOU MEAN, IT CAN'T TALK?
HOW SHOULD I KNOW?
MAYBE IT'S ALL THE BANDAGES. I HAD A HANG-OVER ONE TIME, AND I WRAPPED THIS TOWEL AROUND MY HEAD--
UM, I HATE TO POINT OUT THE obvious...
...BUT DO YOU THINK THAT MAYBE THIS MUMMY IS ONE OF THESE?

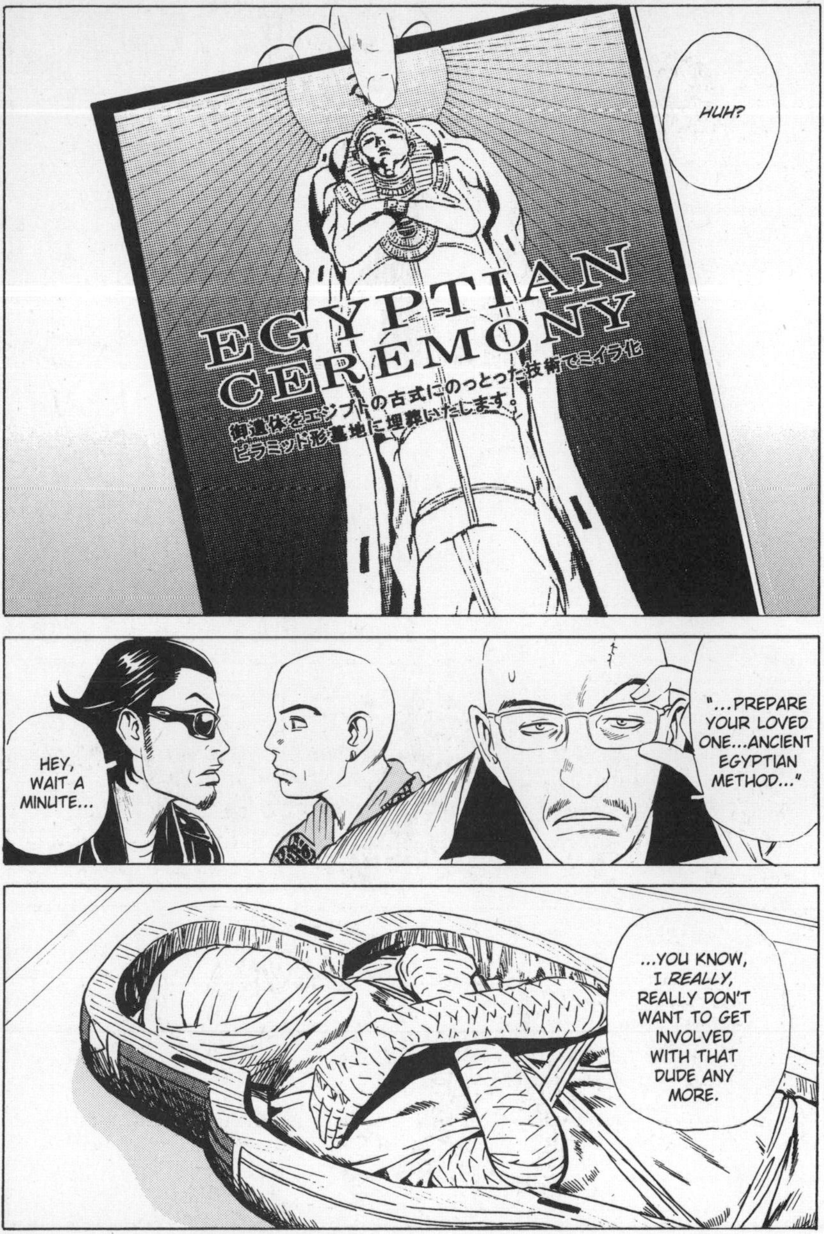
HUH?
EGYPTIAN CEREMONY
御遺体をエジプトの古式にのっとった技術でミイラ化
ピラミッド形墓地に埋葬いたします。
"...PREPARE YOUR LOVED ONE...ANCIENT EGYPTIAN METHOD..."
HEY, WAIT A MINUTE...
...YOU KNOW, I *REALLY*, REALLY DON'T WANT TO GET INVOLVED WITH THAT DUDE ANY MORE.

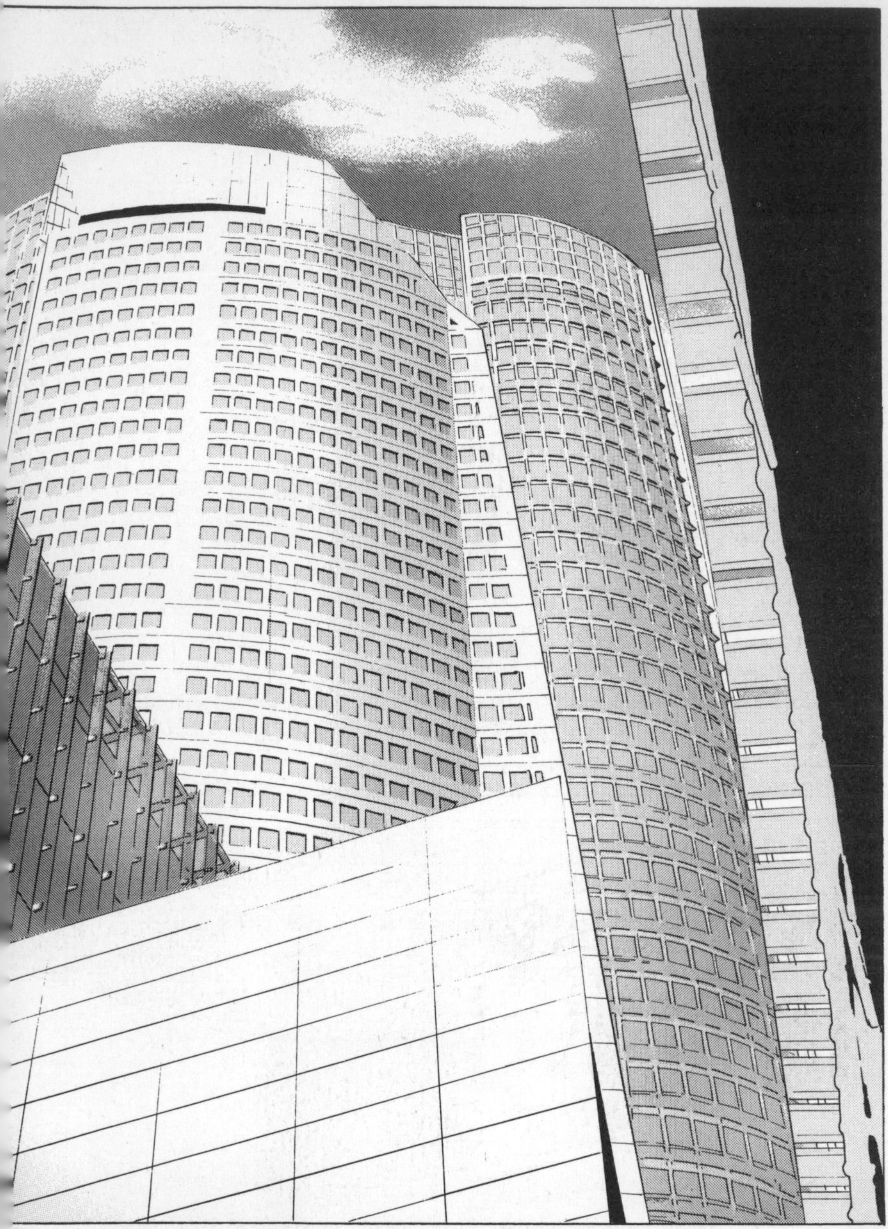

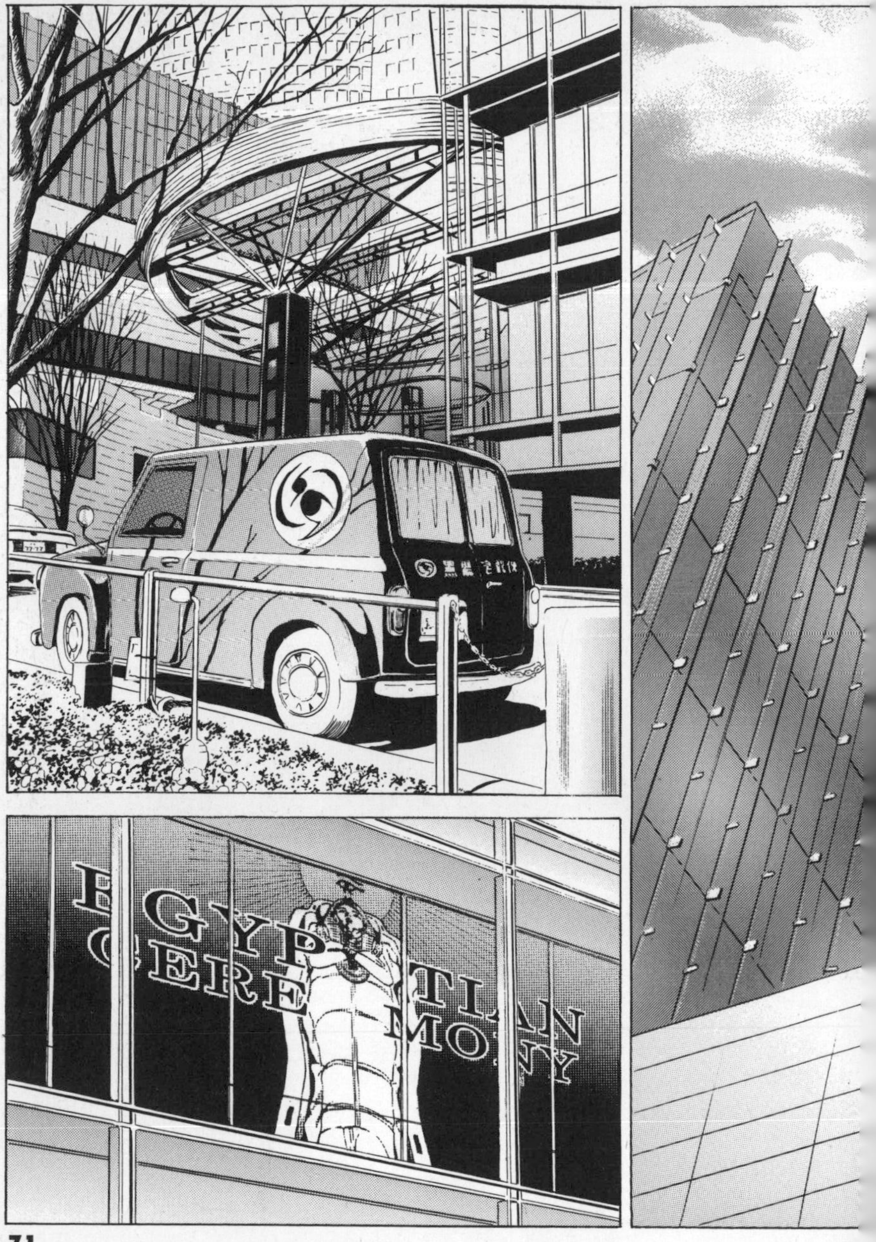
EGYP TIAN
CERE MO NY

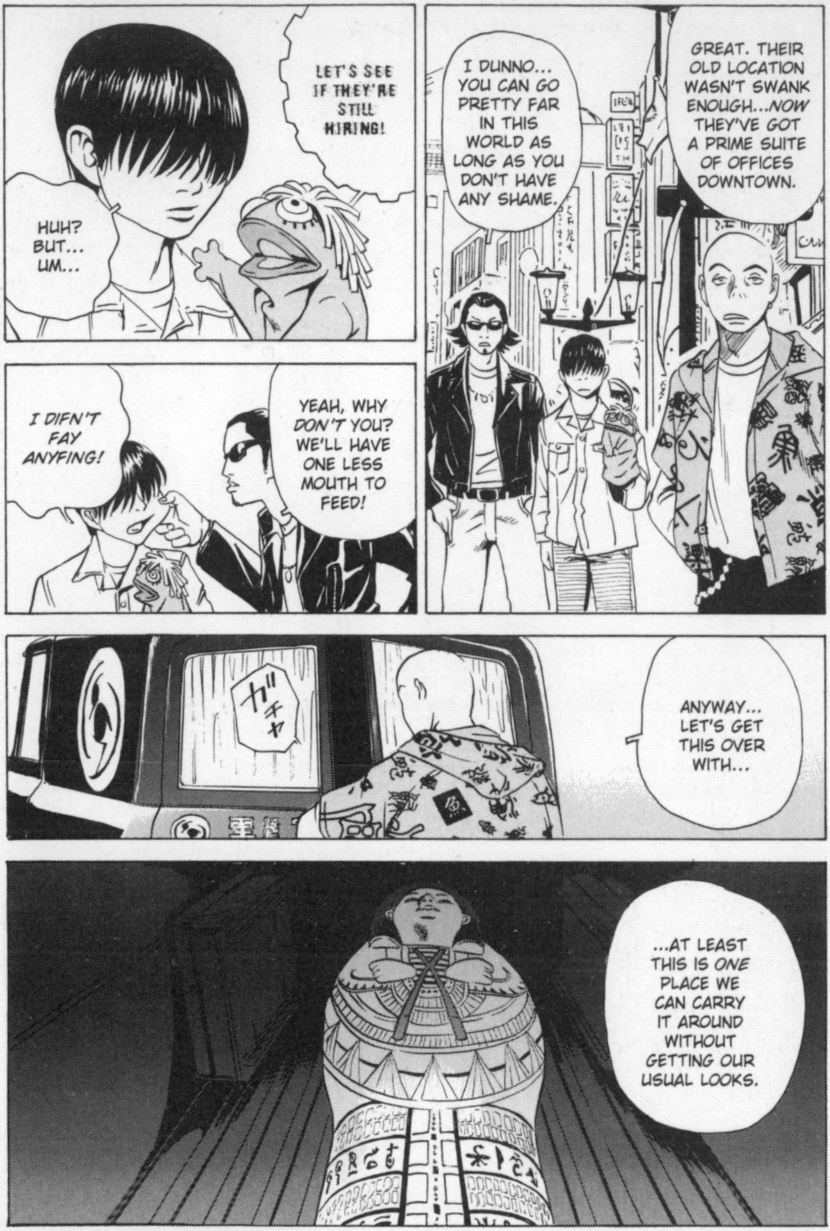
GREAT. THEIR OLD LOCATION WASN'T SWANK ENOUGH...*NOW* THEY'VE GOT A PRIME SUITE OF OFFICES DOWNTOWN.
I DUNNO... YOU CAN GO PRETTY FAR IN THIS WORLD AS LONG AS YOU DON'T HAVE ANY SHAME.
LET'S SEE IF THEY'RE STILL HIRING!
HUH? BUT... UM...
YEAH, WHY *DON'T* YOU? WE'LL HAVE ONE LESS MOUTH TO FEED!
I DIFN'T FAY ANYFING!
ANYWAY... LET'S GET THIS OVER WITH...
ガチャ
...AT LEAST THIS IS *ONE* PLACE WE CAN CARRY IT AROUND WITHOUT GETTING OUR USUAL LOOKS.

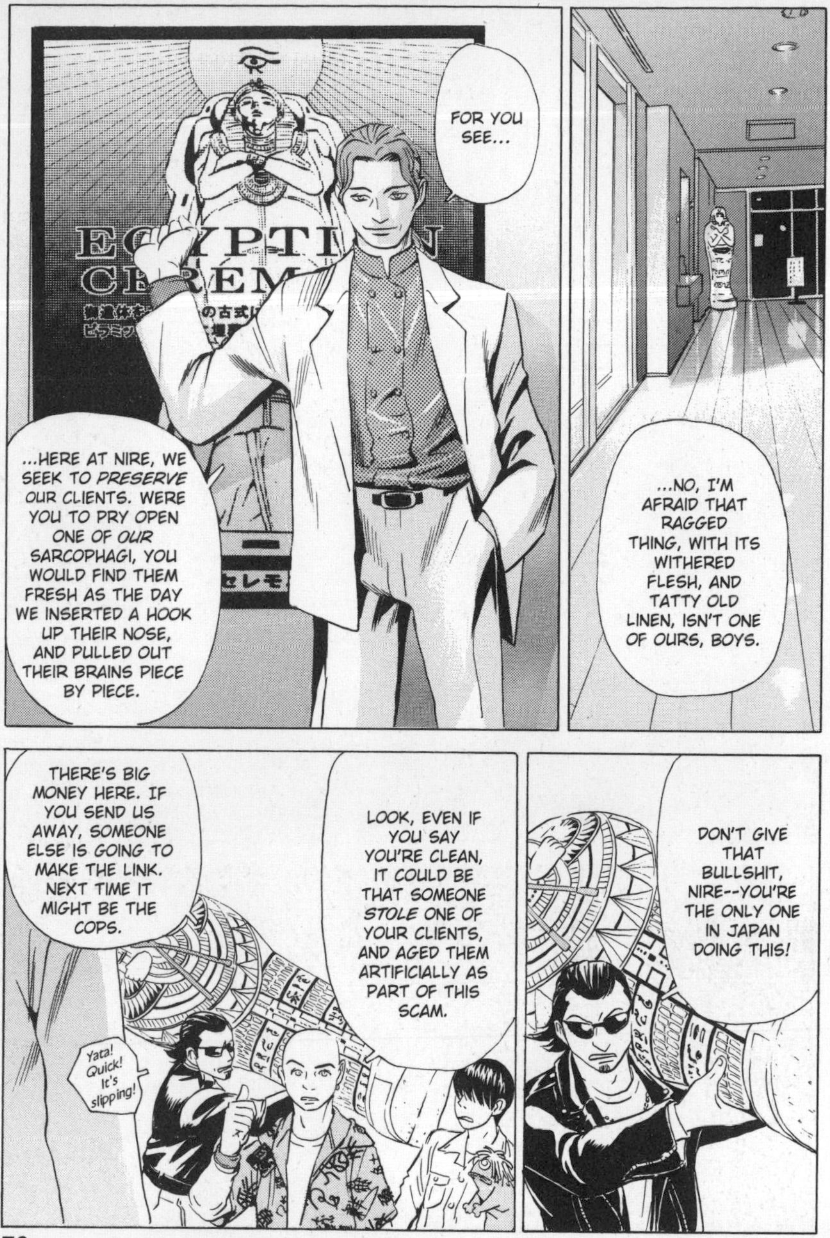
...NO, I'M AFRAID THAT RAGGED THING, WITH ITS WITHERED FLESH, AND TATTY OLD LINEN, ISN'T ONE OF OURS, BOYS.
FOR YOU SEE...
...HERE AT NIRE, WE SEEK TO *PRESERVE* OUR CLIENTS. WERE YOU TO PRY OPEN ONE OF *OUR* SARCOPHAGI, YOU WOULD FIND THEM FRESH AS THE DAY WE INSERTED A HOOK UP THEIR NOSE, AND PULLED OUT THEIR BRAINS PIECE BY PIECE.
DON'T GIVE THAT BULLSHIT, NIRE--YOU'RE THE ONLY ONE IN JAPAN DOING THIS!
LOOK, EVEN IF YOU SAY YOU'RE CLEAN, IT COULD BE THAT SOMEONE *STOLE* ONE OF YOUR CLIENTS, AND AGED THEM ARTIFICIALLY AS PART OF THIS SCAM.
THERE'S BIG MONEY HERE. IF YOU SEND US AWAY, SOMEONE ELSE IS GOING TO MAKE THE LINK. NEXT TIME IT MIGHT BE THE COPS.
Yata! Quick! It's slipping!

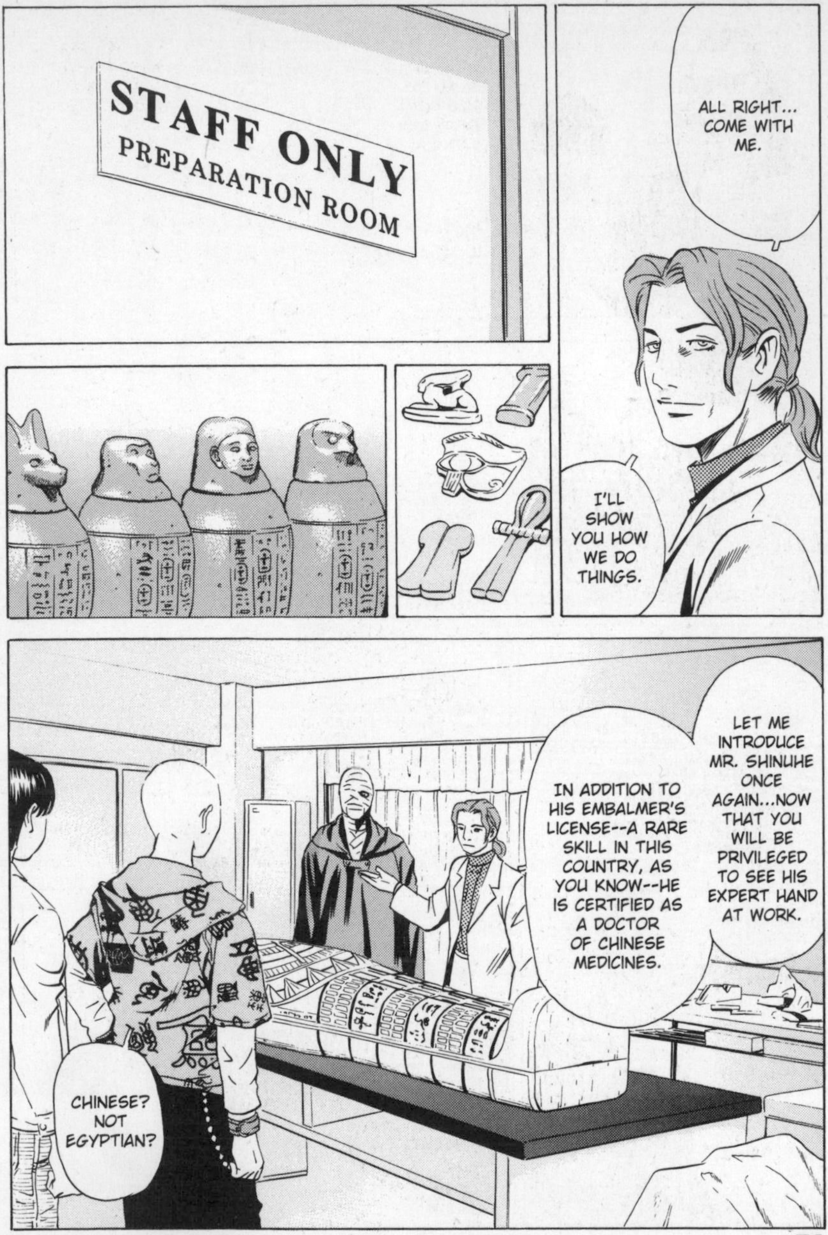
ALL RIGHT... COME WITH ME.
I'LL SHOW YOU HOW WE DO THINGS.
STAFF ONLY
PREPARATION ROOM
LET ME INTRODUCE MR. SHINUHE ONCE AGAIN...NOW THAT YOU WILL BE PRIVILEGED TO SEE HIS EXPERT HAND AT WORK.
IN ADDITION TO HIS EMBALMER'S LICENSE--A RARE SKILL IN THIS COUNTRY, AS YOU KNOW--HE IS CERTIFIED AS A DOCTOR OF CHINESE MEDICINES.
CHINESE? NOT EGYPTIAN?

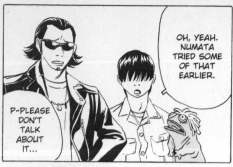

TH...THEY ARE LINKED, FOR IN... THE DAYS OF OLD, MUMMIES WERE USED AS AN INGREDIENT IN CHINESE MEDICINES. E...EVEN IN THE EDO PERIOD, MANY MUMMIES WERE IMPORTED TO JAPAN FOR THAT PURPOSE.
IN...INDEED THERE ARE RECORDS TH...THAT YOSHIMUNE TOKUGAWA ORDERED MUMMIES HIMSELF.
OH, YEAH. NUMATA TRIED SOME OF THAT EARLIER.
P-PLEASE DON'T TALK ABOUT IT...
G...GOOD FOR CURING PROBLEMS OF THE LIVER AND SPLEEN. ALSO E...FFECTIVE WITH RESPIRATORY AILMENTS.
PLEASE... I'M BEGGING YOU...
JUST THINK, NUMATA, YOU HAD THOUSANDS OF YEARS OF HISTORY IN YOUR MOUTH!
YEAH, AND IF HE DOESN'T SHUT UP, YOU'RE ABOUT TO SEE IT EMERGE FROM THE PAST!
N...NOW, LET ME TAKE A LOOK AT TH...THOSE X-RAYS...
HMM...TH... THE AUDITORY OSSICLES ARE STILL PRESENT...
...A...AND... THE HEART IS MISSING. TH...THIS IS DEFINITELY A FAKE.

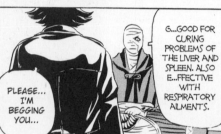

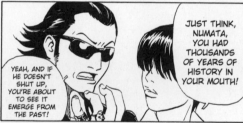

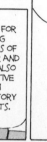

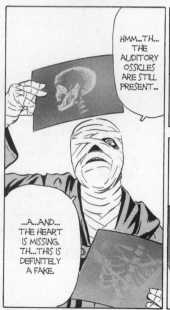

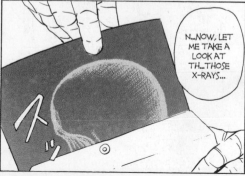

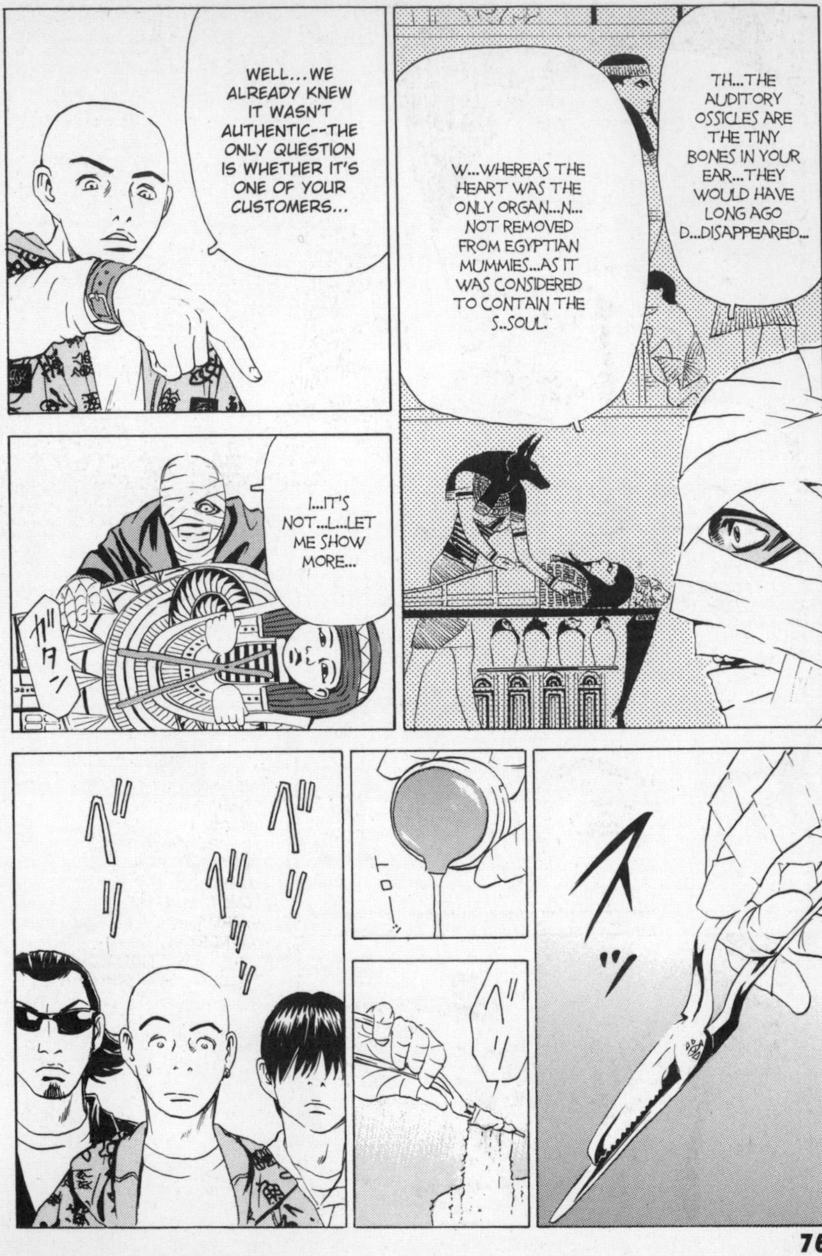
TH...THE AUDITORY OSSICLES ARE THE TINY BONES IN YOUR EAR...THEY WOULD HAVE LONG AGO D...DISAPPEARED...
W...WHEREAS THE HEART WAS THE ONLY ORGAN...N... NOT REMOVED FROM EGYPTIAN MUMMIES...AS IT WAS CONSIDERED TO CONTAIN THE S..SOUL.
WELL...WE ALREADY KNEW IT WASN'T AUTHENTIC--THE ONLY QUESTION IS WHETHER IT'S ONE OF YOUR CUSTOMERS...
I...IT'S NOT...L...LET ME SHOW MORE...
ガタン
スッ
トロー…ッ
ベリ
ベリ
ベリ
ベリッ
ベリッ

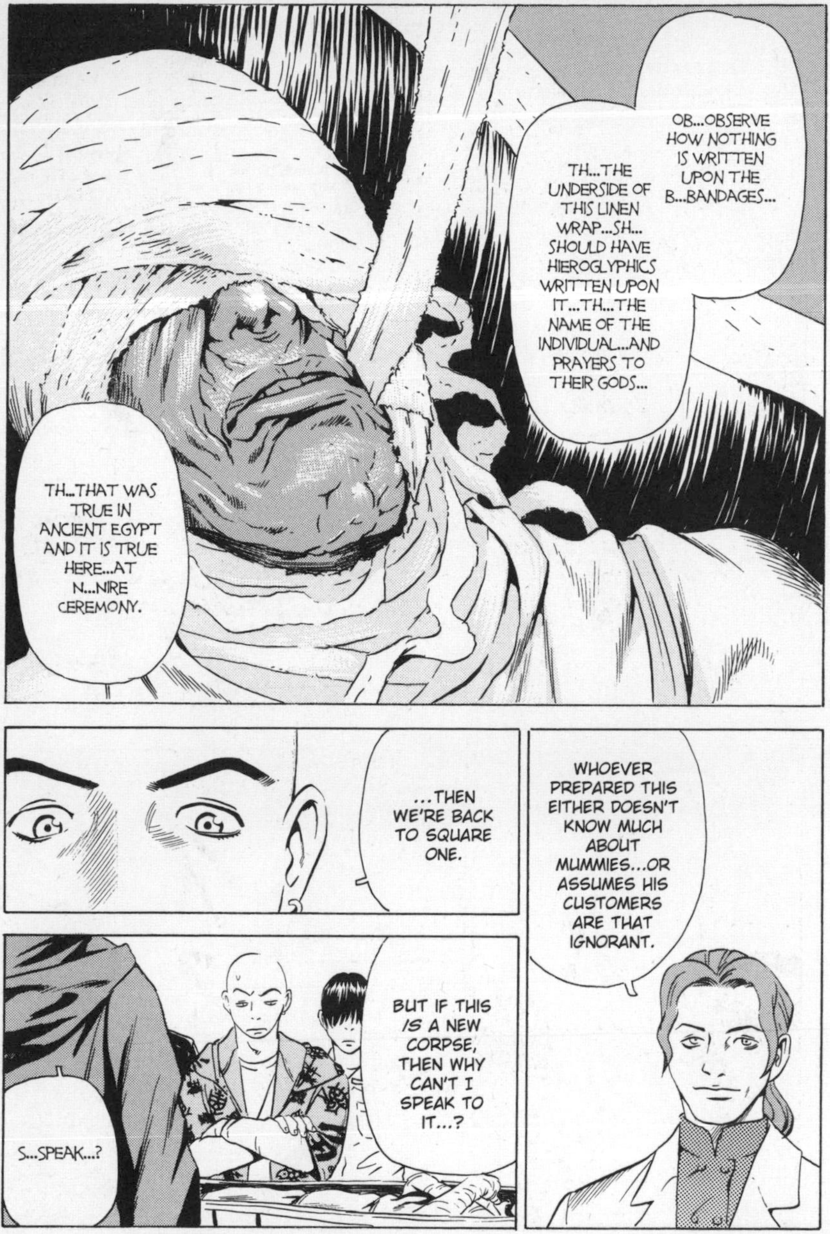
OB...OBSERVE HOW NOTHING IS WRITTEN UPON THE B...BANDAGES...
TH...THE UNDERSIDE OF THIS LINEN WRAP...SH... SHOULD HAVE HIEROGLYPHICS WRITTEN UPON IT...TH...THE NAME OF THE INDIVIDUAL...AND PRAYERS TO THEIR GODS...
TH...THAT WAS TRUE IN ANCIENT EGYPT AND IT IS TRUE HERE...AT N...NIRE CEREMONY.
WHOEVER PREPARED THIS EITHER DOESN'T KNOW MUCH ABOUT MUMMIES...OR ASSUMES HIS CUSTOMERS ARE THAT IGNORANT.
...THEN WE'RE BACK TO SQUARE ONE.
BUT IF THIS *IS* A NEW CORPSE, THEN WHY CAN'T I SPEAK TO IT...?
S...SPEAK...?

...I...I SEE.

OH, YES. HE HAS THE ABILITY TO TALK TO THE DEAD.

T...TALK TO THE DEAD...

...WHAT?

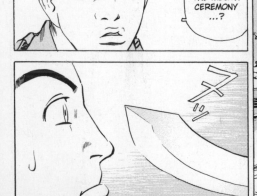

OPENING OF THE MOUTH CEREMONY ...?

I...I BEG YOUR PARDON...IT'S POSSIBLE THAT THE O...OPENING OF THE MOUTH CEREMONY HAS NOT BEEN PERFORMED...YET.

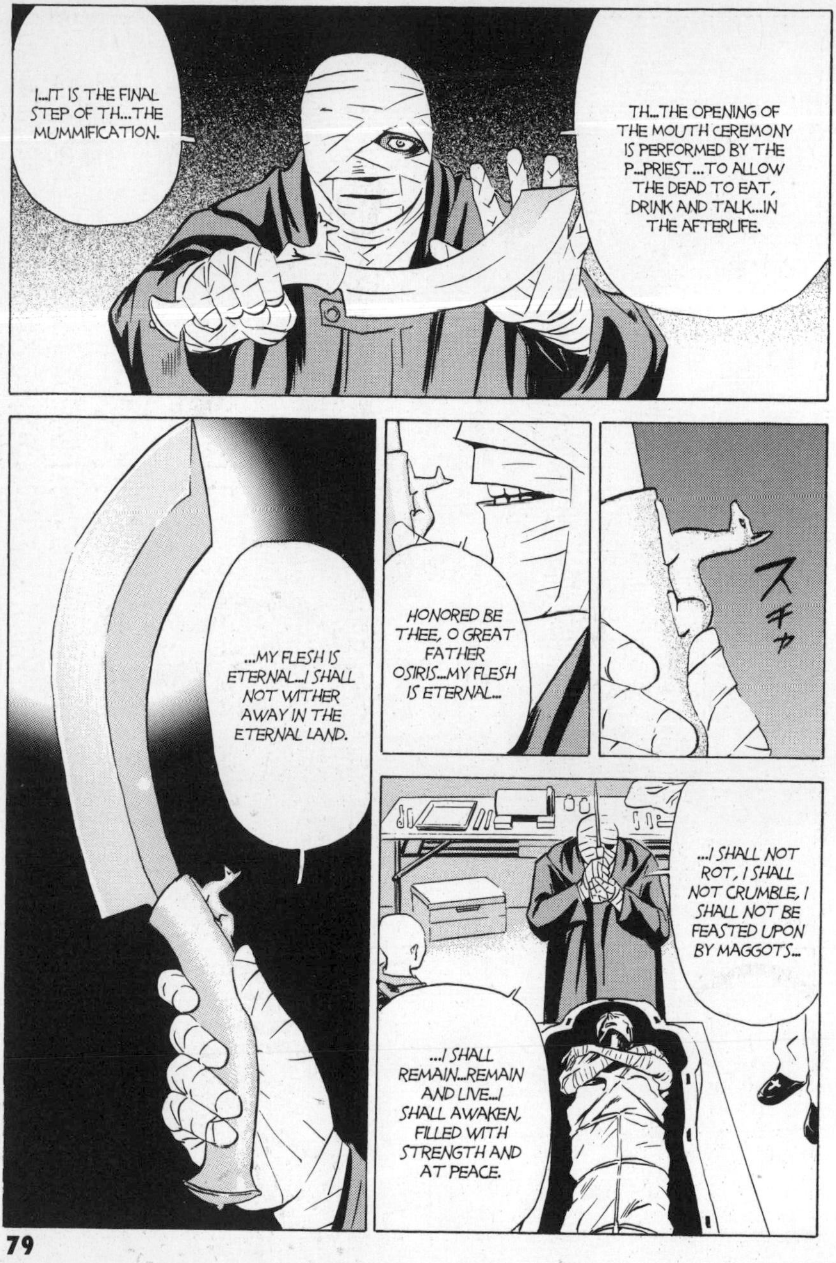
TH...THE OPENING OF THE MOUTH CEREMONY IS PERFORMED BY THE P...PRIEST...TO ALLOW THE DEAD TO EAT, DRINK AND TALK...IN THE AFTERLIFE.
I...IT IS THE FINAL STEP OF TH...THE MUMMIFICATION.
スチャ
HONORED BE THEE, O GREAT FATHER OSIRIS...MY FLESH IS ETERNAL...
...I SHALL NOT ROT, I SHALL NOT CRUMBLE, I SHALL NOT BE FEASTED UPON BY MAGGOTS...
...I SHALL REMAIN...REMAIN AND LIVE...I SHALL AWAKEN, FILLED WITH STRENGTH AND AT PEACE.
...MY FLESH IS ETERNAL...I SHALL NOT WITHER AWAY IN THE ETERNAL LAND.

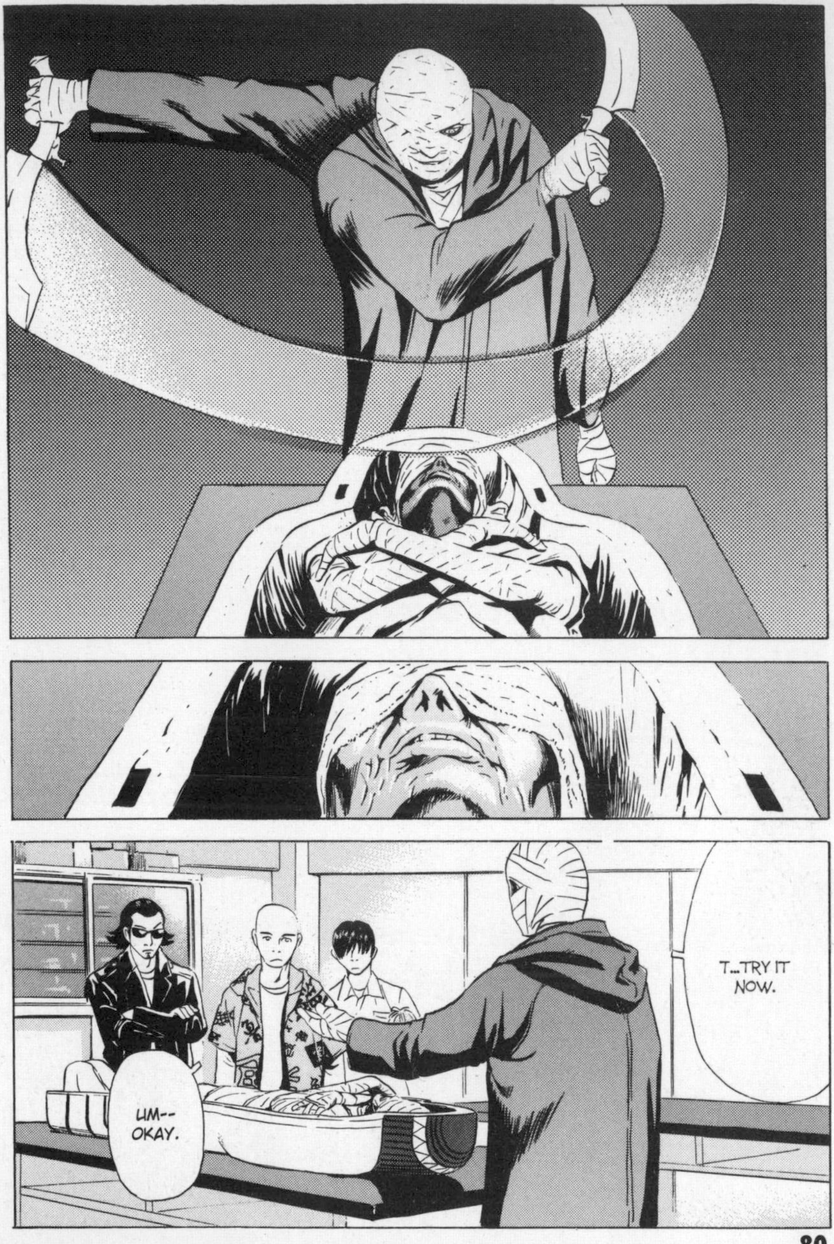
T...TRY IT NOW.
UM-- OKAY.

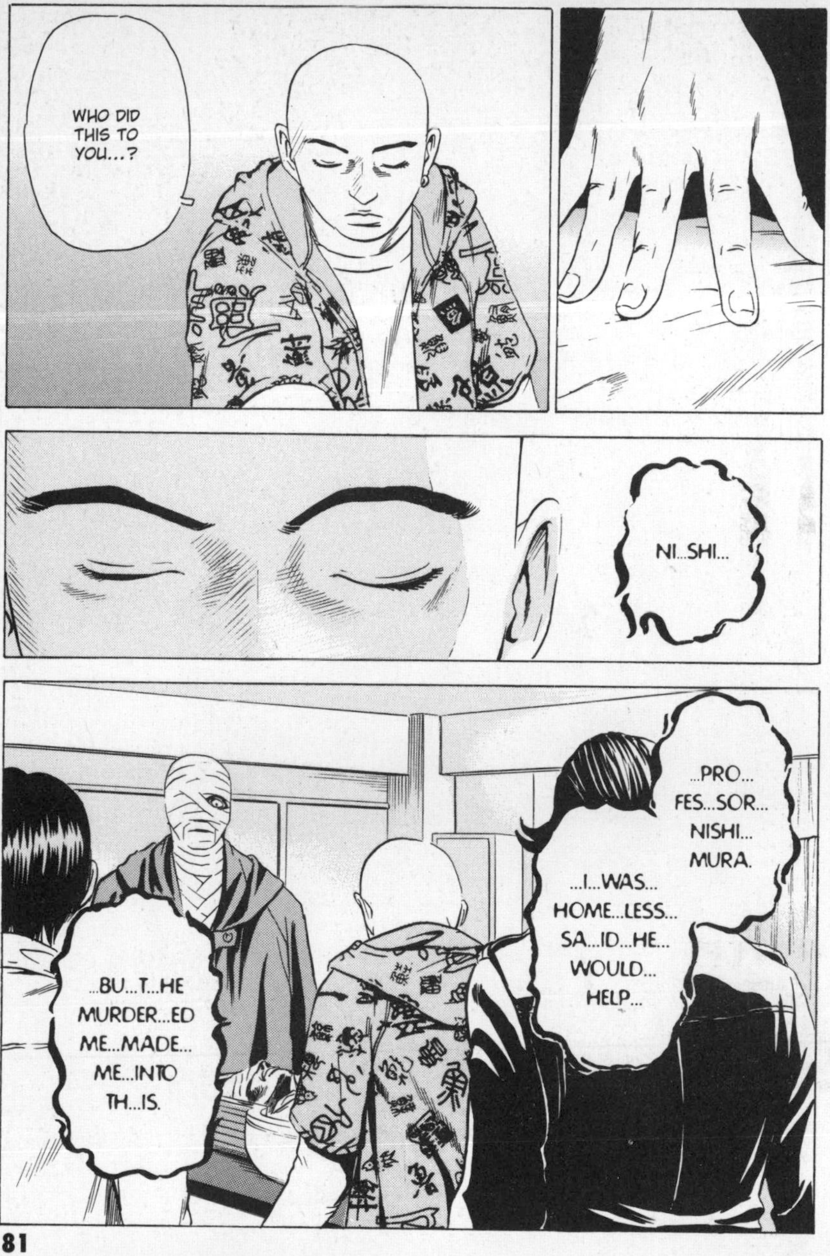
WHO DID THIS TO YOU...?
NI...SHI...
...PRO... FES...SOR... NISHI... MURA.
...I...WAS... HOME...LESS... SA...ID...HE... WOULD... HELP...
...BU...T...HE MURDER...ED ME...MADE... ME...INTO TH...IS.

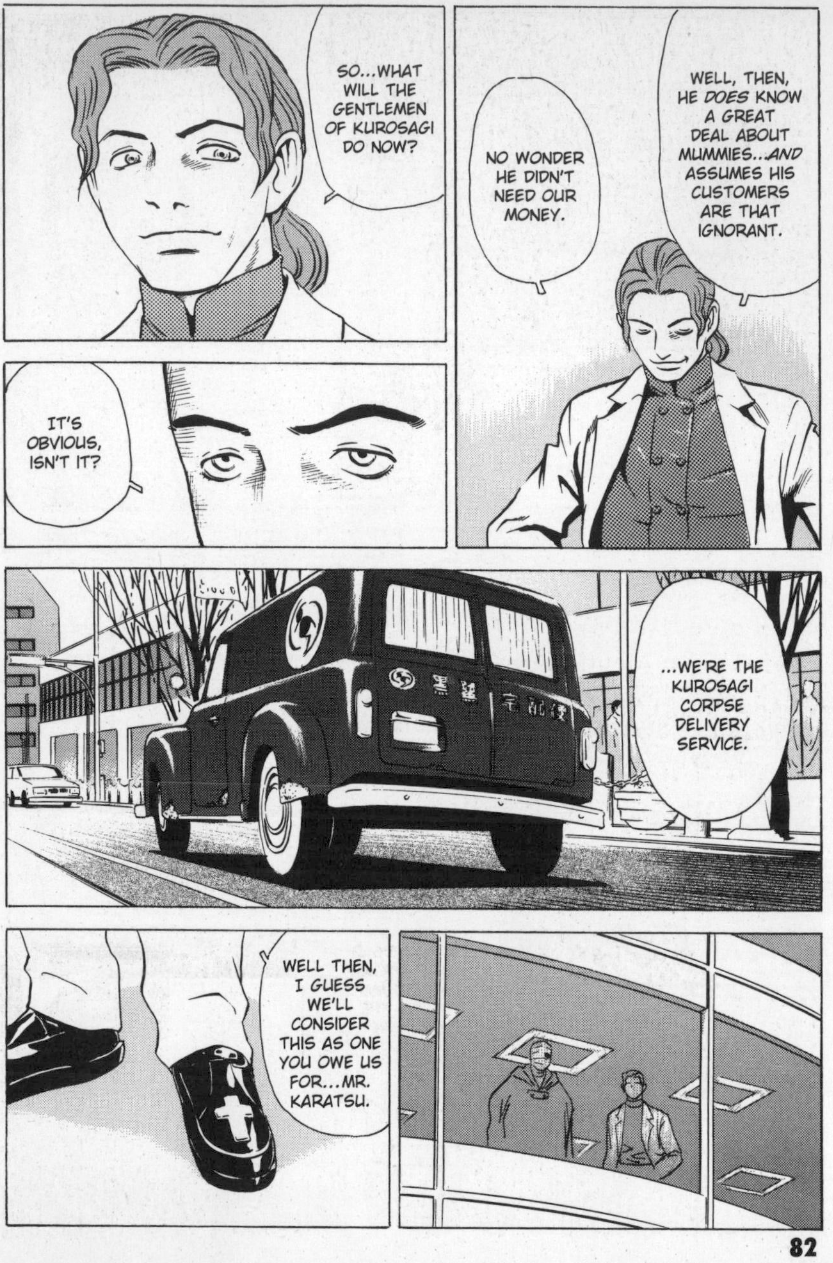
WELL, THEN, HE *DOES* KNOW A GREAT DEAL ABOUT MUMMIES...*AND* ASSUMES HIS CUSTOMERS ARE THAT IGNORANT.
NO WONDER HE DIDN'T NEED OUR MONEY.
SO...WHAT WILL THE GENTLEMEN OF KUROSAGI DO NOW?
IT'S OBVIOUS, ISN'T IT?
...WE'RE THE KUROSAGI CORPSE DELIVERY SERVICE.
WELL THEN, I GUESS WE'LL CONSIDER THIS AS ONE YOU OWE US FOR...MR. KARATSU.

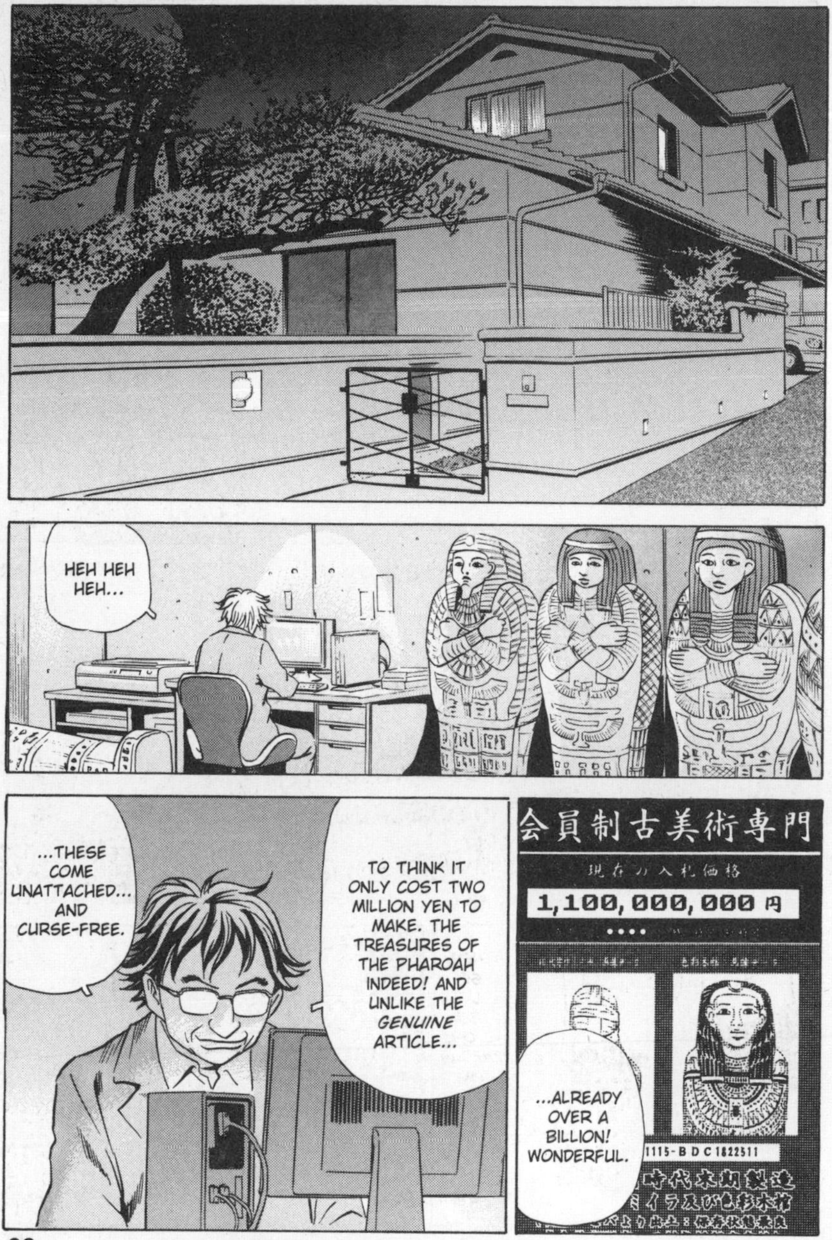
HEH HEH HEH...
会員制古美術専門
現在の入札価格
1,100,000,000 円
1115-BDC1822511
時代末期製造
ミイラ及び色彩木棺
...ALREADY OVER A BILLION! WONDERFUL.
TO THINK IT ONLY COST TWO MILLION YEN TO MAKE. THE TREASURES OF THE PHAROAH INDEED! AND UNLIKE THE *GENUINE* ARTICLE...
...THESE COME UNATTACHED... AND CURSE-FREE.

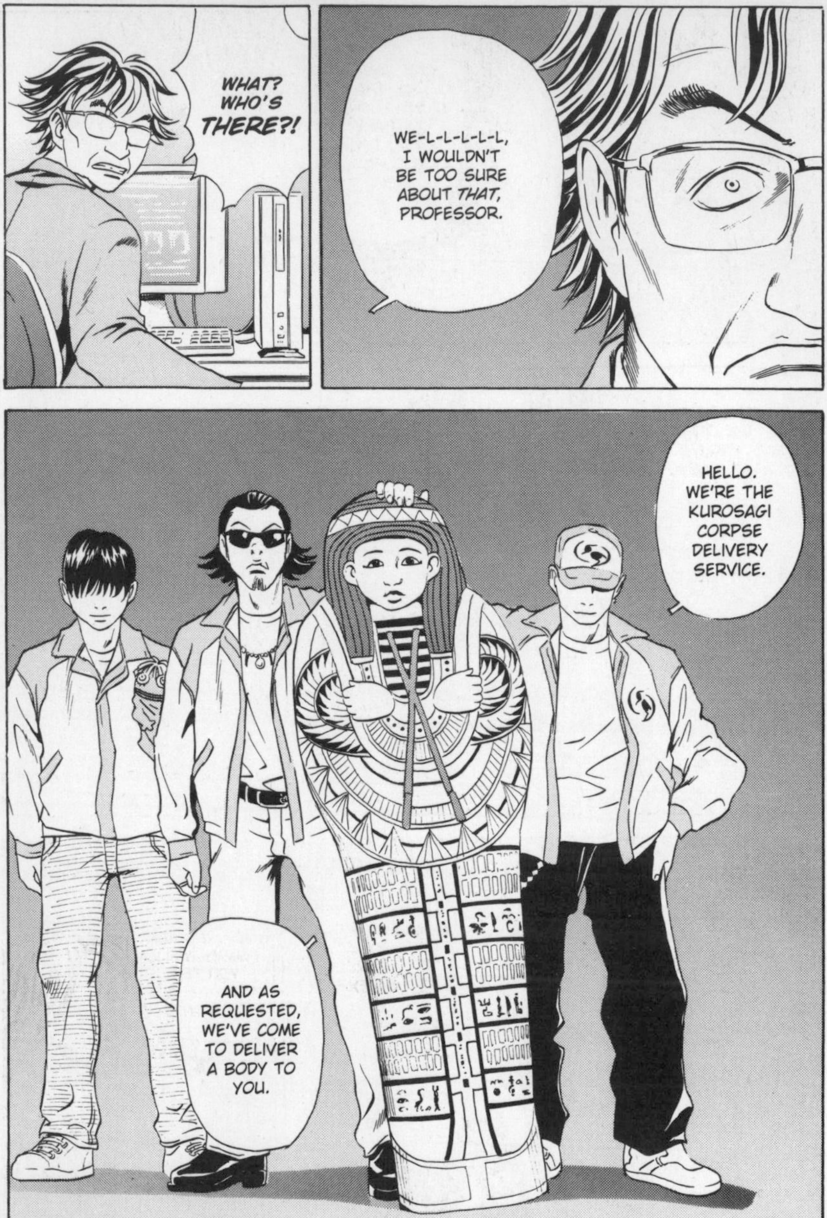
WE-L-L-L-L-L, I WOULDN'T BE TOO SURE ABOUT *THAT*, PROFESSOR.
WHAT? WHO'S **THERE?!**
HELLO. WE'RE THE KUROSAGI CORPSE DELIVERY SERVICE.
AND AS REQUESTED, WE'VE COME TO DELIVER A BODY TO YOU.

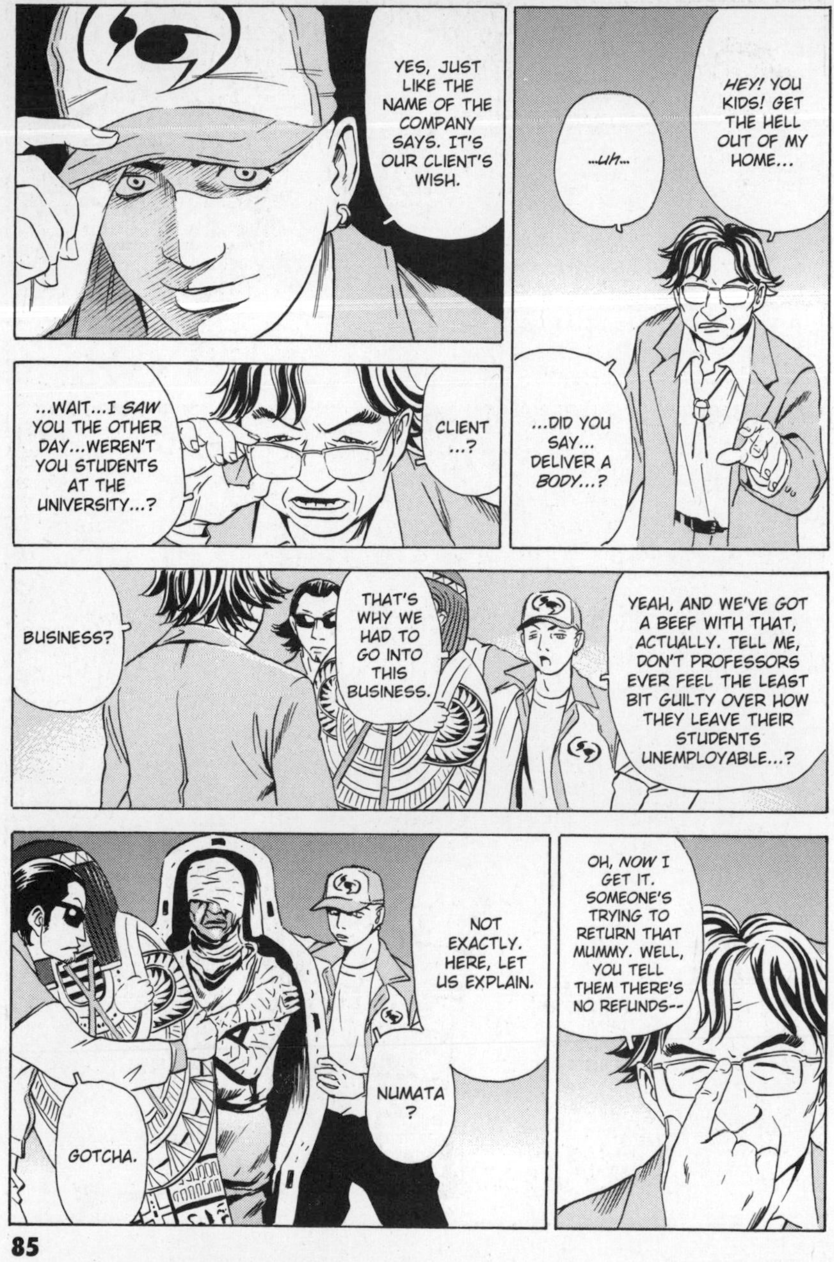
HEY! YOU KIDS! GET THE HELL OUT OF MY HOME...
...uh...
YES, JUST LIKE THE NAME OF THE COMPANY SAYS. IT'S OUR CLIENT'S WISH.
...DID YOU SAY... DELIVER A BODY...?
CLIENT ...?
...WAIT...I SAW YOU THE OTHER DAY...WEREN'T YOU STUDENTS AT THE UNIVERSITY...?
YEAH, AND WE'VE GOT A BEEF WITH THAT, ACTUALLY. TELL ME, DON'T PROFESSORS EVER FEEL THE LEAST BIT GUILTY OVER HOW THEY LEAVE THEIR STUDENTS UNEMPLOYABLE...?
THAT'S WHY WE HAD TO GO INTO THIS BUSINESS.
BUSINESS?
OH, NOW I GET IT. SOMEONE'S TRYING TO RETURN THAT MUMMY. WELL, YOU TELL THEM THERE'S NO REFUNDS--
NOT EXACTLY. HERE, LET US EXPLAIN.
NUMATA ?
GOTCHA.

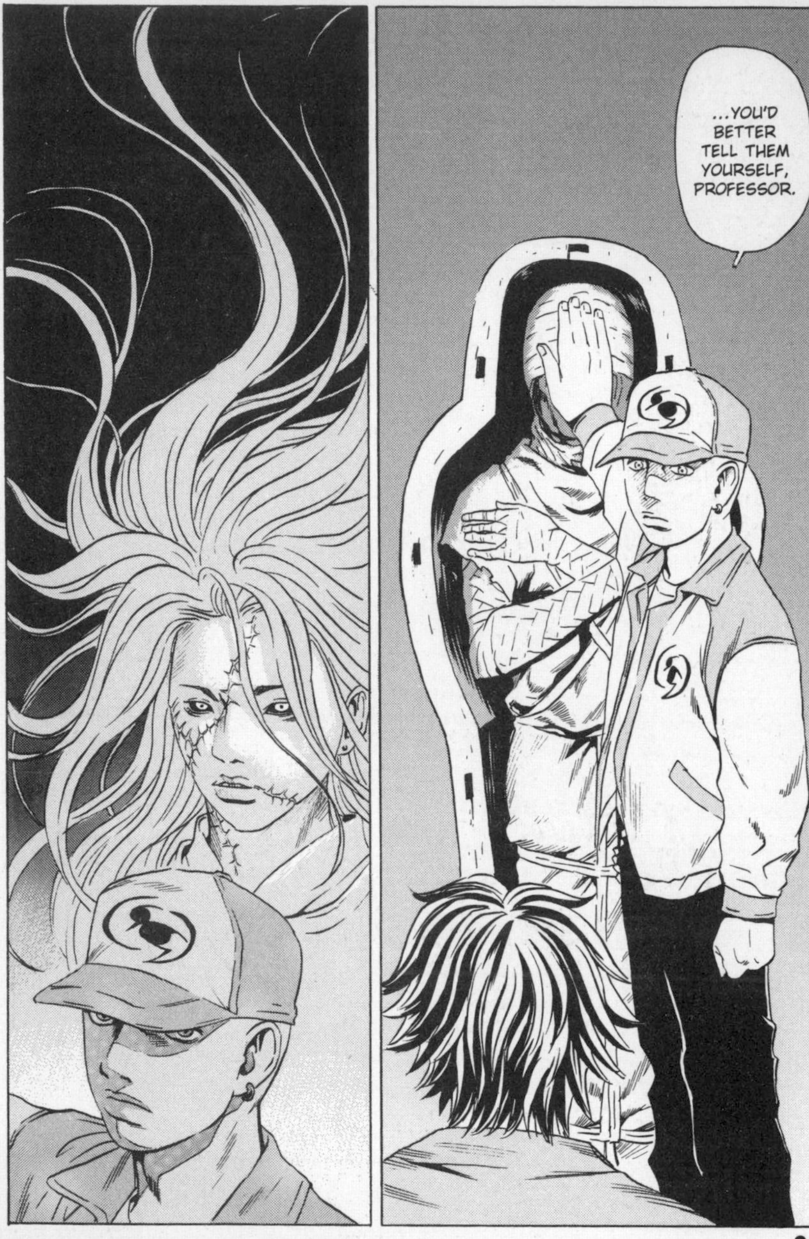
...YOU'D BETTER TELL THEM YOURSELF, PROFESSOR.

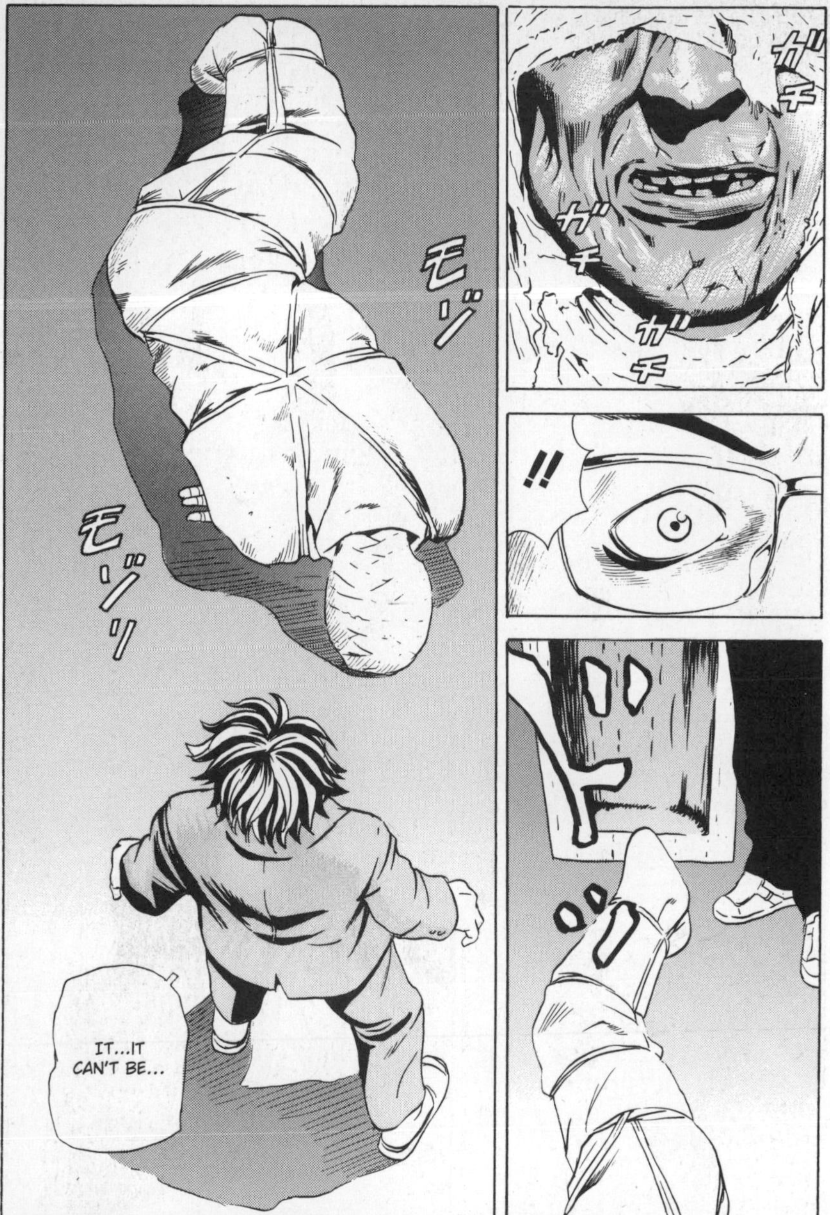
ガチ
ガチ
ガチ
!!
モゾ
モゾッ
IT...IT CAN'T BE...

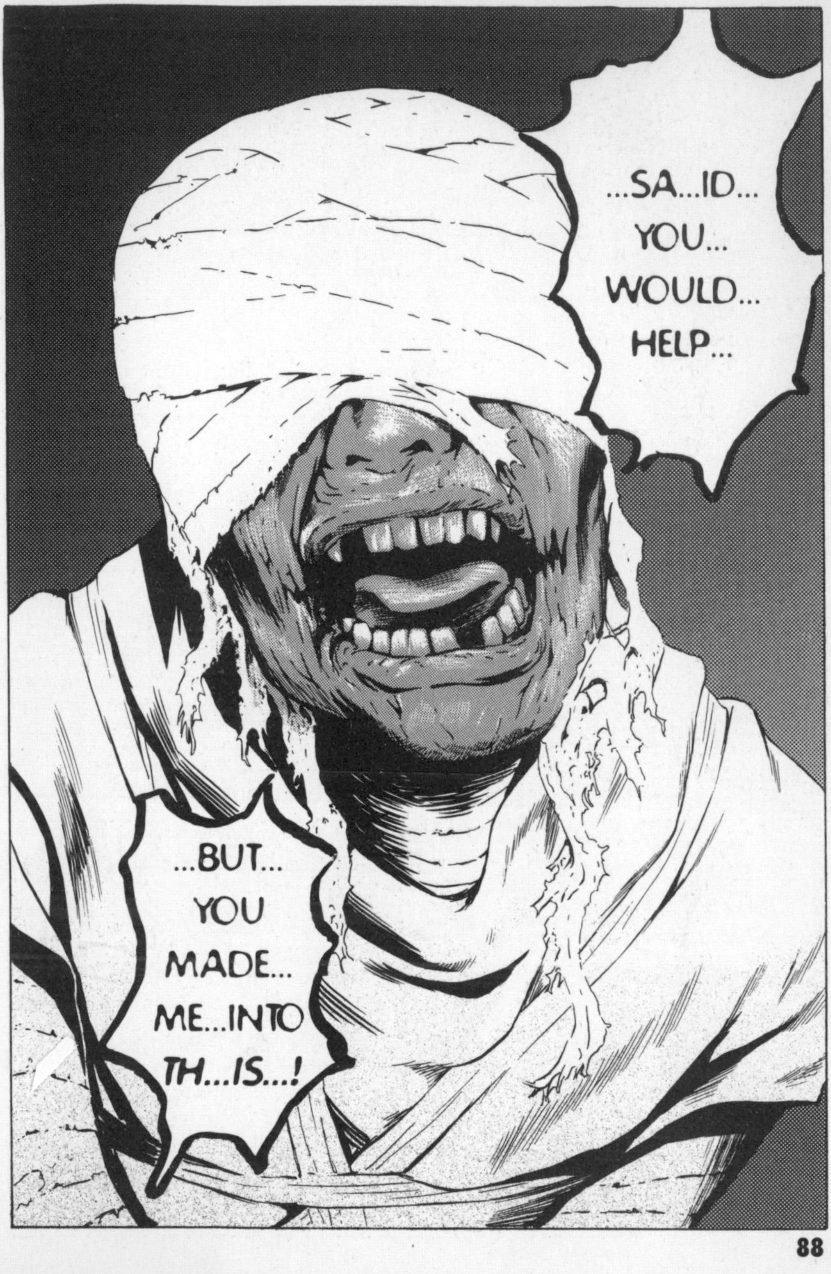
...SA...ID... YOU... WOULD... HELP...
...BUT... YOU MADE... ME...INTO TH...IS...!

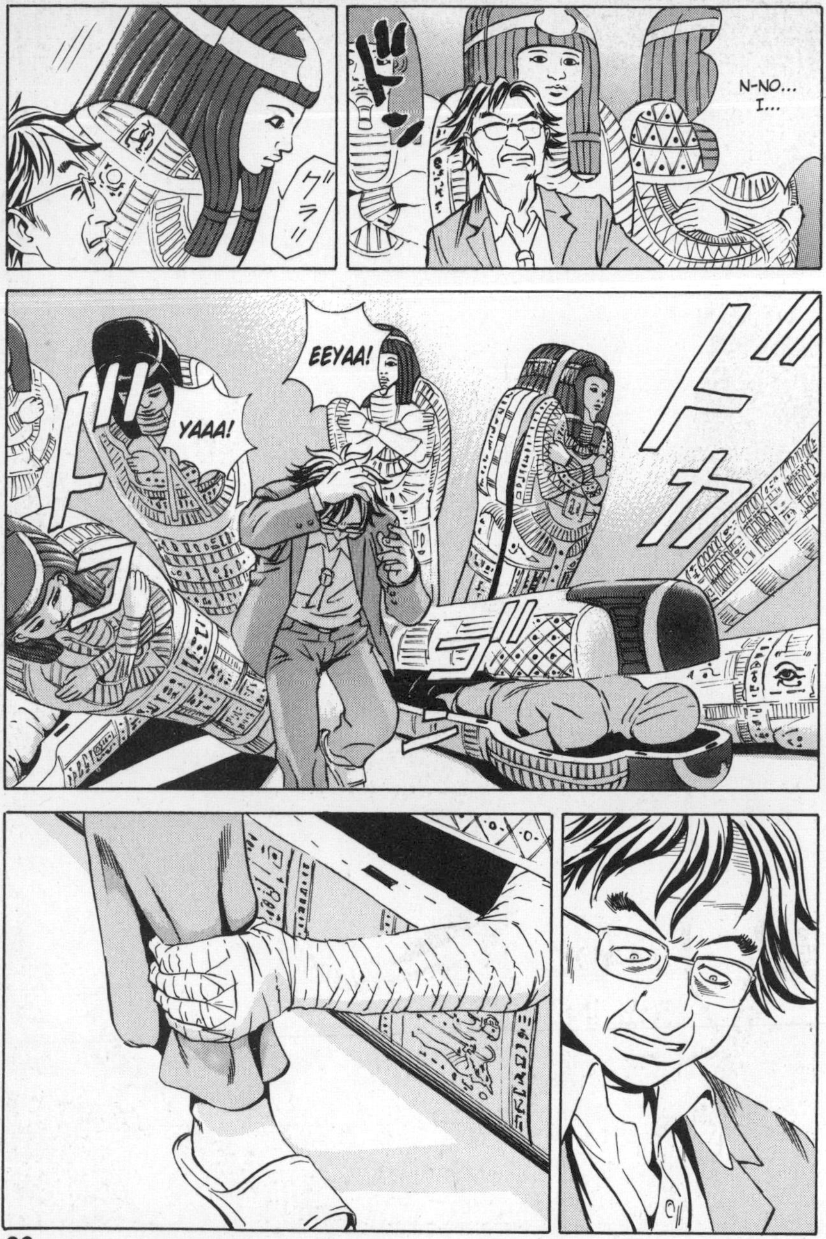
N-NO...
I...
グラ
EEYAA!
YAAA!

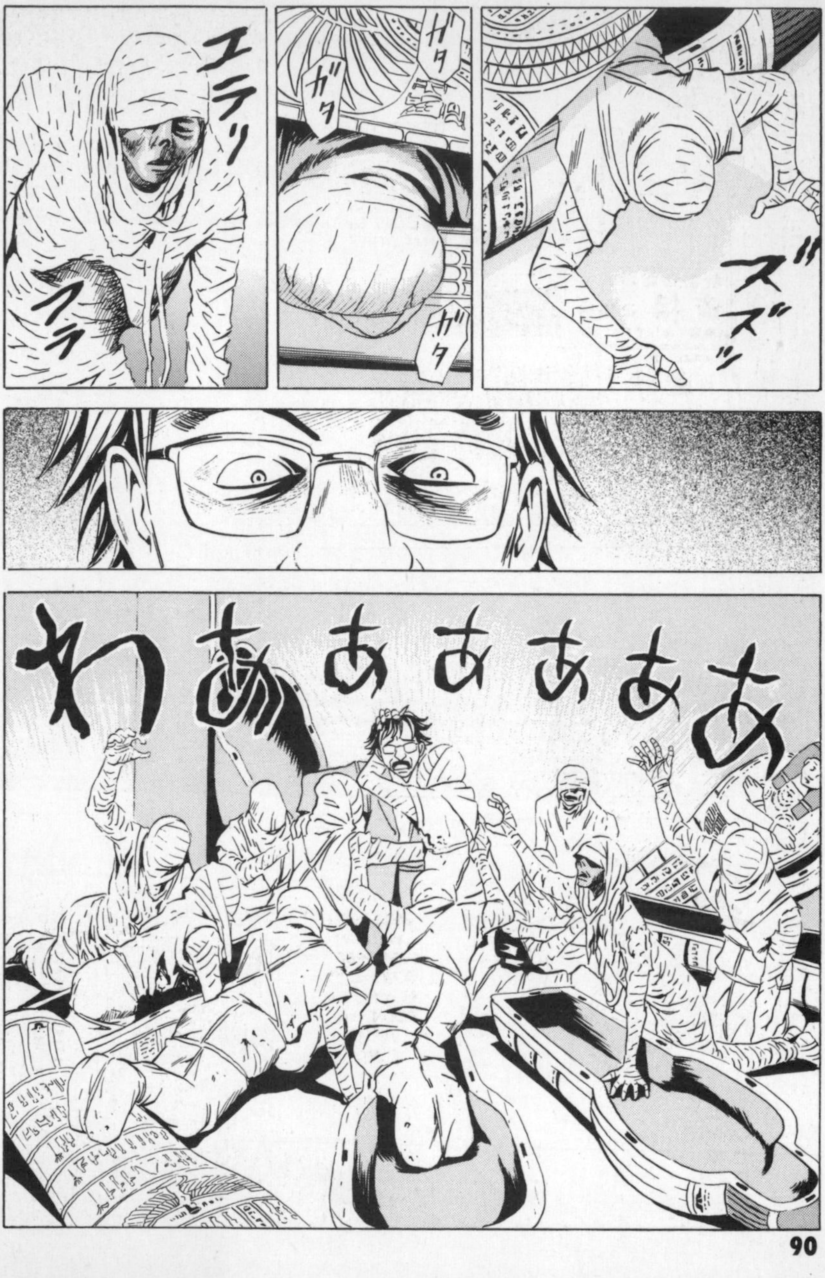
ズズッ
ガタ
ガタ
ガタ
エラッ
フラ
わあああああ

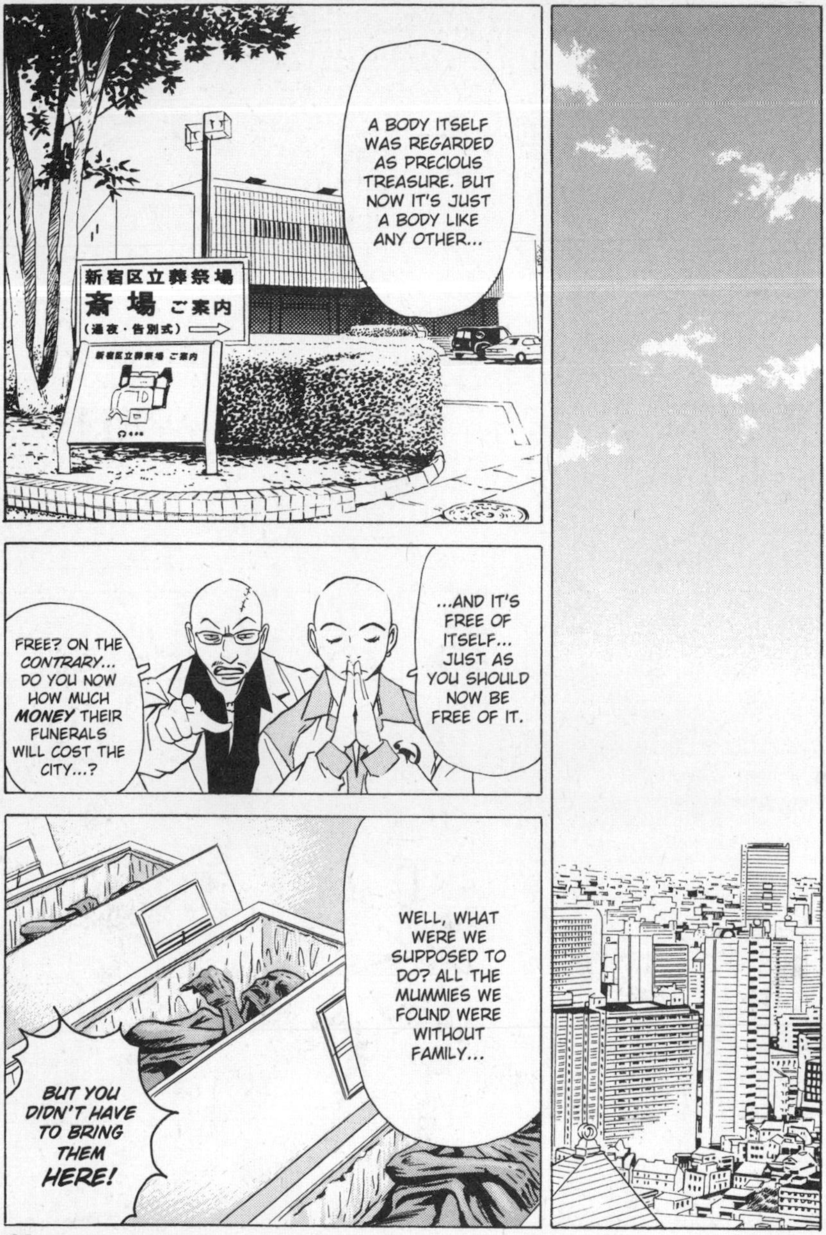
A BODY ITSELF WAS REGARDED AS PRECIOUS TREASURE. BUT NOW IT'S JUST A BODY LIKE ANY OTHER...
新宿区立葬祭場
斎場 ご案内
(通夜・告別式)
新宿区立葬祭場 ご案内
...AND IT'S FREE OF ITSELF... JUST AS YOU SHOULD NOW BE FREE OF IT.
FREE? ON THE *CONTRARY*... DO YOU NOW HOW MUCH ***MONEY*** THEIR FUNERALS WILL COST THE CITY...?
WELL, WHAT WERE WE SUPPOSED TO DO? ALL THE MUMMIES WE FOUND WERE WITHOUT FAMILY...
*BUT YOU DIDN'T HAVE TO BRING THEM **HERE!***

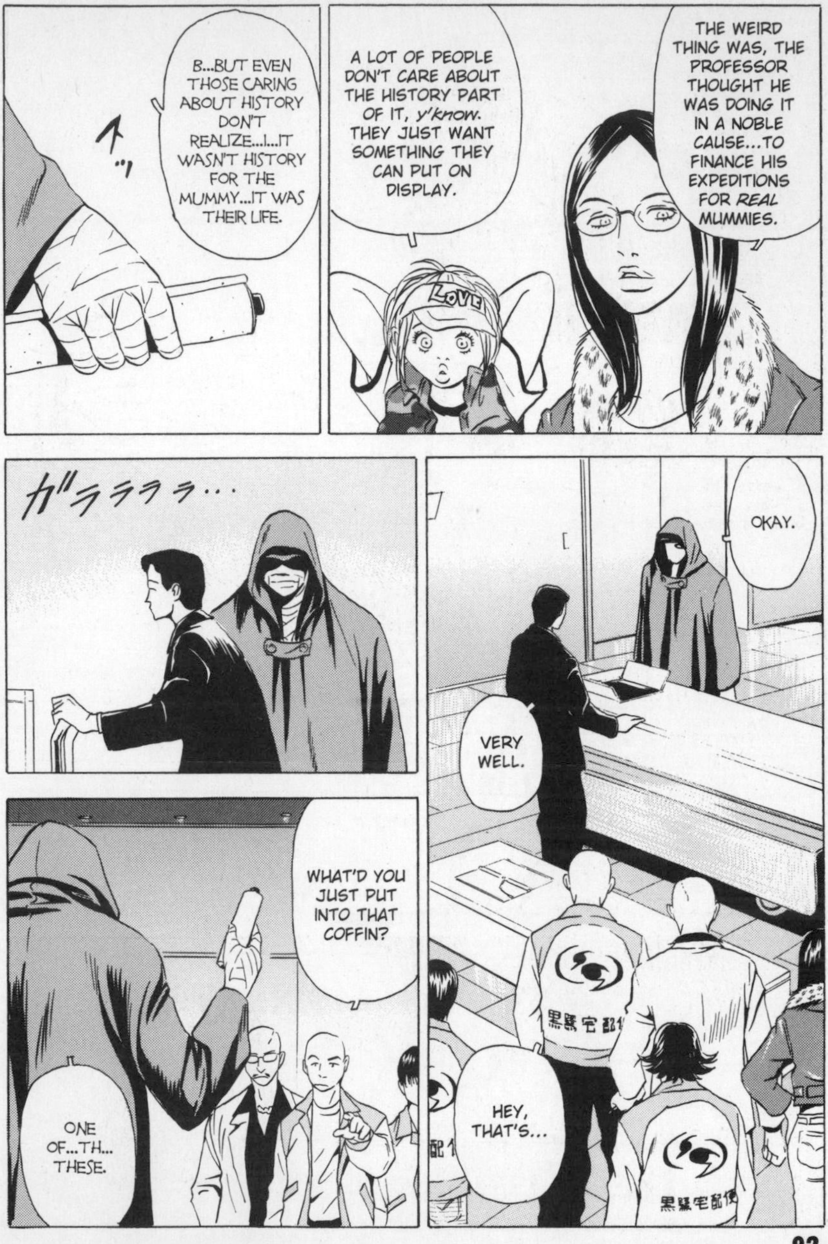
THE WEIRD THING WAS, THE PROFESSOR THOUGHT HE WAS DOING IT IN A NOBLE CAUSE...TO FINANCE HIS EXPEDITIONS FOR *REAL* MUMMIES.
A LOT OF PEOPLE DON'T CARE ABOUT THE HISTORY PART OF IT, *y'know*. THEY JUST WANT SOMETHING THEY CAN PUT ON DISPLAY.
LOVE
B...BUT EVEN THOSE CARING ABOUT HISTORY DON'T REALIZE...I...IT WASN'T HISTORY FOR THE MUMMY...IT WAS THEIR LIFE.
スッ
OKAY.
VERY WELL.
HEY, THAT'S...
黒鷺宅配便
ガラララ ラ...
WHAT'D YOU JUST PUT INTO THAT COFFIN?
ONE OF...TH... THESE.

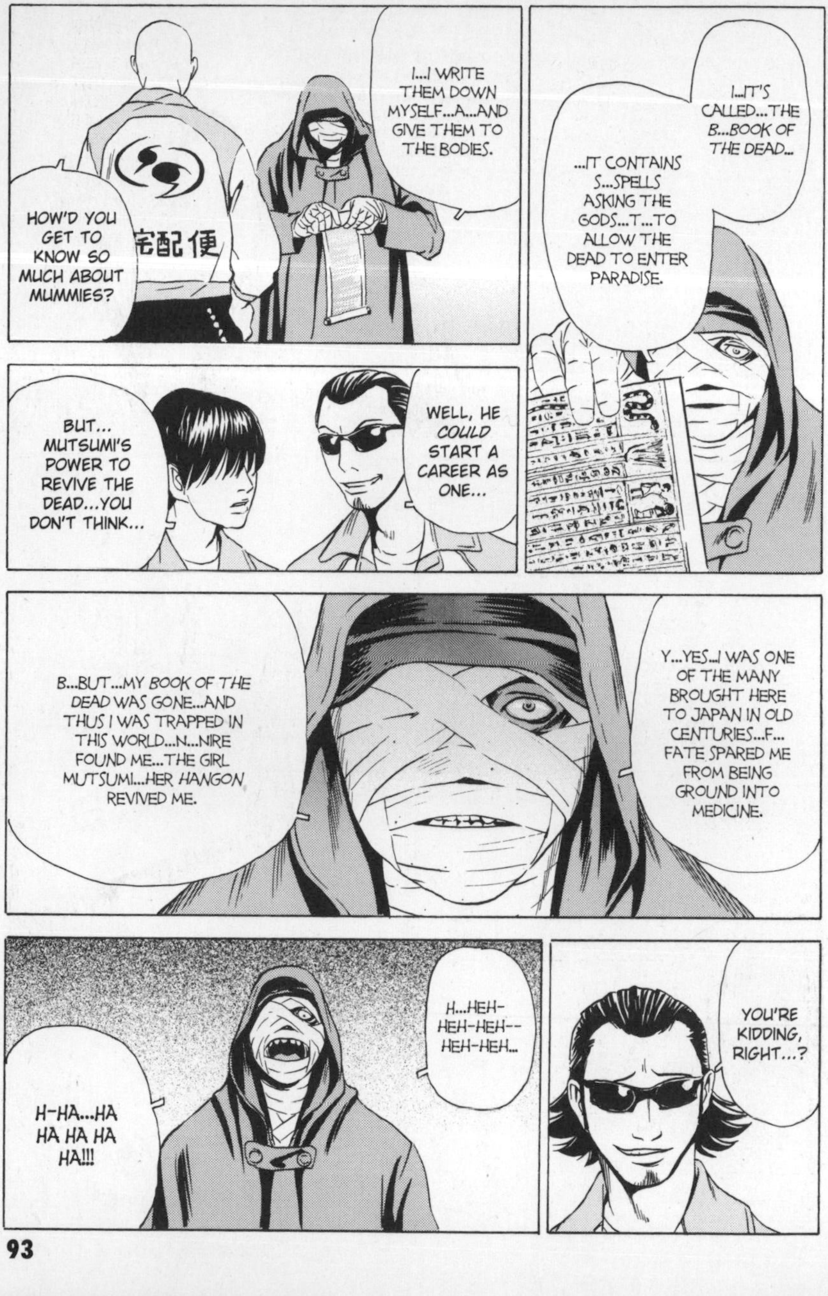
I...IT'S CALLED...THE B...BOOK OF THE DEAD...
...IT CONTAINS S...SPELLS ASKING THE GODS...T...TO ALLOW THE DEAD TO ENTER PARADISE.
I...I WRITE THEM DOWN MYSELF...A...AND GIVE THEM TO THE BODIES.
HOW'D YOU GET TO KNOW SO MUCH ABOUT MUMMIES?
宅配便
WELL, HE *COULD* START A CAREER AS ONE...
BUT... MUTSUMI'S POWER TO REVIVE THE DEAD...YOU DON'T THINK...
Y...YES...I WAS ONE OF THE MANY BROUGHT HERE TO JAPAN IN OLD CENTURIES...F... FATE SPARED ME FROM BEING GROUND INTO MEDICINE.
B...BUT...MY *BOOK OF THE DEAD* WAS GONE...AND THUS I WAS TRAPPED IN THIS WORLD...N...NIRE FOUND ME...THE GIRL MUTSUMI...HER *HANGON* REVIVED ME.
YOU'RE KIDDING, RIGHT...?
H...HEH-HEH-HEH--HEH-HEH...
H-HA...HA HA HA HA HA!!!

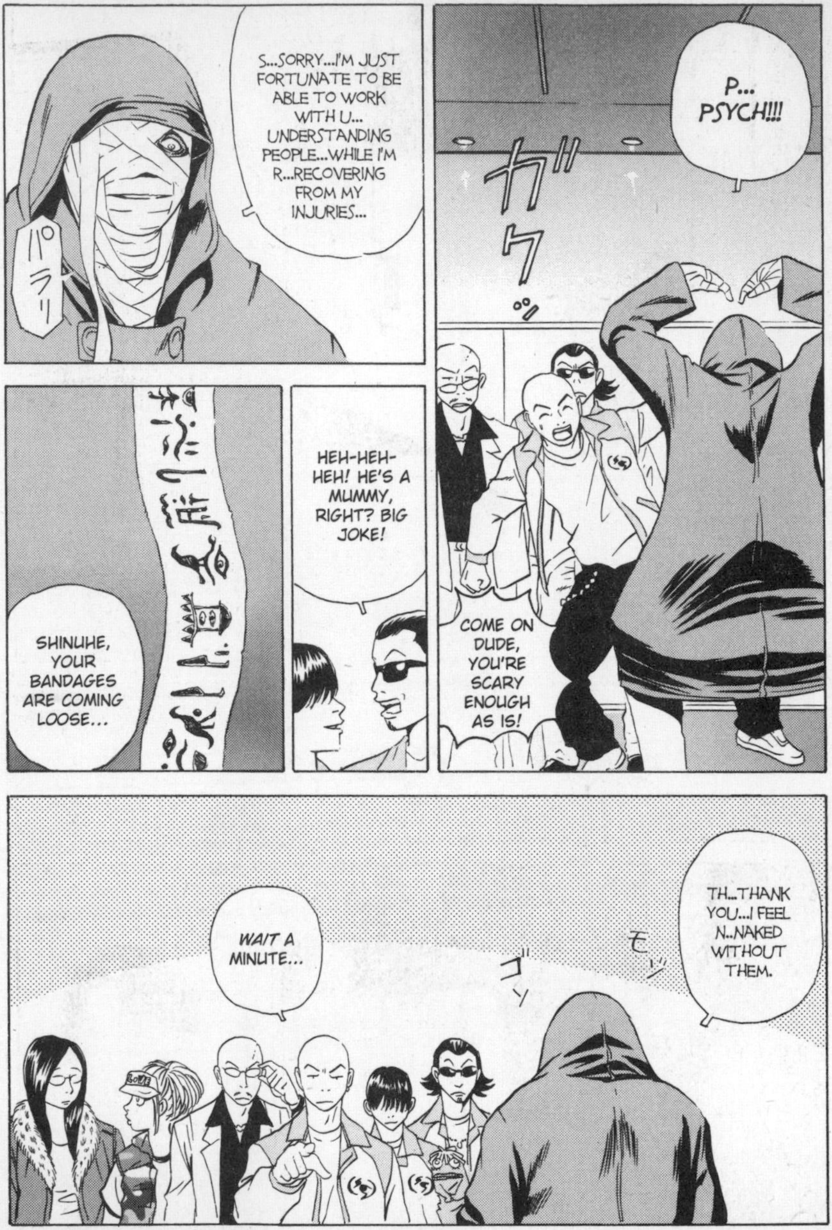
P... PSYCH!!!
ガクッ
COME ON DUDE, YOU'RE SCARY ENOUGH AS IS!
S...SORRY...I'M JUST FORTUNATE TO BE ABLE TO WORK WITH U... UNDERSTANDING PEOPLE...WHILE I'M R...RECOVERING FROM MY INJURIES...
パラリ
HEH-HEH-HEH! HE'S A MUMMY, RIGHT? BIG JOKE!
SHINUHE, YOUR BANDAGES ARE COMING LOOSE...
TH...THANK YOU...I FEEL N..NAKED WITHOUT THEM.
モッ
ゴッ
WAIT A MINUTE...

2nd delivery: password to tomorrow—the end

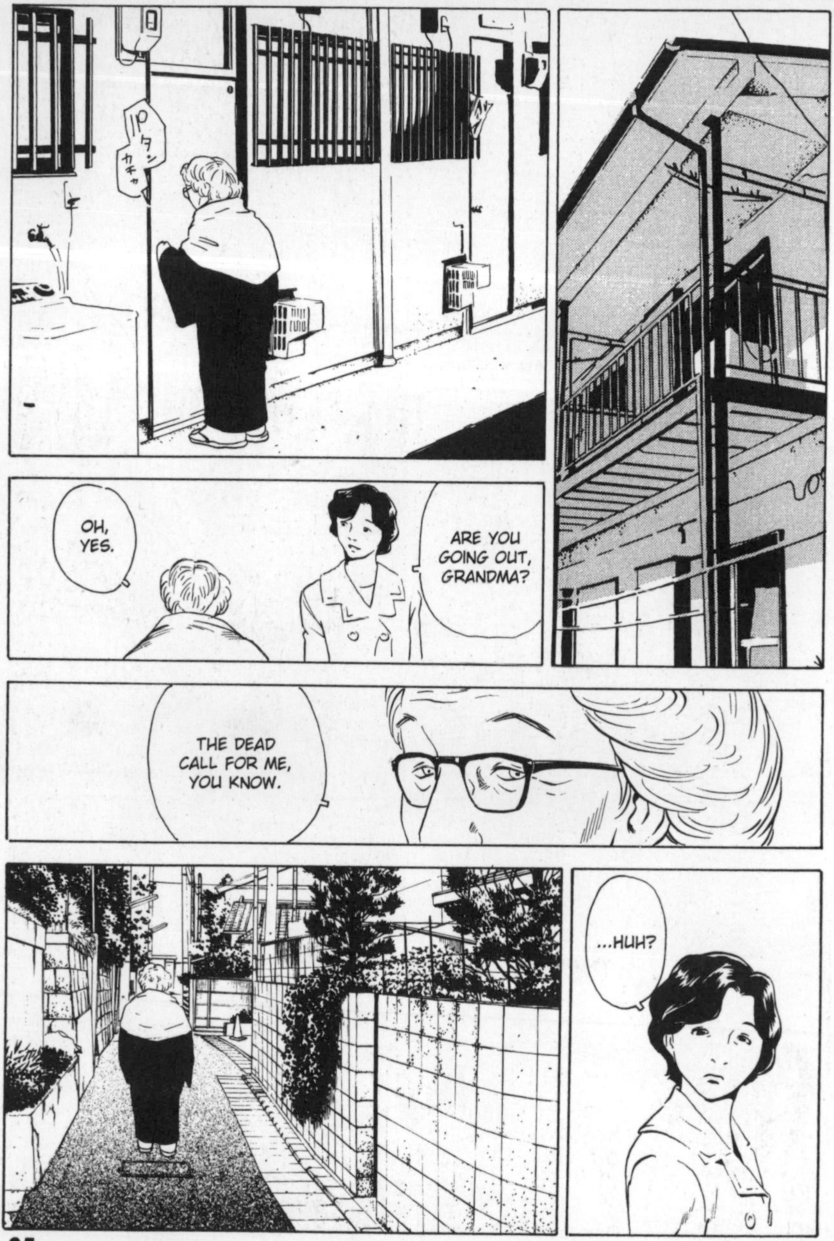
パタン
カチャ
ARE YOU GOING OUT, GRANDMA?
OH, YES.
THE DEAD CALL FOR ME, YOU KNOW.
...HUH?

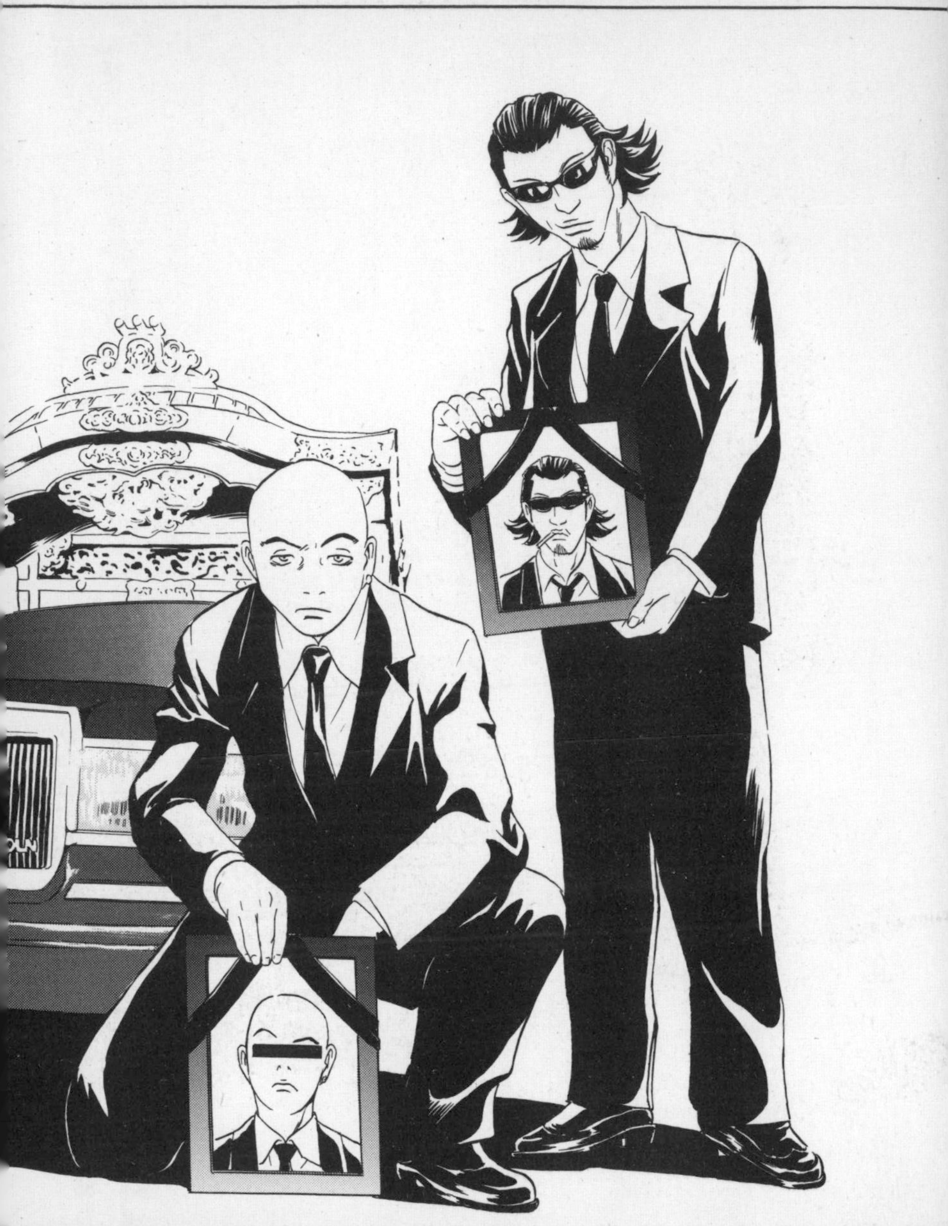

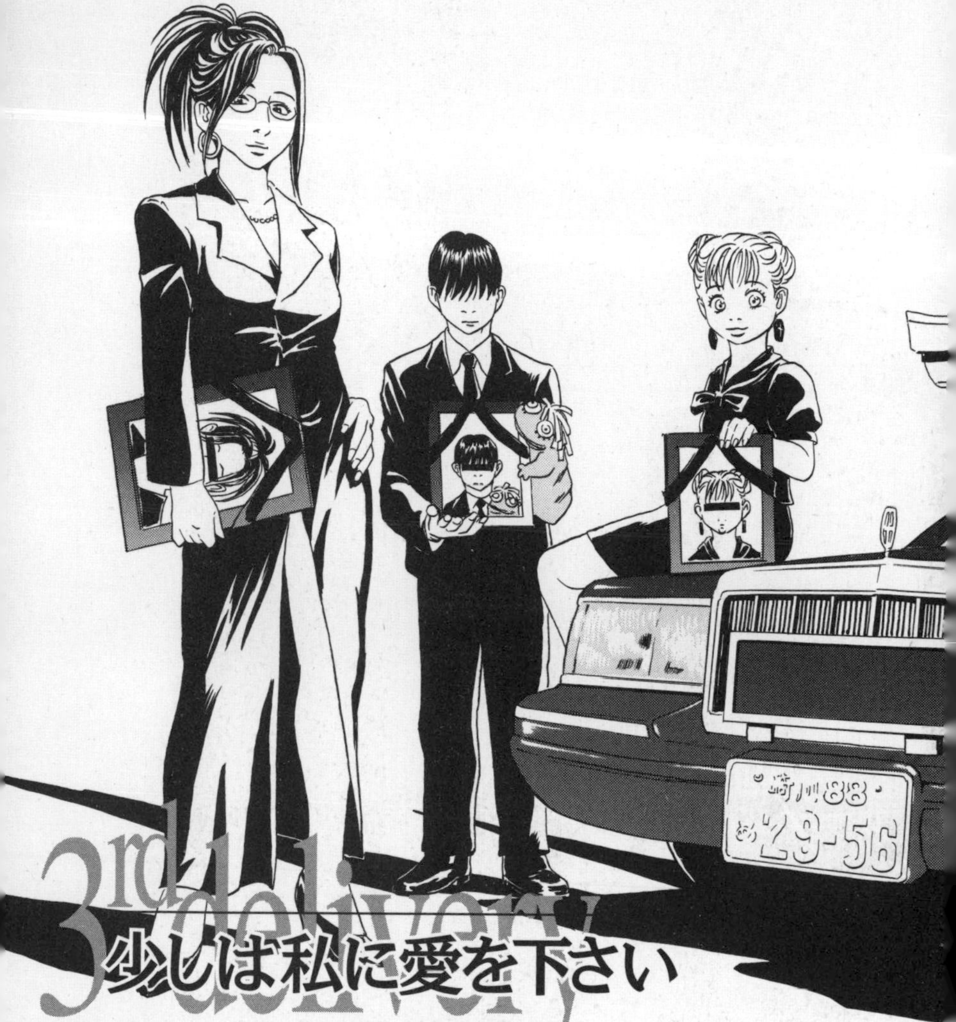

3rd delivery 少しは私に愛を下さい

please give me a little love

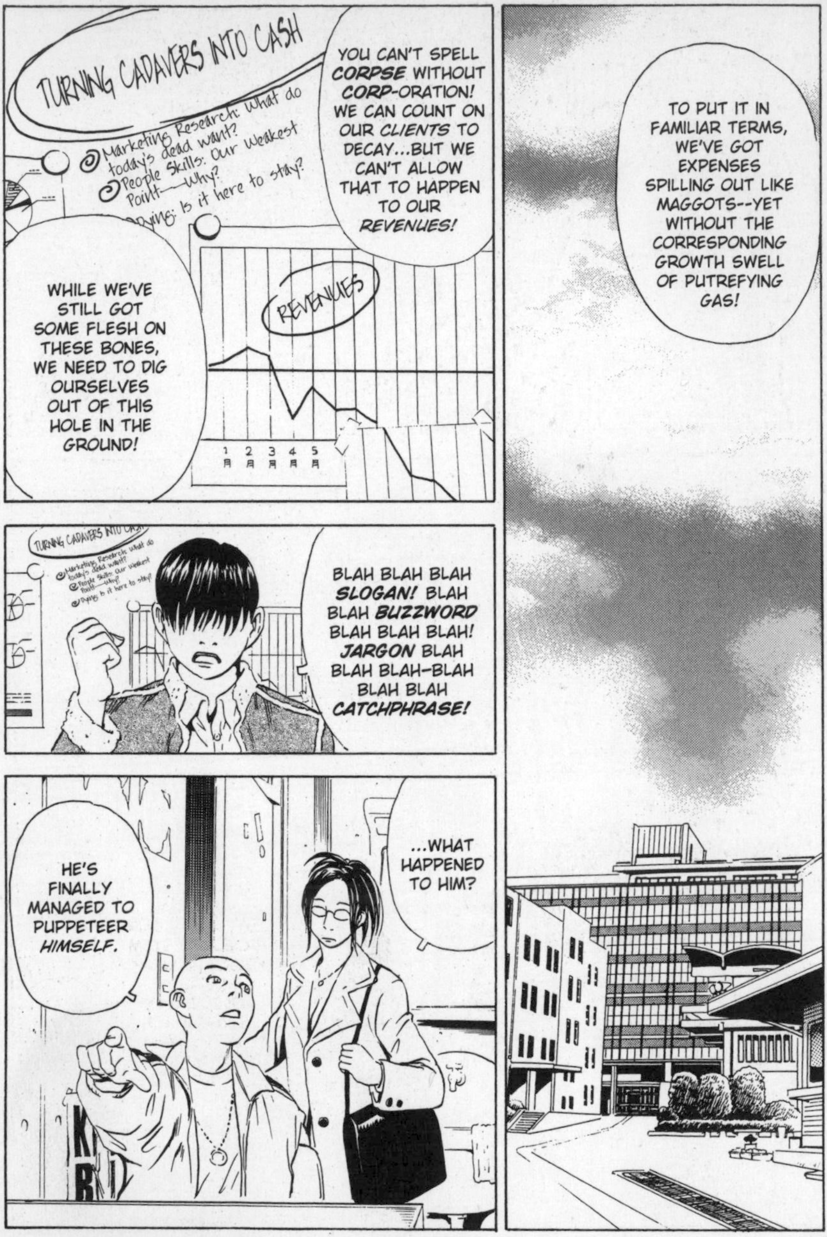
TO PUT IT IN FAMILIAR TERMS, WE'VE GOT EXPENSES SPILLING OUT LIKE MAGGOTS--YET WITHOUT THE CORRESPONDING GROWTH SWELL OF PUTREFYING GAS!
YOU CAN'T SPELL CORPSE WITHOUT CORP-ORATION! WE CAN COUNT ON OUR CLIENTS TO DECAY...BUT WE CAN'T ALLOW THAT TO HAPPEN TO OUR REVENUES!
TURNING CADAVERS INTO CASH
Marketing Research: What do today's dead want?
People Skills: Our Weakest Point——Why?
Is it here to stay?
REVENUES
WHILE WE'VE STILL GOT SOME FLESH ON THESE BONES, WE NEED TO DIG OURSELVES OUT OF THIS HOLE IN THE GROUND!
BLAH BLAH BLAH SLOGAN! BLAH BLAH BUZZWORD BLAH BLAH BLAH! JARGON BLAH BLAH BLAH-BLAH BLAH BLAH CATCHPHRASE!
...WHAT HAPPENED TO HIM?
HE'S FINALLY MANAGED TO PUPPETEER HIMSELF.

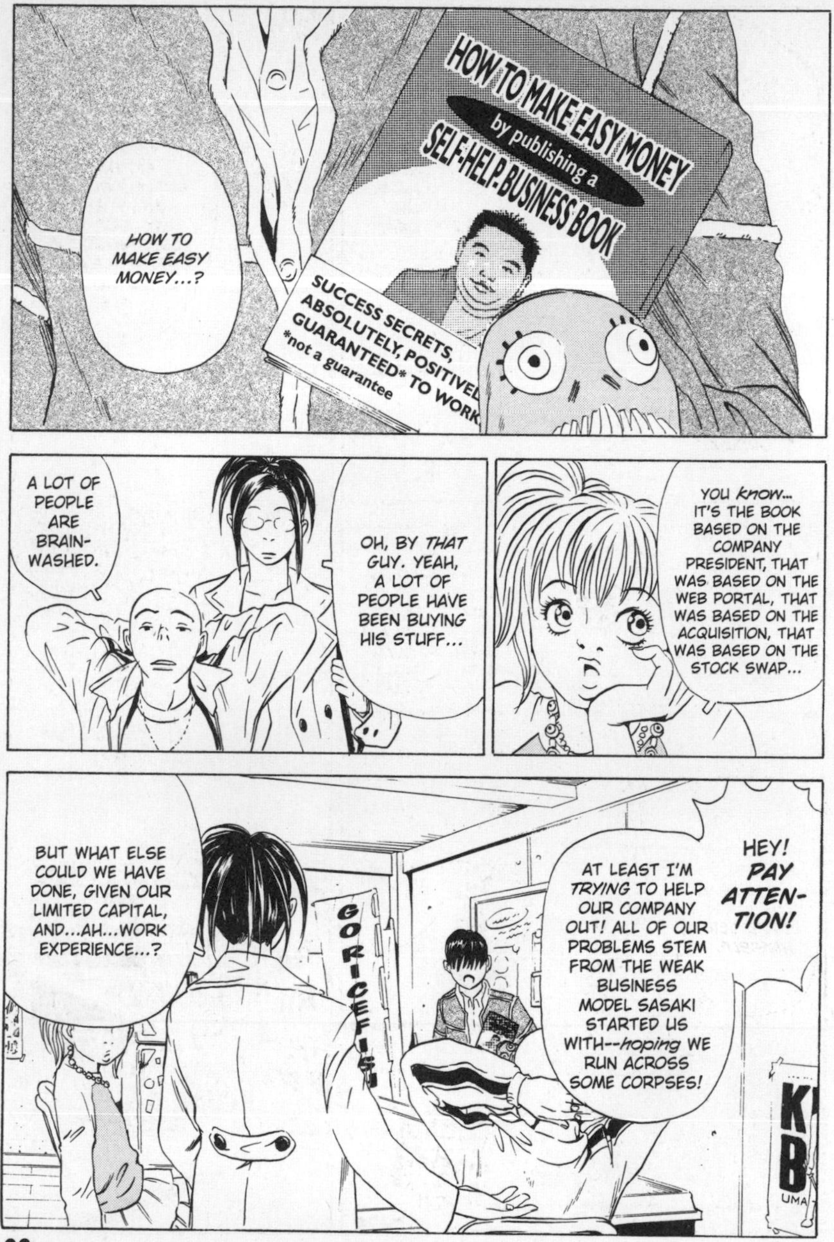
HOW TO MAKE EASY MONEY
by publishing a
SELF-HELP. BUSINESS BOOK
SUCCESS SECRETS, ABSOLUTELY, POSITIVELY GUARANTEED* TO WORK
*not a guarantee
HOW TO MAKE EASY MONEY...?
YOU *know*... IT'S THE BOOK BASED ON THE COMPANY PRESIDENT, THAT WAS BASED ON THE WEB PORTAL, THAT WAS BASED ON THE ACQUISITION, THAT WAS BASED ON THE STOCK SWAP...
OH, BY *THAT* GUY. YEAH, A LOT OF PEOPLE HAVE BEEN BUYING HIS STUFF...
A LOT OF PEOPLE ARE BRAIN-WASHED.
HEY! ***PAY ATTEN-TION!***
AT LEAST I'M *TRYING* TO HELP OUR COMPANY OUT! ALL OF OUR PROBLEMS STEM FROM THE WEAK BUSINESS MODEL SASAKI STARTED US WITH--*hoping* WE RUN ACROSS SOME CORPSES!
BUT WHAT ELSE COULD WE HAVE DONE, GIVEN OUR LIMITED CAPITAL, AND...AH...WORK EXPERIENCE...?

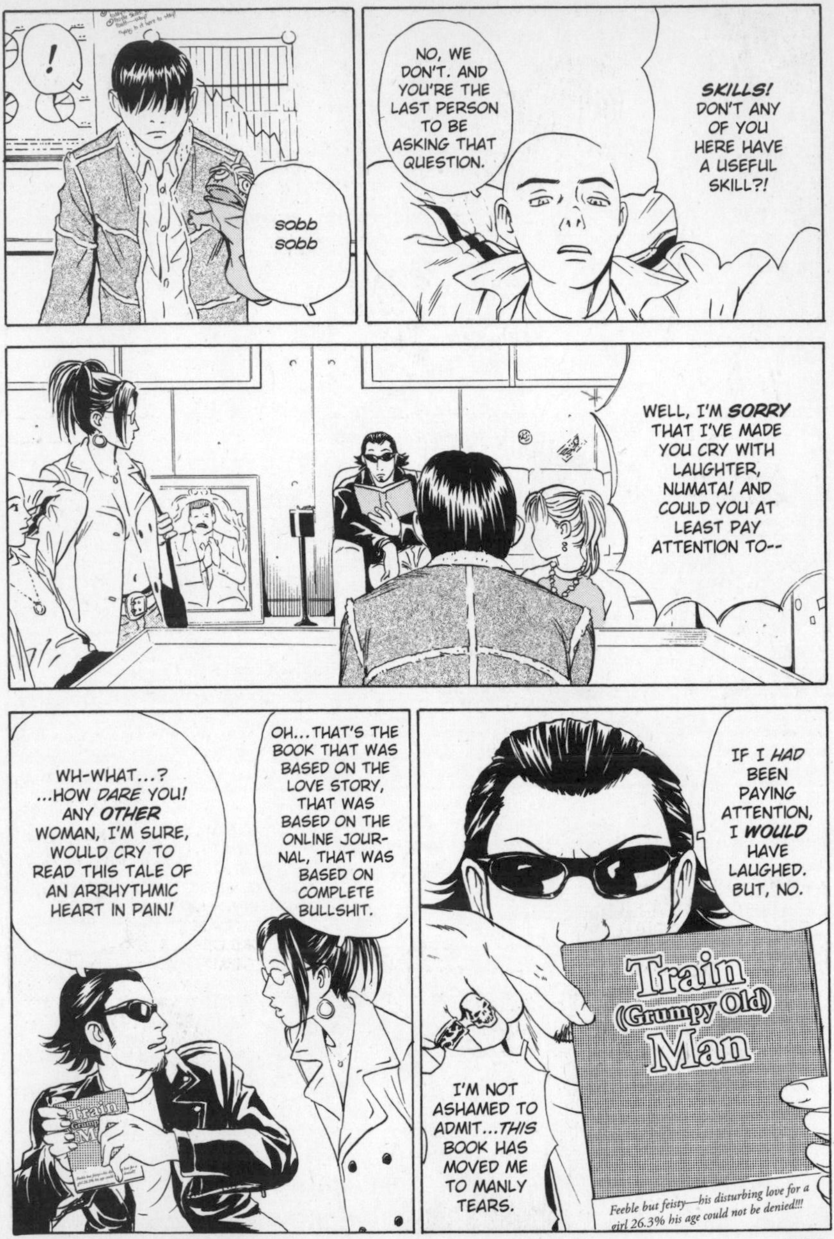
SKILLS! DON'T ANY OF YOU HERE HAVE A USEFUL SKILL?!
NO, WE DON'T. AND YOU'RE THE LAST PERSON TO BE ASKING THAT QUESTION.
!
sobb sobb
WELL, I'M SORRY THAT I'VE MADE YOU CRY WITH LAUGHTER, NUMATA! AND COULD YOU AT LEAST PAY ATTENTION TO--
IF I HAD BEEN PAYING ATTENTION, I WOULD HAVE LAUGHED. BUT, NO.
I'M NOT ASHAMED TO ADMIT...THIS BOOK HAS MOVED ME TO MANLY TEARS.
Train (Grumpy Old) Man
Feeble but feisty—his disturbing love for a girl 26.3% his age could not be denied!!!
OH...THAT'S THE BOOK THAT WAS BASED ON THE LOVE STORY, THAT WAS BASED ON THE ONLINE JOURNAL, THAT WAS BASED ON COMPLETE BULLSHIT.
WH-WHAT...? ...HOW DARE YOU! ANY OTHER WOMAN, I'M SURE, WOULD CRY TO READ THIS TALE OF AN ARRHYTHMIC HEART IN PAIN!

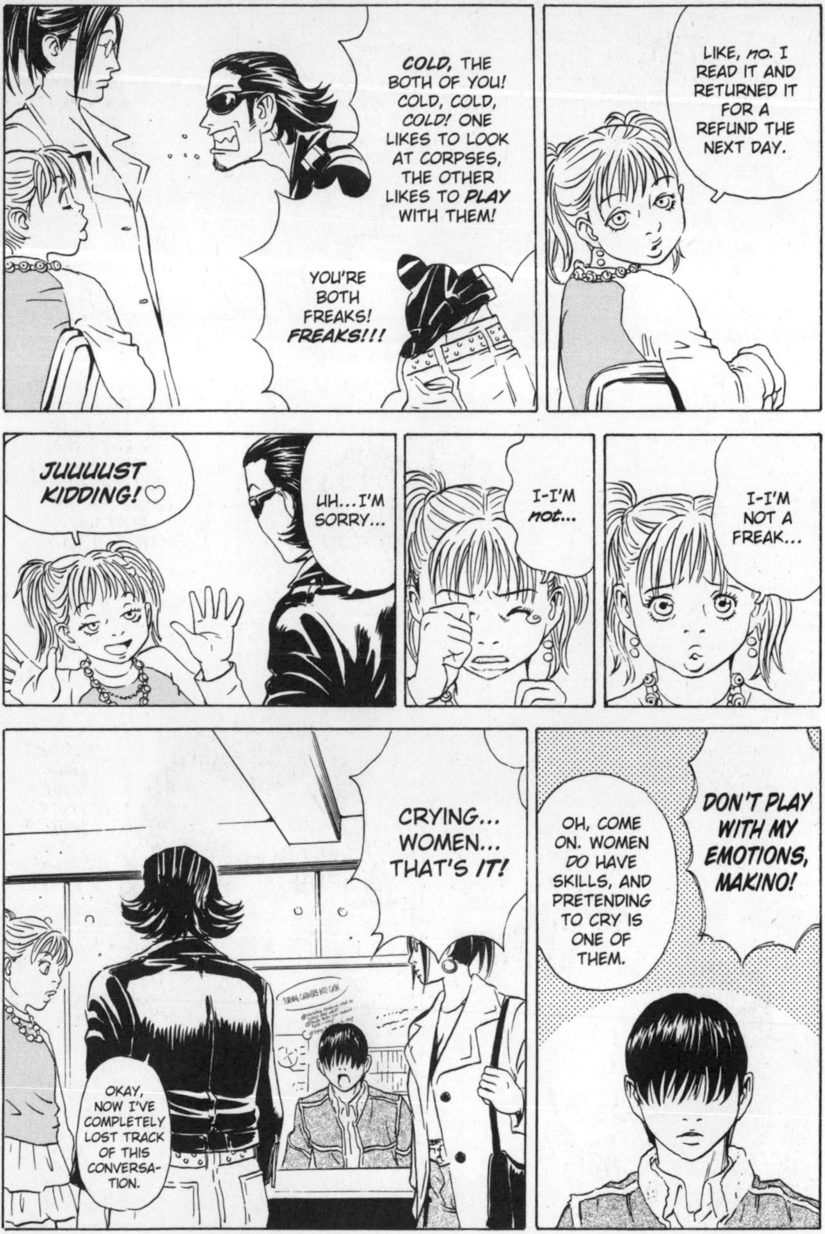
LIKE, *no*. I READ IT AND RETURNED IT FOR A REFUND THE NEXT DAY.
COLD, THE BOTH OF YOU! COLD, COLD, *COLD!* ONE LIKES TO LOOK AT CORPSES, THE OTHER LIKES TO *PLAY* WITH THEM!
. . .
YOU'RE BOTH FREAKS! ***FREAKS!!!***
I-I'M NOT A FREAK...
I-I'M *not*...
UH...I'M SORRY...
JUUUUST KIDDING! ♡
DON'T PLAY WITH MY EMOTIONS, MAKINO!
OH, COME ON. WOMEN *DO* HAVE SKILLS, AND PRETENDING TO CRY IS ONE OF THEM.
CRYING... WOMEN... THAT'S *IT!*
OKAY, NOW I'VE COMPLETELY LOST TRACK OF THIS CONVERSATION.

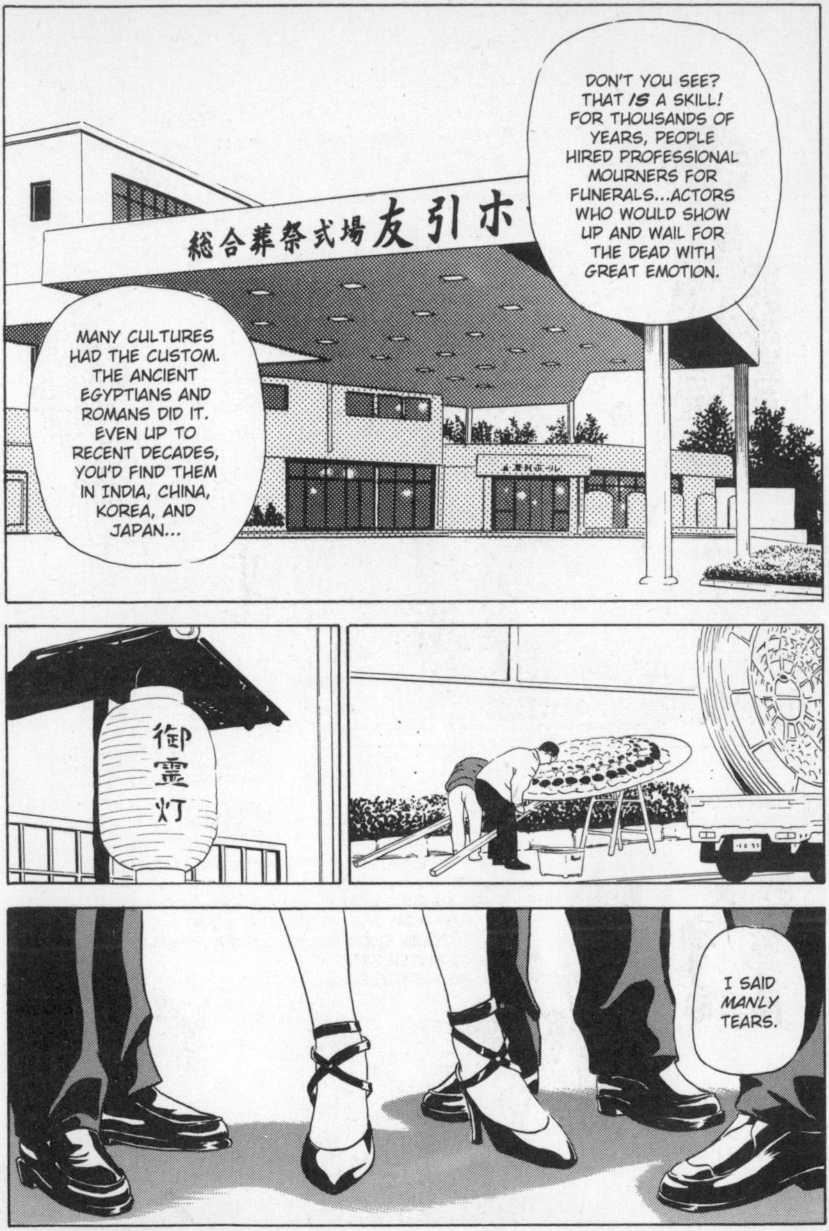
DON'T YOU SEE? THAT *IS* A SKILL! FOR THOUSANDS OF YEARS, PEOPLE HIRED PROFESSIONAL MOURNERS FOR FUNERALS...ACTORS WHO WOULD SHOW UP AND WAIL FOR THE DEAD WITH GREAT EMOTION.
総合葬祭式場友引ホ
MANY CULTURES HAD THE CUSTOM. THE ANCIENT EGYPTIANS AND ROMANS DID IT. EVEN UP TO RECENT DECADES, YOU'D FIND THEM IN INDIA, CHINA, KOREA, AND JAPAN...
御霊灯
I SAID *MANLY* TEARS.

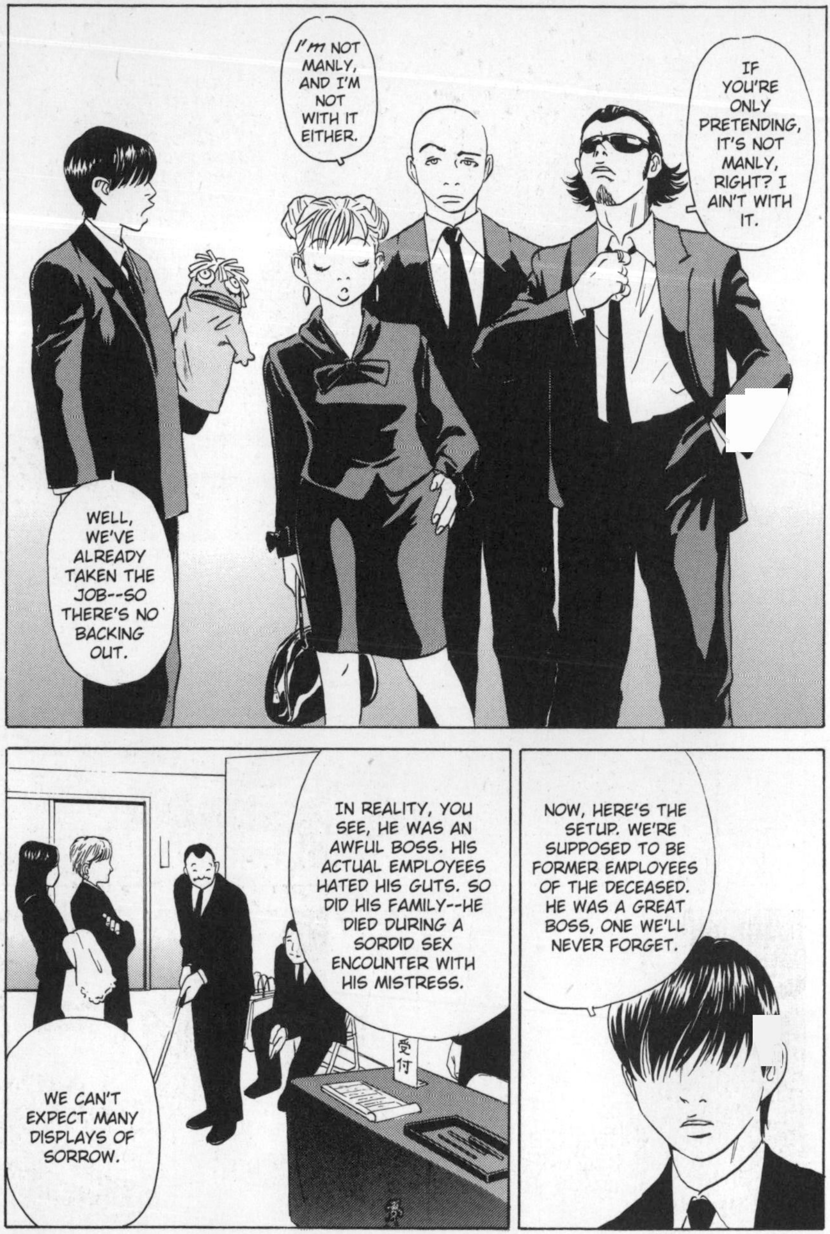
IF YOU'RE ONLY PRETENDING, IT'S NOT MANLY, RIGHT? I AIN'T WITH IT.
I'm NOT MANLY, AND I'M NOT WITH IT EITHER.
WELL, WE'VE ALREADY TAKEN THE JOB--SO THERE'S NO BACKING OUT.
NOW, HERE'S THE SETUP. WE'RE SUPPOSED TO BE FORMER EMPLOYEES OF THE DECEASED. HE WAS A GREAT BOSS, ONE WE'LL NEVER FORGET.
IN REALITY, YOU SEE, HE WAS AN AWFUL BOSS. HIS ACTUAL EMPLOYEES HATED HIS GUTS. SO DID HIS FAMILY--HE DIED DURING A SORDID SEX ENCOUNTER WITH HIS MISTRESS.
受付
WE CAN'T EXPECT MANY DISPLAYS OF SORROW.

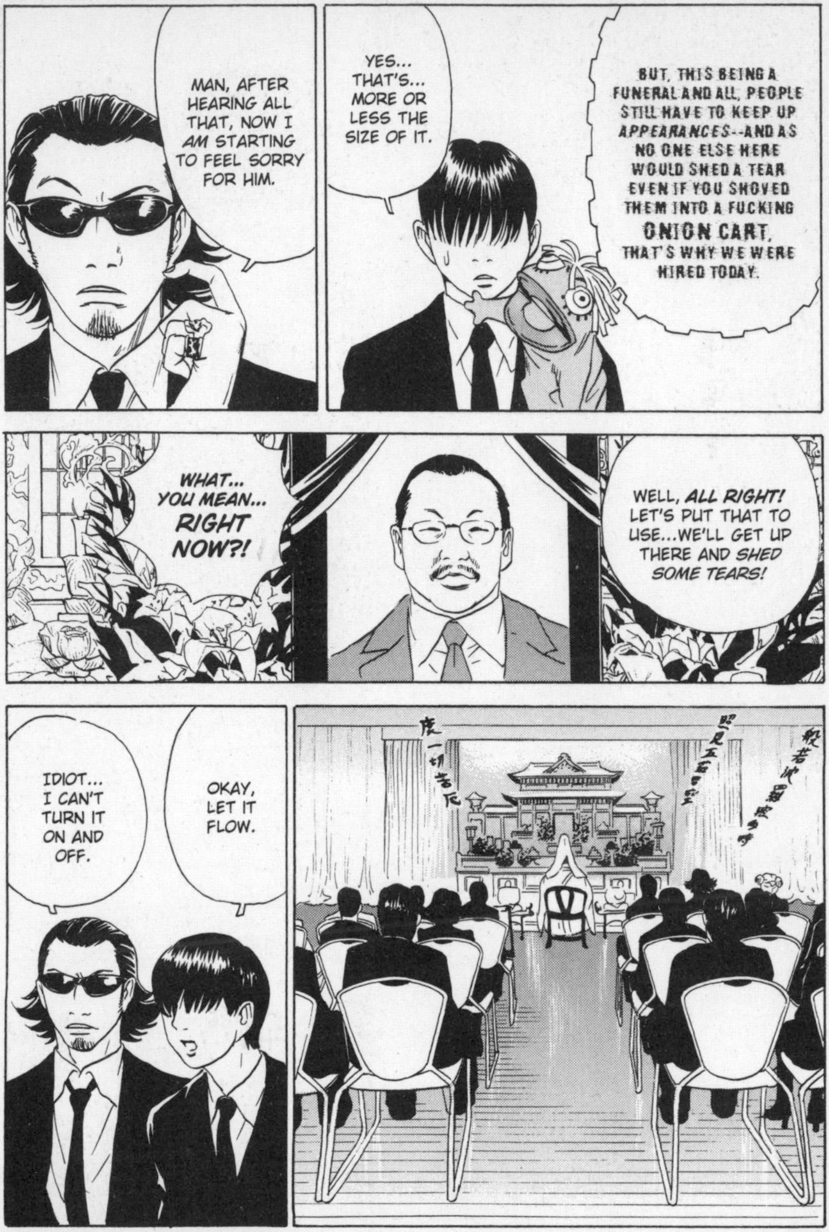
BUT, THIS BEING A FUNERAL AND ALL, PEOPLE STILL HAVE TO KEEP UP *APPEARANCES*--AND AS NO ONE ELSE HERE WOULD SHED A TEAR EVEN IF YOU SHOVED THEM INTO A FUCKING **ONION CART**, THAT'S WHY WE WERE HIRED TODAY.
YES... THAT'S... MORE OR LESS THE SIZE OF IT.
MAN, AFTER HEARING ALL THAT, NOW I *AM* STARTING TO FEEL SORRY FOR HIM.
WELL, ***ALL RIGHT!*** LET'S PUT THAT TO USE...WE'LL GET UP THERE AND *SHED* SOME TEARS!
WHAT... YOU MEAN... ***RIGHT NOW?!***
般若波羅蜜多時
照見五蘊皆空
度一切苦厄
OKAY, LET IT FLOW.
IDIOT... I CAN'T TURN IT ON AND OFF.

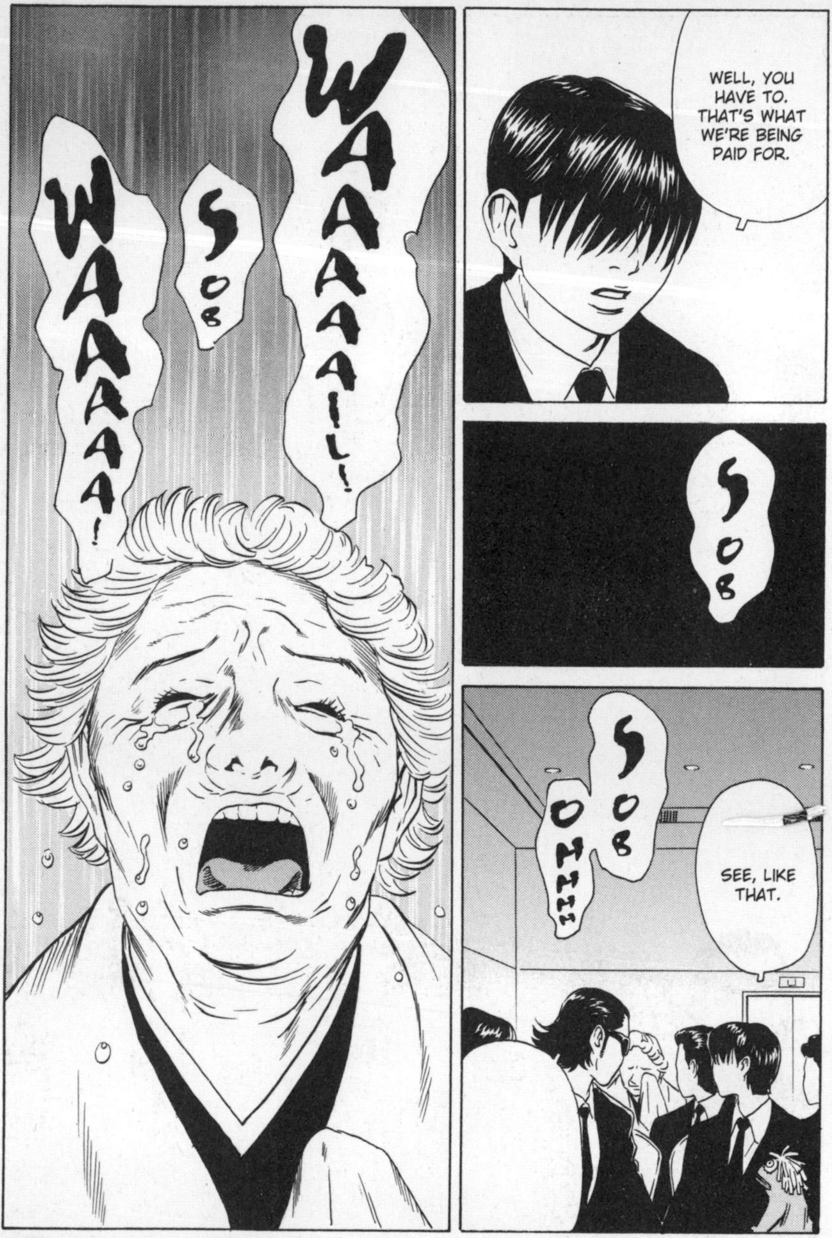
WELL, YOU HAVE TO. THAT'S WHAT WE'RE BEING PAID FOR.
SOB
SEE, LIKE THAT.
SOB
OHHHH
WAAAAAIL!
SOB
WAAAAA!

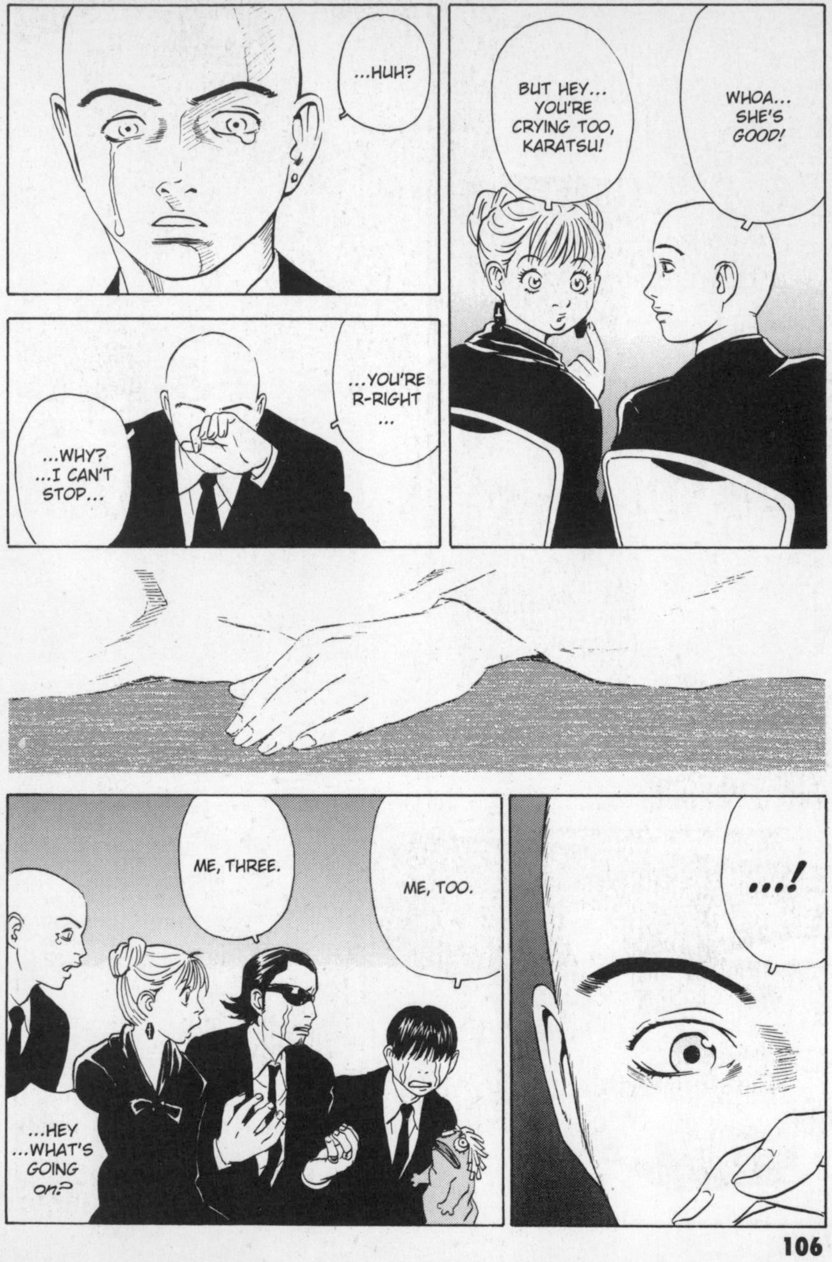
WHOA... SHE'S GOOD!
BUT HEY... YOU'RE CRYING TOO, KARATSU!
...HUH?
...YOU'RE R-RIGHT ...
...WHY? ...I CAN'T STOP...
...!
ME, TOO.
ME, THREE.
...HEY ...WHAT'S GOING on?

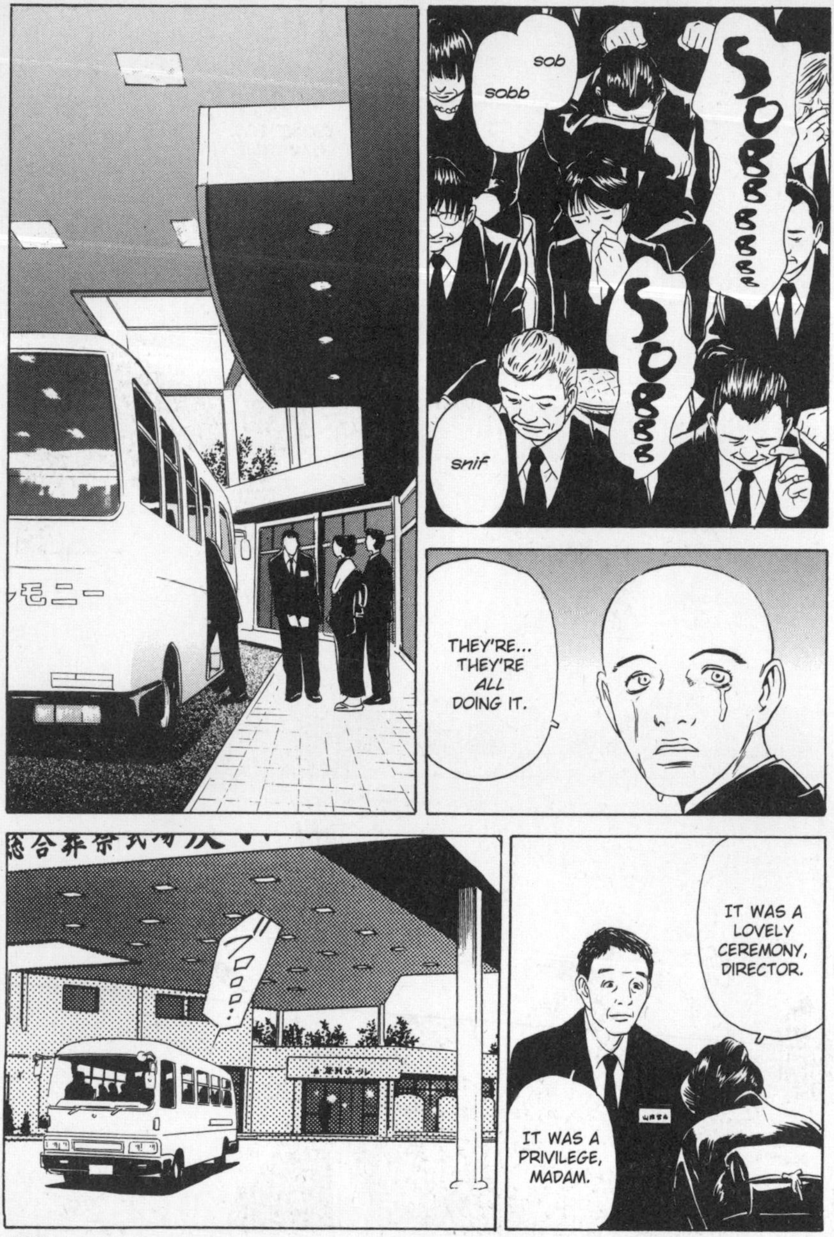
sob
sobb
SOBBBBBB
SOBBB
snif
THEY'RE... THEY'RE *ALL* DOING IT.
IT WAS A LOVELY CEREMONY, DIRECTOR.
IT WAS A PRIVILEGE, MADAM.
総合葬祭式場
ブロロロ…

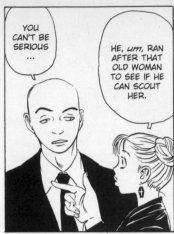

THAT'S REALLY WHAT GOT ME GOING, TOO... THE OLD WOMAN.
WELL, CONSIDER IT A BLESSING, AS THAT MEANS WE'LL GET PAID.
...COME TO THINK OF IT, WHERE DID YATA GO?
HE, *um*, RAN AFTER THAT OLD WOMAN TO SEE IF HE CAN SCOUT HER.
YOU CAN'T BE SERIOUS ...
HEY, *GUYS! GUYS!*
SHE WANTS TO HELP! MEET THE NEWEST MEMBER OF OUR CORPORATION!
...ISN'T THAT RIGHT, GRANDMA? SEE, IT TURNS OUT SHE REALLY *IS* A TRADITIONAL "CRYING WOMAN"... ONE OF THE LAST IN JAPAN!
REALLY?

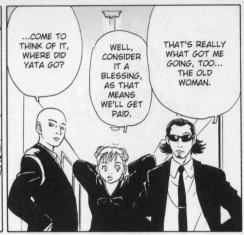

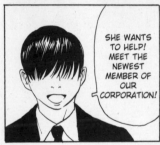

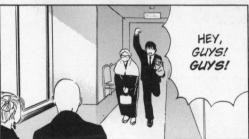

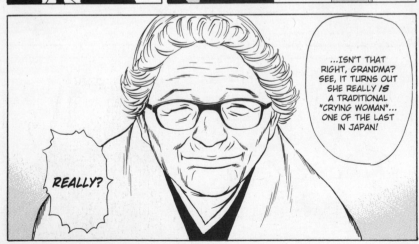

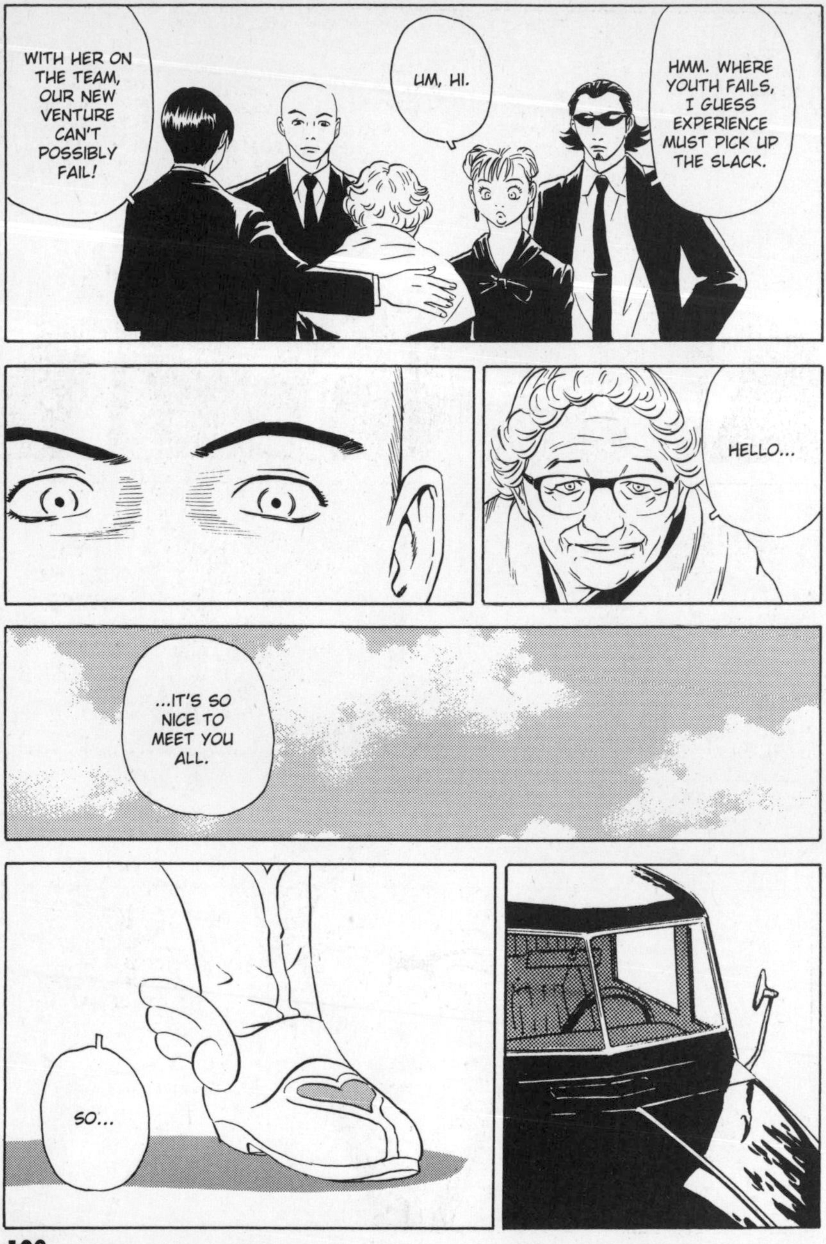
HMM. WHERE YOUTH FAILS, I GUESS EXPERIENCE MUST PICK UP THE SLACK.
UM, HI.
WITH HER ON THE TEAM, OUR NEW VENTURE CAN'T POSSIBLY FAIL!
HELLO...
...IT'S SO NICE TO MEET YOU ALL.
SO...

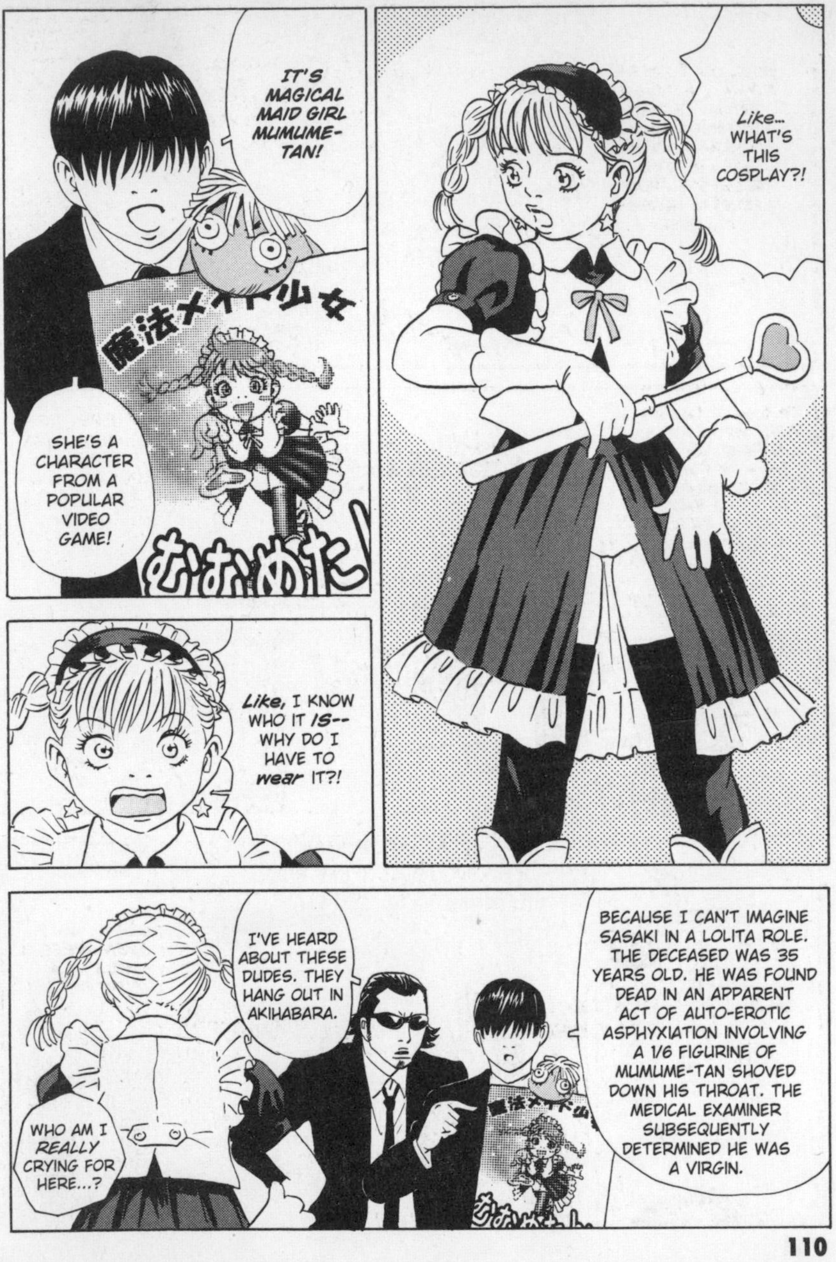
Like... WHAT'S THIS COSPLAY?!
IT'S MAGICAL MAID GIRL MUMUME-TAN!
魔法メイド少女
SHE'S A CHARACTER FROM A POPULAR VIDEO GAME!
Like, I KNOW WHO IT IS-- WHY DO I HAVE TO wear IT?!
BECAUSE I CAN'T IMAGINE SASAKI IN A LOLITA ROLE. THE DECEASED WAS 35 YEARS OLD. HE WAS FOUND DEAD IN AN APPARENT ACT OF AUTO-EROTIC ASPHYXIATION INVOLVING A 1/6 FIGURINE OF MUMUME-TAN SHOVED DOWN HIS THROAT. THE MEDICAL EXAMINER SUBSEQUENTLY DETERMINED HE WAS A VIRGIN.
I'VE HEARD ABOUT THESE DUDES. THEY HANG OUT IN AKIHABARA.
WHO AM I REALLY CRYING FOR HERE...?

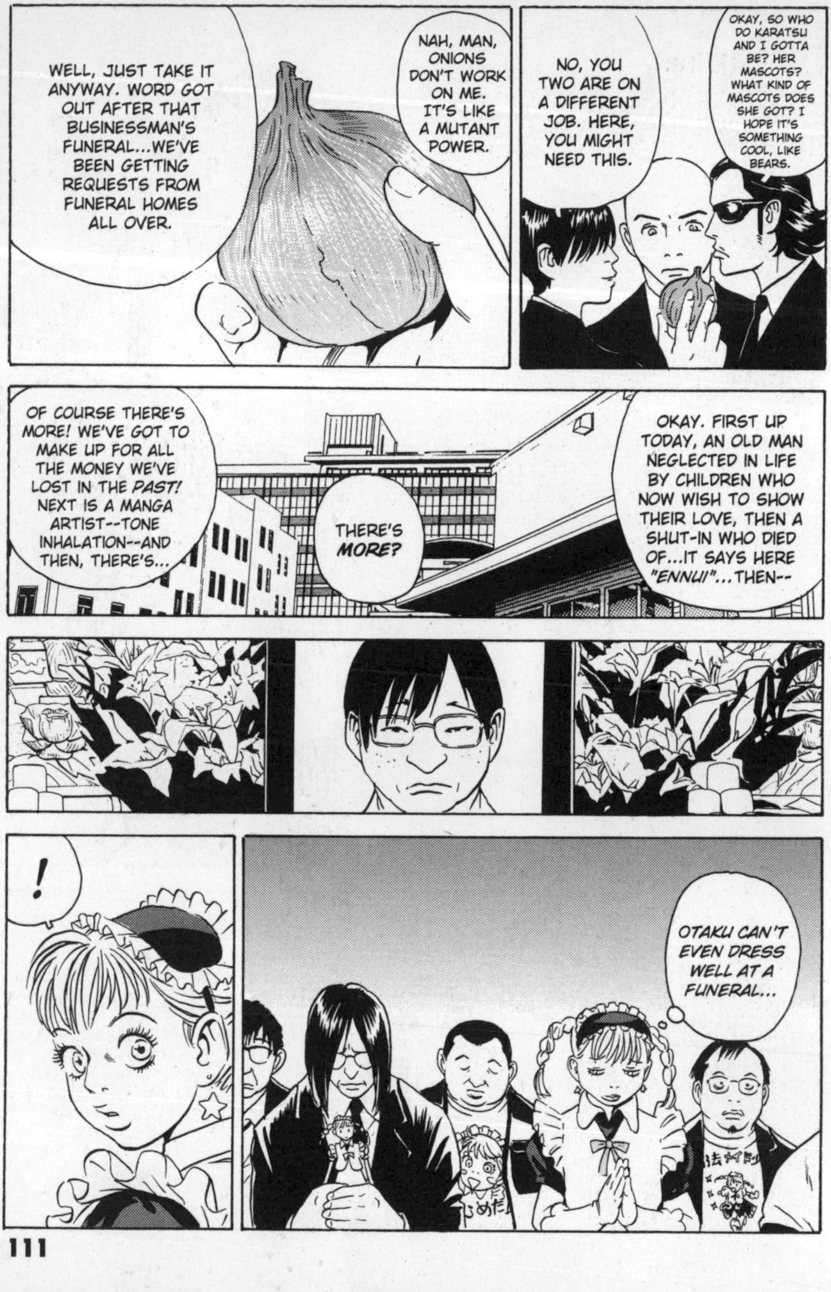
OKAY, SO WHO DO KARATSU AND I GOTTA BE? HER MASCOTS? WHAT KIND OF MASCOTS DOES SHE GOT? I HOPE IT'S SOMETHING COOL, LIKE BEARS.
NO, YOU TWO ARE ON A DIFFERENT JOB. HERE, YOU MIGHT NEED THIS.
NAH, MAN, ONIONS DON'T WORK ON ME. IT'S LIKE A MUTANT POWER.
WELL, JUST TAKE IT ANYWAY. WORD GOT OUT AFTER THAT BUSINESSMAN'S FUNERAL...WE'VE BEEN GETTING REQUESTS FROM FUNERAL HOMES ALL OVER.
OKAY. FIRST UP TODAY, AN OLD MAN NEGLECTED IN LIFE BY CHILDREN WHO NOW WISH TO SHOW THEIR LOVE, THEN A SHUT-IN WHO DIED OF...IT SAYS HERE "ENNUI"...THEN--
THERE'S MORE?
OF COURSE THERE'S MORE! WE'VE GOT TO MAKE UP FOR ALL THE MONEY WE'VE LOST IN THE PAST! NEXT IS A MANGA ARTIST--TONE INHALATION--AND THEN, THERE'S...
OTAKU CAN'T EVEN DRESS WELL AT A FUNERAL...
!

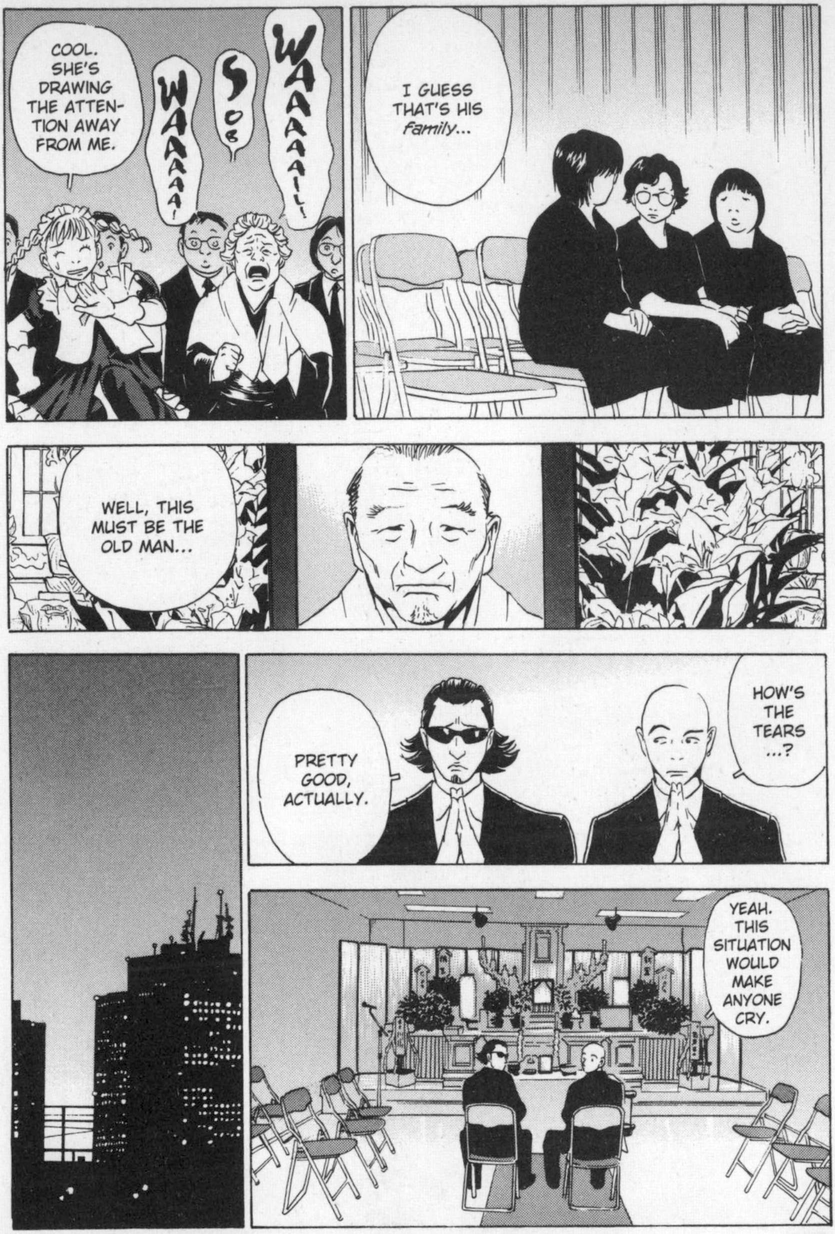
I GUESS THAT'S HIS *family*...
WAAAAAAIL!
SOB
WAAAAA!
COOL. SHE'S DRAWING THE ATTENTION AWAY FROM ME.
WELL, THIS MUST BE THE OLD MAN...
HOW'S THE TEARS ...?
PRETTY GOOD, ACTUALLY.
YEAH. THIS SITUATION WOULD MAKE ANYONE CRY.

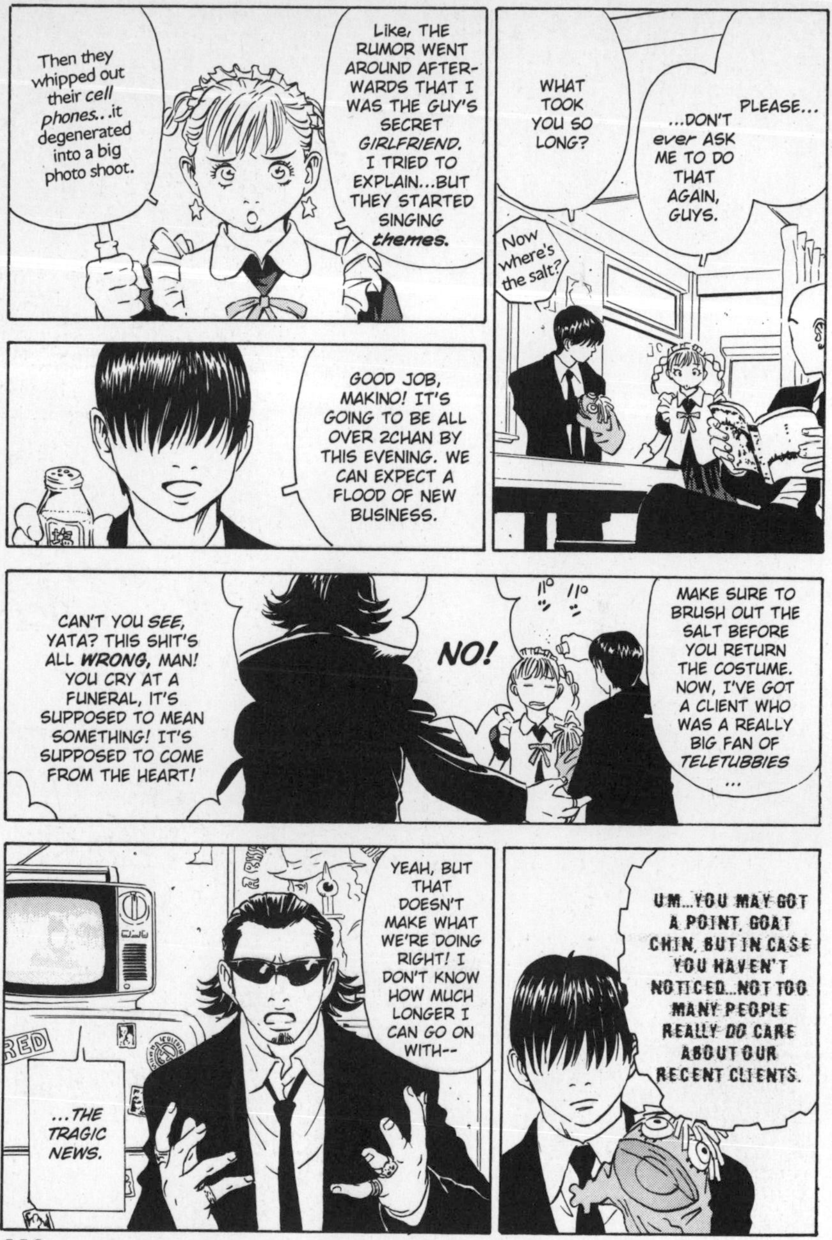
PLEASE...
...DON'T ever ASK ME TO DO THAT AGAIN, GUYS.
WHAT TOOK YOU SO LONG?
Now where's the salt?
Like, THE RUMOR WENT AROUND AFTER-WARDS THAT I WAS THE GUY'S SECRET GIRLFRIEND. I TRIED TO EXPLAIN...BUT THEY STARTED SINGING themes.
Then they whipped out their cell phones...it degenerated into a big photo shoot.
GOOD JOB, MAKINO! IT'S GOING TO BE ALL OVER 2CHAN BY THIS EVENING. WE CAN EXPECT A FLOOD OF NEW BUSINESS.
MAKE SURE TO BRUSH OUT THE SALT BEFORE YOU RETURN THE COSTUME. NOW, I'VE GOT A CLIENT WHO WAS A REALLY BIG FAN OF TELETUBBIES ...
NO!
CAN'T YOU SEE, YATA? THIS SHIT'S ALL WRONG, MAN! YOU CRY AT A FUNERAL, IT'S SUPPOSED TO MEAN SOMETHING! IT'S SUPPOSED TO COME FROM THE HEART!
UM...YOU MAY GOT A POINT, GOAT CHIN, BUT IN CASE YOU HAVEN'T NOTICED...NOT TOO MANY PEOPLE REALLY DO CARE ABOUT OUR RECENT CLIENTS.
YEAH, BUT THAT DOESN'T MAKE WHAT WE'RE DOING RIGHT! I DON'T KNOW HOW MUCH LONGER I CAN GO ON WITH--
...THE TRAGIC NEWS.

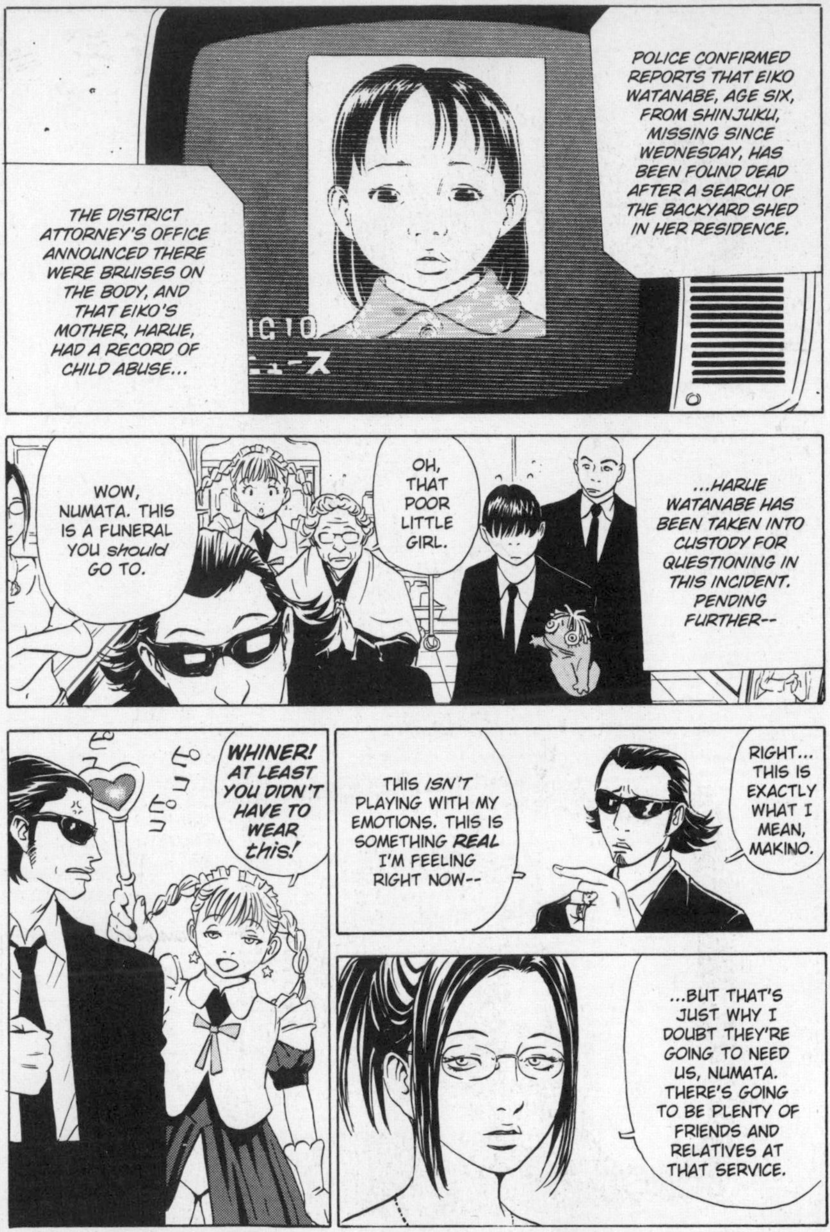
POLICE CONFIRMED REPORTS THAT EIKO WATANABE, AGE SIX, FROM SHINJUKU, MISSING SINCE WEDNESDAY, HAS BEEN FOUND DEAD AFTER A SEARCH OF THE BACKYARD SHED IN HER RESIDENCE.
THE DISTRICT ATTORNEY'S OFFICE ANNOUNCED THERE WERE BRUISES ON THE BODY, AND THAT EIKO'S MOTHER, HARUE, HAD A RECORD OF CHILD ABUSE...
...HARUE WATANABE HAS BEEN TAKEN INTO CUSTODY FOR QUESTIONING IN THIS INCIDENT. PENDING FURTHER--
OH, THAT POOR LITTLE GIRL.
WOW, NUMATA. THIS IS A FUNERAL YOU *should* GO TO.
RIGHT... THIS IS EXACTLY WHAT I MEAN, MAKINO.
THIS *ISN'T* PLAYING WITH MY EMOTIONS. THIS IS SOMETHING ***REAL*** I'M FEELING RIGHT NOW--
...BUT THAT'S JUST WHY I DOUBT THEY'RE GOING TO NEED US, NUMATA. THERE'S GOING TO BE PLENTY OF FRIENDS AND RELATIVES AT THAT SERVICE.
ピコピコ
WHINER! AT LEAST YOU DIDN'T HAVE TO WEAR this!

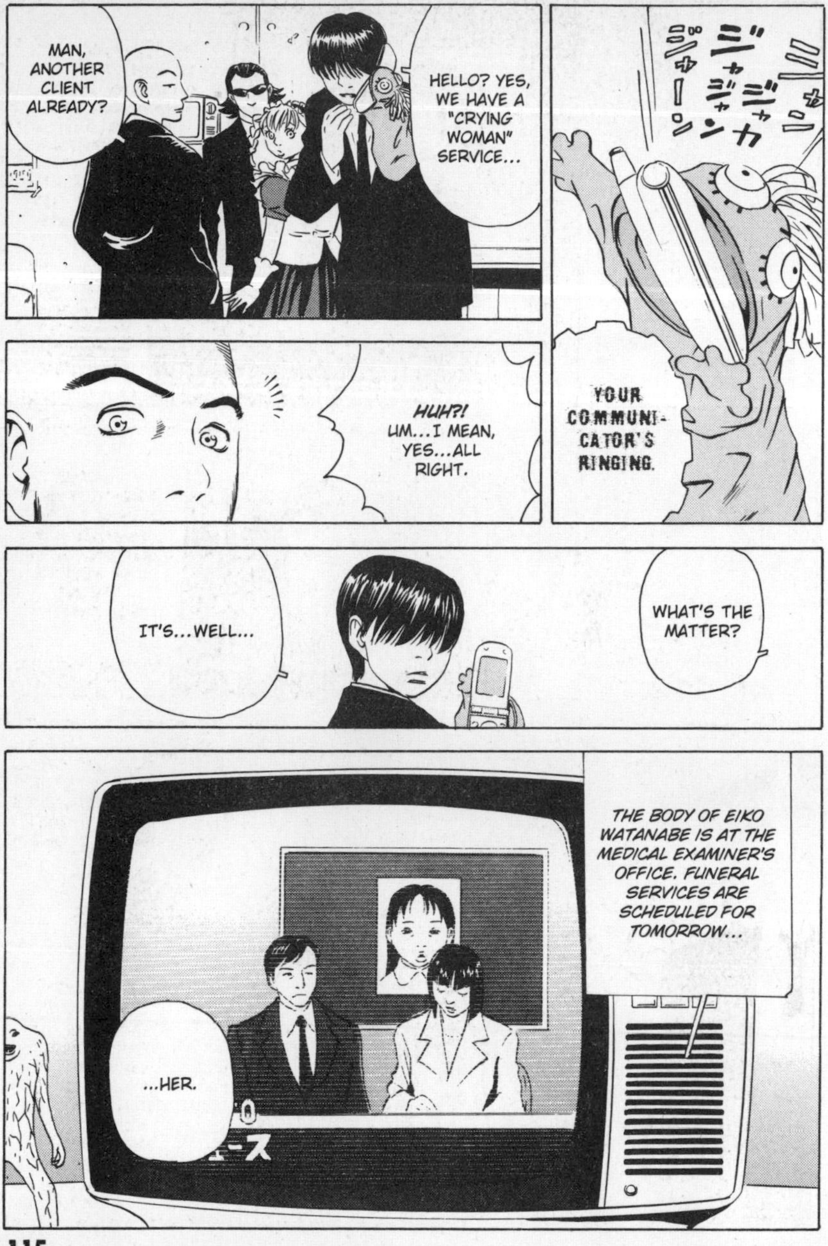
YOUR COMMUNICATOR'S RINGING.
HELLO? YES, WE HAVE A "CRYING WOMAN" SERVICE...
MAN, ANOTHER CLIENT ALREADY?
HUH?! UM...I MEAN, YES...ALL RIGHT.
WHAT'S THE MATTER?
IT'S...WELL...
THE BODY OF EIKO WATANABE IS AT THE MEDICAL EXAMINER'S OFFICE. FUNERAL SERVICES ARE SCHEDULED FOR TOMORROW...
...HER.

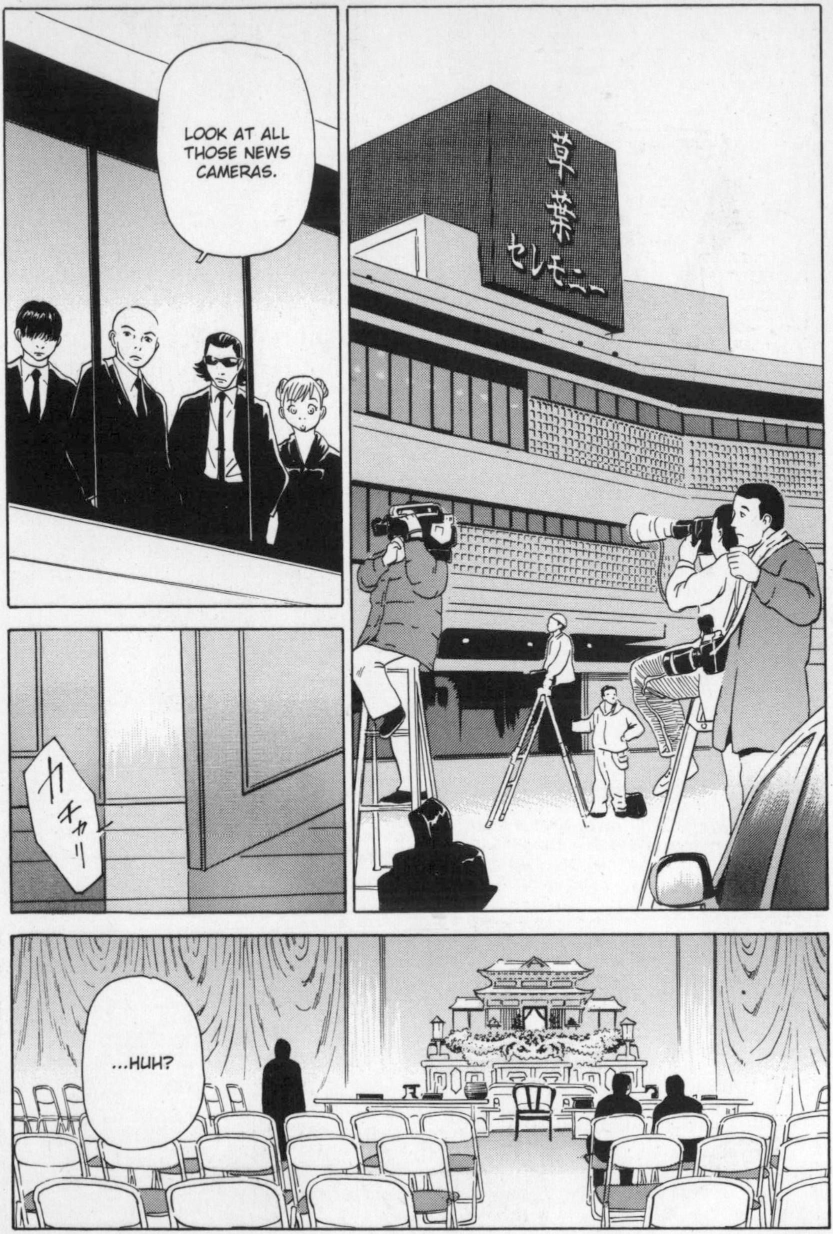
草葉
セレモニー
LOOK AT ALL THOSE NEWS CAMERAS.
カチャリ
...HUH?

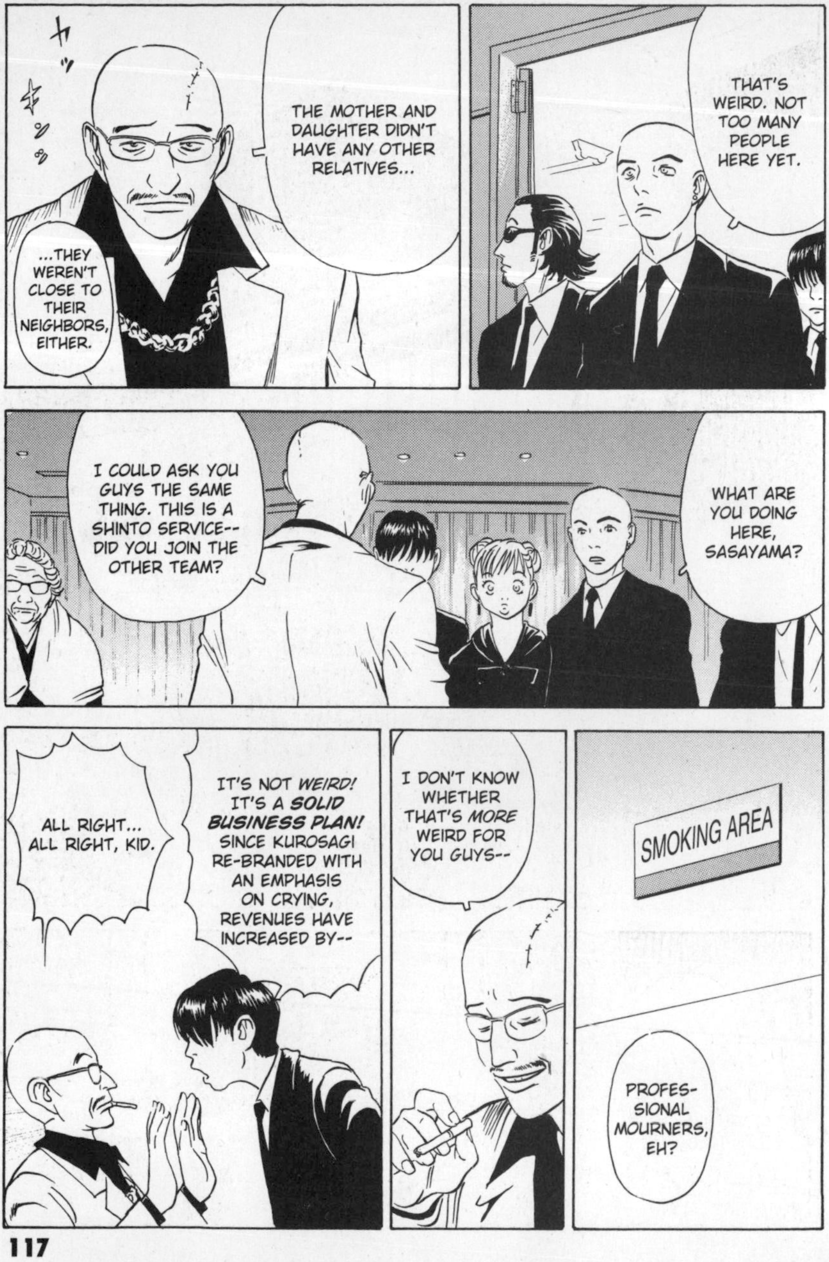
THAT'S WEIRD. NOT TOO MANY PEOPLE HERE YET.
THE MOTHER AND DAUGHTER DIDN'T HAVE ANY OTHER RELATIVES...
...THEY WEREN'T CLOSE TO THEIR NEIGHBORS, EITHER.
WHAT ARE YOU DOING HERE, SASAYAMA?
I COULD ASK YOU GUYS THE SAME THING. THIS IS A SHINTO SERVICE-- DID YOU JOIN THE OTHER TEAM?
SMOKING AREA
PROFES- SIONAL MOURNERS, EH?
I DON'T KNOW WHETHER THAT'S *MORE* WEIRD FOR YOU GUYS--
IT'S NOT *WEIRD!* IT'S A ***SOLID BUSINESS PLAN!*** SINCE KUROSAGI RE-BRANDED WITH AN EMPHASIS ON CRYING, REVENUES HAVE INCREASED BY--
ALL RIGHT... ALL RIGHT, KID.

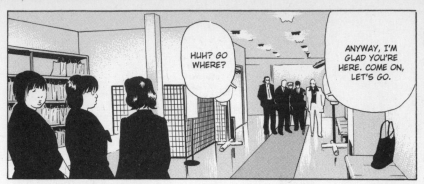

ANYWAY, I'M GLAD YOU'RE HERE. COME ON, LET'S GO.
HUH? GO WHERE?
OH, THAT POOR GIRL... sob.
HEY, WE'VE GOT A JOB HERE...
IT'S RELATED. QUIET.
...?
THIS IS EIKO WATANABE... VICTIM OF MATERNAL CHILD ABUSE...AND EVENTUALLY, MURDER.
THAT IS...IF SHE WAS THE ONE WHO DID IT.

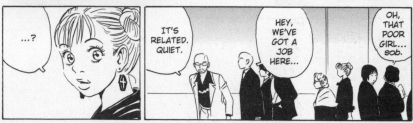

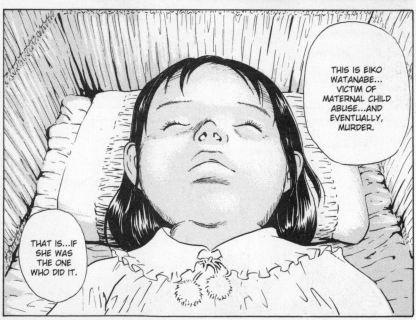

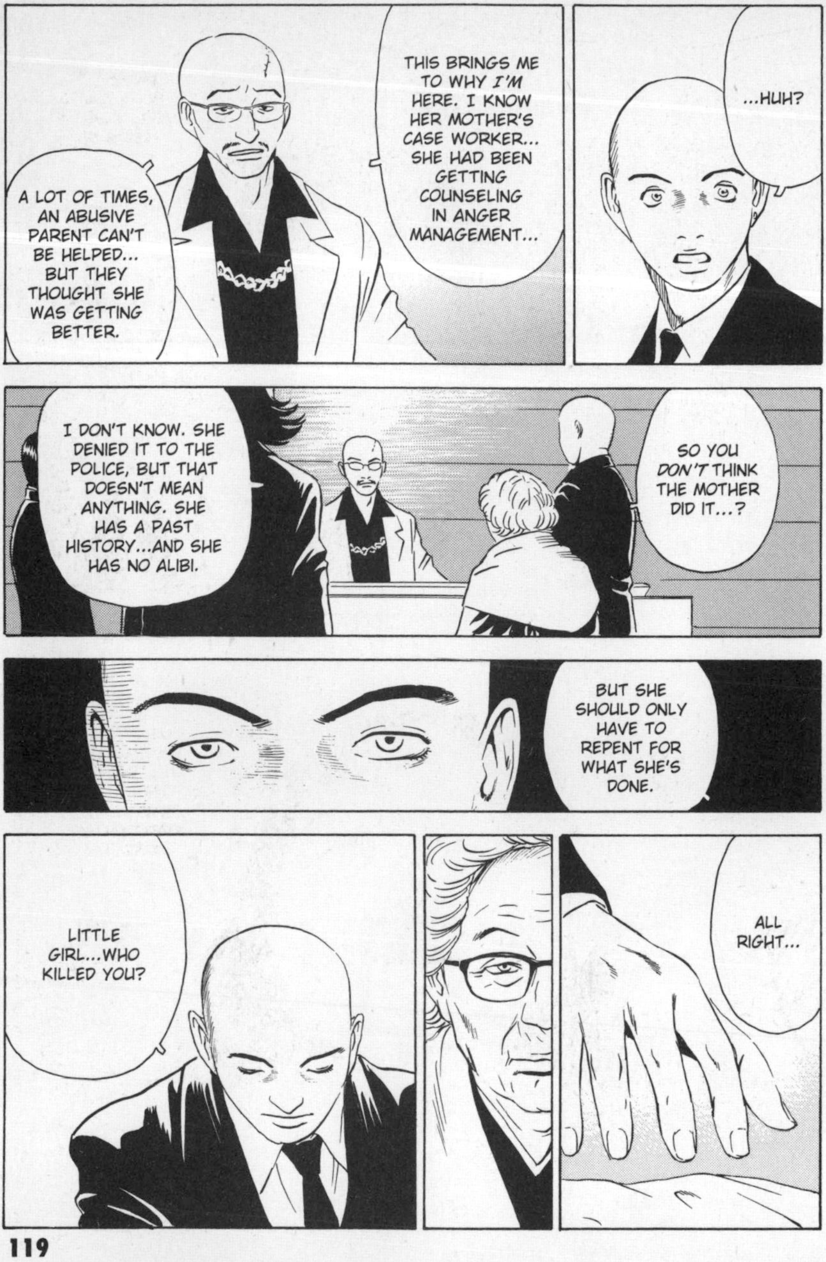
...HUH?
THIS BRINGS ME TO WHY *I'M* HERE. I KNOW HER MOTHER'S CASE WORKER... SHE HAD BEEN GETTING COUNSELING IN ANGER MANAGEMENT...
A LOT OF TIMES, AN ABUSIVE PARENT CAN'T BE HELPED... BUT THEY THOUGHT SHE WAS GETTING BETTER.
SO YOU *DON'T* THINK THE MOTHER DID IT...?
I DON'T KNOW. SHE DENIED IT TO THE POLICE, BUT THAT DOESN'T MEAN ANYTHING. SHE HAS A PAST HISTORY...AND SHE HAS NO ALIBI.
BUT SHE SHOULD ONLY HAVE TO REPENT FOR WHAT SHE'S DONE.
ALL RIGHT...
LITTLE GIRL...WHO KILLED YOU?

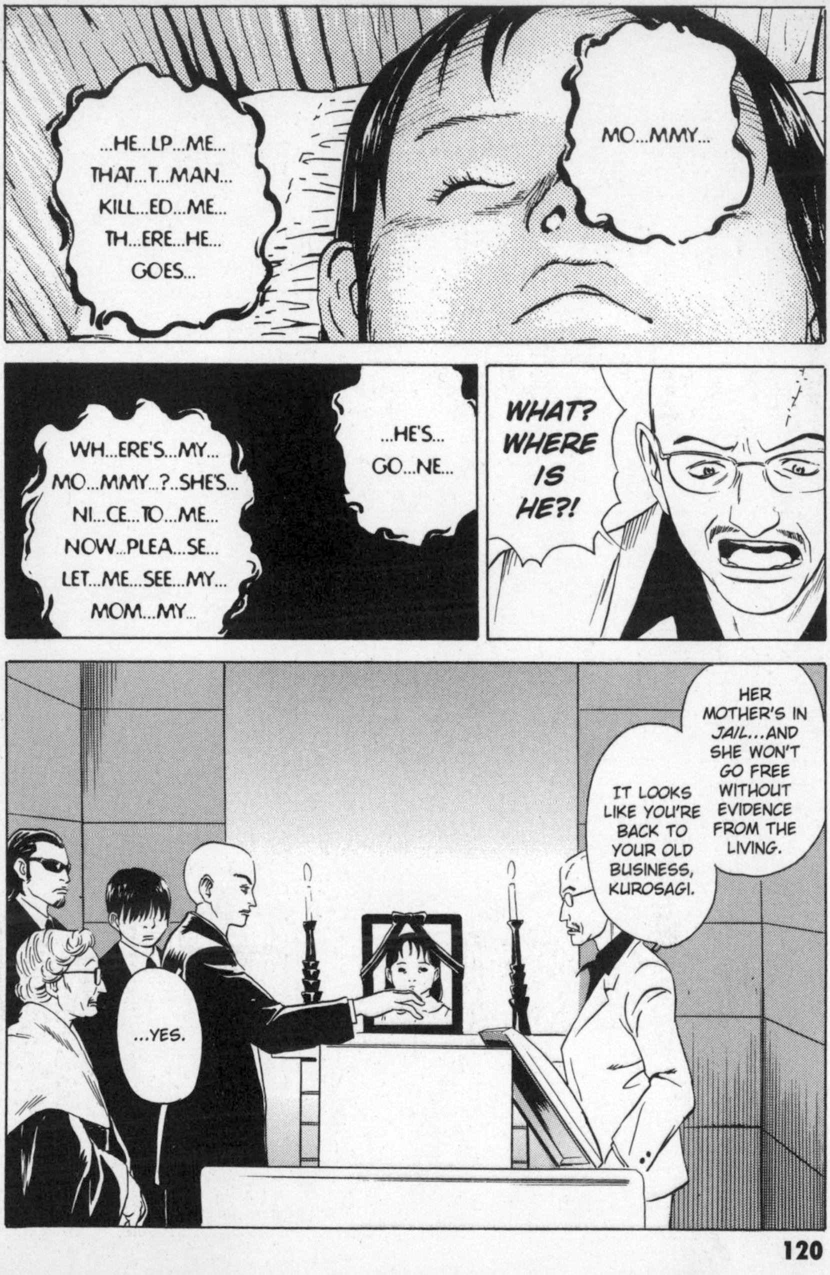
MO...MMY...
...HE...LP...ME... THAT...T...MAN... KILL...ED...ME... TH...ERE...HE... GOES...
WHAT? WHERE IS HE?!
...HE'S... GO...NE...
WH...ERE'S...MY... MO...MMY...?..SHE'S... NI...CE...TO...ME... NOW...PLEA...SE... LET...ME...SEE...MY... MOM...MY...
HER MOTHER'S IN *JAIL*...AND SHE WON'T GO FREE WITHOUT EVIDENCE FROM THE LIVING.
IT LOOKS LIKE YOU'RE BACK TO YOUR OLD BUSINESS, KUROSAGI.
...YES.

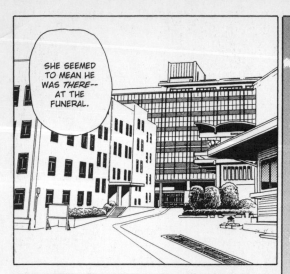

SHE SEEMED TO MEAN HE WAS *THERE*-- AT THE FUNERAL.
WE BORROWED THE GUEST BOOK, BUT I DON'T THINK THE MURDERER WOULD BE STUPID ENOUGH TO SIGN IT...
ANY NAMES IN THERE LOOK SUSPICIOUS?
WHAT, LIKE "I.M. DE KILLER"? HOW ARE WE SUPPOSED TO TELL FROM JUST A NAME?

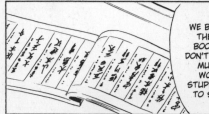

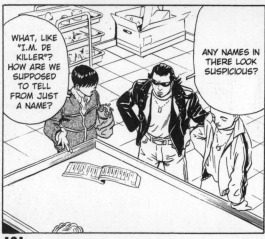

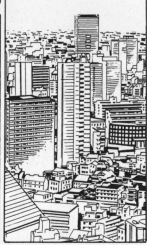

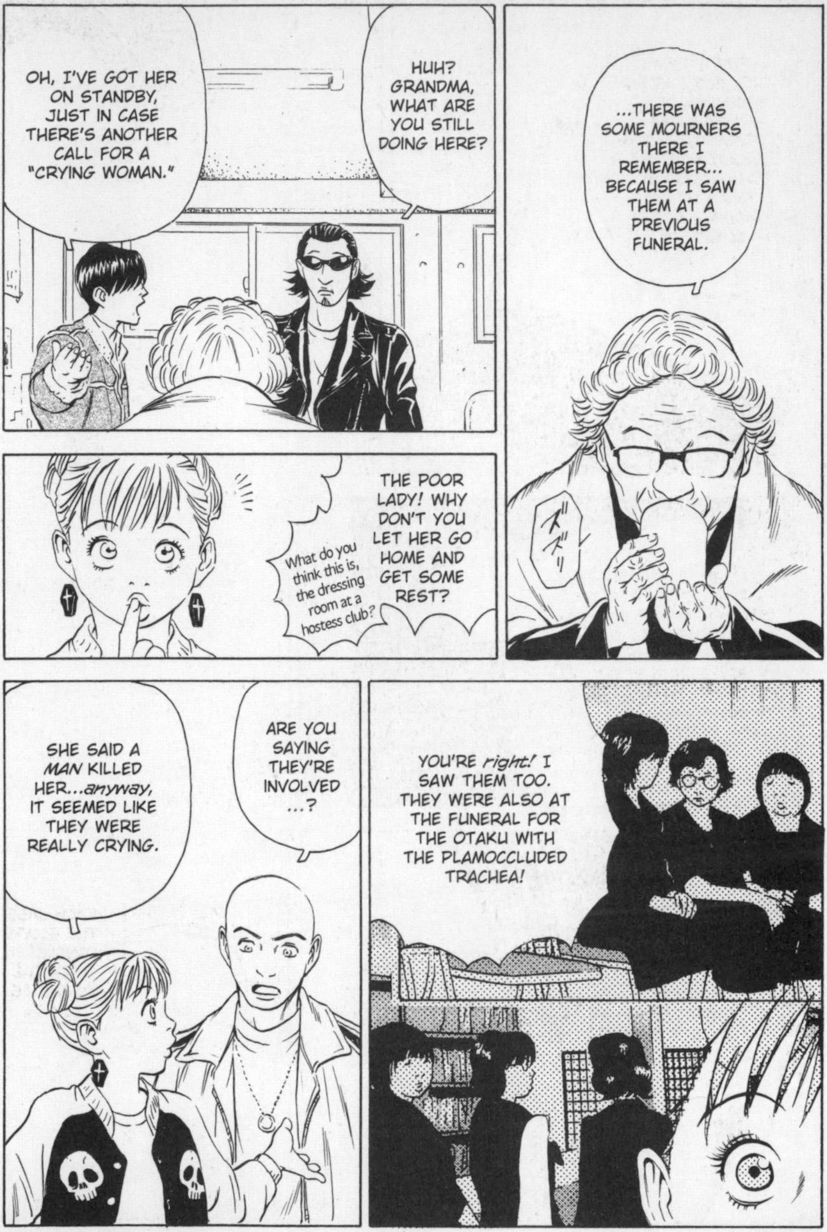
HUH? GRANDMA, WHAT ARE YOU STILL DOING HERE?
OH, I'VE GOT HER ON STANDBY, JUST IN CASE THERE'S ANOTHER CALL FOR A "CRYING WOMAN."
THE POOR LADY! WHY DON'T YOU LET HER GO HOME AND GET SOME REST?
What do you think this is, the dressing room at a hostess club?
...THERE WAS SOME MOURNERS THERE I REMEMBER... BECAUSE I SAW THEM AT A PREVIOUS FUNERAL.
YOU'RE *right!* I SAW THEM TOO. THEY WERE ALSO AT THE FUNERAL FOR THE OTAKU WITH THE PLAMOCCLUDED TRACHEA!
ARE YOU SAYING THEY'RE INVOLVED ...?
SHE SAID A *MAN* KILLED HER...*anyway*, IT SEEMED LIKE THEY WERE REALLY CRYING.

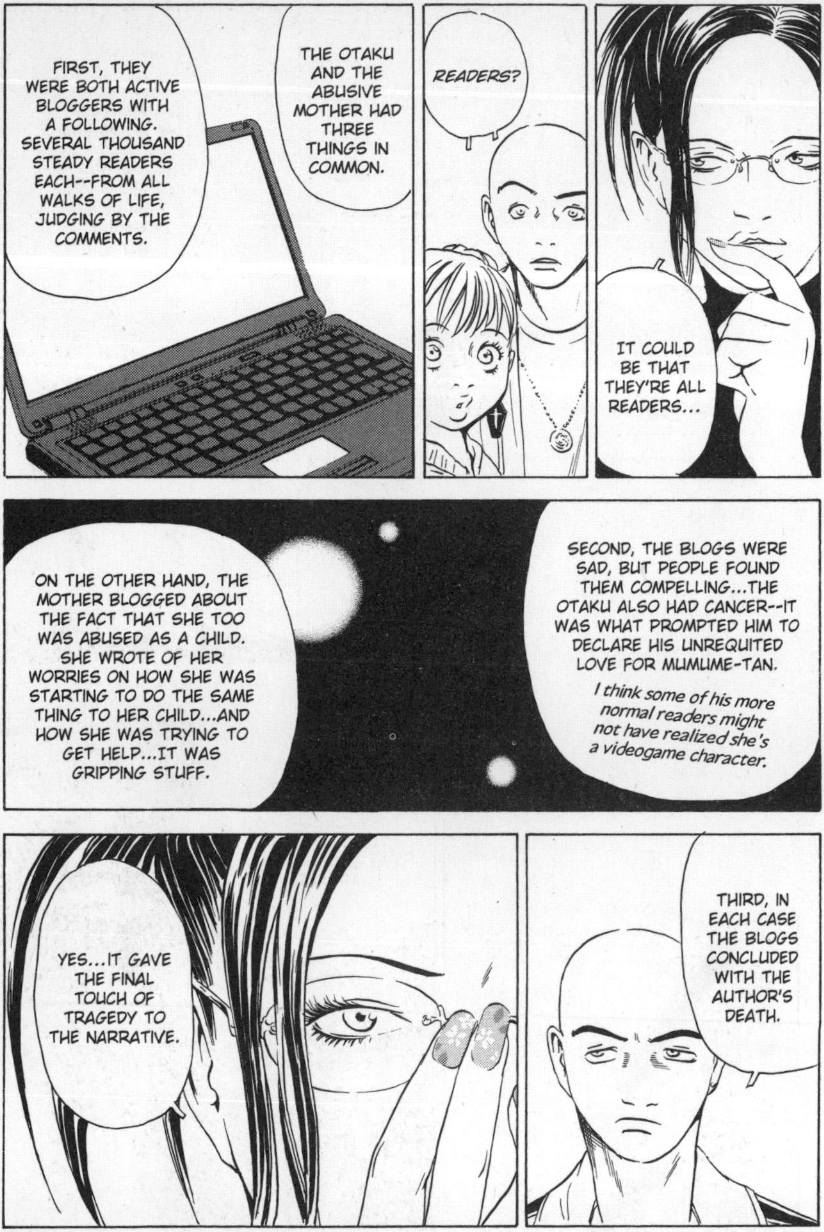
IT COULD BE THAT THEY'RE ALL READERS...
READERS?
THE OTAKU AND THE ABUSIVE MOTHER HAD THREE THINGS IN COMMON.
FIRST, THEY WERE BOTH ACTIVE BLOGGERS WITH A FOLLOWING. SEVERAL THOUSAND STEADY READERS EACH--FROM ALL WALKS OF LIFE, JUDGING BY THE COMMENTS.
SECOND, THE BLOGS WERE SAD, BUT PEOPLE FOUND THEM COMPELLING...THE OTAKU ALSO HAD CANCER--IT WAS WHAT PROMPTED HIM TO DECLARE HIS UNREQUITED LOVE FOR MUMUME-TAN.
I think some of his more normal readers might not have realized she's a videogame character.
ON THE OTHER HAND, THE MOTHER BLOGGED ABOUT THE FACT THAT SHE TOO WAS ABUSED AS A CHILD. SHE WROTE OF HER WORRIES ON HOW SHE WAS STARTING TO DO THE SAME THING TO HER CHILD...AND HOW SHE WAS TRYING TO GET HELP...IT WAS GRIPPING STUFF.
THIRD, IN EACH CASE THE BLOGS CONCLUDED WITH THE AUTHOR'S DEATH.
YES...IT GAVE THE FINAL TOUCH OF TRAGEDY TO THE NARRATIVE.

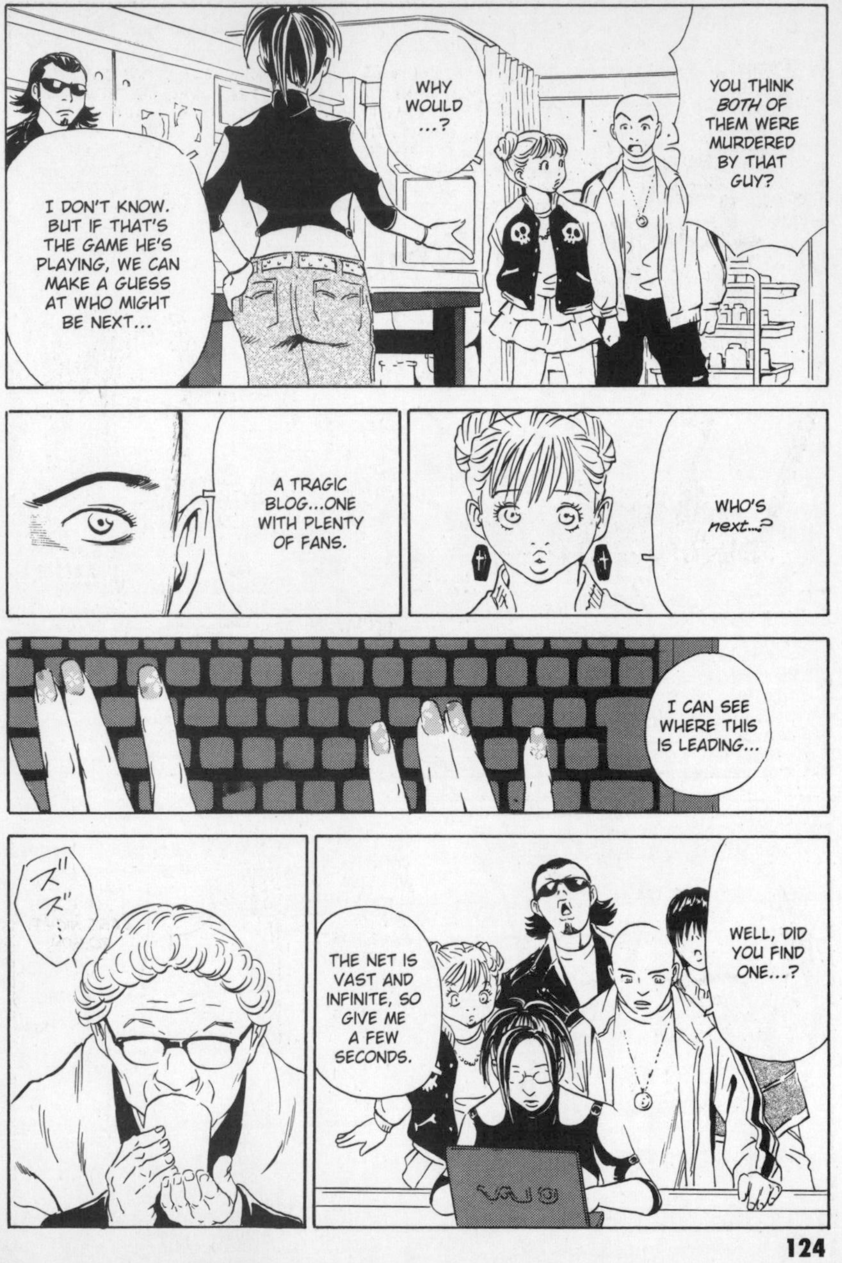
YOU THINK *BOTH* OF THEM WERE MURDERED BY THAT GUY?
WHY WOULD ...?
I DON'T KNOW. BUT IF THAT'S THE GAME HE'S PLAYING, WE CAN MAKE A GUESS AT WHO MIGHT BE NEXT...
WHO'S *next...?*
A TRAGIC BLOG...ONE WITH PLENTY OF FANS.
I CAN SEE WHERE THIS IS LEADING...
WELL, DID YOU FIND ONE...?
THE NET IS VAST AND INFINITE, SO GIVE ME A FEW SECONDS.
ズズ…

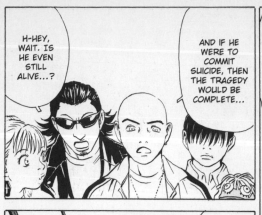

HOW ABOUT THIS ONE? ANOTHER CASE OF TERMINAL DISEASE--BUT *THIS* TIME, IT'S A COUPLE. THEY MET IN A HOSPITAL WARD WHILE UNDERGOING TREATMENT. BUT THE WOMAN WENT FIRST...AND NOW HE'S DYING ALL ALONE. THE NUMBER OF HITS IS ASTRONOMICAL.
AND IF HE WERE TO COMMIT SUICIDE, THEN THE TRAGEDY WOULD BE COMPLETE...
H-HEY, WAIT. IS HE EVEN STILL ALIVE...?
I'M CHECKING NOW...
...NO.
HE KILLED HIMSELF LAST NIGHT. POISON.
I WAS JUST KIDDING!
IF YOU'RE RIGHT--AND WE WANT TO CATCH HIM, WE'VE GOT TO MOVE FAST. IF HE DIED YESTERDAY, THEN TODAY IS THE WAKE...
...THE FUNERAL WOULD BE TOMORROW.

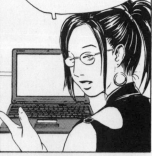

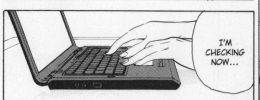

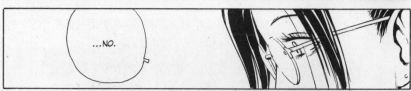

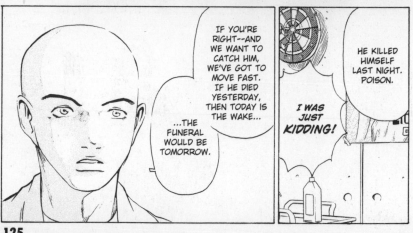

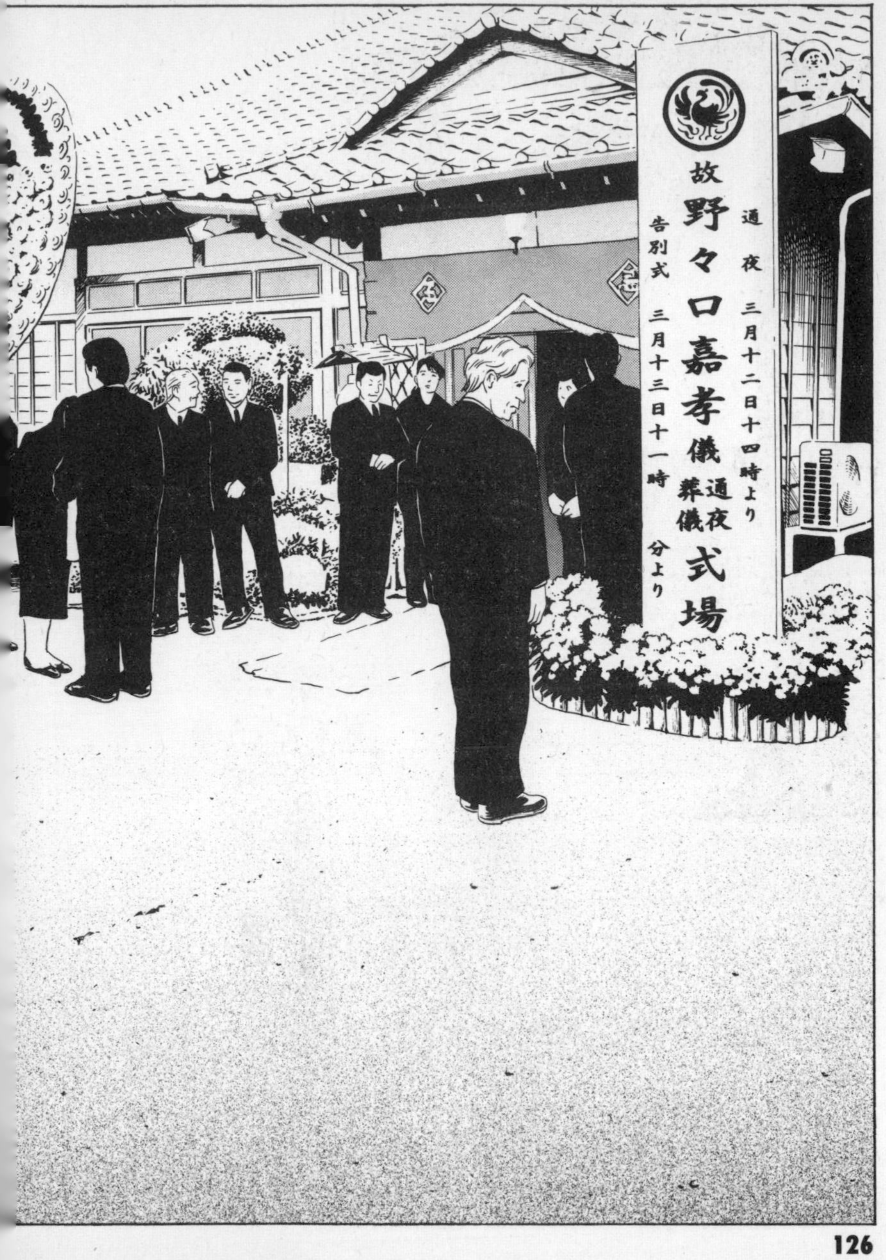
通夜　三月十二日十四時より
故野々口嘉孝儀
通夜
葬儀
式場
告別式　三月十三日十一時　分より

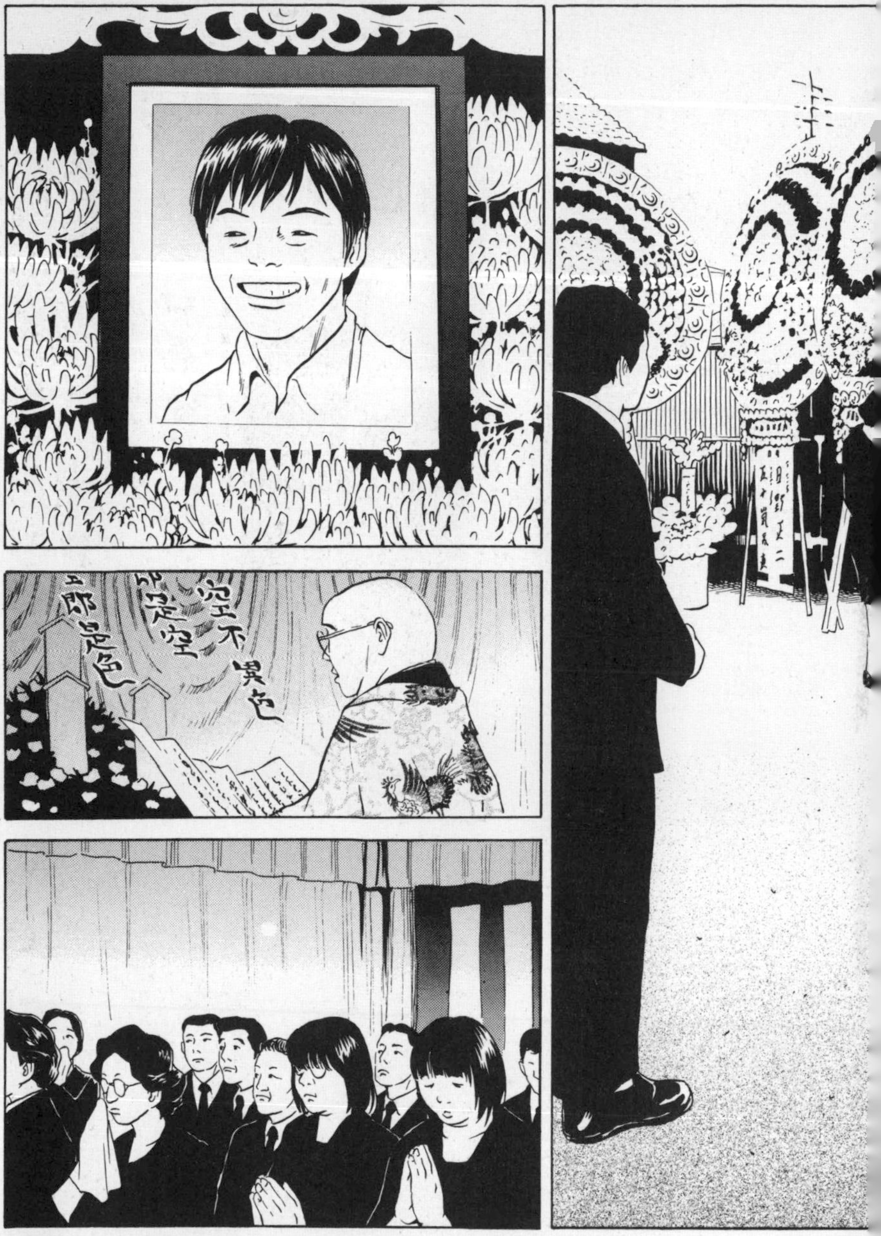

空不異色
即是空
即是色

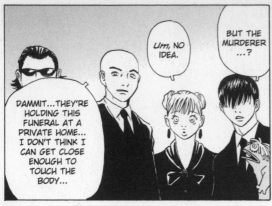

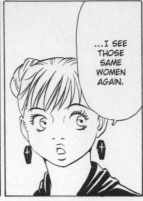

...I SEE THOSE SAME WOMEN AGAIN.
BUT THE MURDERER ...?
Um, NO IDEA.
DAMMIT...THEY'RE HOLDING THIS FUNERAL AT A PRIVATE HOME... I DON'T THINK I CAN GET CLOSE ENOUGH TO TOUCH THE BODY...
スッ
!
GRANDMA, WE'RE NOT HERE TO CRY TODAY...
THE DEAD CALL FOR ME, YOU KNOW.
EXCUSE ME...
UH...SHE WENT ALL THE WAY TO THE FRONT...
B-BUT SHE'S NOT FAMILY...

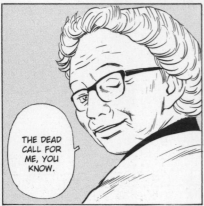

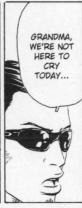

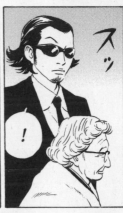

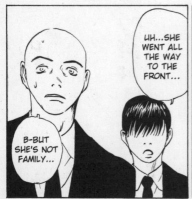

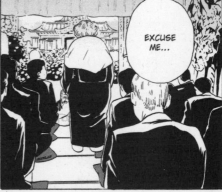

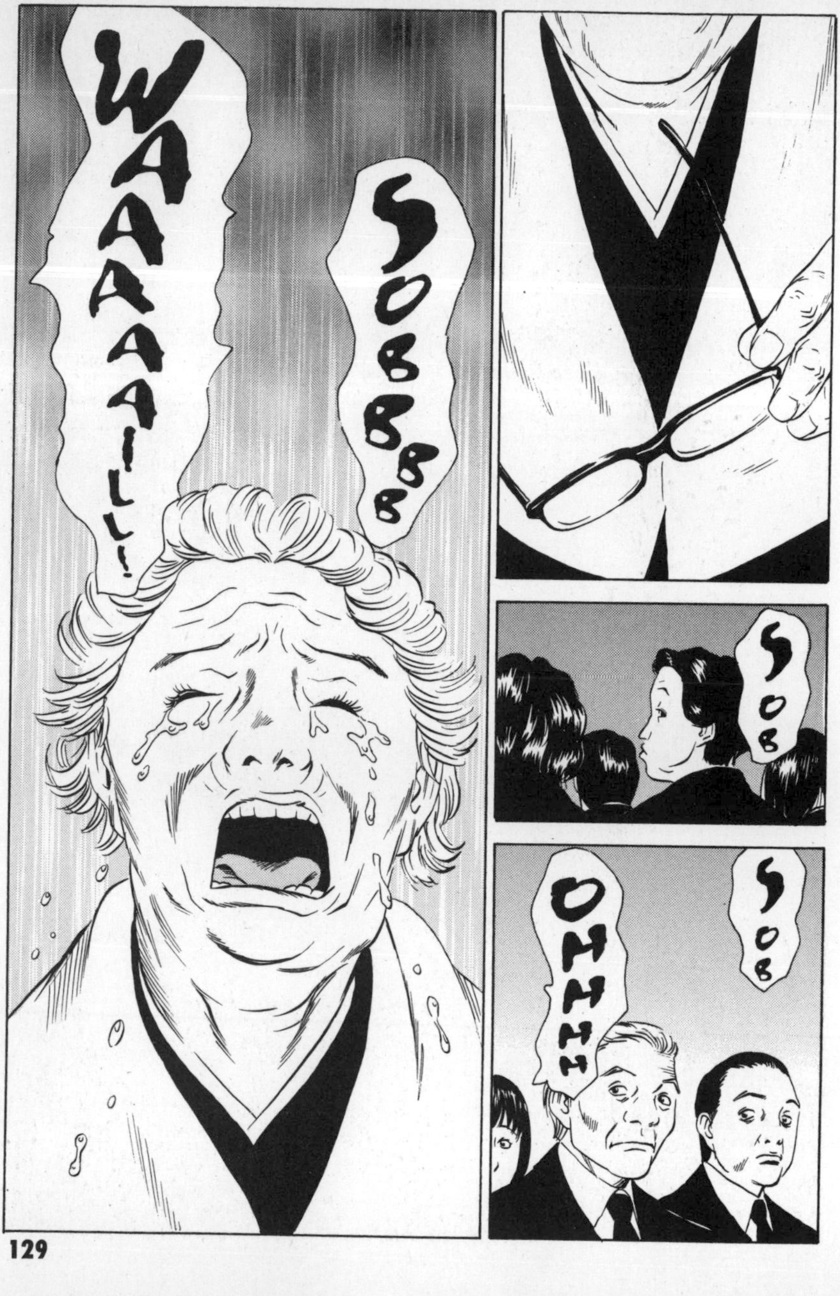
SOB
SOB
OHHHH
SOBBBB
WAAAAILL!

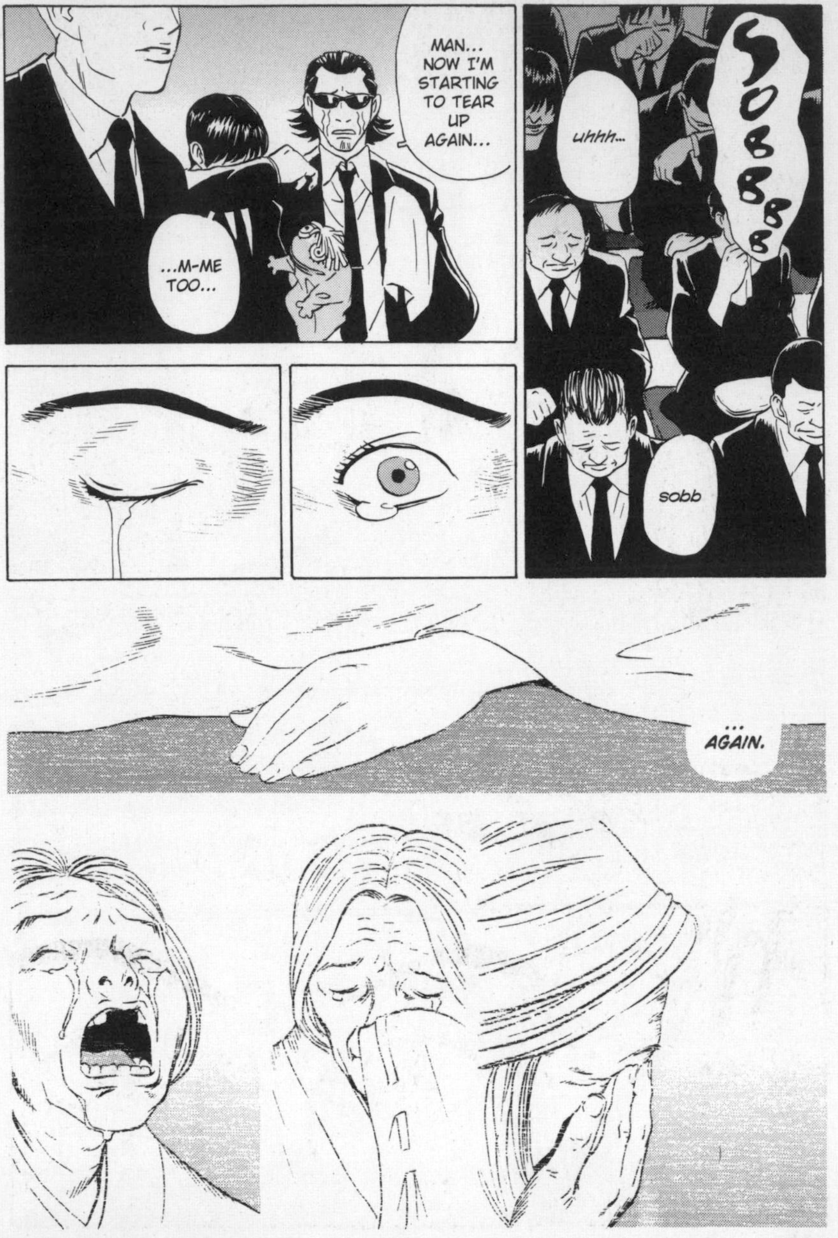
SOBBBB
uhhh...
sobb
MAN... NOW I'M STARTING TO TEAR UP AGAIN...
...M-ME TOO...
... AGAIN.

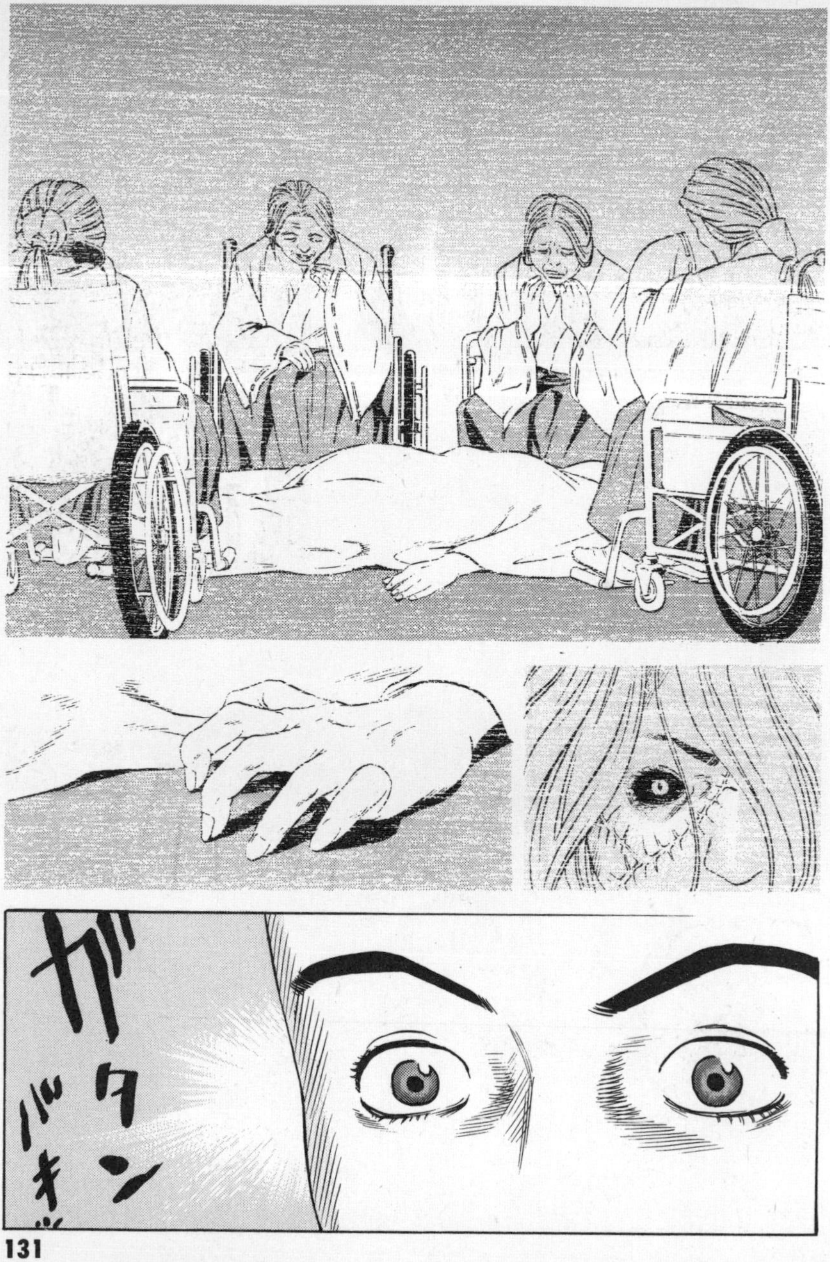
ガタン
バキ

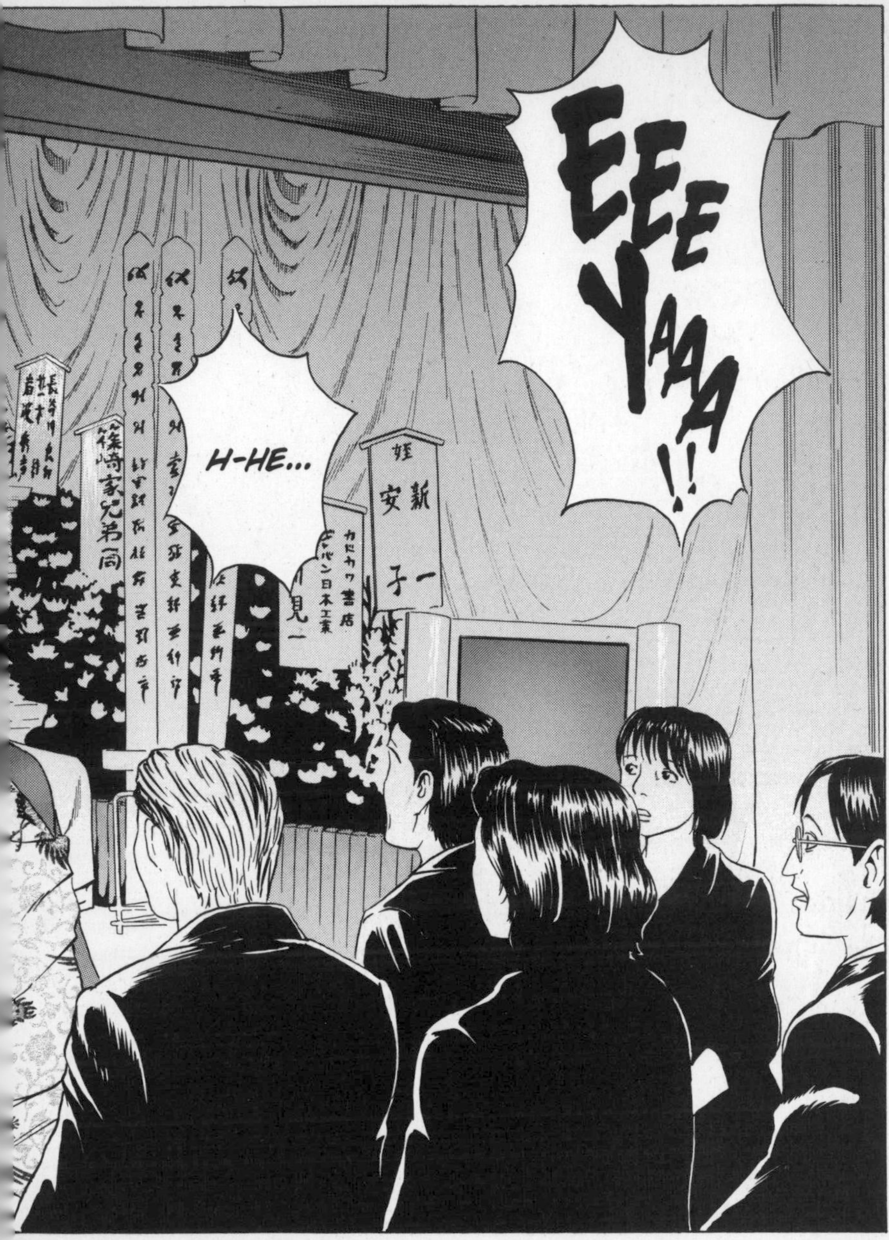
EEEYAAA!!
H-HE...
篠崎家兄弟一同
カドカワ書店

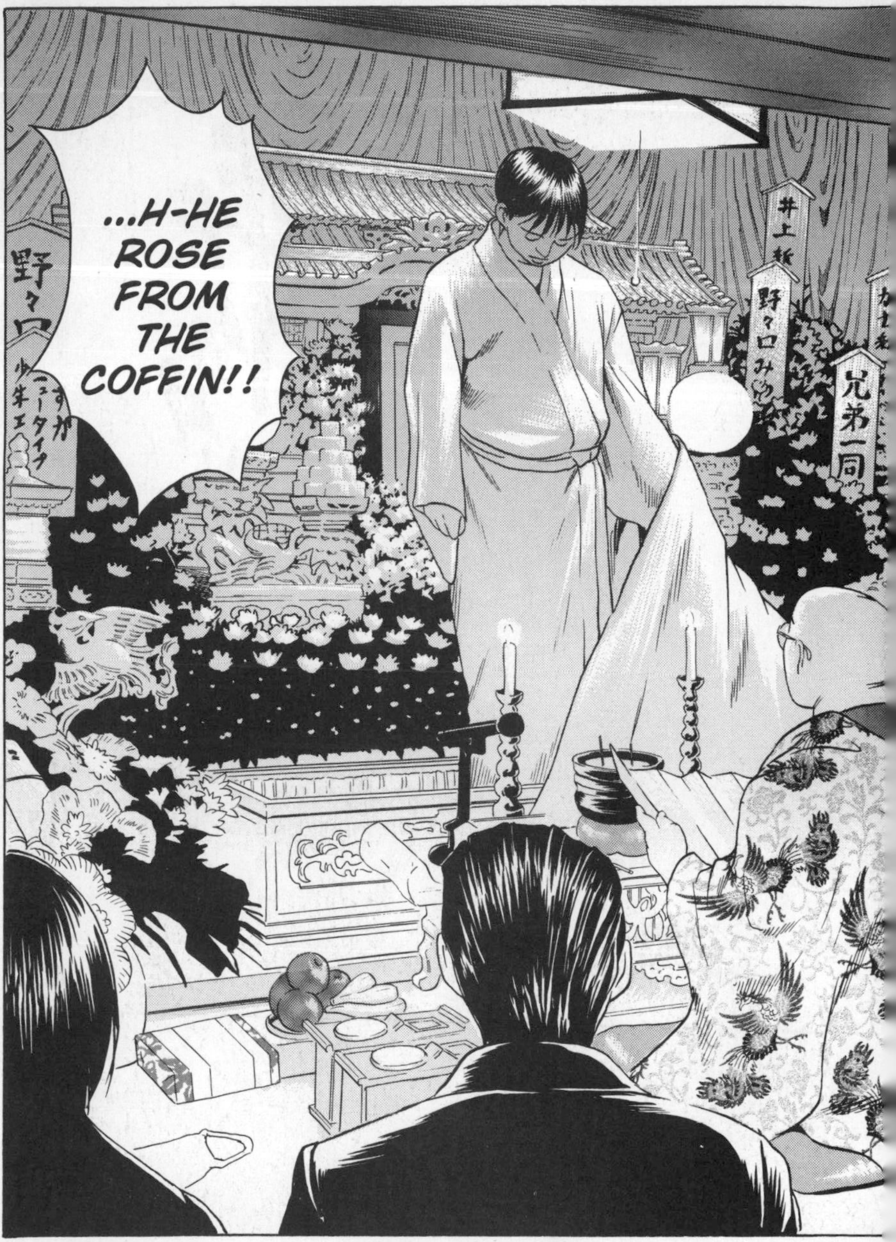
...H-HE ROSE FROM THE COFFIN!!
野々口
兄弟一同

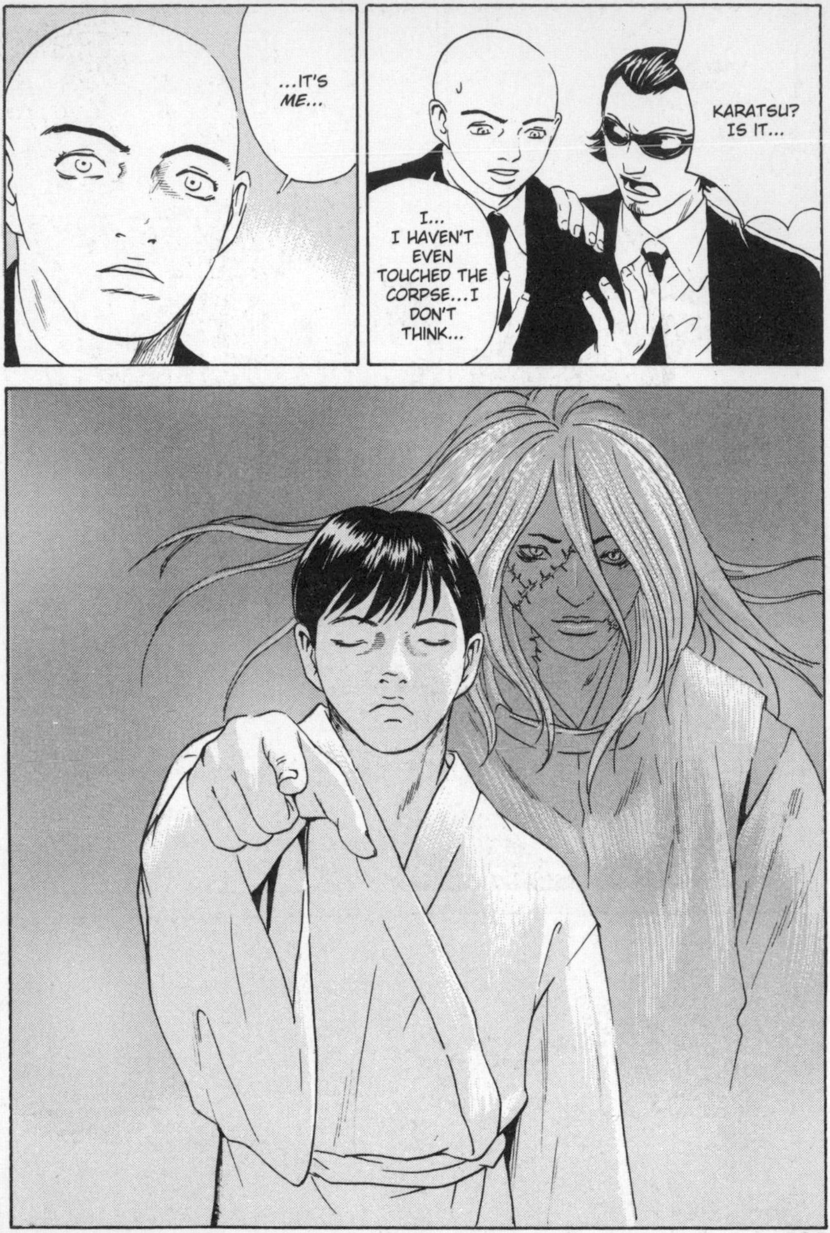
KARATSU? IS IT...
I... I HAVEN'T EVEN TOUCHED THE CORPSE...I DON'T THINK...
...IT'S ME...

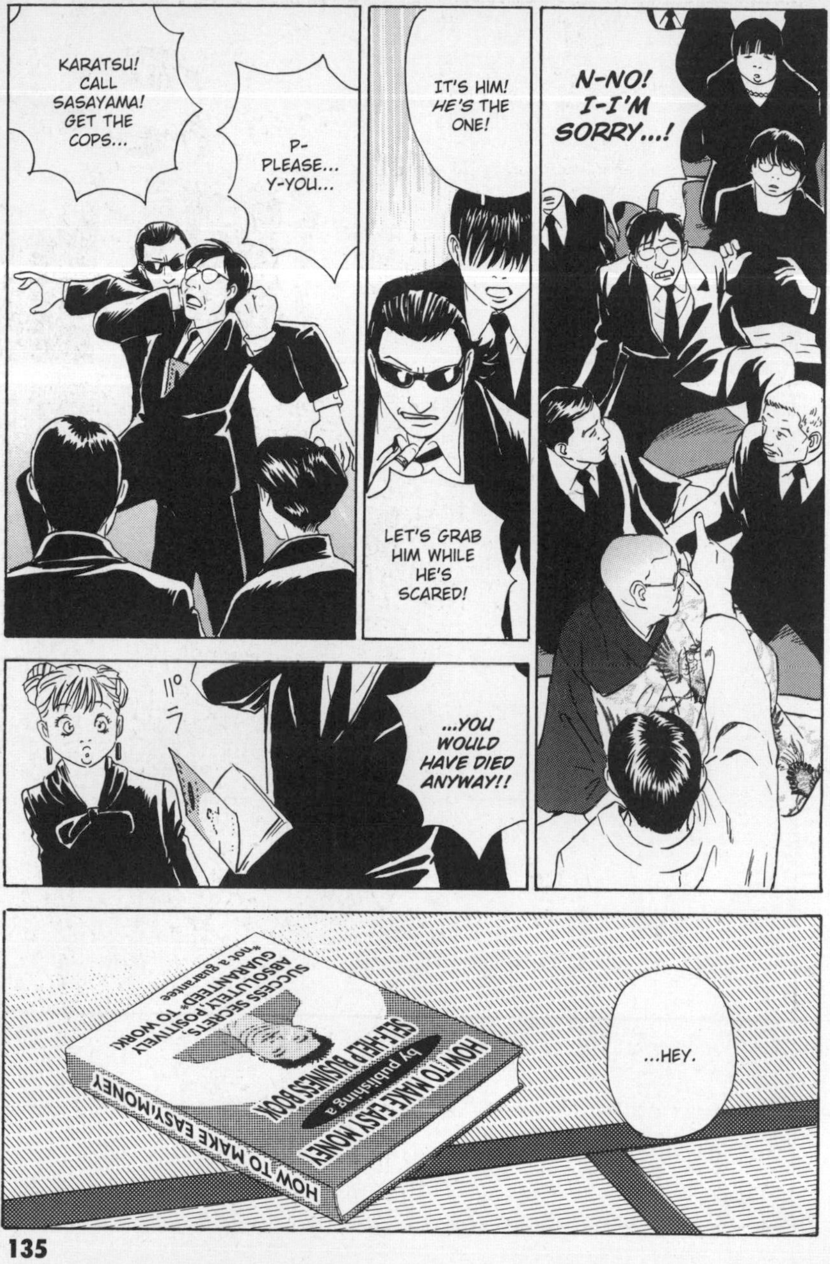
N-NO! I-I'M SORRY...!
IT'S HIM! HE'S THE ONE!
LET'S GRAB HIM WHILE HE'S SCARED!
KARATSU! CALL SASAYAMA! GET THE COPS...
P-PLEASE... Y-YOU...
...YOU WOULD HAVE DIED ANYWAY!!
パラ
HOW TO MAKE EASY MONEY
by publishing a
SELF-HELP BUSINESS BOOK
SUCCESS SECRETS, ABSOLUTELY, POSITIVELY GUARANTEED* TO WORK!
*not a guarantee
HOW TO MAKE EASY MONEY
...HEY.

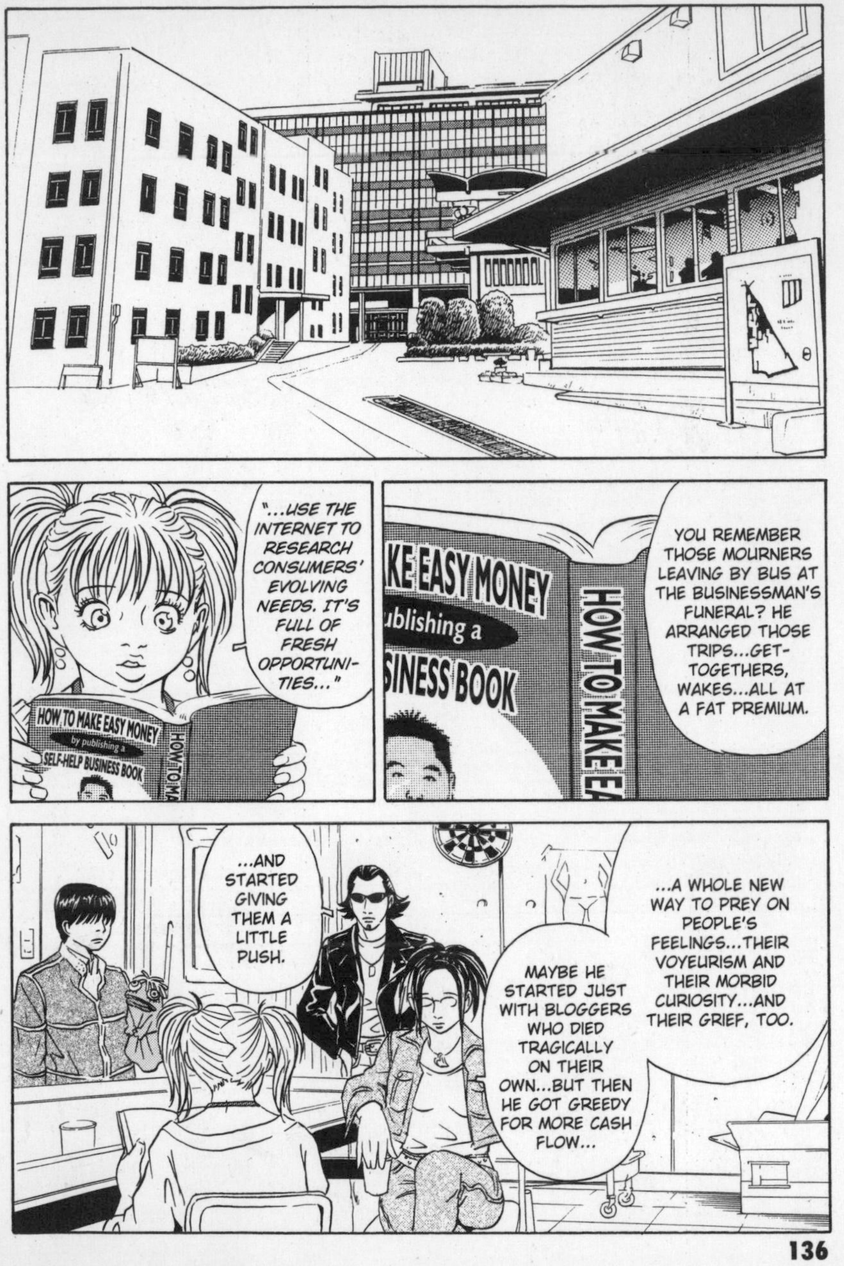
YOU REMEMBER THOSE MOURNERS LEAVING BY BUS AT THE BUSINESSMAN'S FUNERAL? HE ARRANGED THOSE TRIPS...GET-TOGETHERS, WAKES...ALL AT A FAT PREMIUM.
KE EASY MONEY
ublishing a
SINESS BOOK
HOW TO MAKE EA
"...USE THE INTERNET TO RESEARCH CONSUMERS' EVOLVING NEEDS. IT'S FULL OF FRESH OPPORTUNITIES..."
HOW TO MAKE EASY MONEY
by publishing a
SELF-HELP BUSINESS BOOK
HOW TO MA
...A WHOLE NEW WAY TO PREY ON PEOPLE'S FEELINGS...THEIR VOYEURISM AND THEIR MORBID CURIOSITY...AND THEIR GRIEF, TOO.
MAYBE HE STARTED JUST WITH BLOGGERS WHO DIED TRAGICALLY ON THEIR OWN...BUT THEN HE GOT GREEDY FOR MORE CASH FLOW...
...AND STARTED GIVING THEM A LITTLE PUSH.

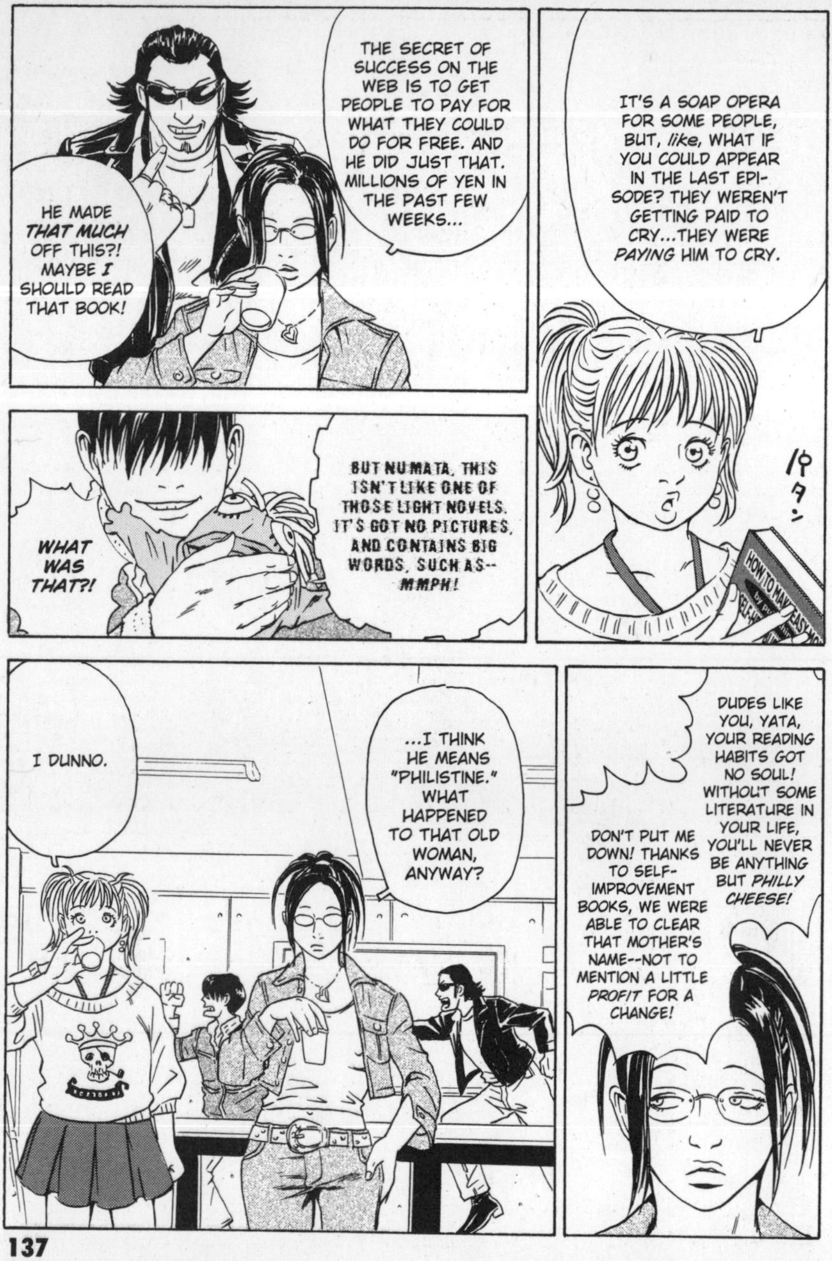
IT'S A SOAP OPERA FOR SOME PEOPLE, BUT, *like*, WHAT IF YOU COULD APPEAR IN THE LAST EPI-SODE? THEY WEREN'T GETTING PAID TO CRY...THEY WERE *PAYING* HIM TO CRY.
パタン
THE SECRET OF SUCCESS ON THE WEB IS TO GET PEOPLE TO PAY FOR WHAT THEY COULD DO FOR FREE. AND HE DID JUST THAT. MILLIONS OF YEN IN THE PAST FEW WEEKS...
HE MADE *THAT MUCH* OFF THIS?! MAYBE *I* SHOULD READ THAT BOOK!
BUT NUMATA, THIS ISN'T LIKE ONE OF THOSE LIGHT NOVELS. IT'S GOT NO PICTURES, AND CONTAINS BIG WORDS, SUCH AS-- MMPH!
WHAT WAS THAT?!
DUDES LIKE YOU, YATA, YOUR READING HABITS GOT NO SOUL! WITHOUT SOME LITERATURE IN YOUR LIFE, YOU'LL NEVER BE ANYTHING BUT *PHILLY CHEESE!*
DON'T PUT ME DOWN! THANKS TO SELF-IMPROVEMENT BOOKS, WE WERE ABLE TO CLEAR THAT MOTHER'S NAME--NOT TO MENTION A LITTLE *PROFIT* FOR A CHANGE!
...I THINK HE MEANS "PHILISTINE." WHAT HAPPENED TO THAT OLD WOMAN, ANYWAY?
I DUNNO.

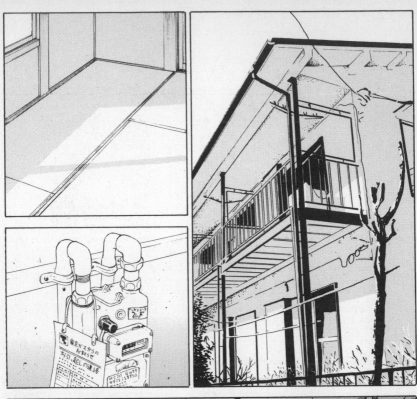

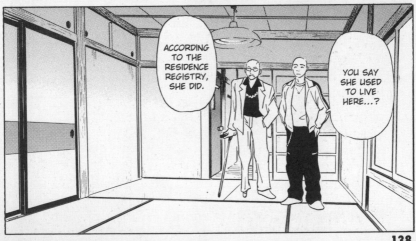

東京ガスからのお知らせ
YOU SAY SHE USED TO LIVE HERE...?
ACCORDING TO THE RESIDENCE REGISTRY, SHE DID.

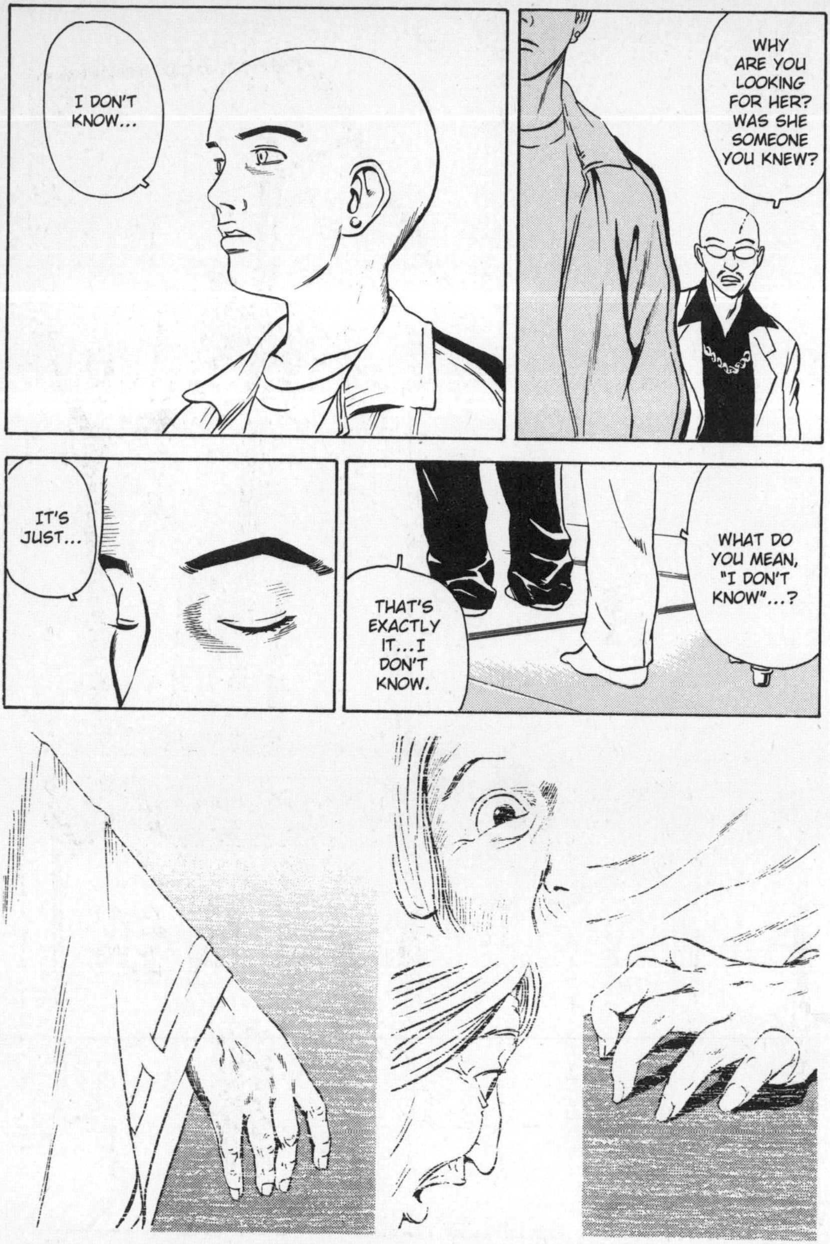
WHY ARE YOU LOOKING FOR HER? WAS SHE SOMEONE YOU KNEW?
I DON'T KNOW...
WHAT DO YOU MEAN, "I DON'T KNOW"...?
THAT'S EXACTLY IT...I DON'T KNOW.
IT'S JUST...

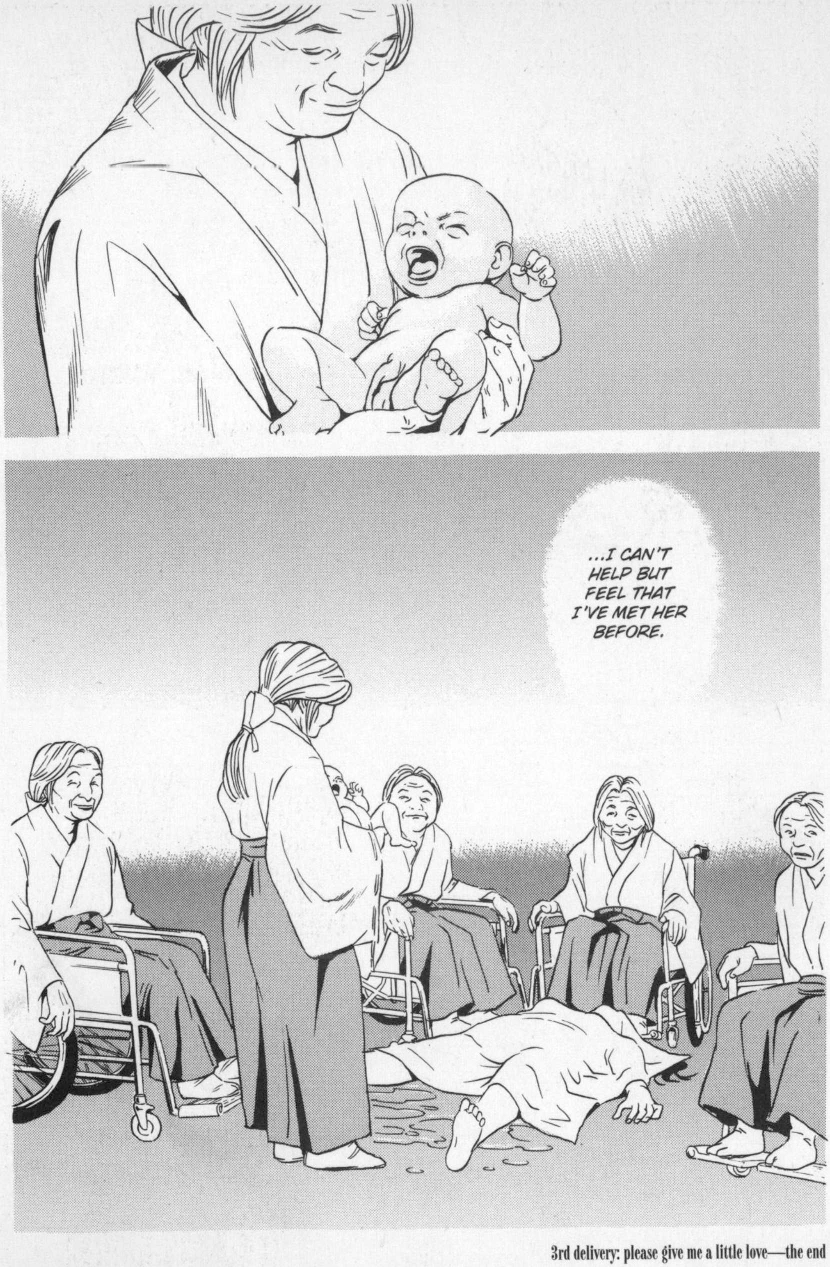
...I CAN'T HELP BUT FEEL THAT I'VE MET HER BEFORE.

3rd delivery: please give me a little love—the end

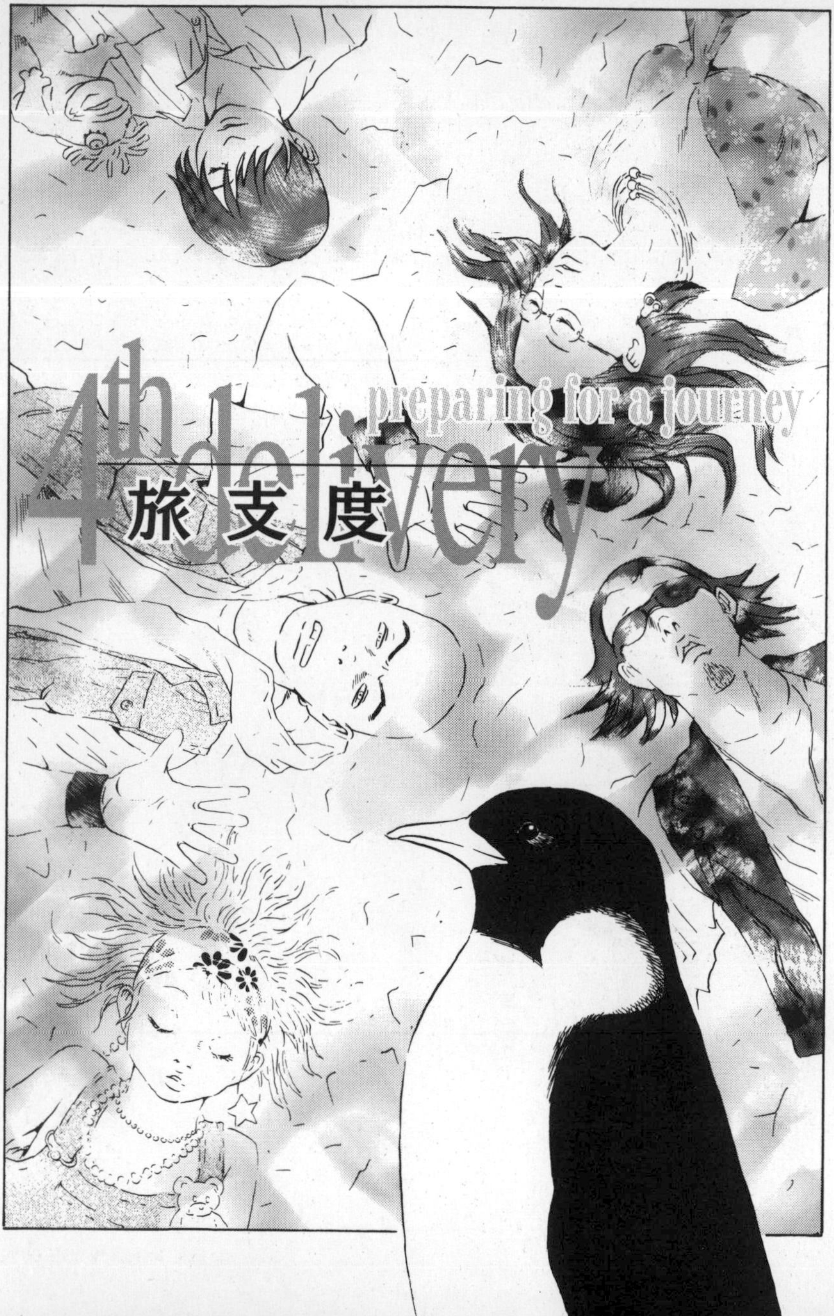
4th delivery
preparing for a journey
旅支度

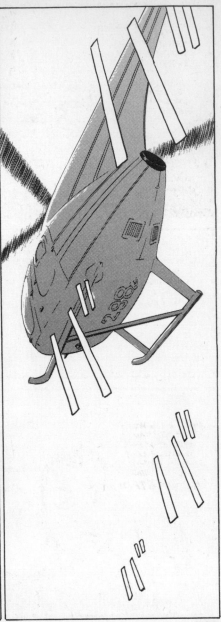

...AND *THIS* IS THE SPOT WHERE A PLASTIC BAG CONTAINING *25 MILLION YEN* WAS FOUND BURIED IN THE *GROUND!*

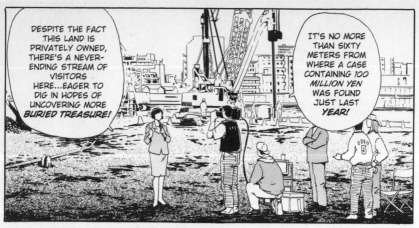

IT'S NO MORE THAN SIXTY METERS FROM WHERE A CASE CONTAINING 100 MILLION YEN WAS FOUND JUST LAST YEAR!
DESPITE THE FACT THIS LAND IS PRIVATELY OWNED, THERE'S A NEVER-ENDING STREAM OF VISITORS HERE...EAGER TO DIG IN HOPES OF UNCOVERING MORE BURIED TREASURE!
...I HEARD STORIES THAT OLD MAN HABAMA BURIED MOST OF THE MONEY HE MADE IN STOCKS...
...HID THEM IN SEVERAL PLACES, THEY SAY...
ME? I WAS JUST DIGGING A HOLE TO BURY SOME OF MY TRASH.
YEAH, SO WHAT? HE HID THE MONEY SO HE WOULDN'T HAVE TO PAY TAX, AMIRITE?
AND I HEAR WE GET TO SPLIT ANY MONEY WE FIND WITH THE LAND OWNER FIFTY-FIFTY! SO DON'T SIMPLY GO, BUT GTFO!

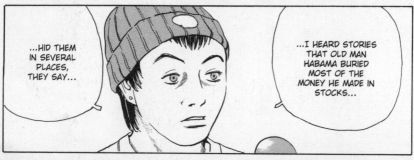

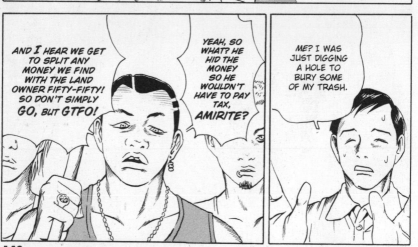

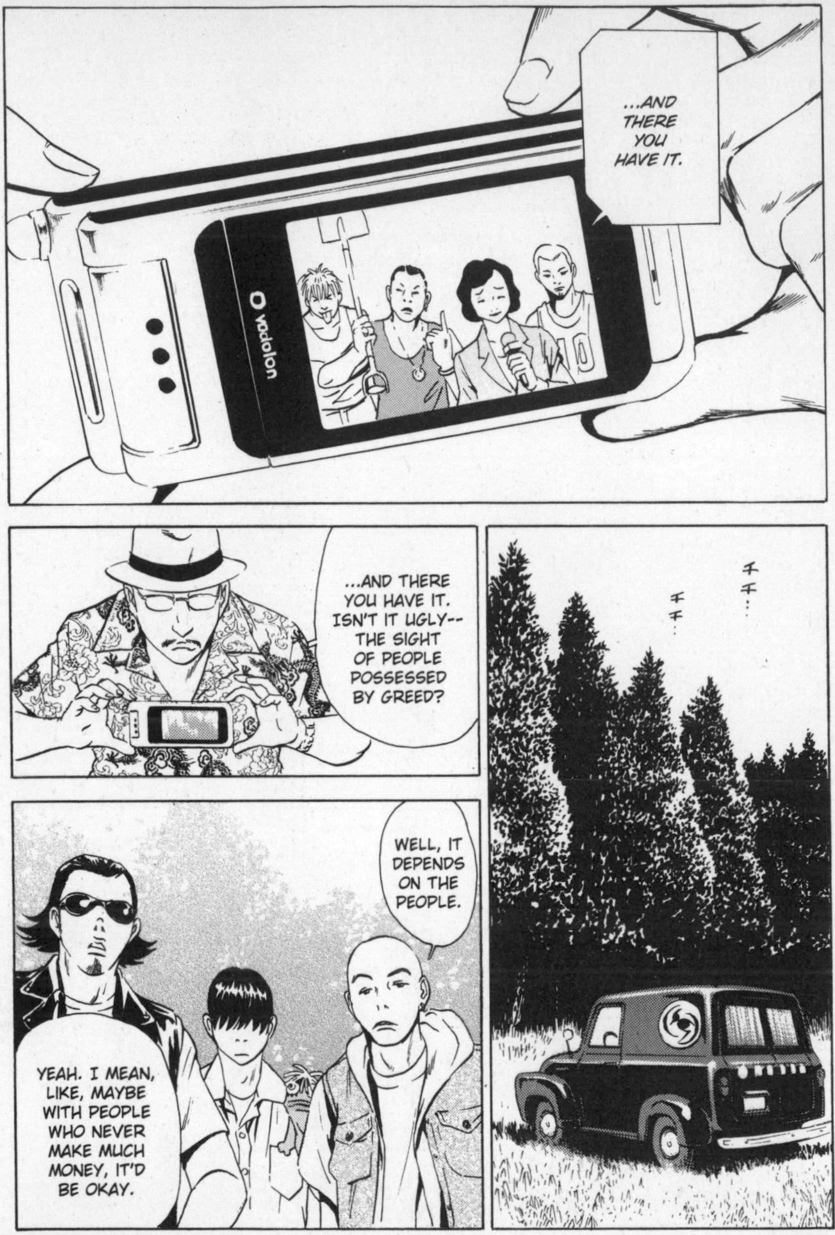
...AND THERE YOU HAVE IT.
チチ…
チチ…
...AND THERE YOU HAVE IT. ISN'T IT UGLY-- THE SIGHT OF PEOPLE POSSESSED BY GREED?
WELL, IT DEPENDS ON THE PEOPLE.
YEAH. I MEAN, LIKE, MAYBE WITH PEOPLE WHO NEVER MAKE MUCH MONEY, IT'D BE OKAY.

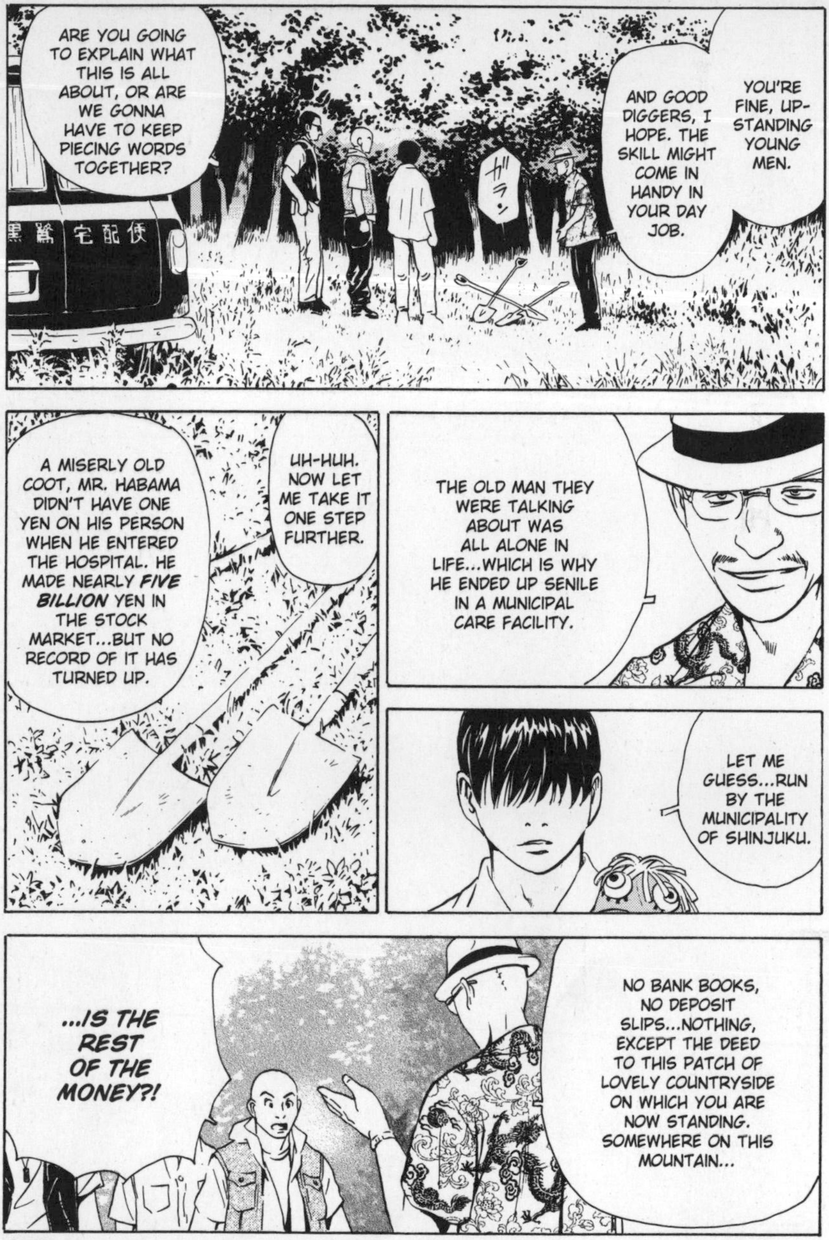
YOU'RE FINE, UP-STANDING YOUNG MEN.
AND GOOD DIGGERS, I HOPE. THE SKILL MIGHT COME IN HANDY IN YOUR DAY JOB.
ガラン
ARE YOU GOING TO EXPLAIN WHAT THIS IS ALL ABOUT, OR ARE WE GONNA HAVE TO KEEP PIECING WORDS TOGETHER?
THE OLD MAN THEY WERE TALKING ABOUT WAS ALL ALONE IN LIFE...WHICH IS WHY HE ENDED UP SENILE IN A MUNICIPAL CARE FACILITY.
LET ME GUESS...RUN BY THE MUNICIPALITY OF SHINJUKU.
UH-HUH. NOW LET ME TAKE IT ONE STEP FURTHER.
A MISERLY OLD COOT, MR. HABAMA DIDN'T HAVE ONE YEN ON HIS PERSON WHEN HE ENTERED THE HOSPITAL. HE MADE NEARLY FIVE BILLION YEN IN THE STOCK MARKET...BUT NO RECORD OF IT HAS TURNED UP.
NO BANK BOOKS, NO DEPOSIT SLIPS...NOTHING, EXCEPT THE DEED TO THIS PATCH OF LOVELY COUNTRYSIDE ON WHICH YOU ARE NOW STANDING. SOMEWHERE ON THIS MOUNTAIN...
...IS THE REST OF THE MONEY?!

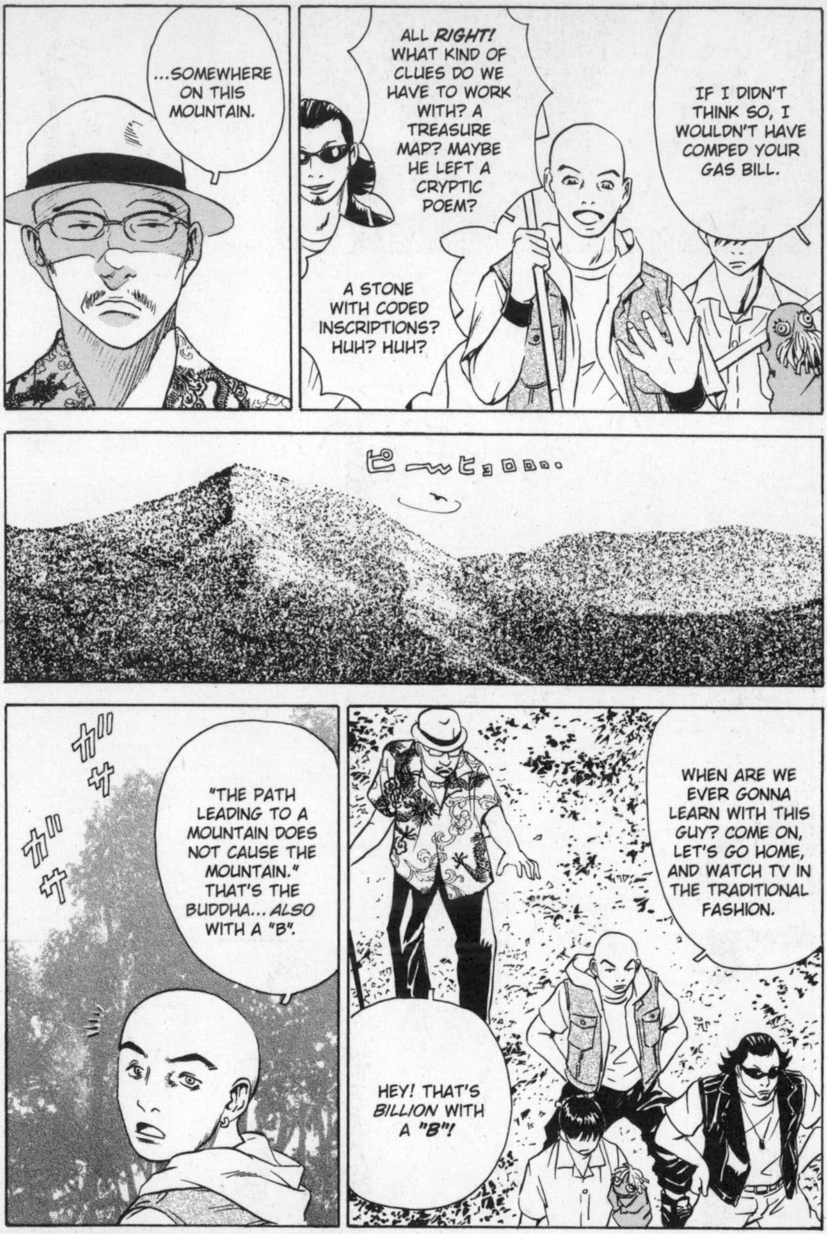
IF I DIDN'T THINK SO, I WOULDN'T HAVE COMPED YOUR GAS BILL.
ALL *RIGHT!* WHAT KIND OF CLUES DO WE HAVE TO WORK WITH? A TREASURE MAP? MAYBE HE LEFT A CRYPTIC POEM?
A STONE WITH CODED INSCRIPTIONS? HUH? HUH?
...SOMEWHERE ON THIS MOUNTAIN.
ピ〜ッヒョロロロ。。
WHEN ARE WE EVER GONNA LEARN WITH THIS GUY? COME ON, LET'S GO HOME, AND WATCH TV IN THE TRADITIONAL FASHION.
HEY! THAT'S *BILLION* WITH A *"B"*!
ガサ
ガサ
"THE PATH LEADING TO A MOUNTAIN DOES NOT CAUSE THE MOUNTAIN." THAT'S THE BUDDHA... *ALSO* WITH A "B".

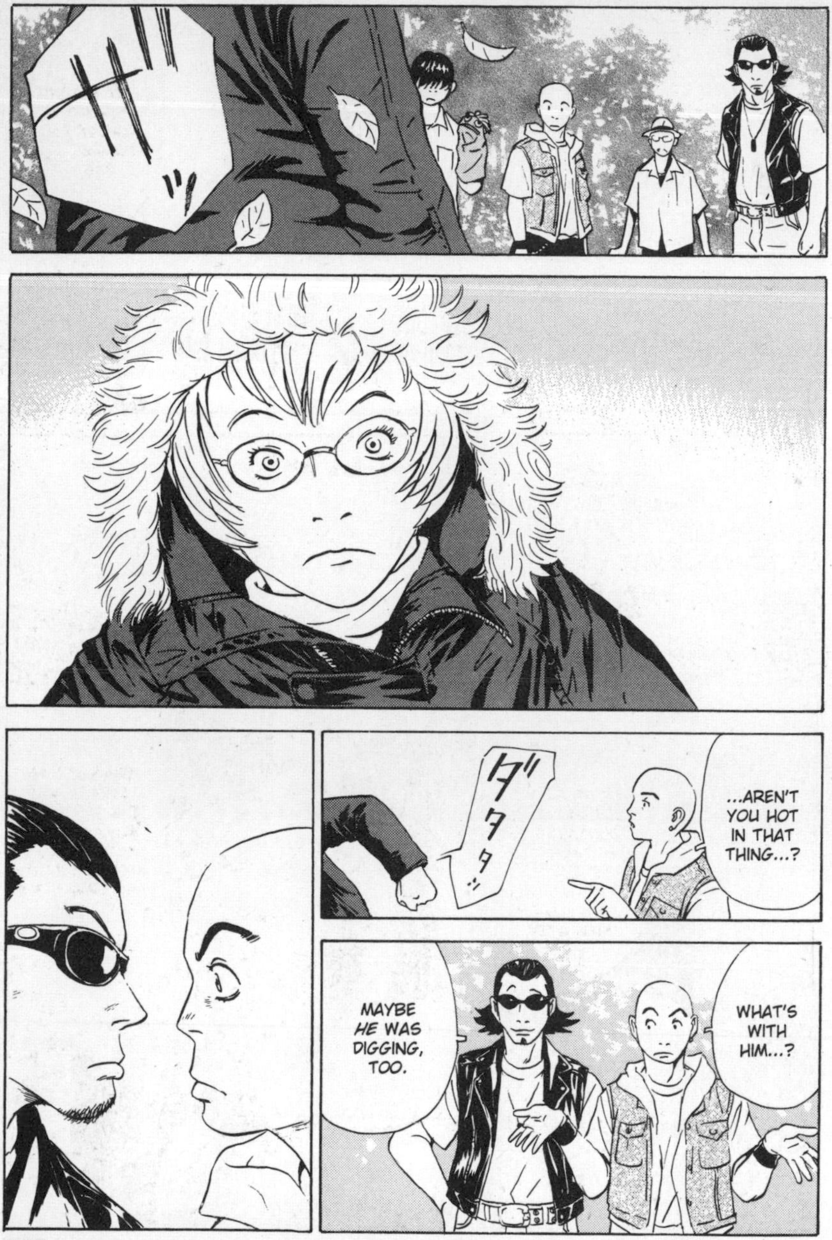
ダタタ
...AREN'T YOU HOT IN THAT THING...?
WHAT'S WITH HIM...?
MAYBE *HE* WAS DIGGING, TOO.

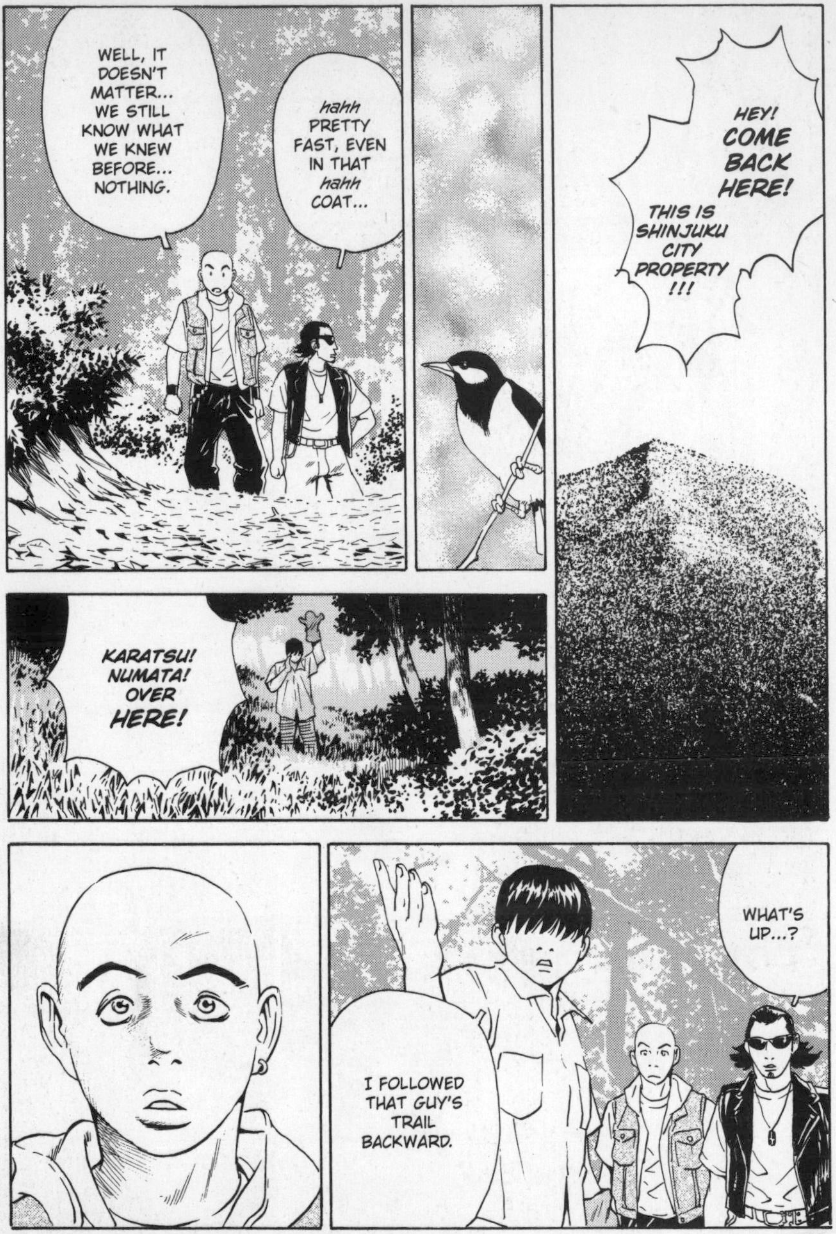
HEY! COME BACK HERE!
THIS IS SHINJUKU CITY PROPERTY !!!
hahh PRETTY FAST, EVEN IN THAT hahh COAT...
WELL, IT DOESN'T MATTER... WE STILL KNOW WHAT WE KNEW BEFORE... NOTHING.
KARATSU! NUMATA! OVER HERE!
WHAT'S UP...?
I FOLLOWED THAT GUY'S TRAIL BACKWARD.

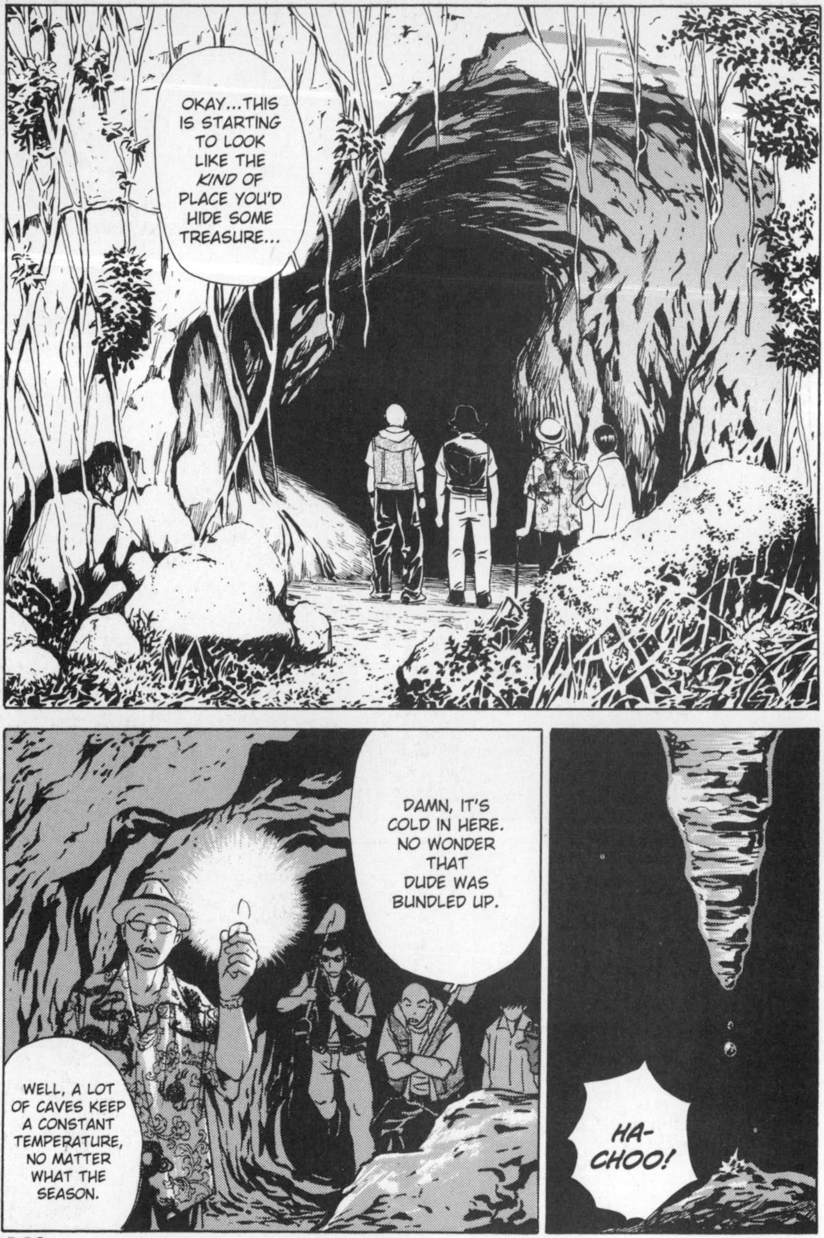
OKAY...THIS IS STARTING TO LOOK LIKE THE *KIND* OF PLACE YOU'D HIDE SOME TREASURE...
HA-CHOO!
DAMN, IT'S COLD IN HERE. NO WONDER THAT DUDE WAS BUNDLED UP.
WELL, A LOT OF CAVES KEEP A CONSTANT TEMPERATURE, NO MATTER WHAT THE SEASON.

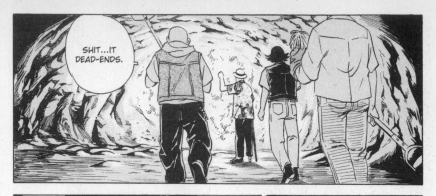

SHIT...IT DEAD-ENDS.
HOLD ON A SEC...THOSE BUMPS IN THE FLOOR LOOK A LITTLE SUSPICIOUS TO ME.
BUMPS ...?
WHAT DO YOU WANT TO BET THIS IS THE LOOT? C'MON, LET'S DIG!
UM...
HEY... THERE *IS* SOMETHING DOWN THERE!
...Looks kind of like a gachapon.

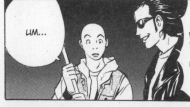

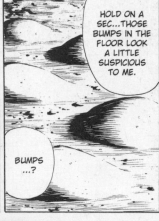

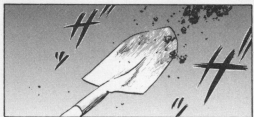

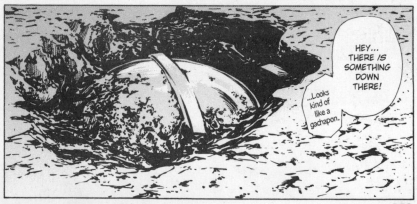

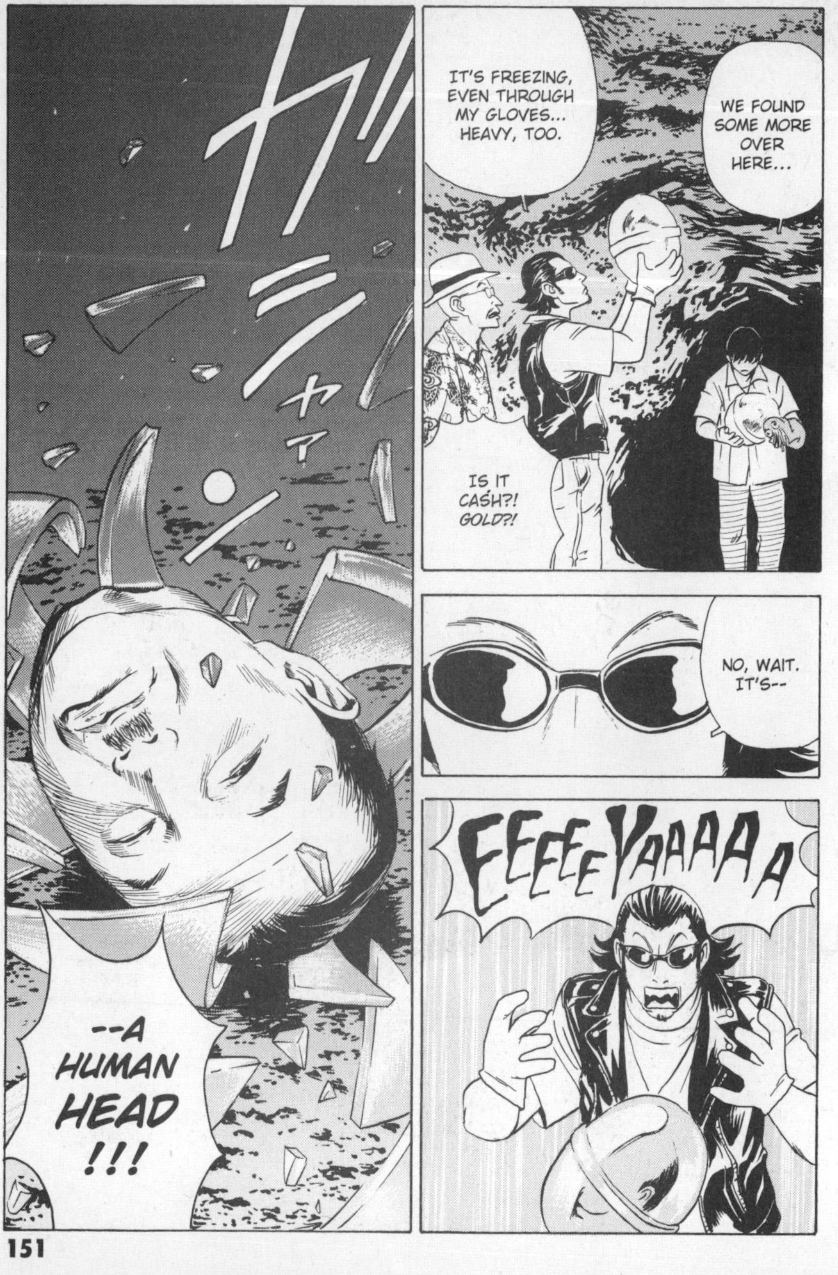
WE FOUND SOME MORE OVER HERE...
IT'S FREEZING, EVEN THROUGH MY GLOVES... HEAVY, TOO.
IS IT CASH?! GOLD?!
NO, WAIT. IT'S--
EEEEE YAAAAAA
ガシャア
--A HUMAN HEAD!!!

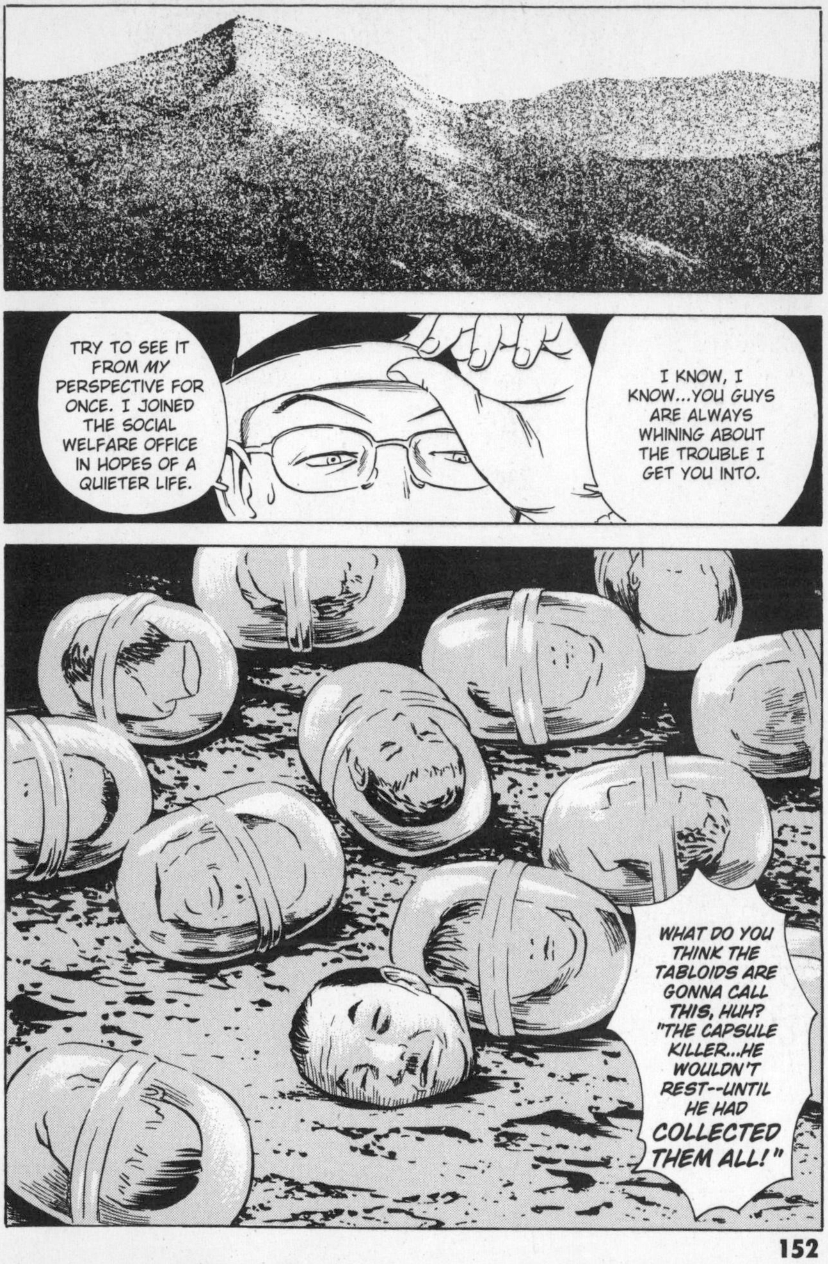
I KNOW, I KNOW...YOU GUYS ARE ALWAYS WHINING ABOUT THE TROUBLE I GET YOU INTO.
TRY TO SEE IT FROM *MY* PERSPECTIVE FOR ONCE. I JOINED THE SOCIAL WELFARE OFFICE IN HOPES OF A QUIETER LIFE.
WHAT DO YOU THINK THE TABLOIDS ARE GONNA CALL THIS, HUH? "THE CAPSULE KILLER...HE WOULDN'T REST--UNTIL HE HAD **COLLECTED THEM ALL!**"

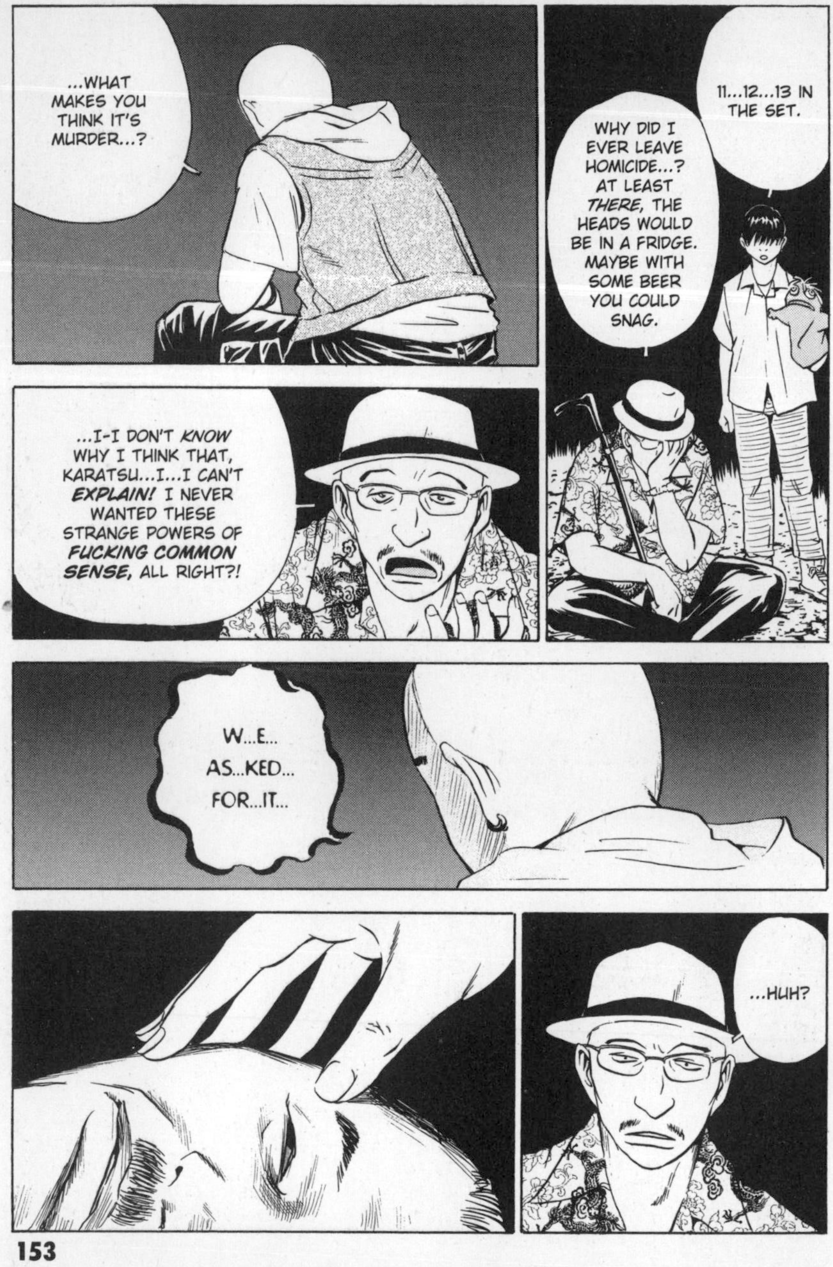
11...12...13 IN THE SET.
WHY DID I EVER LEAVE HOMICIDE...? AT LEAST *THERE*, THE HEADS WOULD BE IN A FRIDGE. MAYBE WITH SOME BEER YOU COULD SNAG.
...WHAT MAKES YOU THINK IT'S MURDER...?
...I-I DON'T *KNOW* WHY I THINK THAT, KARATSU...I...I CAN'T ***EXPLAIN!*** I NEVER WANTED THESE STRANGE POWERS OF ***FUCKING COMMON SENSE***, ALL RIGHT?!
W...E... AS...KED... FOR...IT...
...HUH?

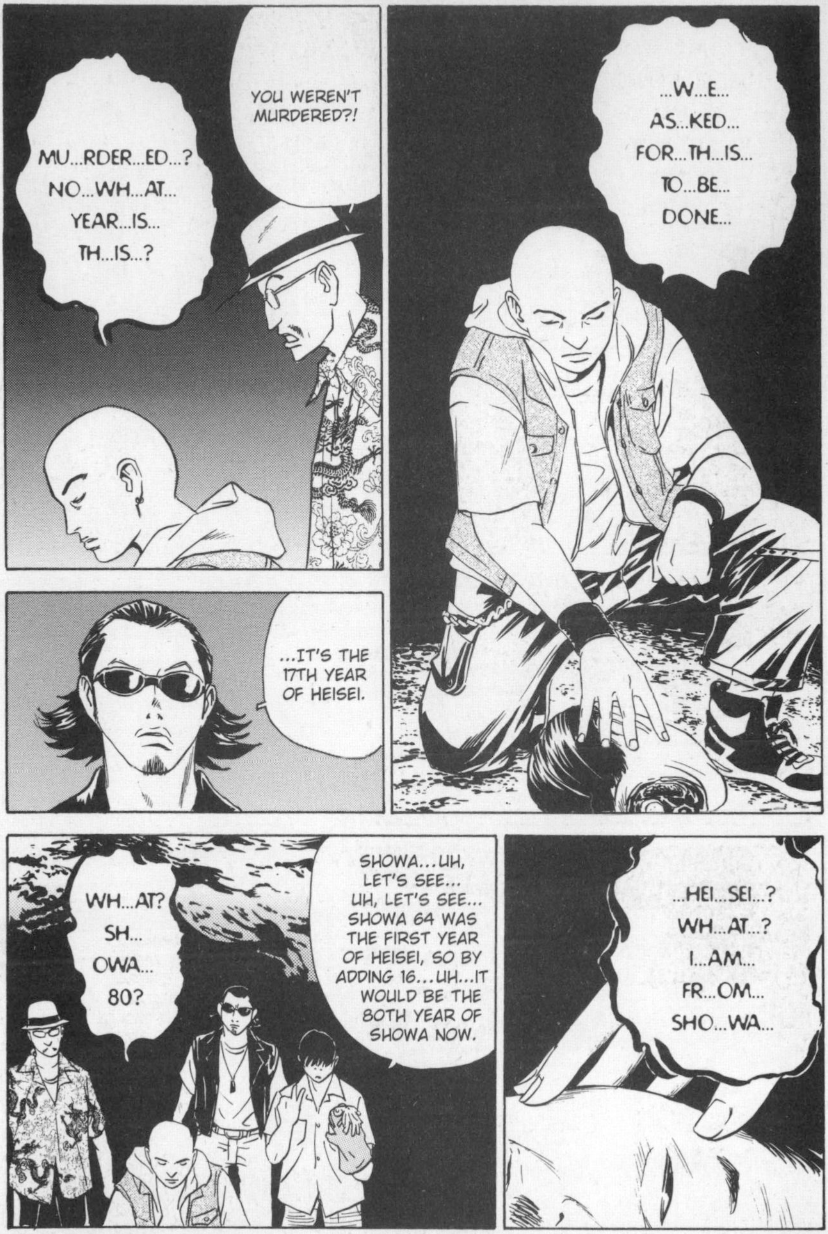
...W...E... AS...KED... FOR...TH...IS... TO...BE... DONE...
YOU WEREN'T MURDERED?!
MU...RDER...ED...? NO...WH...AT... YEAR...IS... TH...IS...?
...IT'S THE 17TH YEAR OF HEISEI.
...HEI...SEI...? WH...AT...? I...AM... FR...OM... SHO...WA...
SHOWA...UH, LET'S SEE... UH, LET'S SEE... SHOWA 64 WAS THE FIRST YEAR OF HEISEI, SO BY ADDING 16...UH...IT WOULD BE THE 80TH YEAR OF SHOWA NOW.
WH...AT? SH... OWA... 80?

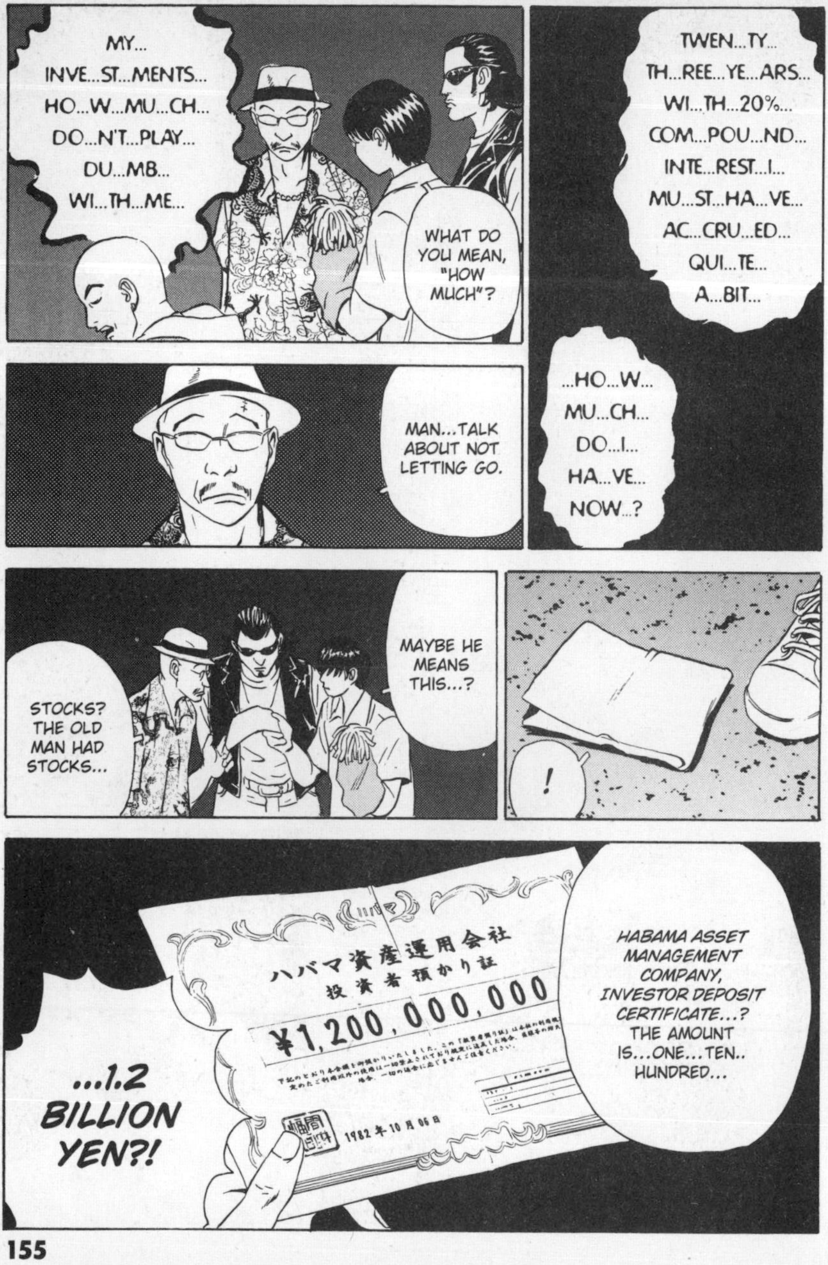
TWEN...TY... TH...REE...YE...ARS... WI...TH...20%... COM...POU...ND... INTE...REST...I... MU...ST...HA...VE... AC...CRU...ED... QUI...TE... A...BIT...
...HO...W... MU...CH... DO...I... HA...VE... NOW...?
MY... INVE...ST...MENTS... HO...W...MU...CH... DO...N'T...PLAY... DU...MB... WI...TH...ME...
WHAT DO YOU MEAN, "HOW MUCH"?
MAN...TALK ABOUT NOT LETTING GO.
!
MAYBE HE MEANS THIS...?
STOCKS? THE OLD MAN HAD STOCKS...
HABAMA ASSET MANAGEMENT COMPANY, INVESTOR DEPOSIT CERTIFICATE...? THE AMOUNT IS...ONE...TEN.. HUNDRED...
ハバマ
ハバマ資産運用会社
投資者預かり証
¥1,200,000,000
1982年10月06日
...1.2 BILLION YEN?!

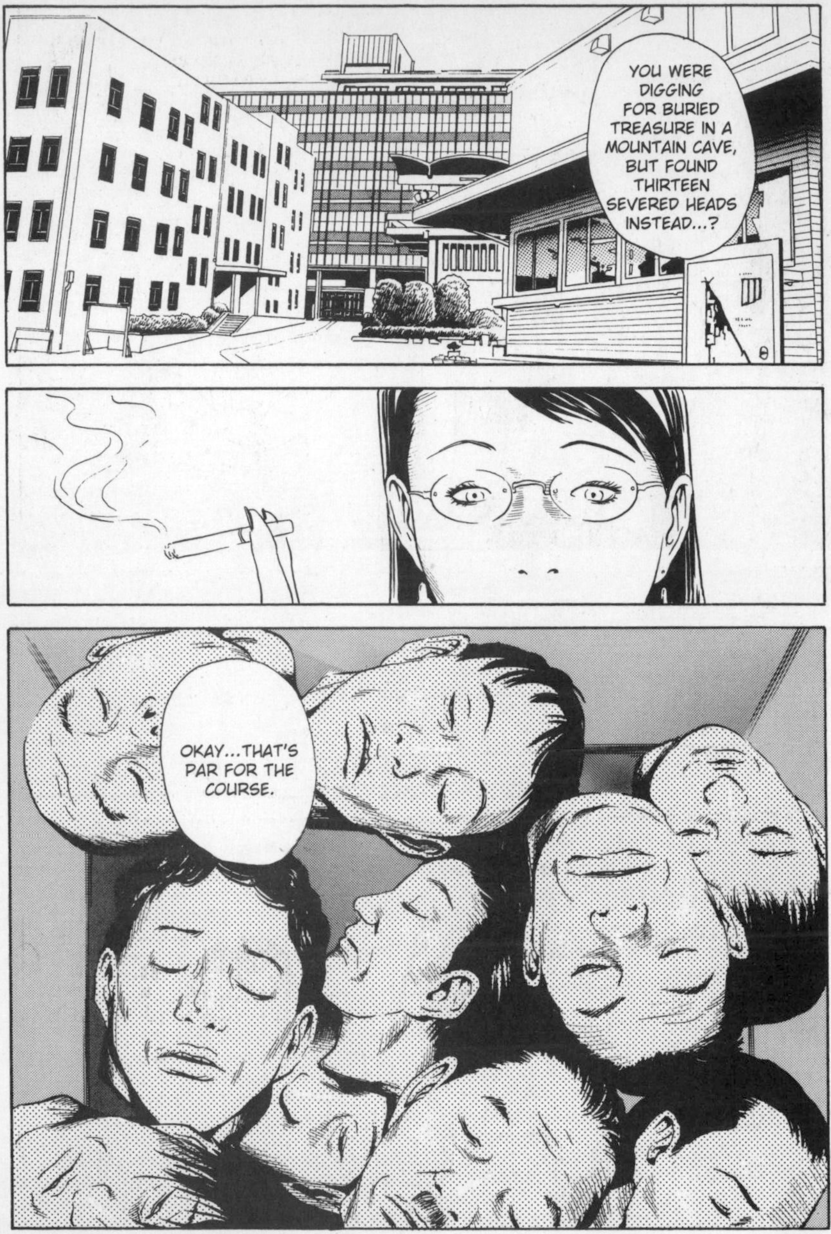
YOU WERE DIGGING FOR BURIED TREASURE IN A MOUNTAIN CAVE, BUT FOUND THIRTEEN SEVERED HEADS INSTEAD...?
OKAY...THAT'S PAR FOR THE COURSE.

SHUT THE COOLER. AT ROOM TEMPERATURE, THEY'LL START TO DECOMPOSE, AND I'LL NEVER HEAR THE END OF IT FROM THE OLD MAN--
HEYO...
WERE YOU ABLE TO FIND ANYTHING OUT, MR. SASAYAMA...?
HE SAID HE WASN'T MURDERED... MAYBE IT'S NOT JUST BAD MEMORY.
I TRACED THE NAMES FROM THE SHARE CERTIFICATES. ALL OF THEM DIED OF NATURAL CAUSES. DIFFERENT HOSPITALS AND DOCTORS SIGNED OFF...LOOKS LEGIT.
AH-HA, ELDER BALDY...BUT ISN'T IT STILL A CRIME TO ABANDON BODIES IN THE WILDERNESS LIKE THAT...?
ガタ
THEY WEREN'T ABANDONED. HABAMA MUST HAVE HAD SOME SMARTS IN THE OLD DAYS... THAT WHOLE MOUNTAIN IS REGISTERED AS A PRIVATE CEMETERY--PERFECTLY LEGAL.

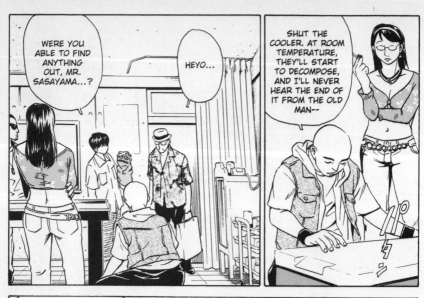

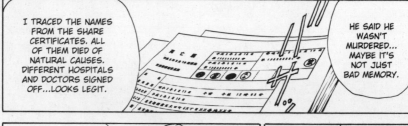

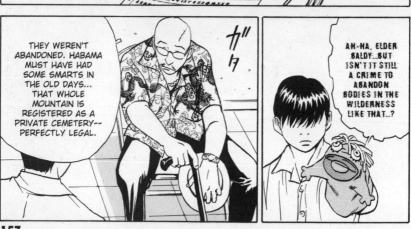

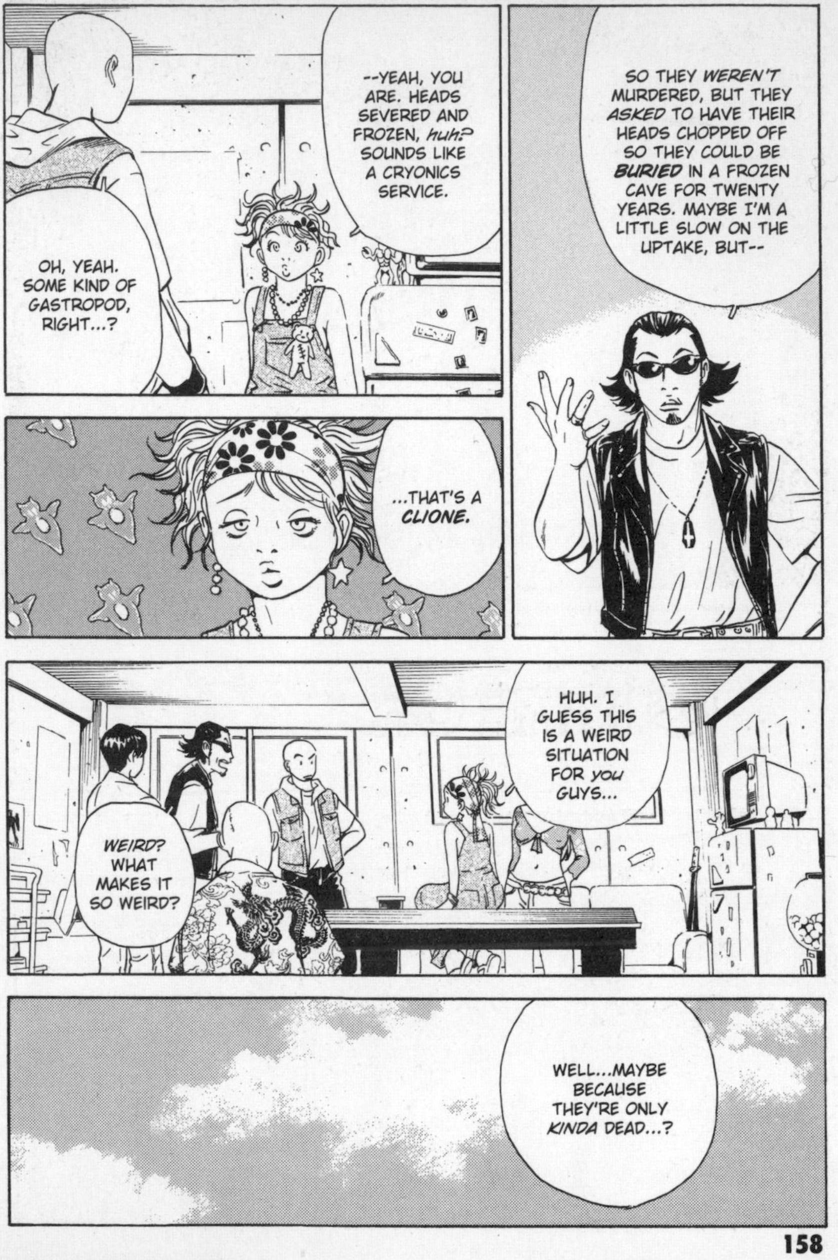
SO THEY *WEREN'T* MURDERED, BUT THEY *ASKED* TO HAVE THEIR HEADS CHOPPED OFF SO THEY COULD BE **BURIED** IN A FROZEN CAVE FOR TWENTY YEARS. MAYBE I'M A LITTLE SLOW ON THE UPTAKE, BUT--
--YEAH, YOU ARE. HEADS SEVERED AND FROZEN, *huh?* SOUNDS LIKE A CRYONICS SERVICE.
OH, YEAH. SOME KIND OF GASTROPOD, RIGHT...?
...THAT'S A ***CLIONE.***
HUH. I GUESS THIS IS A WEIRD SITUATION FOR *you* GUYS...
WEIRD? WHAT MAKES IT SO WEIRD?
WELL...MAYBE BECAUSE THEY'RE ONLY *KINDA* DEAD...?

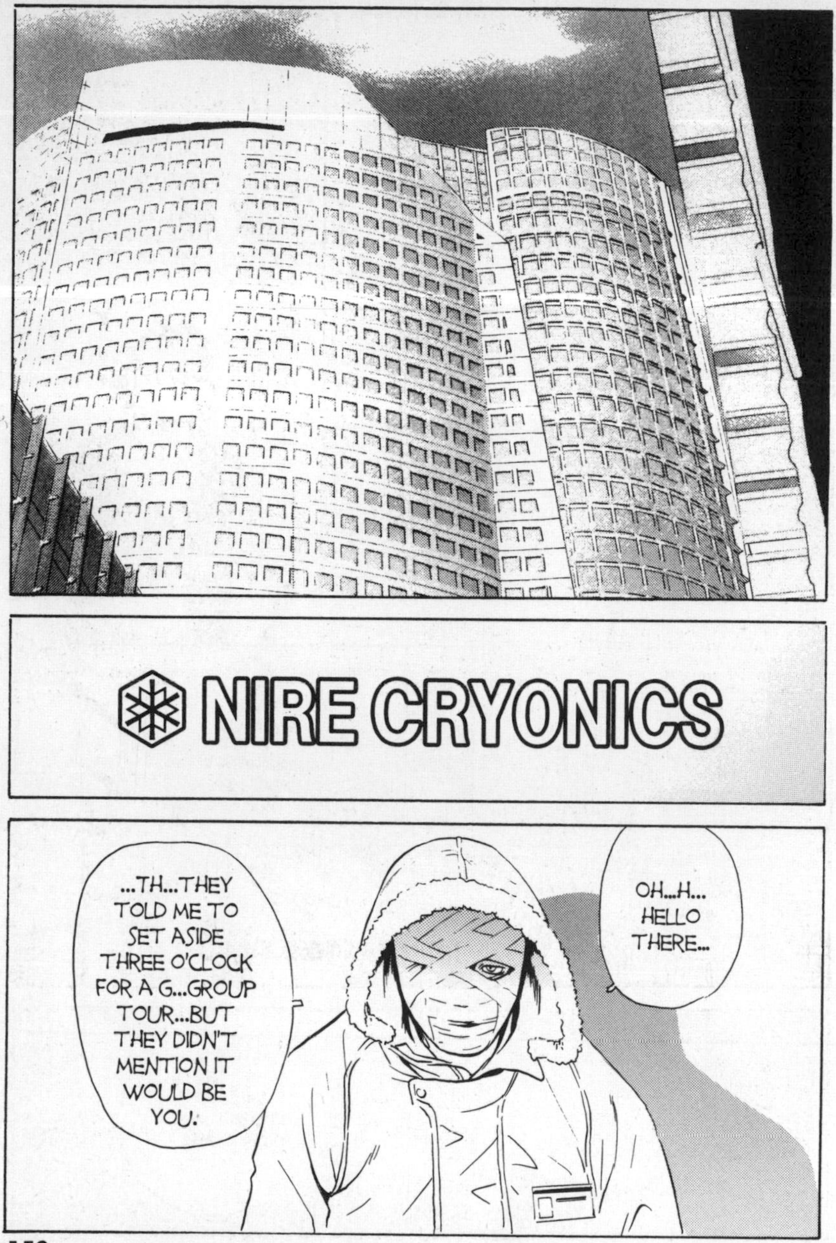
NIRE CRYONICS
OH...H... HELLO THERE...
...TH...THEY TOLD ME TO SET ASIDE THREE O'CLOCK FOR A G...GROUP TOUR...BUT THEY DIDN'T MENTION IT WOULD BE YOU.

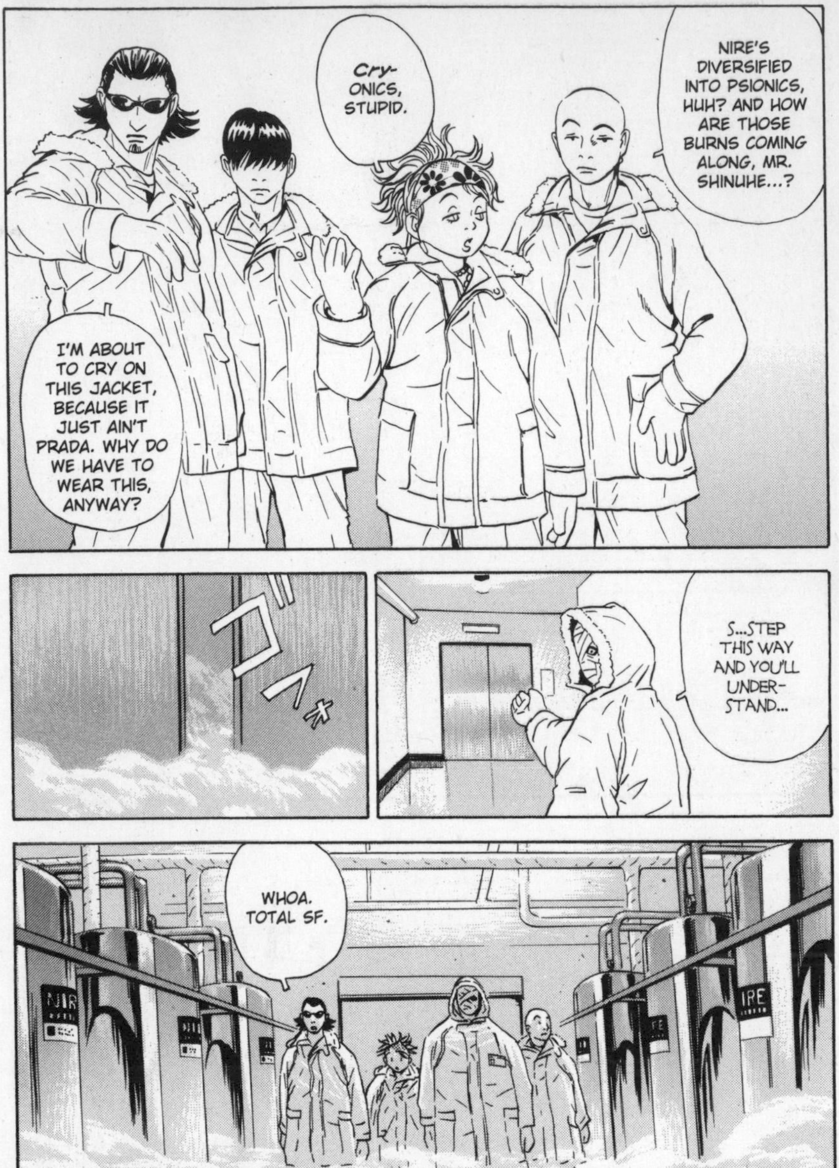
NIRE'S DIVERSIFIED INTO PSIONICS, HUH? AND HOW ARE THOSE BURNS COMING ALONG, MR. SHINUHE...?
Cry-ONICS, STUPID.
I'M ABOUT TO CRY ON THIS JACKET, BECAUSE IT JUST AIN'T PRADA. WHY DO WE HAVE TO WEAR THIS, ANYWAY?
S...STEP THIS WAY AND YOU'LL UNDER-STAND...
WHOA. TOTAL SF.
NIRE

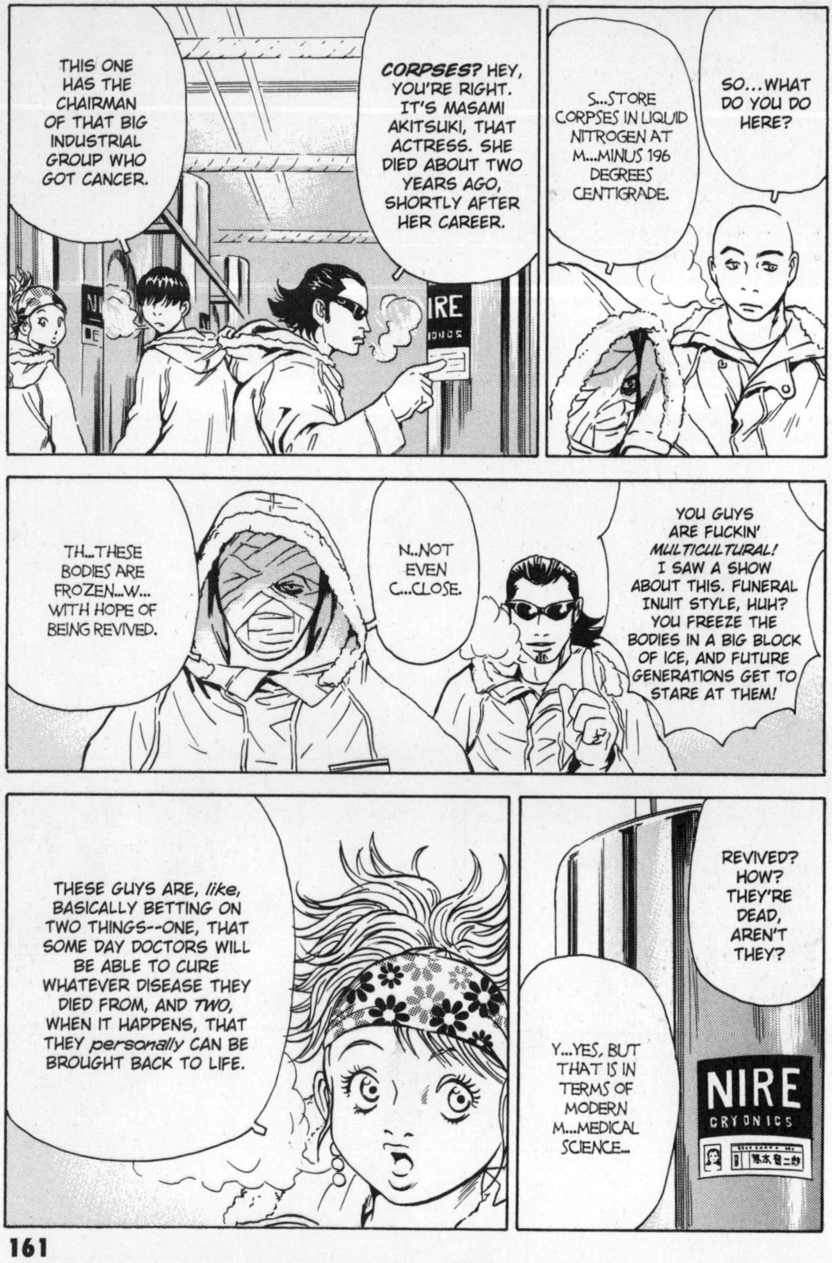
SO...WHAT DO YOU DO HERE?
S...STORE CORPSES IN LIQUID NITROGEN AT M...MINUS 196 DEGREES CENTIGRADE.
CORPSES? HEY, YOU'RE RIGHT. IT'S MASAMI AKITSUKI, THAT ACTRESS. SHE DIED ABOUT TWO YEARS AGO, SHORTLY AFTER HER CAREER.
THIS ONE HAS THE CHAIRMAN OF THAT BIG INDUSTRIAL GROUP WHO GOT CANCER.
YOU GUYS ARE FUCKIN' *MULTICULTURAL!* I SAW A SHOW ABOUT THIS. FUNERAL INUIT STYLE, HUH? YOU FREEZE THE BODIES IN A BIG BLOCK OF ICE, AND FUTURE GENERATIONS GET TO STARE AT THEM!
N..NOT EVEN C...CLOSE.
TH...THESE BODIES ARE FROZEN...W... WITH HOPE OF BEING REVIVED.
REVIVED? HOW? THEY'RE DEAD, AREN'T THEY?
Y...YES, BUT THAT IS IN TERMS OF MODERN M...MEDICAL SCIENCE...
NIRE
CRYONICS
THESE GUYS ARE, *like*, BASICALLY BETTING ON TWO THINGS--ONE, THAT SOME DAY DOCTORS WILL BE ABLE TO CURE WHATEVER DISEASE THEY DIED FROM, AND *TWO*, WHEN IT HAPPENS, THAT THEY *personally* CAN BE BROUGHT BACK TO LIFE.

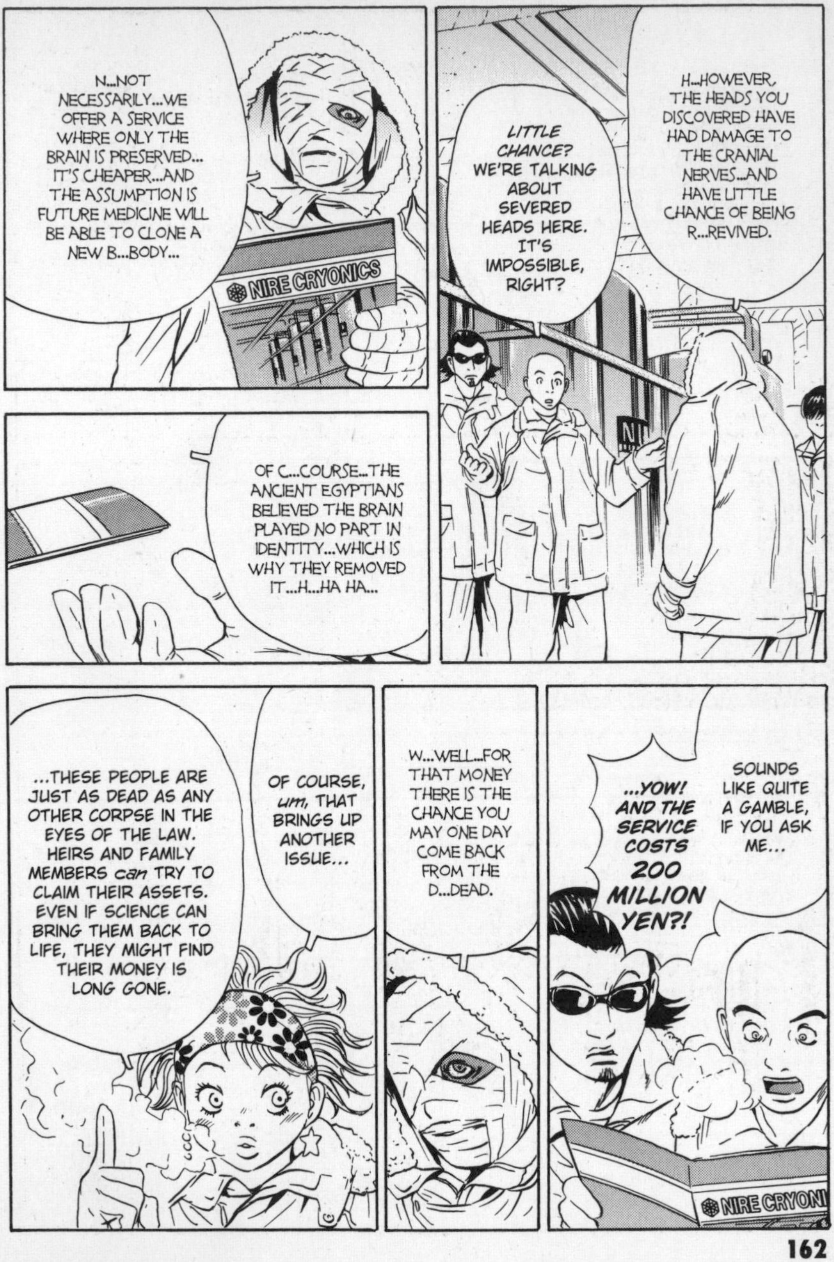
H...HOWEVER, THE HEADS YOU DISCOVERED HAVE HAD DAMAGE TO THE CRANIAL NERVES...AND HAVE LITTLE CHANCE OF BEING R...REVIVED.
LITTLE CHANCE? WE'RE TALKING ABOUT SEVERED HEADS HERE. IT'S IMPOSSIBLE, RIGHT?
N...NOT NECESSARILY...WE OFFER A SERVICE WHERE ONLY THE BRAIN IS PRESERVED... IT'S CHEAPER...AND THE ASSUMPTION IS FUTURE MEDICINE WILL BE ABLE TO CLONE A NEW B...BODY...
NIRE CRYONICS
OF C...COURSE...THE ANCIENT EGYPTIANS BELIEVED THE BRAIN PLAYED NO PART IN IDENTITY...WHICH IS WHY THEY REMOVED IT...H...HA HA...
SOUNDS LIKE QUITE A GAMBLE, IF YOU ASK ME...
...YOW! AND THE SERVICE COSTS 200 MILLION YEN?!
NIRE CRYONI
W...WELL...FOR THAT MONEY THERE IS THE CHANCE YOU MAY ONE DAY COME BACK FROM THE D...DEAD.
OF COURSE, *um*, THAT BRINGS UP ANOTHER ISSUE...
...THESE PEOPLE ARE JUST AS DEAD AS ANY OTHER CORPSE IN THE EYES OF THE LAW. HEIRS AND FAMILY MEMBERS *can* TRY TO CLAIM THEIR ASSETS. EVEN IF SCIENCE CAN BRING THEM BACK TO LIFE, THEY MIGHT FIND THEIR MONEY IS LONG GONE.

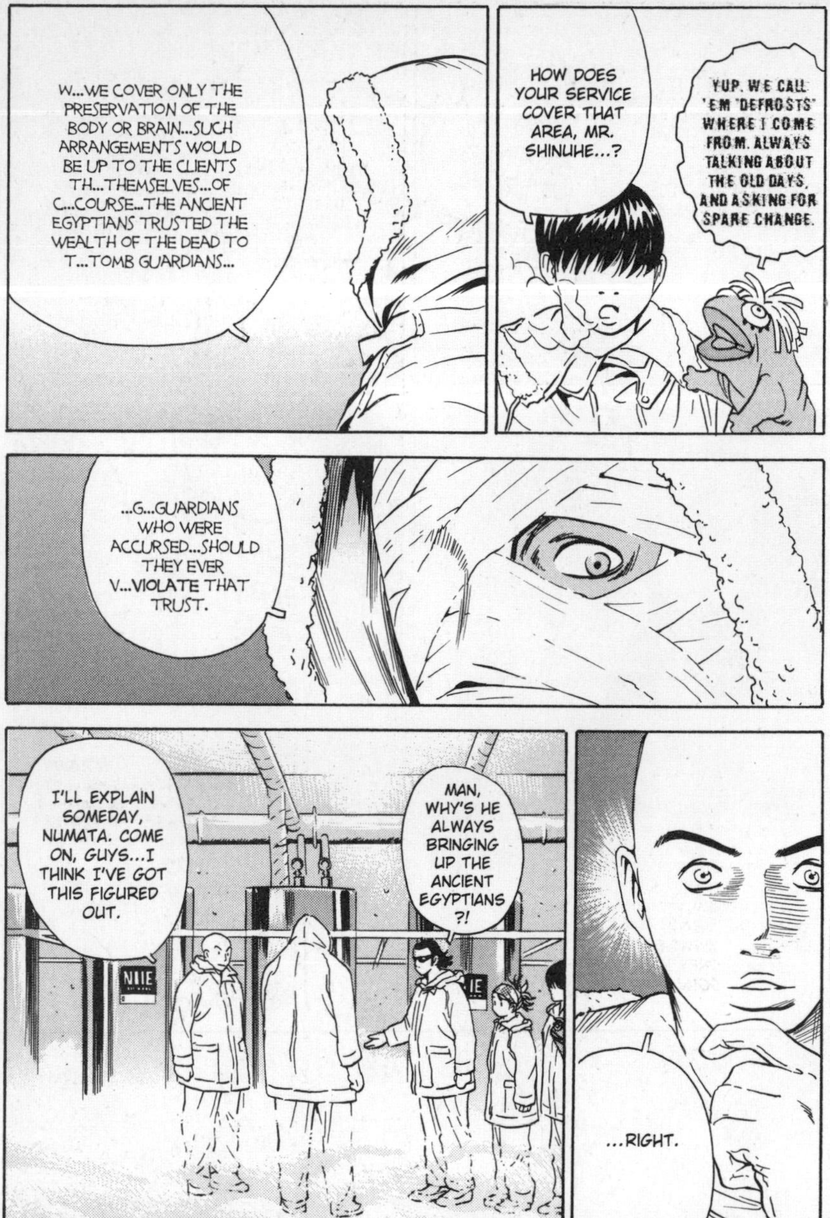
YUP. WE CALL 'EM "DEFROSTS" WHERE I COME FROM. ALWAYS TALKING ABOUT THE OLD DAYS, AND ASKING FOR SPARE CHANGE.
HOW DOES YOUR SERVICE COVER THAT AREA, MR. SHINUHE...?
W...WE COVER ONLY THE PRESERVATION OF THE BODY OR BRAIN...SUCH ARRANGEMENTS WOULD BE UP TO THE CLIENTS TH...THEMSELVES...OF C...COURSE...THE ANCIENT EGYPTIANS TRUSTED THE WEALTH OF THE DEAD TO T...TOMB GUARDIANS...
...G...GUARDIANS WHO WERE ACCURSED...SHOULD THEY EVER V...VIOLATE THAT TRUST.
...RIGHT.
MAN, WHY'S HE ALWAYS BRINGING UP THE ANCIENT EGYPTIANS ?!
I'LL EXPLAIN SOMEDAY, NUMATA. COME ON, GUYS...I THINK I'VE GOT THIS FIGURED OUT.

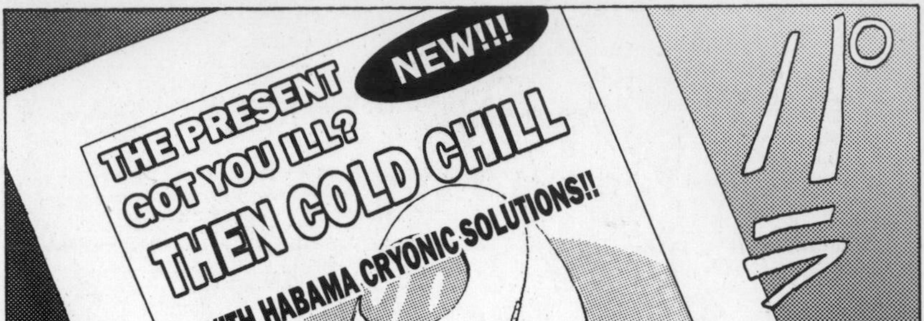
THE PRESENT GOT YOU ILL?
NEW!!!
THEN COLD CHILL
WITH HABAMA CRYONIC SOLUTIONS!!
HOT, RECKLESS, TOTALLY INSANE.
EXPERTS PREDICT FOR THE FUTURE
1997: Manhattan is maximum-security prison
2019: A new life awaits you in the off-world colonies
2052: One billionth Betamax sold
*"HOT" is a term of art meaning "gnarly," and should not be here interpreted as to refer to an elevated temperature. Clients are stored at a temperature of -196° C. Quality tested by Habama V-P Tosuke Himuro!
Still fresh after six months!
HABAMA CORPORATION
TEL03-0XX-22XX
パラ
LOOK...

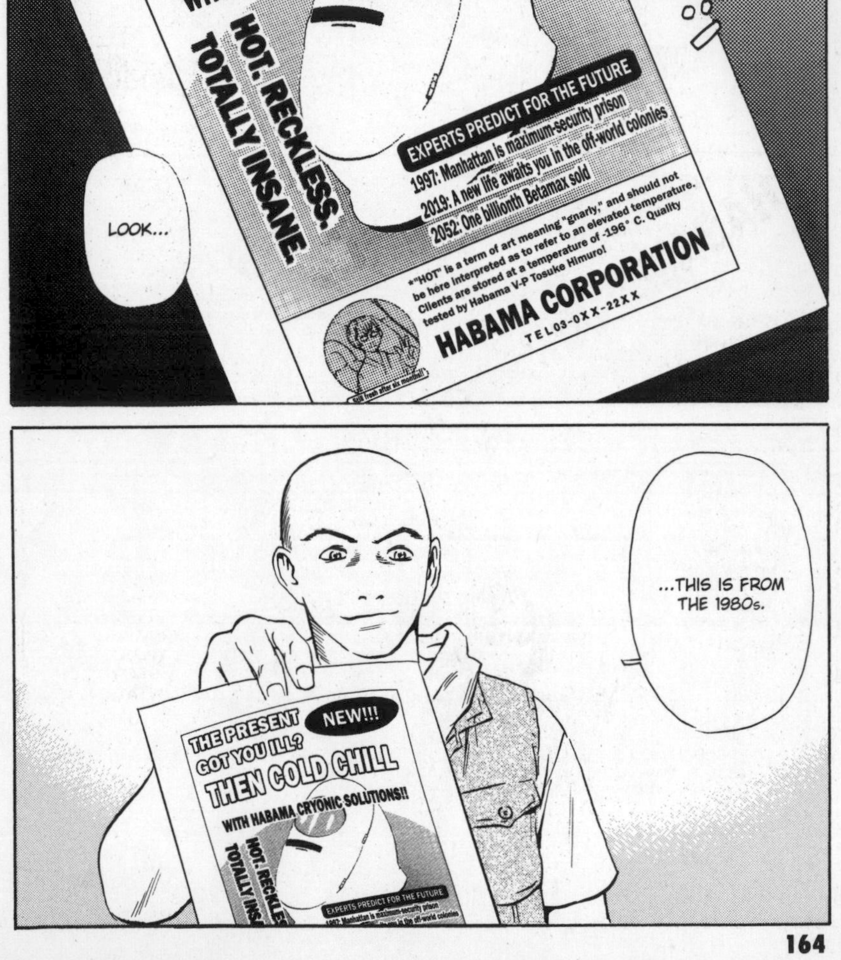
...THIS IS FROM THE 1980s.
THE PRESENT GOT YOU ILL?
NEW!!!
THEN COLD CHILL
WITH HABAMA CRYONIC SOLUTIONS!!
EXPERTS PREDICT FOR THE FUTURE

What does "gnarly" mean?
I USED THAT ADVANCED METHOD OF INFORMATION RETRIEVAL KNOWN AS THE PUBLIC LIBRARY. YOU KNOW, THERE ARE ALL KINDS OF BOOKS AND MAGAZINES OUT THERE THAT HAVE NEVER BEEN SCANNED.
HOW DID YOU FIND IT...?
I looked all over the net.
...IF IT MAKES YOU FEEL BETTER, THOUGH, THEY HARDLY HAD ANY PORN.
ANYHOW, THESE ARE THE GUYS.
THIS IS THE AD THEY MUST HAVE TAKEN OUT TO HELP REEL IN THE SUCKERS.
HABAMA CORPORAT
by Habama V-P Tosuke
TEL 03-0XX-22XX
WE'RE GOING TO HAVE SOME DIFFICULTY PROVING A CRIME, THOUGH...THE STATUTE OF LIMITATIONS IS...
WHAT KIND OF IDIOT WOULD HAVE BELIEVED THIS ANYWAY?
Um, THEY CLAIMED THAT THEIR VICE-PRESIDENT TESTED THE TECHNOLOGY...

THAT'S THEIR VICE-PRESIDENT... TOSUKE HIMURO...?
...YOU DON'T THINK HE WAS THAT SAME GUY WHO...
HA
Still fresh after six months!!
BUT THAT'S GOTTA BE A LIE, TOO. YOU SAID THAT EVEN TODAY, NO ONE KNOWS HOW TO REVIVE PEOPLE YET!
THERE WAS A TOSUKE HIMURO WHO HABAMA WORKED WITH ON OCCASION... BUT...
WELL, HABAMA'S DEAD--THIS GUY'S GOTTA KNOW WHERE THE BODIES ARE BURIED!
OR AT LEAST THE HEADS.
I WISH I COULD SAY THAT WAS A METAPHOR ...
...BUT I JUST CAN'T.

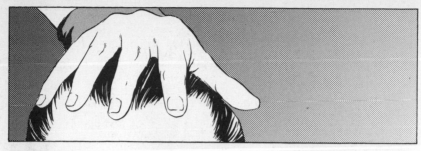

A...SC..AM...
WE'VE...BE...EN...
RO...BBED...

PLEA...SE...
GE...T...O...UR...
MO...NEY...
B...ACK...FOR...
US...

UH, YEAH...
IT'S A LITTLE
LATE TO
FIGURE THAT
OUT--ABOUT
TWENTY-
THREE
YEARS.

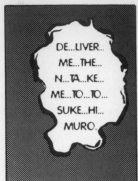

...BUT WE'RE NOT EXACTLY DEBT COLLECTORS. WE'VE GOT PLENTY OF DEBT ON OUR OWN.
YEAH. OUR JOB IS TO DELIVER BODIES WHEREVER THEY WANT TO GO.
DE...LIVER... ME...THE... N...TA...KE... ME...TO...TO... SUKE...HI... MURO.
JU...ST...IN... CAS...E...I...KE... PT...SOM...E... FUN...DS...ON... ME...
...I...CA...N.... PA...Y...YOU.
KEPT?
HOW?!

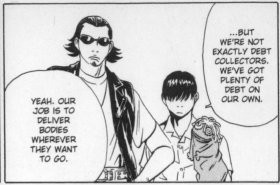

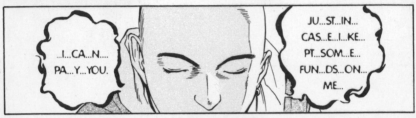

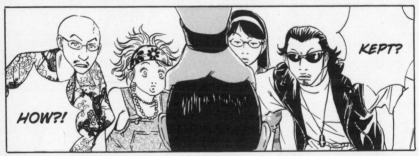

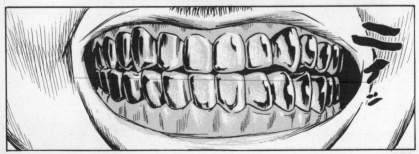

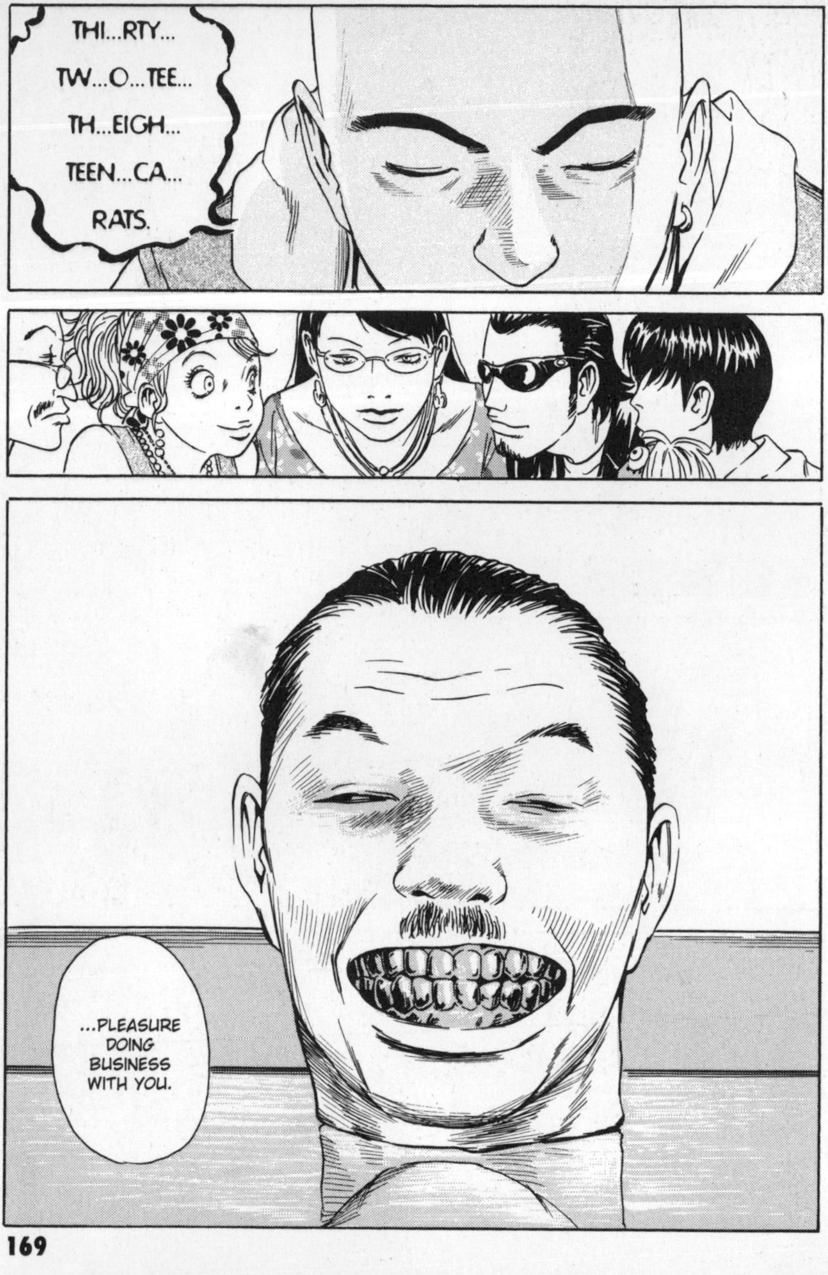
THI...RTY... TW...O...TEE... TH...EIGH... TEEN...CA... RATS.
...PLEASURE DOING BUSINESS WITH YOU.

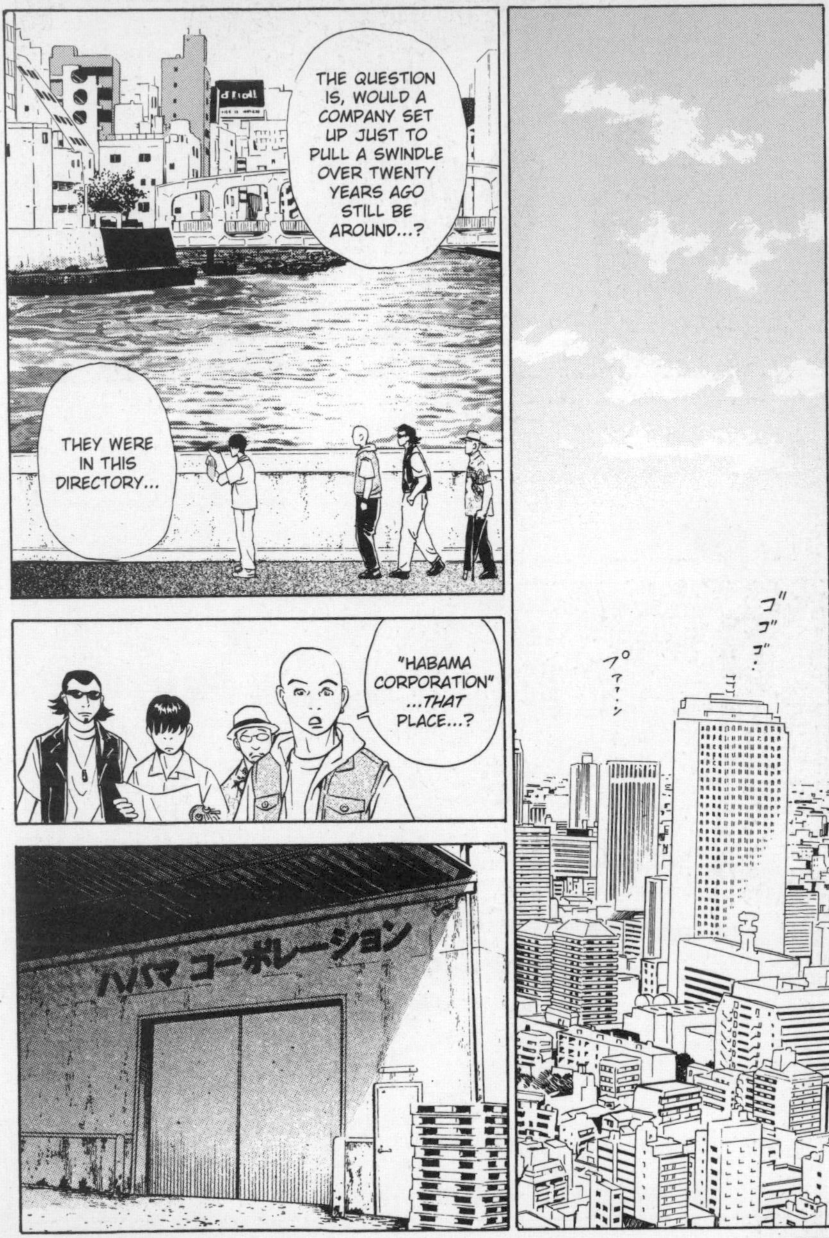
ゴゴゴ‥
プァァ‥ン
THE QUESTION IS, WOULD A COMPANY SET UP JUST TO PULL A SWINDLE OVER TWENTY YEARS AGO STILL BE AROUND...?
THEY WERE IN THIS DIRECTORY...
"HABAMA CORPORATION" ...*THAT* PLACE...?
ハバマ コーポレーション

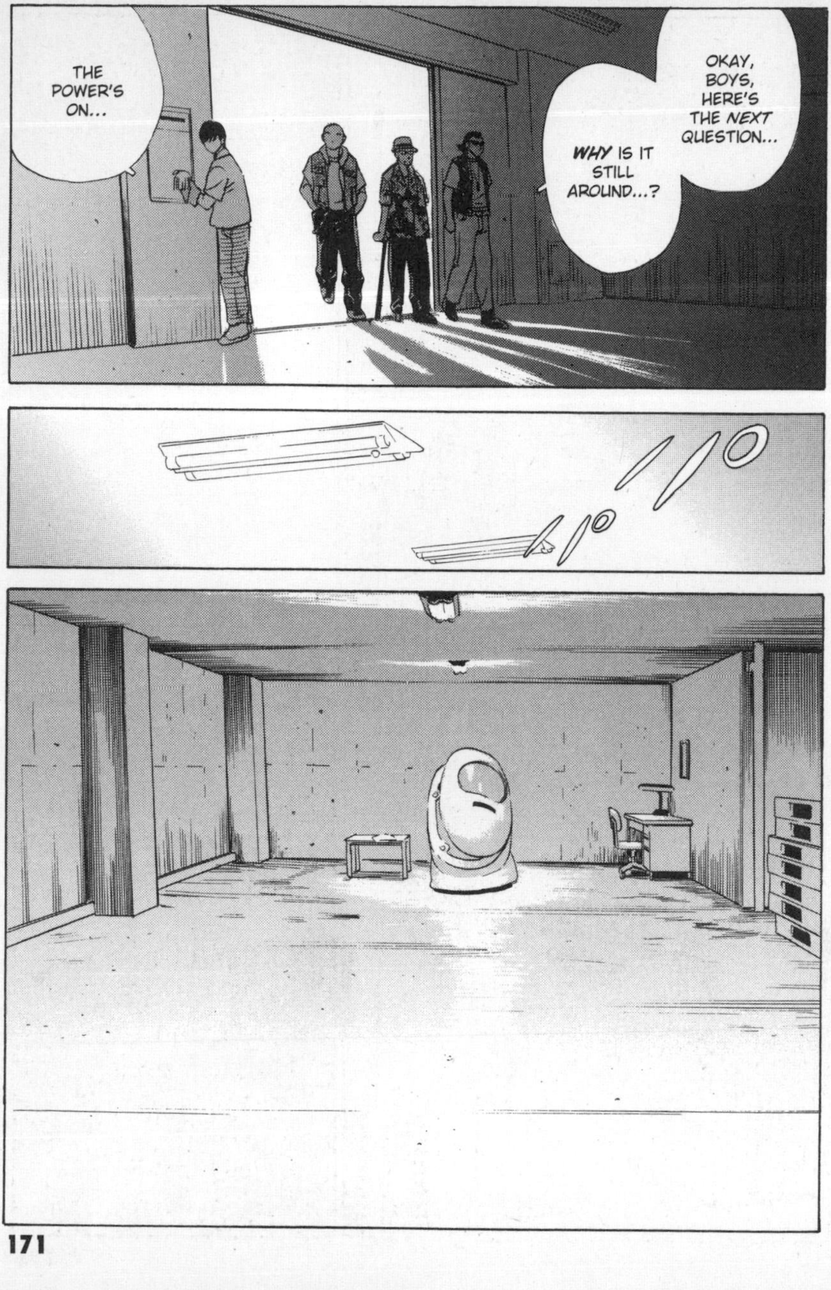
OKAY, BOYS, HERE'S THE *NEXT* QUESTION...
WHY IS IT STILL AROUND...?
THE POWER'S ON...

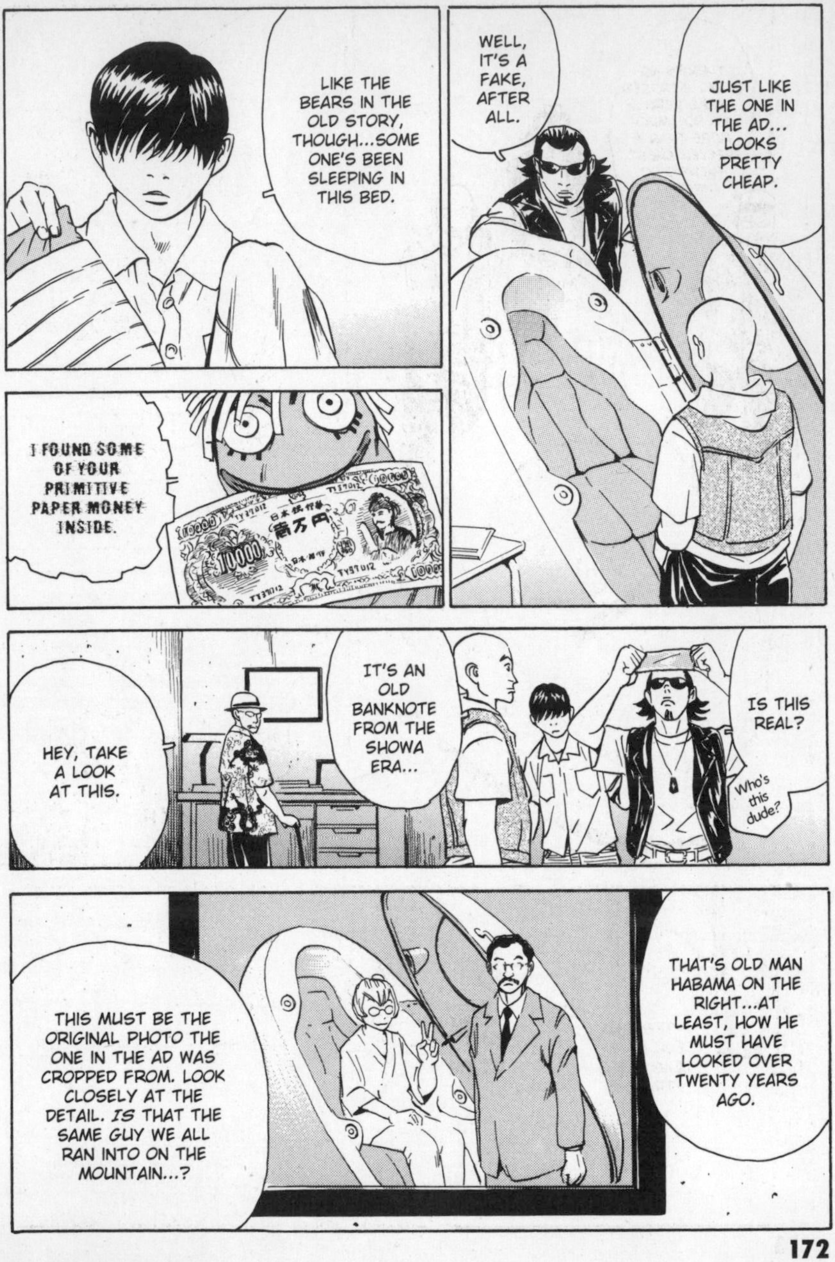
JUST LIKE THE ONE IN THE AD... LOOKS PRETTY CHEAP.
WELL, IT'S A FAKE, AFTER ALL.
LIKE THE BEARS IN THE OLD STORY, THOUGH...SOME ONE'S BEEN SLEEPING IN THIS BED.
I FOUND SOME OF YOUR PRIMITIVE PAPER MONEY INSIDE.
IS THIS REAL?
Who's this dude?
IT'S AN OLD BANKNOTE FROM THE SHOWA ERA...
HEY, TAKE A LOOK AT THIS.
THAT'S OLD MAN HABAMA ON THE RIGHT...AT LEAST, HOW HE MUST HAVE LOOKED OVER TWENTY YEARS AGO.
THIS MUST BE THE ORIGINAL PHOTO THE ONE IN THE AD WAS CROPPED FROM. LOOK CLOSELY AT THE DETAIL. *IS* THAT THE SAME GUY WE ALL RAN INTO ON THE MOUNTAIN...?

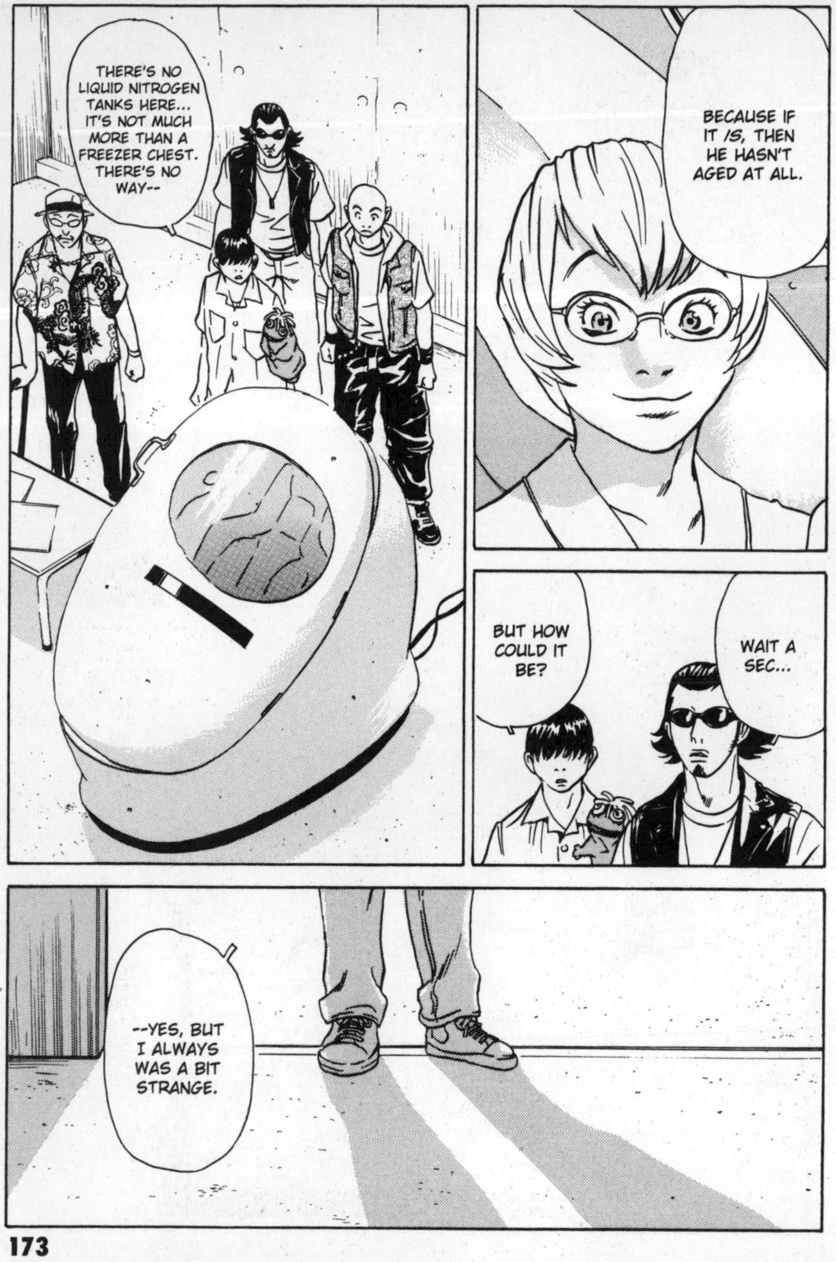
BECAUSE IF IT *IS*, THEN HE HASN'T AGED AT ALL.
WAIT A SEC...
BUT HOW COULD IT BE?
THERE'S NO LIQUID NITROGEN TANKS HERE... IT'S NOT MUCH MORE THAN A FREEZER CHEST. THERE'S NO WAY--
--YES, BUT I ALWAYS WAS A BIT STRANGE.

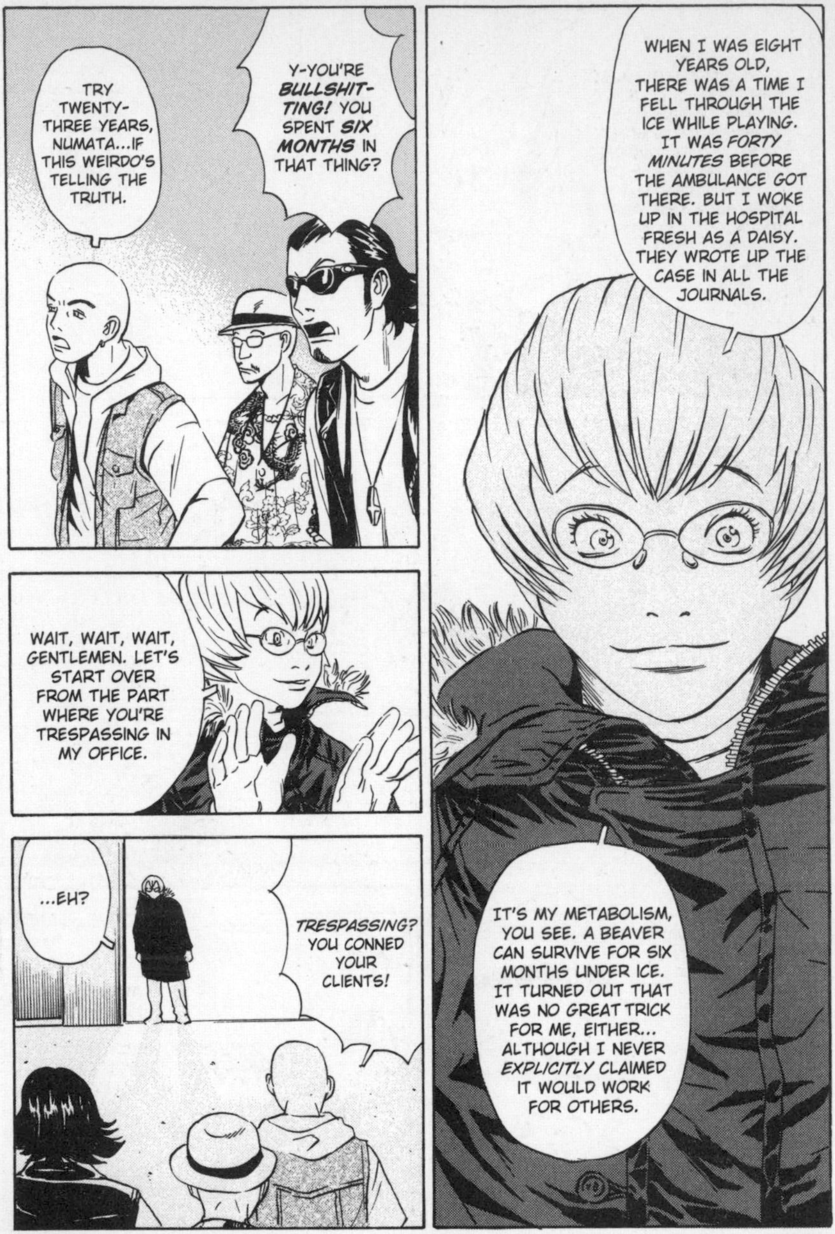
WHEN I WAS EIGHT YEARS OLD, THERE WAS A TIME I FELL THROUGH THE ICE WHILE PLAYING. IT WAS *FORTY MINUTES* BEFORE THE AMBULANCE GOT THERE. BUT I WOKE UP IN THE HOSPITAL FRESH AS A DAISY. THEY WROTE UP THE CASE IN ALL THE JOURNALS.
IT'S MY METABOLISM, YOU SEE. A BEAVER CAN SURVIVE FOR SIX MONTHS UNDER ICE. IT TURNED OUT THAT WAS NO GREAT TRICK FOR ME, EITHER... ALTHOUGH I NEVER *EXPLICITLY* CLAIMED IT WOULD WORK FOR OTHERS.
Y-YOU'RE ***BULLSHITTING!*** YOU SPENT ***SIX MONTHS*** IN THAT THING?
TRY TWENTY-THREE YEARS, NUMATA...IF THIS WEIRDO'S TELLING THE TRUTH.
WAIT, WAIT, WAIT, GENTLEMEN. LET'S START OVER FROM THE PART WHERE YOU'RE TRESPASSING IN MY OFFICE.
TRESPASSING? YOU CONNED YOUR CLIENTS!
...EH?

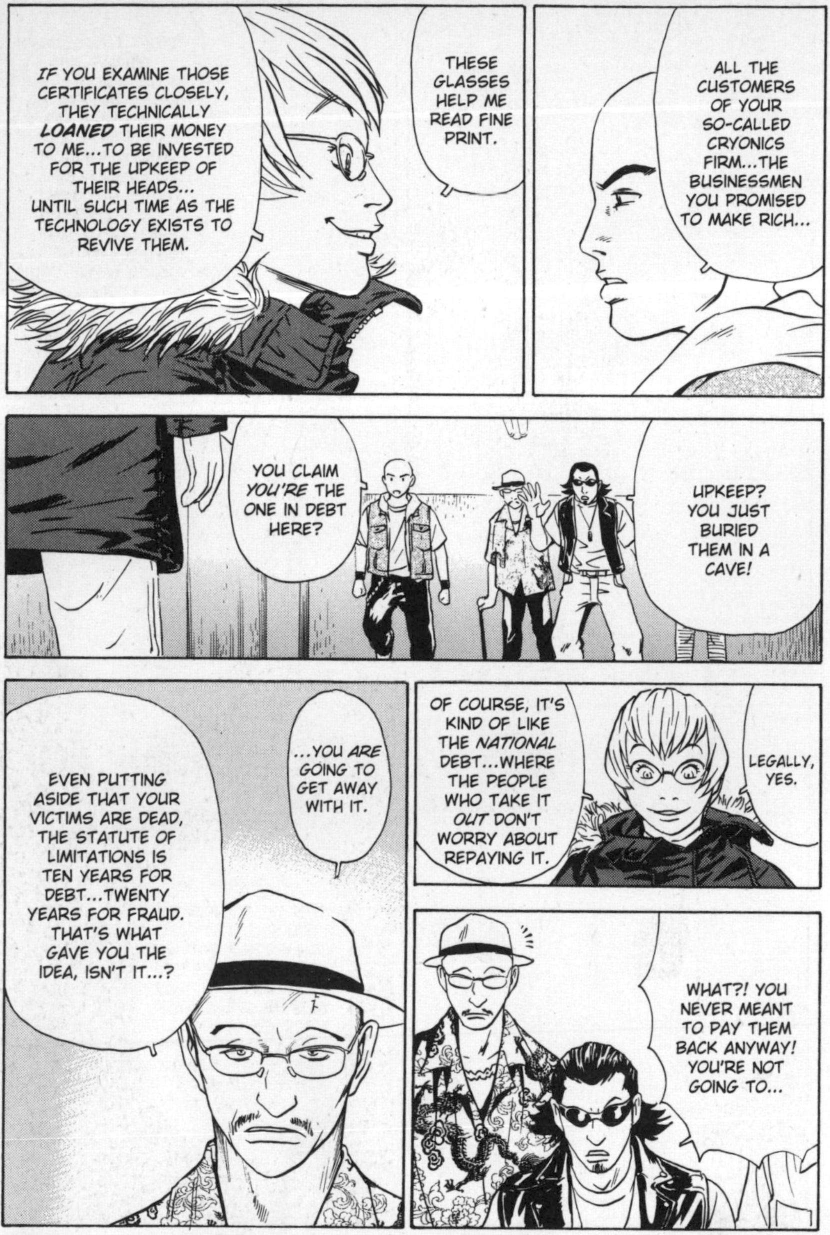
ALL THE CUSTOMERS OF YOUR SO-CALLED CRYONICS FIRM...THE BUSINESSMEN YOU PROMISED TO MAKE RICH...
THESE GLASSES HELP ME READ FINE PRINT.
IF YOU EXAMINE THOSE CERTIFICATES CLOSELY, THEY TECHNICALLY ***LOANED*** THEIR MONEY TO ME...TO BE INVESTED FOR THE UPKEEP OF THEIR HEADS... UNTIL SUCH TIME AS THE TECHNOLOGY EXISTS TO REVIVE THEM.
UPKEEP? YOU JUST BURIED THEM IN A CAVE!
YOU CLAIM *YOU'RE* THE ONE IN DEBT HERE?
LEGALLY, YES.
OF COURSE, IT'S KIND OF LIKE THE *NATIONAL* DEBT...WHERE THE PEOPLE WHO TAKE IT *OUT* DON'T WORRY ABOUT REPAYING IT.
WHAT?! YOU NEVER MEANT TO PAY THEM BACK ANYWAY! YOU'RE NOT GOING TO...
...YOU *ARE* GOING TO GET AWAY WITH IT.
EVEN PUTTING ASIDE THAT YOUR VICTIMS ARE DEAD, THE STATUTE OF LIMITATIONS IS TEN YEARS FOR DEBT...TWENTY YEARS FOR FRAUD. THAT'S WHAT GAVE YOU THE IDEA, ISN'T IT...?

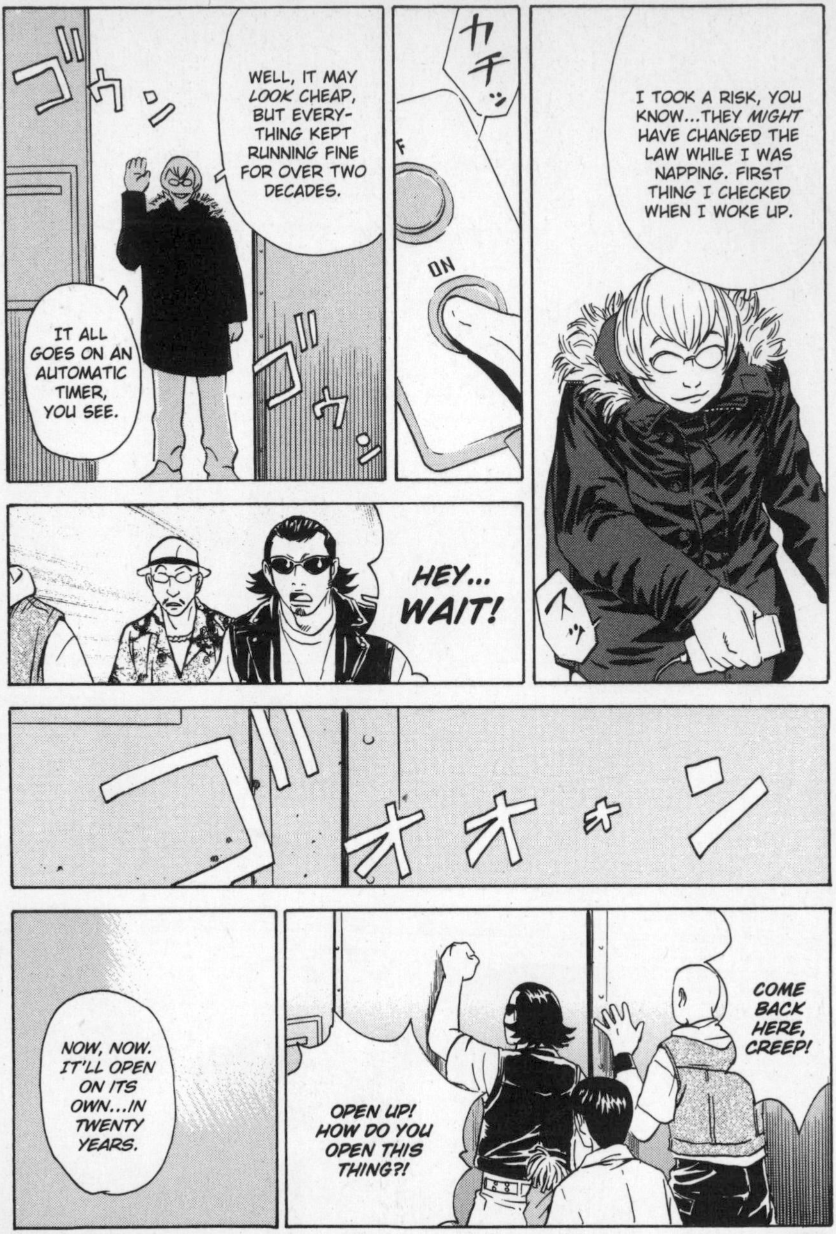
I TOOK A RISK, YOU KNOW...THEY *MIGHT* HAVE CHANGED THE LAW WHILE I WAS NAPPING. FIRST THING I CHECKED WHEN I WOKE UP.
ON
WELL, IT MAY *LOOK* CHEAP, BUT EVERY-THING KEPT RUNNING FINE FOR OVER TWO DECADES.
IT ALL GOES ON AN AUTOMATIC TIMER, YOU SEE.
HEY... WAIT!
COME BACK HERE, CREEP!
OPEN UP! HOW DO YOU OPEN THIS THING?!
NOW, NOW. IT'LL OPEN ON ITS OWN...IN TWENTY YEARS.

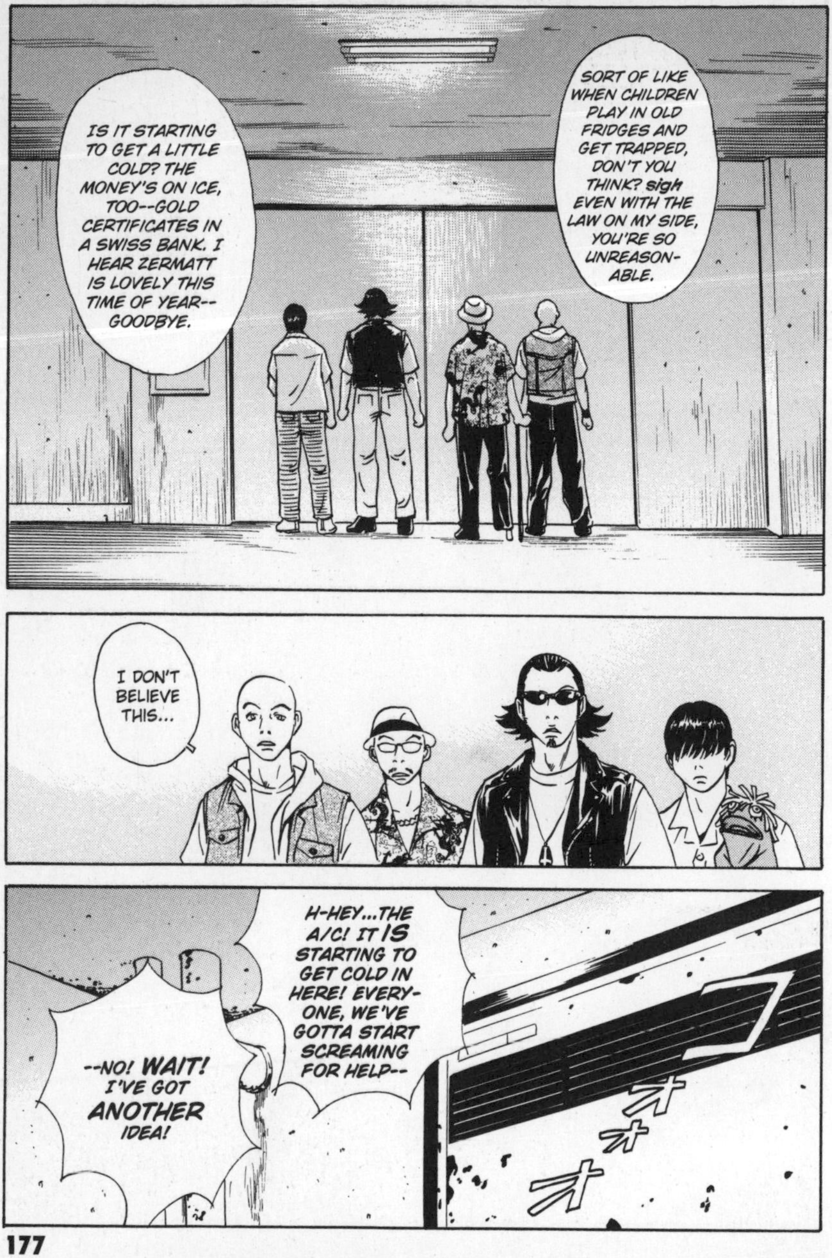
SORT OF LIKE WHEN CHILDREN PLAY IN OLD FRIDGES AND GET TRAPPED, DON'T YOU THINK? sigh EVEN WITH THE LAW ON MY SIDE, YOU'RE SO UNREASON-ABLE.
IS IT STARTING TO GET A LITTLE COLD? THE MONEY'S ON ICE, TOO--GOLD CERTIFICATES IN A SWISS BANK. I HEAR ZERMATT IS LOVELY THIS TIME OF YEAR-- GOODBYE.
I DON'T BELIEVE THIS...
オオオ
H-HEY...THE A/C! IT IS STARTING TO GET COLD IN HERE! EVERY-ONE, WE'VE GOTTA START SCREAMING FOR HELP--
--NO! WAIT! I'VE GOT ANOTHER IDEA!

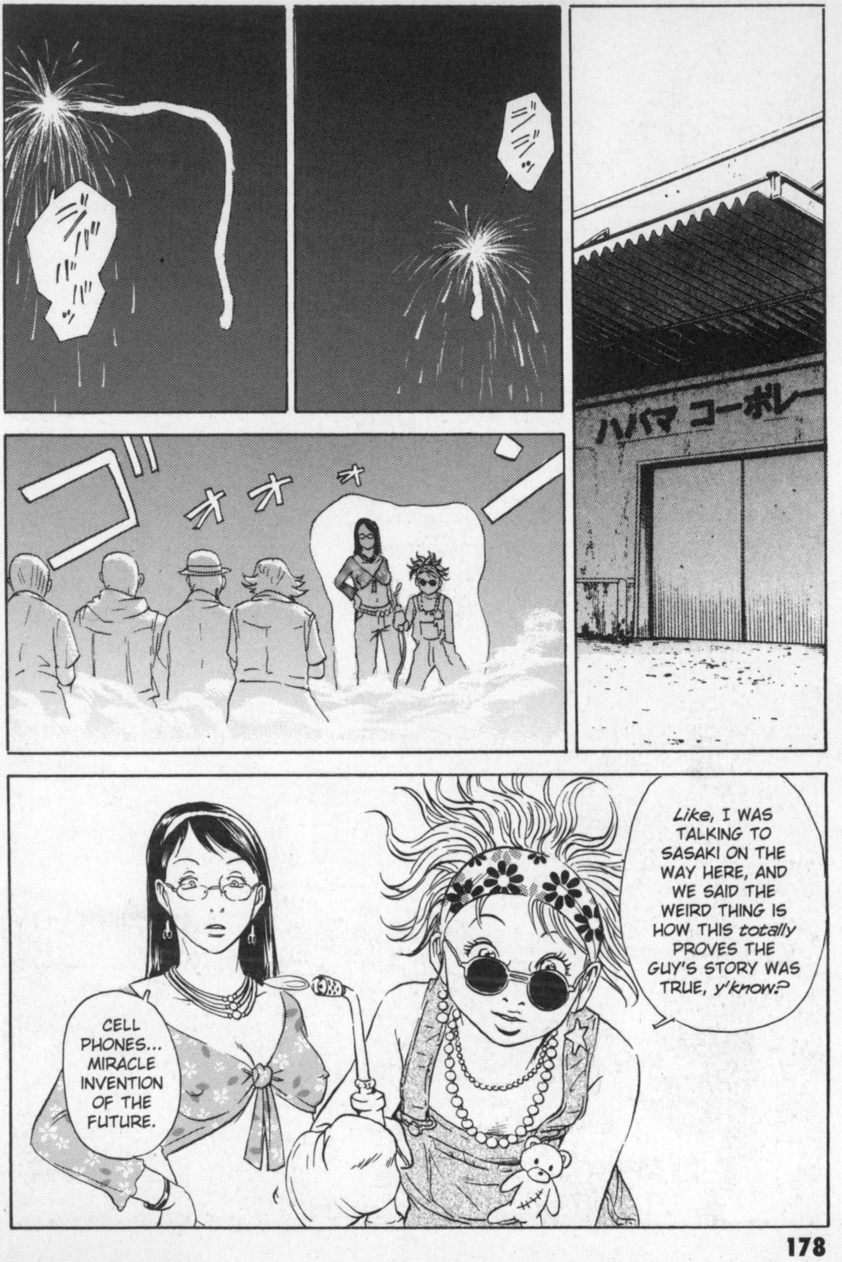
ハバマ コーポレー
ジジジッ
ゴオオオン
Like, I WAS TALKING TO SASAKI ON THE WAY HERE, AND WE SAID THE WEIRD THING IS HOW THIS *totally* PROVES THE GUY'S STORY WAS TRUE, *y'know?*
CELL PHONES... MIRACLE INVENTION OF THE FUTURE.

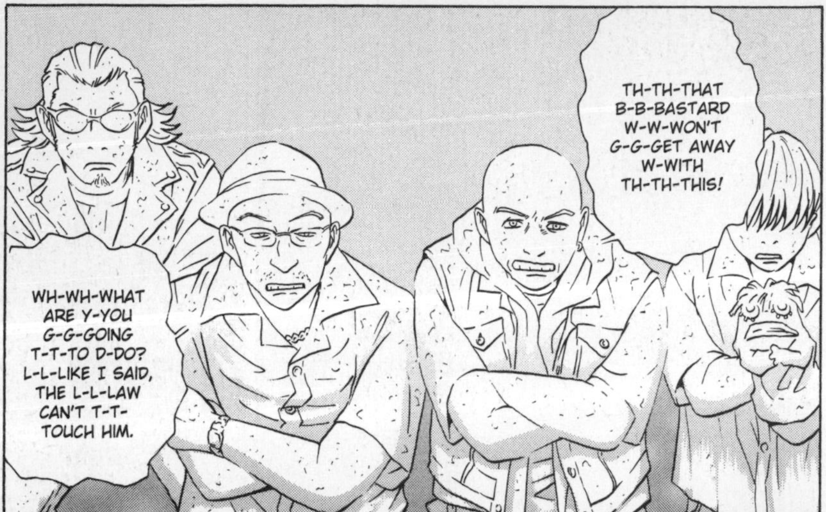
TH-TH-THAT B-B-BASTARD W-W-WON'T G-G-GET AWAY W-WITH TH-TH-THIS!
WH-WH-WHAT ARE Y-YOU G-G-GOING T-T-TO D-DO? L-L-LIKE I SAID, THE L-L-LAW CAN'T T-T-TOUCH HIM.
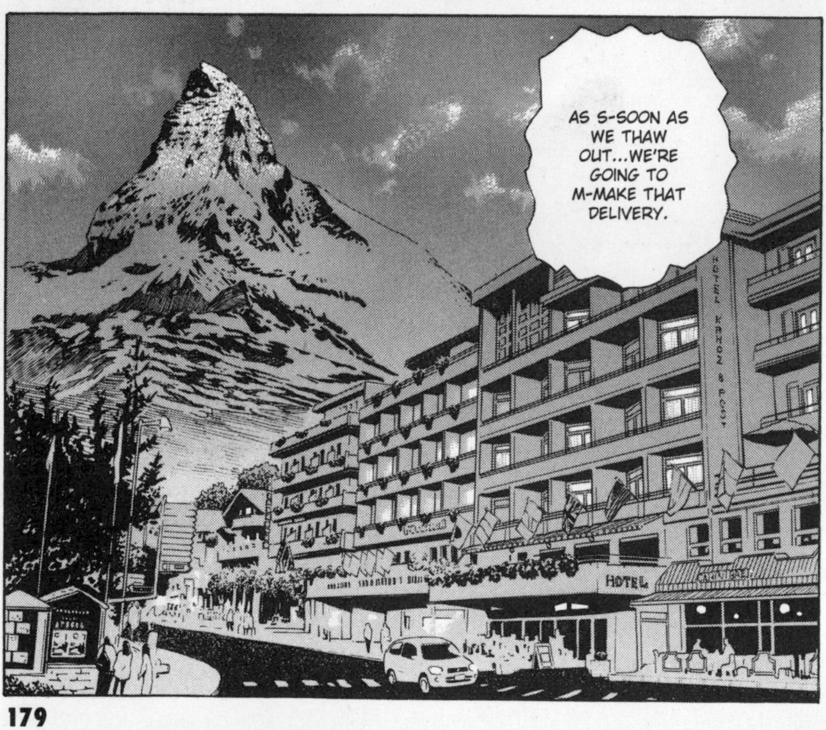
AS S-SOON AS WE THAW OUT...WE'RE GOING TO M-MAKE THAT DELIVERY.
HOTEL

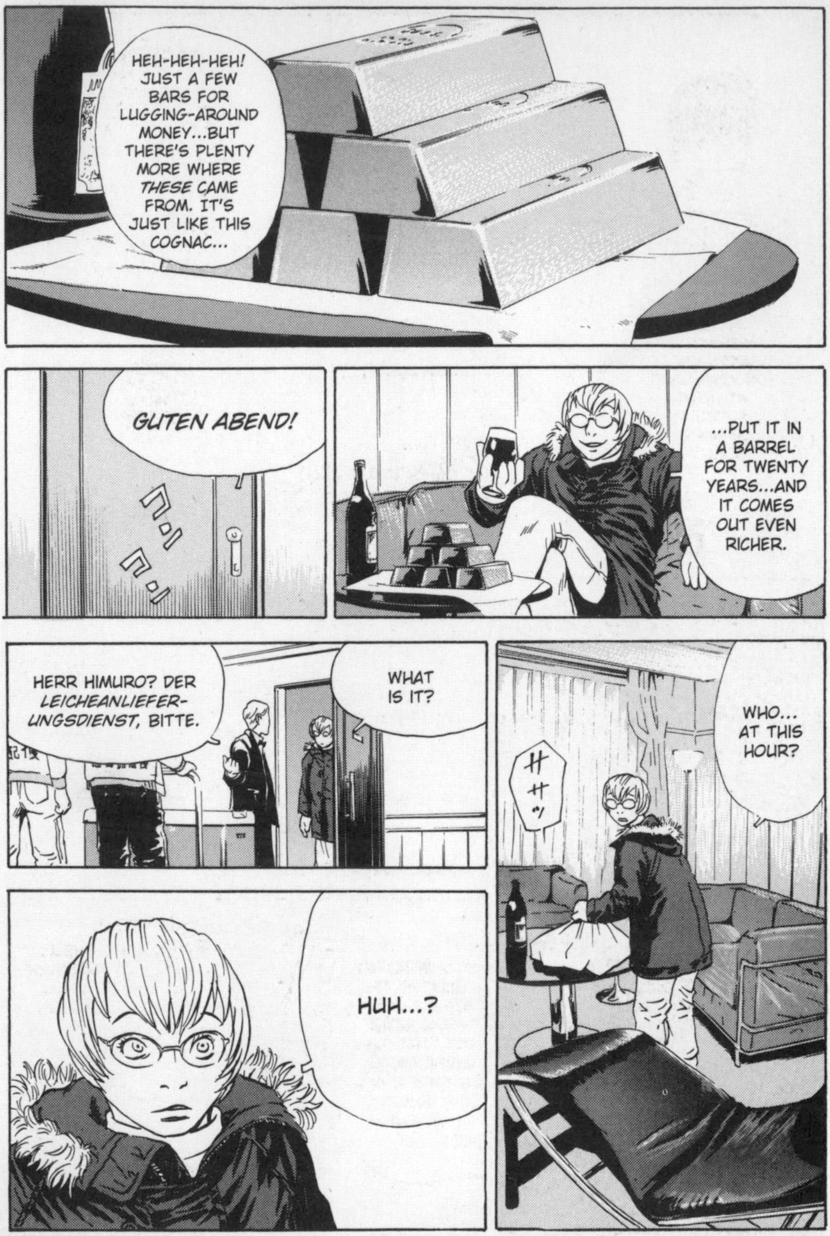
HEH-HEH-HEH! JUST A FEW BARS FOR LUGGING-AROUND MONEY...BUT THERE'S PLENTY MORE WHERE *THESE* CAME FROM. IT'S JUST LIKE THIS COGNAC...
...PUT IT IN A BARREL FOR TWENTY YEARS...AND IT COMES OUT EVEN RICHER.
GUTEN ABEND!
WHO... AT THIS HOUR?
WHAT IS IT?
HERR HIMURO? DER *LEICHEANLIEFER-UNGSDIENST*, BITTE.
HUH...?

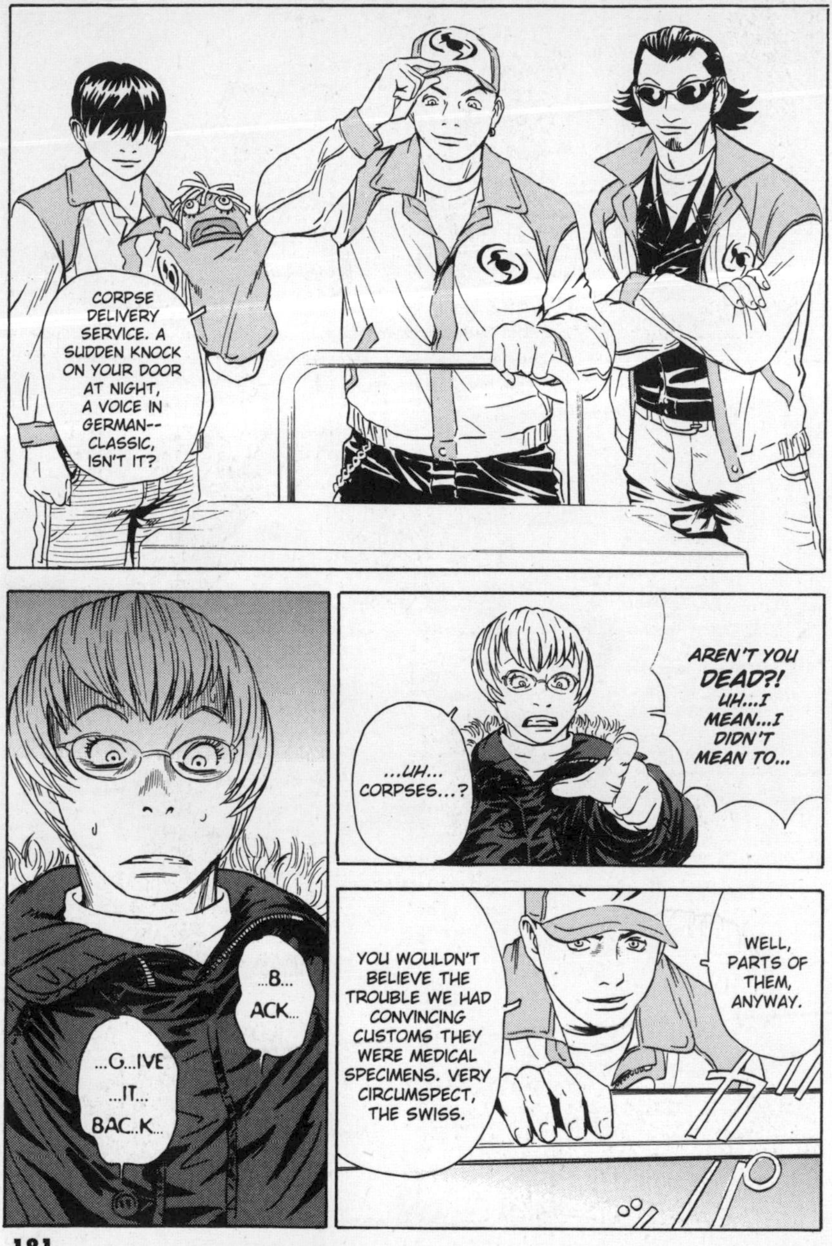
CORPSE DELIVERY SERVICE. A SUDDEN KNOCK ON YOUR DOOR AT NIGHT, A VOICE IN GERMAN-- CLASSIC, ISN'T IT?
AREN'T YOU **DEAD?!** UH...I MEAN...I DIDN'T MEAN TO...
...UH... CORPSES...?
WELL, PARTS OF THEM, ANYWAY.
YOU WOULDN'T BELIEVE THE TROUBLE WE HAD CONVINCING CUSTOMS THEY WERE MEDICAL SPECIMENS. VERY CIRCUMSPECT, THE SWISS.
...B... ACK...
...G..IVE ...IT... BAC..K...

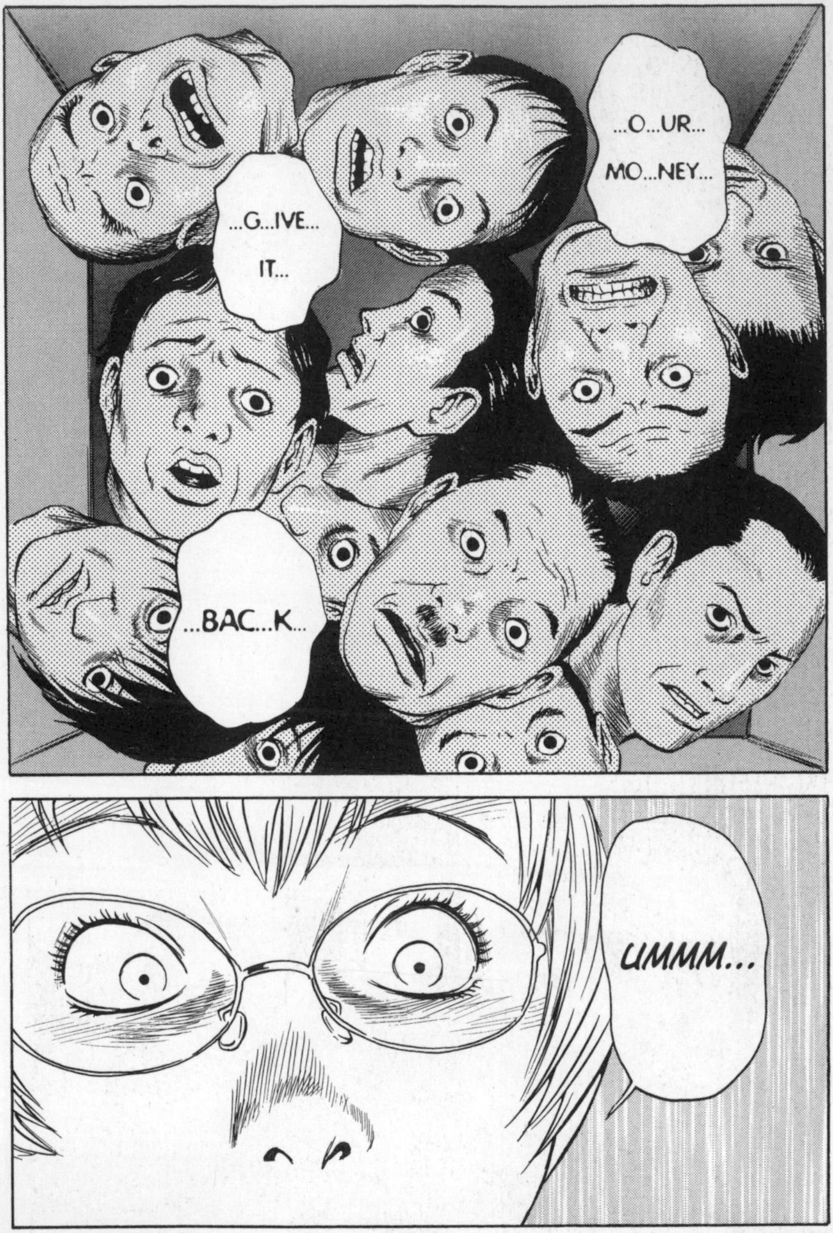
...O...UR... MO...NEY...
...G...IVE... IT...
...BAC...K...
UMMM...

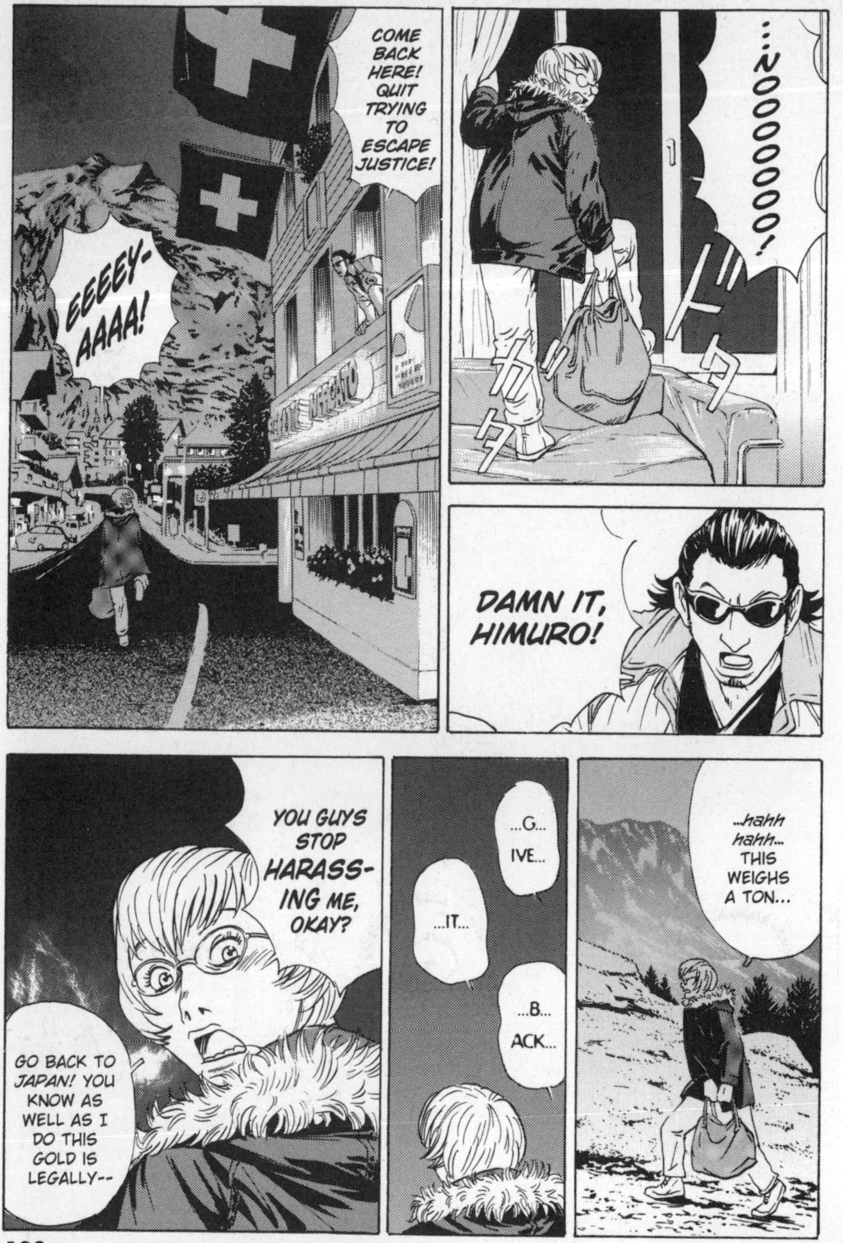
...NOOOOOOOO!
DAMN IT, HIMURO!
COME BACK HERE! QUIT TRYING TO ESCAPE JUSTICE!
EEEEY-AAAA!
...hahh hahh... THIS WEIGHS A TON...
...G... IVE...
...IT...
...B... ACK...
YOU GUYS STOP HARASS-ING ME, OKAY?
GO BACK TO JAPAN! YOU KNOW AS WELL AS I DO THIS GOLD IS LEGALLY--

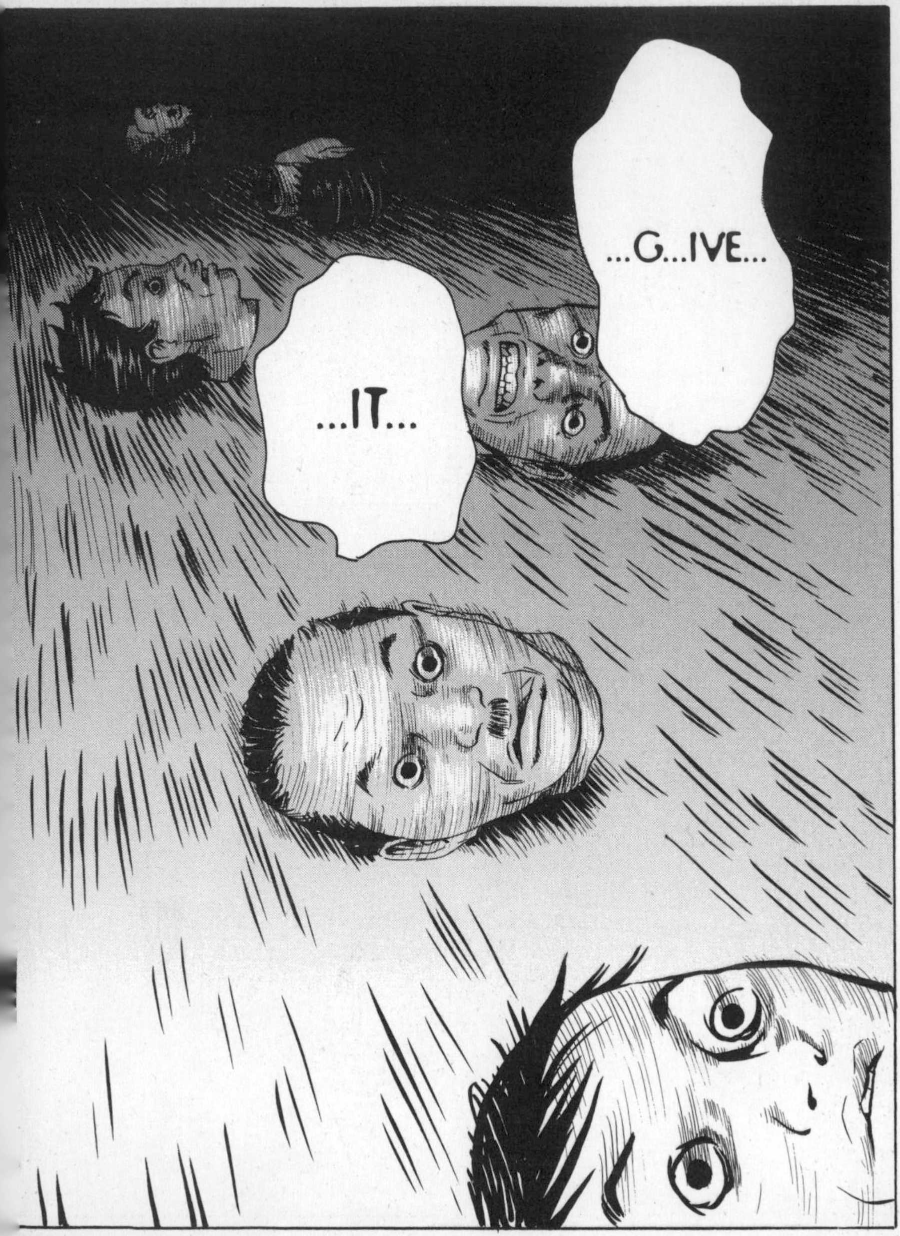
...G...IVE...
...IT...

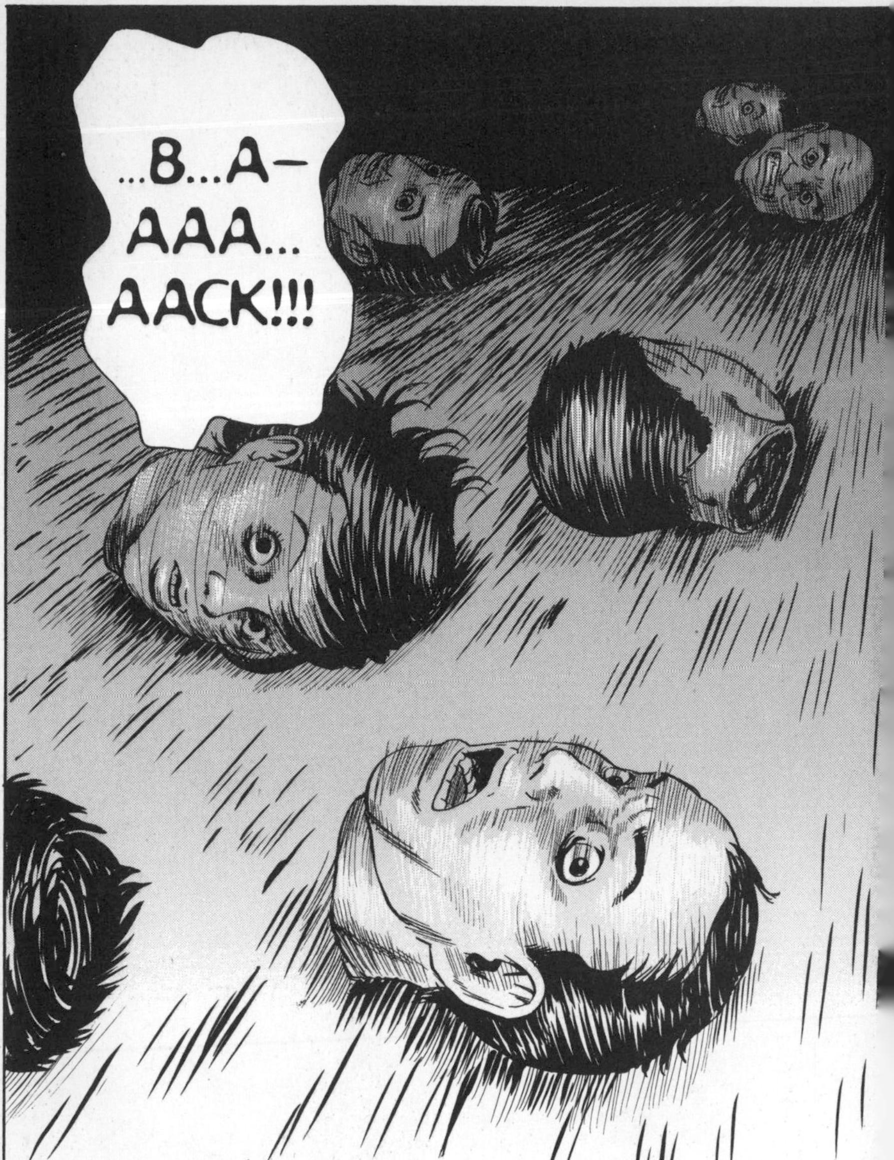
...B...A—
AAA...
AACK!!!

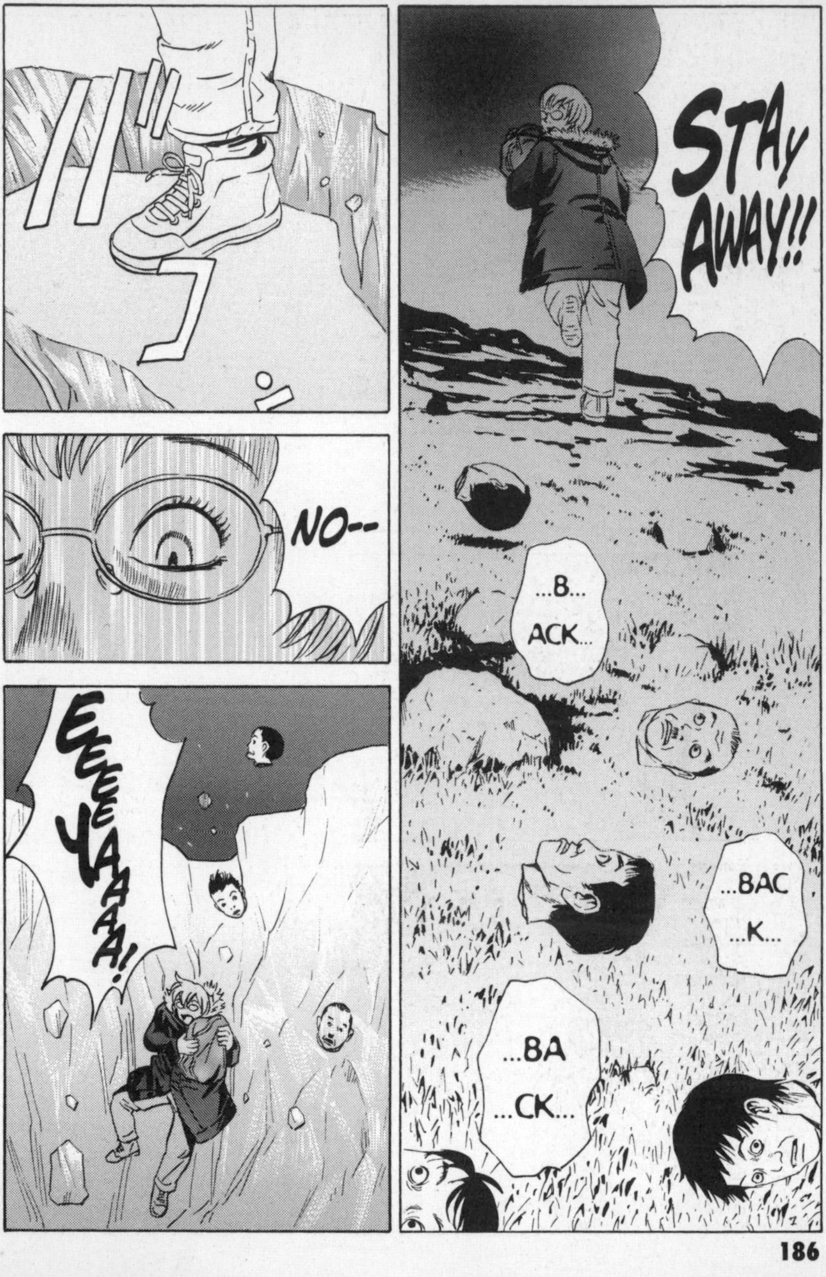
STAY AWAY!!
...B... ACK...
...BAC ...K...
...BA ...CK...
NO--
EEEEEYAAAA!

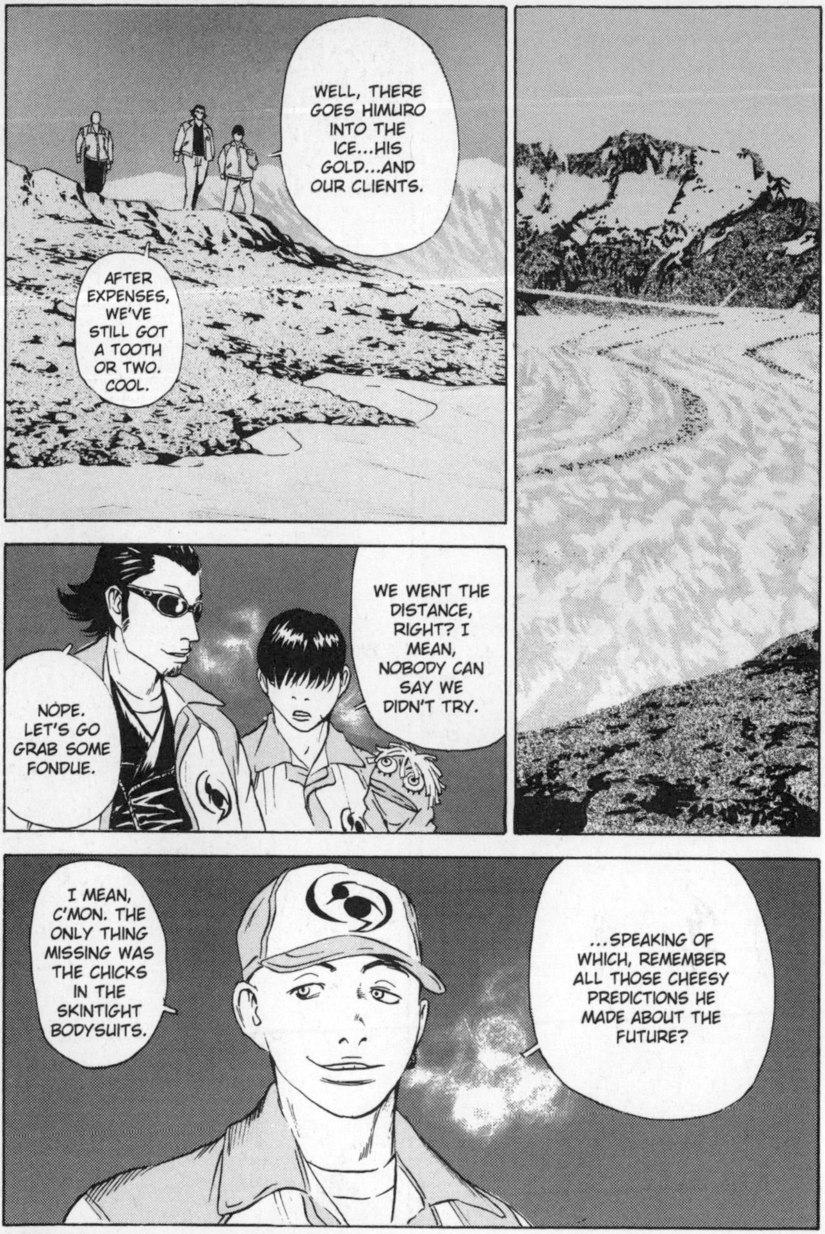
WELL, THERE GOES HIMURO INTO THE ICE...HIS GOLD...AND OUR CLIENTS.
AFTER EXPENSES, WE'VE STILL GOT A TOOTH OR TWO. COOL.
WE WENT THE DISTANCE, RIGHT? I MEAN, NOBODY CAN SAY WE DIDN'T TRY.
NOPE. LET'S GO GRAB SOME FONDUE.
I MEAN, C'MON. THE ONLY THING MISSING WAS THE CHICKS IN THE SKINTIGHT BODYSUITS.
...SPEAKING OF WHICH, REMEMBER ALL THOSE CHEESY PREDICTIONS HE MADE ABOUT THE FUTURE?

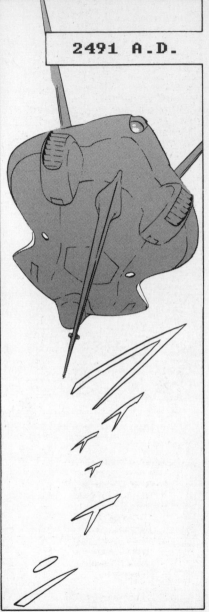

2491 A.D.

...THE DISCOVERY MADE BY RESEARCHERS STUDYING THE KLEIN MATTERHORN GLACIER, ONE OF THE FEW TO SURVIVE THE PERIOD OF GLOBAL WARMING.

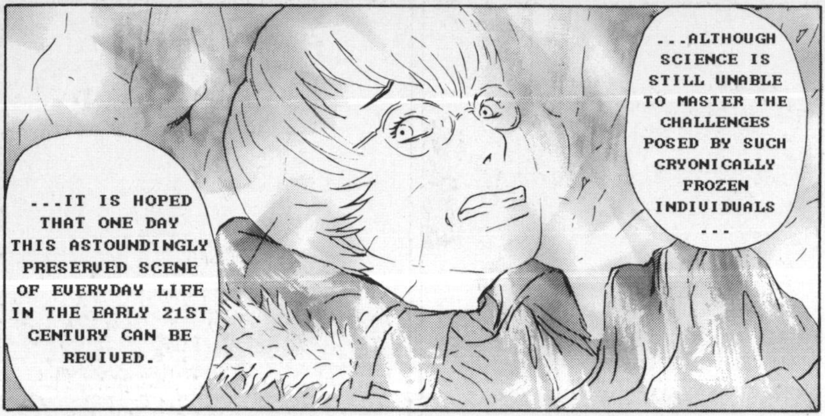
...ALTHOUGH SCIENCE IS STILL UNABLE TO MASTER THE CHALLENGES POSED BY SUCH CRYONICALLY FROZEN INDIVIDUALS ...
...IT IS HOPED THAT ONE DAY THIS ASTOUNDINGLY PRESERVED SCENE OF EVERYDAY LIFE IN THE EARLY 21ST CENTURY CAN BE REVIVED.

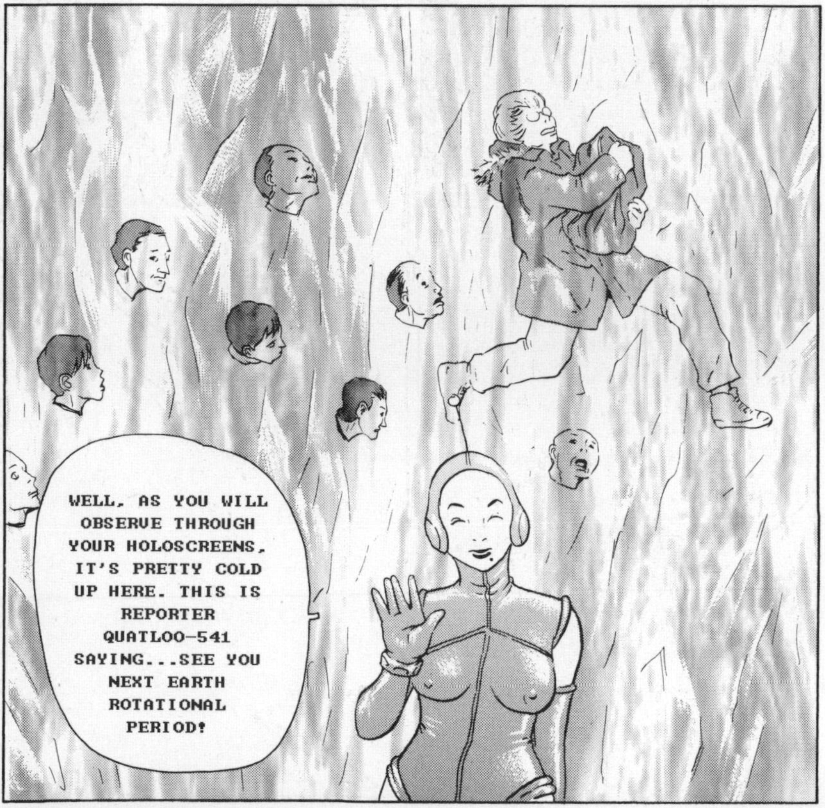
WELL, AS YOU WILL OBSERVE THROUGH YOUR HOLOSCREENS, IT'S PRETTY COLD UP HERE. THIS IS REPORTER QUATLOO-541 SAYING...SEE YOU NEXT EARTH ROTATIONAL PERIOD!

4th delivery: preparing for a journey—the end

the KUROSAGI corpse delivery service

黒鷺死体宅配便

eiji otsuka 大塚英志 housui yamazaki 山崎峰水

designer **HEIDI FAINZA**
editorial assistant **RACHEL MILLER**
art director **LIA RIBACCHI**
publisher **MIKE RICHARDSON**

English-language version
produced by Dark Horse Comics

THE KUROSAGI CORPSE DELIVERY SERVICE VOL. 5
© EIJI OTSUKA OFFICE 2005, © HOUSUI YAMAZAKI 2005. First published in
Japan in 2005 by KADOKAWA SHOTEN Publishing Co., Ltd., Tokyo. English
translation rights arranged with KADOKAWA SHOTEN Publishing Co., Ltd., Tokyo,
through TOHAN CORPORATION, Tokyo. This English language edition ©2007 by
Dark Horse Comics, Inc. All other material ©2007 by Dark Horse Comics, Inc. All
rights reserved. No portion of this publication may be reproduced or transmitted,
in any form or by any means, without the express written permission of the copyright
holders. Names, characters, places, and incidents featured in this publication
are either the product of the author's imagination or are used fictitiously. Any
resemblance to actual persons (living or dead), events, institutions, or locales,
without satiric intent, is coincidental. Dark Horse Manga™ is a trademark of Dark
Horse Comics, Inc. All rights reserved.

Published by
Dark Horse Manga
A division of Dark Horse Comics, Inc.
10956 SE Main Street
Milwaukie, OR 97222
www.darkhorse.com

To find a comics shop in your area,
call the Comic Shop Locator Service
toll-free at 1-888-266-4226

First edition: November 2007
ISBN 978-1-59307-596-5

1 3 5 7 9 10 8 6 4 2

PRINTED IN CANADA

DISJECTA MEMBRA

SOUND FX GLOSSARY AND NOTES ON *KUROSAGI* VOL. 5 BY TOSHIFUMI YOSHIDA
introduction and additional comments by the editor

TO INCREASE YOUR ENJOYMENT of the distinctive Japanese visual style of this manga, we've included a guide to the sound effects (or "FX") used in this manga. It is suggested the reader *not* constantly consult this glossary as they read through, but regard it as supplemental information, in the manner of footnotes. If you want to imagine it being read aloud by Osaka, after the manner of her lecture to Sakaki on hemorrhoids in episode five, please go right ahead. In either Yuki Matsuoka or Kira Vincent-Davis's voice—I like them both.

Japanese, like English, did not independently invent its own writing system, but instead borrowed and modified the system used by the then-dominant cultural power in their part of the world. We still call the letters we use to write English today the "Roman" alphabet, for the simple reason that about 1600 years ago the earliest English speakers, living on the frontier of the Roman Empire, began to use the same letters the Romans used to write their Latin language to write out English.

Around that very same time, on the other side of the planet, Japan, like England, was another example of an island civilization lying across the sea from a great empire, in this case, that of China. Likewise the Japanese borrowed from the Chinese writing system, which then as now consists of thousands of complex symbols—today in China officially referred to in the Roman alphabet as *hanzi*, but which the Japanese pronounce as *kanji*. For example, all the Japanese characters you see on the front cover of The Kurosagi Corpse Delivery Service—the seven which make up the original title and the four each which make up the creators' names—are examples of kanji. Of course, all of them were hanzi first; although the Japanese did invent some original kanji of their own, just as new hanzi have been created over the centuries as Chinese evolved.

Note that whereas both *kanji* and *hanzi* are methods of writing foreign words in Roman letters, "kanji" gives English-speakers a fairly good idea of how the Japanese word is really pronounced—*khan-gee*—whereas "hanzi" does not—in Mandarin Chinese it sounds something like *n-tsuh*. The reason is fairly simple: whereas the most commonly used method of writing Japanese in Roman letters, called the Hepburn system, was developed by a native English speaker, the most commonly used method of writing Chinese in Roman letters, called the *Pinyin* system, was developed by native Mandarin speakers. In fact Pinyin was developed to help teach Mandarin pronunciation to speakers of other Chinese dialects; unlike Hepburn, it was not intended as a learning tool for English-speakers *per se*, and hence has no particular obligation to "make sense" to English speakers or, indeed, users of other languages spelled with the Roman alphabet.

Whereas the various dialects of Chinese are written entirely in hanzi, it is impractical to render the Japanese language entirely in them. To compare once more, English is a notoriously difficult language in which to spell properly, and this is in part because it uses an alphabet designed for another language, Latin, whose sounds are different. The challenges the Japanese faced in using the Chinese writing system for their own language were even greater, for whereas spoken English and Latin are at least from a common language family, spoken Japanese is unrelated to any of the various dialects of spoken Chinese. The complicated writing system Japanese evolved represents an adjustment to these differences.

When the Japanese borrowed hanzi to become kanji, what they were getting was a way to write out (remember, they already had ways to *say*) their vocabulary. Nouns, verbs, many adjectives, the names of places and people—that's what kanji are used for, the fundamental data of the written language. The practical use and processing of that "data"—its grammar and pronunciation—is another matter entirely. Because spoken Japanese neither sounds nor functions like Chinese, the first work-around tried was a system called *manyogana*, where individual kanji were picked to represent certain syllables in Japanese. A similar method is still used in Chinese today to spell out foreign names; companies and individuals often try to choose hanzi for this purpose that have an auspicious, or at least not insulting meaning. As you will also observe in *Kurosagi* and elsewhere,

the meaning behind the characters that make up a personal name are an important literary element of Japanese as well.

The commentary in *Katsuya Terada's The Monkey King* (also available from Dark Horse, and also translated by Toshifumi Yoshida) notes the importance that not only Chinese, but Indian culture had on Japan at this time in history—particularly, Buddhism. It is believed the Northeast Indian *Siddham* script studied by Kukai (died 835 AD), founder of the Shingon sect of Japanese Buddhism, inspired him to create the solution for writing Japanese still used today. Kukai is credited with the idea of taking the manyogana and making shorthand versions of them now known simply as *kana*. The improvement in efficiency was dramatic—a kanji, used previously to represent a sound, that might have taken a dozen strokes to draw, was now reduced to three or four.

Unlike the original kanji it was based on, the new kana had *only* a sound meaning. And unlike the thousands of kanji, there are only 46 kana, which can be used to spell out any word in the Japanese language, including the many ordinarily written with kanji (Japanese keyboards work on this principle). The same set of 46 kana is written two different ways depending on their intended use: cursive style, *hiragana*, and block style, *katakana*. Naturally, sound FX in manga are almost always written out using kana.

Kana works somewhat differently than the Roman alphabet. For example, while there are separate kana for each of the five vowels (the Japanese order is not A-E-I-O-U as in English, but A-I-U-E-O), except for "n," there are no separate kana for consonants (the middle "n" in the word *ninja* illustrates this exception). Instead, kana work by grouping together consonants with vowels: for example, there are five kana for sounds starting with "k," depending on which vowel follows it—in Japanese vowel order, they go KA, KI, KU, KE, KO. The next set of kana begins with "s" sounds, so SA, SHI, SU, SE, SO, and so on. You will observe this kind of consonant-vowel pattern in the FX listings for *Kurosagi* Vol. 4 below.

Katakana are almost always the kind that get used for manga sound FX, but on occasion (often when the sound is one associated with a person's body) hiragana are used instead. In *Kurosagi* Vol. 5 you can see one of several examples on 90.5, when Nishimura screams with a "WAAAAAA" sound, which in hiragana style is written わあああああ. Note its more cursive appearance compared to the other FX. If it had been written in katakana style, it would look like ワアアアアアア.

To see how to use this glossary, take an example from page 5: "5.2 FX: GO—footstep." 5.2 means the FX is the one on page 5, in panel 2. GO is the sound these kana—ゴツ—literally stand for. After the dash comes an explanation of what the sound represents (in some cases, it will be less obvious than others). Note that in cases where there are two or more different sounds in a single panel, an extra number is used to differentiate them from right to left; or, in cases where right and left are less clear, in clockwise order.

The use of kana in these FX also illustrates another aspect of written Japanese—its flexible reading order. For example, the way you're reading the pages and panels of this book in general: going from right-to-left, and from top to bottom—is similar to the order in which Japanese is also written in most forms of print: books, magazines, and newspapers. However, many of the FX in *Kurosagi* (and manga in general) read left-to-right. This kind of flexibility is also to be found on Japanese web pages, which usually also read left-to-right. In other words, Japanese doesn't simply read "the other way" from English; the Japanese themselves are used to reading it in several different directions.

As might be expected, some FX "sound" short, and others "sound" long. Manga represent this in different ways. One of many instances of "short sounds" in *Kurosagi* Vol. 5 is to be found in the example from 5.2 given above: GO. Note the small ツ mark it has at the end. This ordinarily represents the sound "tsu," but its half-size use at the end of FX like this means the sound is the kind which stops or cuts off suddenly; that's why the sound is written as GO and not GOTSU—you don't "pronounce" the TSU in such cases. Note the small "tsu" has another occasional use *inside*, rather than at the end, of a particular FX, where it indicates a doubling of the consonant sound that follows it.

There are three different ways you may see "long sounds"—where a vowel sound is extended—written out as FX. One is with an ellipsis, as in 4.1's SHIIIIN. Another is with an extended line, as in 42.2's GOOOO. Still another is by simply repeating a vowel several times, as in 176.5's GOOOON. You will note that 42.2 has a "tsu" at its end, suggesting an elongated sound that's suddenly cut off; the methods may be combined within a single FX. As a visual element in manga, FX are an art rather than a science, and are used in a less rigorous fashion than kana are in standard written Japanese.

The explanation of what the sound represents may sometimes be surprising; but every culture "hears" sounds differently. Note that manga FX do not even necessarily represent literal sounds; for example 4.1 FX: SHIIIIN—in manga this is the figurative "sound" of silence, in this case the silence of Yata's joke bombing. Such "mimetic" words, which represent an imagined sound, or even a state of mind, are called *gitaigo* in Japanese. Like the onomatopoeic *giseigo* (the words used to represent literal sounds— i.e., most FX in this glossary are classed as giseigo), they are also used in colloquial speech and writing. A Japanese, for example, might say that something bounced by saying PURIN, or talk about eating by saying MUGU MUGU. It's something like describing chatter in English by saying "yadda yadda yadda" instead.

One important last note: all these spelled-out kana vowels should be pronounced as they are in Japanese: "A" as *ah*, "I" as *eee*, "U" as *ooh*, "E" as *eh*, and "O" as *oh*.

2   As has been Eiji Otsuka's style in *The Kurosagi Corpse Delivery Service*, the chapter titles here in Vol. 5 are again song names. For this volume, the songs are those of Kei Ogura. A singer, composer, and lyricist, Ogura was unusual in that he was a professional musician who nevertheless openly maintained his regular day job as a banker! Often characterized as a folk singer, he has branched out several times, working with people such as Hibari Misora, the most famous postwar female *enka* singer (a style sometimes compared to American honky-tonk in theme, although the instrumentation is more Japanese), and balladeer Akira Fuse (whose songs were used for the opening and ending of the recent *Kamen Rider Hibiki* TV series). Ogura himself worked on the end credits for Noboru Ishiguro's epic anime adaptation of the *Legend of the Galactic Heroes* novel series.

4.1   FX: SHIIIIN—sound of silence

4.2   FX: BA—grabbing sound

5.2   FX:GO—footstep

6.1   FX:YURARI YURA YURARI— pendulum starting to swing

8   I just wanted to say that one of the things I've always loved best about manga is its chapter title pages, and especially the way they often relate to the story obliquely, or sometimes not at all. It's a charming element not usually found in traditional American comics. I suppose that's because with only 22 pages or so of art per month in an American comic, it's felt every page is needed for storytelling; yet there are plenty of manga in Japanese monthly magazines with that kind of chapter length. It may be, rather, that the convention of manga title pages arose to make the transition between different stories all sharing the same magazine more clear.

10.4   FX:JARA—cuffs rattling

11.5   FX: PA—pulling up handkerchief
The traditional magician's phrase, "hocus pocus," is often said to be a corruption of *hoc est (enim) corpus (meum)*, "for this is my body," a phase

invoked during the Latin Rite of the Catholic Eucharist, so the joke seemed fairly obvious in this case. The original Japanese phrase spoken by Sasayama was "Arabiin . . . dobiin . . . Hagechabin!"—as *hage* means "bald," it was possibly a self-referential joke on his part.

13.4 **FX: SU**—placing hand on body

15.2 **FX/balloons: GOTON GATA GAN**—car bouncing along a bumpy dirt road

16.3 **FX: CHAN CHAKA CHAKA CHAKA ZUN CHA CHA**—ringtone

17.2 That seems at first like a fairly shameless bit of product placement on Kadokawa's part, but it won't be the last reference to *Kurosagi*'s publisher in this volume—as you shall see.

19.1 **FX/balloon: BAN**—car door closing

20.4 **FX: ZAN**—slashing sound

22.2 **FX/balloon: FU**—sound of the *torii* gate passing by quickly

The name of the town in the original Japanese version was *Osugita*, spelled with the kanji 大杉田 (you can clearly see them on Sasaki's computer screen in 17.3). The homophonic *osugita*, spelled 多すぎた, means "too many." I feel somewhat guilty that *Tumani* is not an actual Japanese word, although it theoretically could be one under the Japanese Ministry of Education's own romanization system, the *kunrei-shiki*. Under the better-known (to foreigners) Hepburn system discussed in the intro, it would be

tsumani—which isn't a real Japanese word either, although people sometimes misspell *tsumani* that way.

22.4 **FX/balloon: CHIRA**—peering into mirror

23.6 **FX/balloons: CHUN CHUN CHUCHUN**—sound of chirping birds

26.1 **FX/balloon: GAPO**—pulling a cooking pot out of the mud

26.4 **FX: CHARAN**—sound of chain dangling

26.5 **FX: HYUN HYUN HYUN**—sound of swinging pendulum

29.4 In this case, the "alkaline conditions" giving rise to saponification within American caskets would come from the use of embalming fluid.

30.6 **FX: DOSA**—dropping body bag

31.2 **FX: SU**—placing hand on body

32.5 **FX: ZAAA**—sound of rain

32.6 **FX: OGYAA OGYAA**—sound of a crying baby

33.5 **FX/balloon: BOKO**—sound of something coming out of the mud

34-35.1 **FX: BOKO BOKO**—sound of dried mud breaking up

34-35.2 **FX: KUN KUKUN**—sound of exposed leg moving back and forth

34-35.3 **FX: BATAN BATAN**—sound of torso flopping back and forth

36.1 **FX: BOKO BOKON**—another body coming out of mud

36.2 **FX: ZU**—starting to pull sword out of the mud

36.3 **FX: ZUZUZU**—continuing to pull the sword out of the mud

37.3 FX: HYUN HYUN—swinging sword

39.2 FX: BYUN—sound of something zipping by head

39.3 FX: DOKO—sound of spear hitting body

40.1 FX: DWOON—thud

40.5 FX: PATA—arm falling to the ground

41.1 FX: GORO GORORO—sound of the sky rumbling

41.2 FX: POTSU POTSU—sound of raindrops

41.3 FX: ZAAA—sound of pouring rain

41.4 The editor was recently on a radio show for KQED discussing manga along with the much more resonantly-voiced (and cosmically better-informed) Fred Schodt, and was asked by the host whether he'd ever come across any mention of the Nanking massacre in a manga. I said no, but talked about how *Kurosagi* made reference to Unit 731 in Volume 4. Now, with this story, we do see the massacre (also known as the Rape of Nanking—the "rape" part having been quite literal as well) make an appearance. Although some fairly prominent Japanese figures have been known to assert this event never happened, or that it's used by the Chinese government to whip up a sense of nationalist hatred, the editor would say both are unfortunately true; that is, the Rape of Nanking did happen and was as horrible as they say, *and* it is used in a cynical fashion by the Chinese government that itself has a terrible human rights record towards its own people. Japan has plenty to be proud of—its culture, its economic and technological achievements, the fact it is the most democratic nation in Asia. Nor need it be ashamed it was militarily defeated by the United States—it's not like they didn't put up a fight, after all; it took longer for America to beat Japan than Nazi Germany, and in the end atomic bombs were necessary to force an unconditional surrender—in a sense this terrible weapon was a measure of Japan's terrible will. But the imperialist and racist reasons behind the war itself were nothing for Japan to be proud of—not that they are the only nation that has a problem with mis-placed pride.

42.2 FX: GOOOO—sound of the incinerator

42.3 FX/balloon: KIN—sound of the metal tip of the cane hitting floor

44.4 FX: ZAAAA—sound of rain

44.6 FX: OGYAA OGYAA—sound of a crying baby

45.2 FX: OGYAA OGYAA OGYAA OGYAA OGYAA—crying baby sound

45.4 FX: OGYAA OGYAA—crying baby

50.5 FX: HYUN HYUN HYUN—pendulum swinging

54.3 It wouldn't be a real manga without an eating contest in there somewhere.

54.4 FX: GA GA GA—fierce eating sounds

56.2 FX: GATAAN—sound of Numata falling over

58.1 *Maitreyavyakarana* is the ancient Sanskrit text that prophesied the coming of a future incarnation of the Buddha, known as Maitreya (or Miroku in Japanese). As a sort of messianic figure within Buddhism, there have been many claimants to the role over the centuries, and Maitreya has inspired apocalyptic and revolutionary movements, particularly in China. Numata must have been under great duress indeed to actually remember anything from his classes.

60.2 The kanji in Shinhue's name are 死戸, meaning "death" and "door." Not at all foreboding.

61.4 **FX: PON**—tossing crumpled check

63.1 The editor has often thought that we're being remiss to archaeologists of the future by our rather minimalist burial practices. How are generations to come supposed to learn anything about us, if we leave ourselves in just a simple box with no possessions hoarded for the afterlife? Not to mention our modern lack of tombs that throw in a few challenges, like pit traps and spring-loaded spears.

64.2 **FX: CHARAAN JARARARAN JAKA JAN**—ringtone

64.3 **FX: PI**—answering phone

66.3 **FX: BASA**—x-ray pictures being tossed onto the table

67.3 **FX: SU**—reaching out to touch

FX: GACHA—opening door

73.2 That's how it was done. Although we have an image of a human brain as a rubbery organ, the ones you might see in anatomy classes were specially treated to acquire a firm consistency; fresh human brains have a texture more like scrambled eggs. A not dissimilar procedure is used in a trans-orbital lobotomy, although the goal there is to damage brain tissue rather than remove it. Well, this is a horror manga.

75.1 Yoshimune Tokugawa was the eighth of the Tokugawa shoguns, reigning from 1716 to 1745. He was known in particular for reforming the finances of the shogunate, a task which was largely ideological, since the Confucian principles that were used to help justify political obedience in the samurai era also contained a disdain for money and trade.

75.3 I regret to say the stuff about eating mummies is true as well.

75.5 **FX: SU**—sliding out x-ray

76.1 The organs that were removed included the lungs, liver, stomach, and intestines, and (at least in traditional practice) were not discarded like the brain, but were placed in the tomb within so-called *canopic jars* decorated with the likenesses of the sons of the god Horus, whose indestructible eye (portrayed on the cover of Vol. 5) was regarded as a talisman of rebirth. The canopic jars themselves can be seen in 74.4; note that if the cover design suggests that the brain, like the lungs, would be within such a "pot," (i.e., canopic jar), it would be inaccurate.

76.4 **FX: SU**—picking up tool

76.5 **FX: TORO**—pouring viscous fluid sound

76.6 **FX: BERI**—ripping up bandages

76.7 **FX: BERI BERI BERI**—sound of bandages being ripped up

78.6 **FX: NU**—blade being presented

79.2 **FX: SUCHA**—brandishing blade

87.1 **FX: GACHI GACHI GACHI**—mouth moving

87.3 **FX: DO**—mummy falling over

87.4 **FX: MOZO MOZO**—mummy wiggling closer

89.1 **FX: DON**—bumping into a sarcophagus

89.2 **FX: GURA**—sarcophagus starting to topple

89.3 **FX: DOKA GON DOKO**—sarcophagi hitting floor

90.1 **FX: ZU ZU**—mummy moving

90.2.1 **FX: GATA**—mummy moving to get free

90.2.2 **FX: GATA**—mummy moving to get free

90.2.3 **FX: GATA**—mummy moving to get free

90.3 **FX: YURARI**—another mummy slowly getting up

90.5 **FX: WAAAAAAAAAA**—scream of fear

92.2 **FX: SU**—placing a scroll into a coffin

92.4 **FX: GARARARARA**—sound of wheels rolling

94.1 **FX: GAKU**—pratfall sound

94.2 **FX: PARARI**—bandage starting to unravel

94.5 **FX: MOZO GOSO**—putting bandage back on

95.2.1 **FX/balloon: PATAN**—closing door

95.2.2 **FX/balloon: KACHA**—locking door

99.3 The author of this book is believed to be a riff on Takafumi Horie, formerly a dot-com billionaire (his assets are now said to be considerably reduced, although still considerable) through his founding of Livedoor, an internet portal. He was later investigated for securities fraud and sentenced to 30 months' imprisonment in March of this year—although some commentators have charged an establishment bias against Horie for his younger, non-conformist, and entrepreneurial business style, seen as disruptive to the established order.

104.4 This is an excerpt (apparently being chanted by the priest sitting before the altar) of the opening passage of the *Hannya Shingyo*, the Heart of Wisdom Sutra, commonly read at Buddhist funerals in Japan. Going from right to left, the first line is said *Hannya Haramita Ji*, the second line *Sho Ken Go Un Kai Ku*, and the third line *Do Issai Ku Yaku*. One translation of the complete passage (there are a few words missing from the beginning and ending of what is given here) is, "When a sincere truth seeker finds the wisdom of enlighten- ment, he realizes that the five senses are empty, and he transcends every suffering." Note that the Hannya Shingyo, admired for its brief but resonant expression of essential Buddhist beliefs, is not a funeral service per se; in a manner comparable to the Lord's Prayer or the 23rd Psalm in Christianity, it is said at regular devotions (particularly in Zen practice) as well as for the dead.

107.5 FX: BURORORO—bus driving away

110.4 It's moments like these that assuage the bitter sting of *Welcome to the N.H.K.* not being a Dark Horse title.

113.4 FX: PA PA—shaking salt on Makino. Japanese (among other cultures) use salt for ritual purification after a funeral; readers may have noted its use also in Vol. 3 of Housui Yamazaki's other manga from Dark Horse, *Mail*.

114.5 FX: PIKO PIKO PIKO—hitting Numata with toy magical girl wand

115.1 FX: JAN JYAKA JAJAN JAAN—ringtone

116.1 The sign says "Kusaha Ceremony," which will immediately put the reader in mind of "Nire Ceremony." In real-life Japan, it is common for funeral homes to use the English loan-word *seremonii* in their company names, signifying their readiness to perform the ceremonies of various different religious rites.

116.3 FX: KACHA—door opening

117.2.1 FX/black: KA—footstep

117.2.2 FX/white: KIN—sound of the metal tip on cane hitting floor

117.3 Although funerals in Japan are usually held with Buddhist rites, a few are conducted with Shinto rites (in fact a major reason so many Japanese funerals are Buddhist is so as to avoid spiritual "pollution" of Shinto rites through the presence of death). A Shinto altar, or *kamidana* (meaning "shelf for the gods") can be seen at the front of the room on 116.4.

122.1 FX/balloon: ZUZURI—sipping tea

122.3 The typical practice in a Japanese host or hostess club (of which today's maid cafes are only one modern incarnation) is that you pay one of the respective hosts or hostesses attached to the establishment 20 minutes at a time to sit with you at a table in a club, make conversation, and drink watered brandy (Michael Gombos maintains he's seen even the leftover watered brandy in the glasses poured back into the bottles from whence they came at closing time). It's just conversation, but if the client wants to try to convince the host/hostess to meet them after work, that's considered their business. At standard rates, you don't get to choose the specific person to sit with you; instead, as long as you keep paying, the old one will leave and a new one will arrive from a waiting room "backstage" such as Numata alludes to here. This system has its advantages for the host/hostess and client; if it's not going well for them, at least it will be over fairly soon. For extra money, of course, you can request a specific person to sit with you, and some of a club's most popular "stars" can command high rates. But why am I explaining all this? You guys probably read *Ouran High School Host Club.*

124.6 FX/balloon: ZUZU—sipping tea

126 The sign reads "Funeral and wake site for the deceased, Yoshitaka Nonoguchi. Wake: March 12, 4pm on; Funeral: March 13, 1pm on." Note that Kadokawa's logo (the phoenix) is at the top of the sign!

127.3 Another excerpt from the Hannya Shingyo (see 104.4 above). Although partially obscured, the three lines of kanji in this passage read, going from right to left, *Ku Fu I Shiki, Shiki Soku Ze Ku, Ku Soku Ze Shiki.* One translation of this passage would be, "Emptiness is not different from all things; form is emptiness; emptiness is form."

128.3 FX: SU—old woman stepping forward

131.4 FX: GATAN BAKIN—sound of the coffin moving, then wood breaking

135.4 FX: PARA—book falling out

137.1 FX: PATAN—closing book

137.4 http://www.angel-cp.com/. Exclusively distributed in Japan through the Morinaga Milk Co., Ltd.—who are also makers of the world-famous non-dairy creamer, "Creap."

142.1 FX: BABABABA—helicopter sounds

142.2 FX: BATATATA—distant helicopter sounds

144.2 FX: CHICHI . . . CHICHI . . . —chirping birds

145.1 FX/balloon: GARAN—shovels clattering on the ground

146.3 FX: PIIHYORO—sound of a bird

147.1 FX/balloon: ZA—footstep

147.3 FX/balloon: DADADA—running sound

147.4 The editor thought Himuro was a *she,* some kind of sinister riff on Rei Ayanami (of whom Natsuki Kato performed a truly spectacular cosplay in the September 18th issue of *Kurosagi*'s home magazine, *Comic Charge*). But in a manga written by Eiji Otsuka, you never really know. Actually in manga you never really know, period.

150.4 FX: ZA ZA—digging sounds

150.5 *Gachapon* are the kind of capsules Japanese vending machine toys come in; their name is a perfect example of how sound effects make their way into everyday Japanese speech—GACHA being the mechanical sound of the vending machine knob being turned, and PON being the subsequent popping forth of the capsule.

151.4 FX: GASHAAAN—shattering sound

154.5 As noted before, for many business and official purposes, Japanese use not only the Western year, but the corresponding year of the imperial reign. The late Emperor Hirohito, whose era was known as *Showa* (posthumously, he too is known as the Showa Emperor) died in 1989, the 64th and final year of Showa. The last year of the old era was also considered to be the first of the new—the *Heisei* era of the current Emperor, Akihito. This story takes place in 2005, but the current year is Heisei 17.

157.3 FX: BASA—tossing down a stack of paper

157.5 FX: GATA—sitting down into chair

160.3 FX: GOFWOO—sound of heavy doors opening

162.2 Cryonics services of the kind described here (preserving bodies and/or brains with liquid nitrogen or other techniques) actually exist, although no more than a few hundred people are known to have used them; the two main cryonics companies in the U.S. are the Cryonics Institute in Michigan, and the Alcor Life Extension Foundation in Arizona. Cryonics "patients" are, in fact, dead—under U.S. law, the procedure can only be applied after death (and would probably in any case kill a living person) and it should not be confused with the classic science fiction idea of "suspended animation," since that usually implies a living person put into a state of long-term hibernation (something not yet possible under current medical science, just as the revival of cryonics patients is not yet possible). It should be noted that, at least in the United States, it is much cheaper to be cryonically preserved than the 200 million yen figure quoted here; Alcor, for example, charges

US$150,000 for the whole body treatment—about 17 million yen at current rates. Presumably Nire's unfortunate customers are having to pick up the tab for the firm's prime downtown location.

164.1 FX: PARA—sound of a piece of paper being presented

165.1 As a child of the 1980s, I suppose I had better enjoy its current revival for however long it lasts. Well, these things do seem to go in cycles; the 1990s saw a lot of rediscovery of the '70s, whereas the 1970s were known for the '50s nostalgia of *Grease* and *Happy Days*. This, of course, leaves how the 1980s felt about the '60s, an ambiguity reflected by the fact my high school had a themed dress-up called "Hippie/Bum Day." Gen-X are the natural enemies of the Boomers, which is why I'm voting Obama.

166.2 The To in "Tosuke" is spelled using the character for "winter," 冬, whereas the "Himuro" is composed of the characters for "ice" and room," 氷室.

168.5 FX: NII—smirking sound

169.1 The editor's mother came from a generation where it was considered prudent to always keep a little gold in your teeth; her reasoning was, "What if you need to bribe the camp guards"?

170.1 FX: GOGOGO PUWAAAN—construction and traffic noise

171.2 FX: PA PA—lights coming on

172.4 The "dude" in question is Prince Shotoku (died 621 A.D.) who is credited with establishing the first centralized government in Japan, and is therefore considered in some respects the founder of the Japanese nation. He was on the 10,000 yen banknote until 1986 (the current 10,000 yen note has Yukichi Fukuzawa, one of Japan's great modernizers in the 19th century).

176.2 FX: KACHI—pushing button

176.3 FX: GOWUN GOWUN—door closing

176.5 FX: GOOOON—door closing

177.3 FX: KOOOOO—sound of the AC starting up

178.2 FX/balloon: JIJI—sound of sparks

178.3 FX: JIBABABAB—sound of a cutting torch working

178.4 FX: GOWOOOON—heavy door thudding

180.3 FX: KON KON—knocking

180.4 FX: SASA—hiding gold

180.5 *Leicheanlieferungsdienst* is, as you might expect, a somewhat dubious way of saying "Corpse Delivery Service" in German. (unlike in France, there is no German edition of the manga as yet). The *dienst* ending makes it sound somewhat like a government agency ("service" as in "Secret Service"), but thanks to Sasayama, they sort of now are anyway.

186.2 FX: BAKO—ice breaking

188.1 FX: FWEEEEN—flying ship sound

188.2 FX: EEEEN—distant flying ship sound

189.2 Powell's Bookstore in Portland, which the city is proud of (and it speaks well of a city that it's proud of its bookstore) claims to accept quatloos; they do accept euros, pounds sterling, yen, and pesos, reflecting the truly international clientele of what is probably the largest bookstore in the Western Hemisphere.

If you enjoyed this book, be sure to check out *Mail*, a new mature-readers manga series from the artist of *The Kurosagi Corpse Delivery Service!*

山崎峰水 housui yamazaki

Private detective Reiji Akiba has a theory about those awkward moments and weird coincidences we all encounter in life. They are actually encounters with the dead—their way of sending us a message! But you may not want to open such strange mail from beyond—not unless you can see the ghostly attachment, like Akiba can. And not unless you carry a tool that can kill what isn't alive, like Akiba's sanctified gun, *Kagutsuchi!*

Volume 1:
ISBN-10: 1-59307-566-9
ISBN-13: 978-1-59307-566-8

Volume 2:
ISBN-10: 1-59307-591-X
ISBN-13: 978-1-59307-591-0

$10.95 each!

The first book in a highly successful series of novels from Japan,
Blood: The Last Vampire—*Night of the Beasts*
is a startling, fast-paced thriller full of chilling surprises.

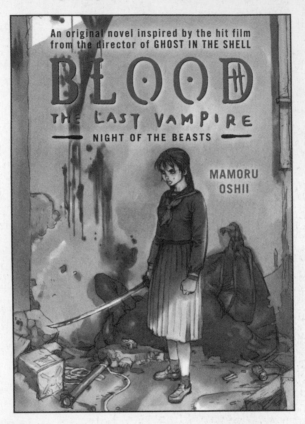

At Yokota Base in Japan, American soldiers stand guard at the brink of the Vietnam War. Although they fear the enemy outside their base, an even more dangerous enemy waits within—bloodthirsty vampires walk among them! Saya, a fierce and beautiful vampire hunter, leads a team of undercover agents who must wipe out the vampires before they can wipe out the base. But even though Saya is a powerful warrior, her ferocity may not be enough!

ISBN-10: 1-59582-029-9 / ISBN-13: 978-1-59582-029-7 | $8.95

dhpressbooks.com

AVAILABLE AT YOUR LOCAL COMICS SHOP OR BOOKSTORE
To find a comics shop in your area, call 1-888-266-4266
For more information or to order direct: •On the web: darkhorse.com •E-mail: mailorder@darkhorse.com
•Phone: 1-800-862-0052 Mon.-Fri. 9 A.M. to 5 P.M. Pacific Time.
BLOOD THE LAST VAMPIRE: NIGHT OF THE BEASTS (KEMONO TACHI NO YORU BLOOD THE LAST VAMPIRE) © Mamoru Oshii 2000. © Production I.G. 2000.
Originally published in Japan in 2000 by KADOKAWA SHOTEN PUBLISHING Co., Ltd., Tokyo. English Translation rights arranged with KADOKAWA SHOTEN
PUBLISHING Co., Ltd., Tokyo through TOHAN CORPORATION, Tokyo. DH Press™ is a trademark of Dark Horse Comics, Inc. All rights reserved. (BL7000)

the Ring

Plunge into the depths of manga horror with *The Ring* saga. Based on the best-selling horror novels by Koji Suzuki, these books are perfect for horror and manga fans alike, as well as fans of the hit Japanese and American *Ring* movies!

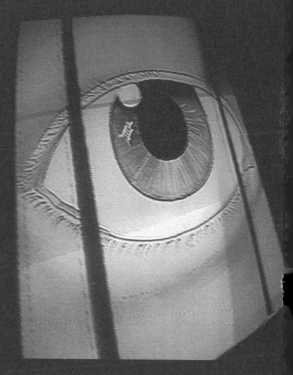

THE RING, VOLUME 0
ISBN-10: 1-59307-306-2
ISBN-13: 978-1-59307-306-0
$12.95

THE RING, VOLUME 1
ISBN-10: 1-59307-054-3
ISBN-13: 978-1-59307-054-0
$14.95

THE RING, VOLUME 2
ISBN-10: 1-59307-055-1
ISBN-13: 978-1-59307-055-7
$12.95

SPIRAL
ISBN-10: 1-59307-215-5
ISBN-13: 978-1-59307-215-5
$12.95

BIRTHDAY
ISBN-10: 1-59307-267-8
ISBN-13: 978-1-59307-267-4
$12.95

AVAILABLE AT YOUR LOCAL COMICS SHOP OR BOOKSTORE! • TO FIND A COMICS SHOP IN YOUR AREA, CALL 1-888-266-4226.

For more information or to order direct visit darkhorse.com or call 1-800-862-0052 Mon.-Fri. 9 A.M. to 5 P.M. Pacific Time.
*Prices and availability subject to change without notice. THE RING 0 © 2000 THE RING 0 Production Group. © MEIMU 2000. THE RING © 1998 THE RING Production Group. © MISAO INAGAKI 1999. THE RING 2 © 1999 THE RING 2 Production Group. © MEIMU 1999. SPIRAL © 1999 SPIRAL Production Group. © 1999 SAKURA MIZUKI. BIRTHDAY © 1999 Koji SUZUKI. © 1999 MEIMU. Originally published in Japan in 1999, 2000 by KADOKAWA SHOTEN PUBLISHING Co., Ltd. English translation rights arranged with KADOKAWA SHOTEN PUBLISHING Co., Ltd., TOKYO through TOHAN CORPORATION, TOKYO. English text translation by Digital Manga, Inc. and Dark Horse Comics, Inc. All rights reserved. (BL7042)

DARK
HORSE
MANGA

STOP!

THIS IS THE BACK OF THE BOOK!

This manga collection is translated into English, but arranged in right-to-left reading format to maintain the artwork's visual orientation as originally drawn and published in Japan. If you've never read comics this way before, take a look at the diagram below to give yourself an idea of how to go about it. Basically, you'll be starting in the upper right-hand corner, and will read each word balloon and panel moving right-to-left. It may take a little getting used to, but you should get the hang of it very quickly. Have fun! If this is the millionth manga you've read this way, never mind. ^_^

1
...
2
THEY TALK TO YOU BECAUSE YOU'RE THE KIND OF GUY WHO CAN'T SAY NO.
3
...YES.
4
RIGHT. SO LET'S TAKE THIS HORRIBLE, STINKING, ROTTING THING BACK TO CAMPUS. QUICK, BEFORE THE COPS NOTICE.
5
BACK TO CAMPUS?!
6
KARATSU, THERE'S NOTHING IN THE HANDBOOK THAT SAYS STUDENTS CAN'T POSSESS CORPSES--OR, IN YOUR CASE, VICE-VERSA.

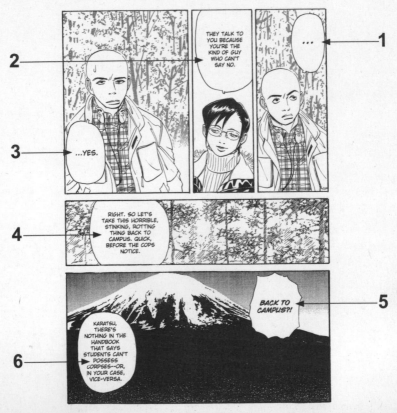